Managing Software Development Projects
Formula for Success

Second Edition

Neal Whitten

John Wiley & Sons, Inc.

New York • Chichester • Brisbane • Toronto • Singapore

Publisher: Katherine Schowalter
Senior Editor: Diane D. Cerra
Managing Editor: Robert Aronds
Text Design & Composition: North Market Street Graphics

Designations used by companies to distinguish their products are often claimed as trademarks. In all instances where John Wiley & Sons, Inc. is aware of a claim, the product names appear in initial capital or all capital letters. Readers, however, should contact the appropriate companies for more complete information regarding trademarks and registration.

This text is printed on acid-free paper.

This publication is designed to provide accurate and authoritative information in regard to the subject matter covered. It is sold with the understanding that the publisher is not engaged in rendering legal, accounting, or other professional service. If legal advice or other expert assistance is required, the services of a competent professional person should be sought.

Chapters 4 and 5 include material on project scheduling and tracking that the author wrote (1993) while employed at IBM. IBM has granted permission for the use of this material in this book.

Library of Congress Cataloging-in-Publication Data:

Whitten, Neal.
    Managing software development projects : formula for success /
Neal Whitten. — 2nd ed.
        p.   cm.
    Includes bibliographical references.
    ISBN 0-471-07683-X
    1. Computer software—Development—Management.   I. Title.
QA76.76.D47W49   1995
005.1'068—dc20   94-45409
                                                                         CIP

10 9 8

Dedication

To
Ann and Debi

Preface

There is no such thing as instant experience, but this book is the next best thing. It cuts to the quick by revealing the most common, major problems that plague software projects today and presents effective approaches to address and, in many cases, prevent these problems from taking root in your project.

If you want the big-ticket results for your project of higher satisfaction with your customers, greater competitiveness, higher product quality, higher productivity of project members, lower project costs, and shorter schedule cycles, then you must focus your time, resources, and energy on the big-ticket problems—the major problems—that haunt software projects. The objective of this book is to focus your attention on these major problems—and their solutions.

This book offers results—many that can be immediate. This book is not about theories or history. This book is a how-to, real-world, no-nonsense, practical guide to identifying and resolving the most common, major problems prevalent in software projects. This book is what project managers, project leaders, and project members want and need.

How do I know this? Since the publication of the first edition of *Managing Software Development Projects: Formula for Success* in 1990, I have worked with thousands of people and dozens of projects through my speaking, instructing, and consulting engagements. I also have received personal correspondence from hundreds of people who have read and are using the first edition. Their feedback tells me that the strategies and techniques given in the first edition work. This second edition offers even more useful, practical, and up-to-date information than the first edition. New subjects are addressed and old subjects are reworked based on the abundant feedback that I received.

Software development problems occur in all aspects of a project, from its people, to its processes, to its specific activities. The major problem-prone areas discussed in this book are:

- Project Discipline
- People Communications
- Software Development Process
- Scheduling
- Tracking
- Quality
- Managing Priorities

- Customer Requirements
- Product Objectives
- Product Specifications
- Product Ease of Use
- Development Testing
- Project Reviews
- Vendor Relationships

A full chapter is dedicated to each of these problem-prone areas. Each chapter begins with one or more revealing, true-life stories to show how the problem can be traced through a project and its people. Then a recovery or avoidance approach is recommended.

This book collects the experiences and wisdom of virtually thousands of people and hundreds of projects and attempts to present this treasure of information in a format that allows the reader to learn from the misfortunes and successes of others. A legion of us have learned from these common but costly mistakes the hard way—by making them. But by applying the hard-earned experience in this book, you can identify these major problems and target effective approaches to solving these problems. Project success doesn't just happen; for the most part, it is predictable and controllable.

It is my objective that your investment in acquiring this book and in learning about and using its recommendations will be rewarded many, many times over on your current or next project.

Neal Whitten

Acknowledgments

The views and opinions expressed in this book are mine alone and do not necessarily represent the opinions and views of any other person or company.

I am grateful to the hundreds of people who have contacted me regarding the first edition. Their feedback has been most appreciated and helpful. Many of the enhancements to the Second Edition are a direct result of requests, comments and observations that they have shared with me.

I am especially appreciative to the following people for their candid and helpful input: John McDonald, Wendy Miller, Bob Rosenman, Lori Vandegrift, Vince Vila, and Larry Whittington.

And finally I am grateful to Diane Cerra and the highly professional staff at John Wiley & Sons for their invaluable support and guidance during the manuscript development, editing and production. I would especially like to acknowledge the special contributions of Robert Aronds and Tammy Boyd.

About the Author

Neal Whitten is a popular speaker, trainer, and consultant in the areas of project management, software development, and employee development. To contact him, write to his Internet address at nwhitten@ix.netcom.com, or write to:

Neal Whitten
P.O. Box 858
Roswell, GA 30077-0858

Contents

.

2   Discipline: The Glue That Holds It All Together   47

3   Communicating in Harmony   71

4   Project Schedule Planning: Getting in Control   89

5   Project Tracking: Staying in Control   139

6   Planning for Quality   181

Introduction

Look at the software development projects in your company and throughout the software industry today. Are any of them slipping their schedules, overrunning their budgets, even compromising product quality?

That is more the norm than the exception. But why is this so? After all, every new year ushers in thousands of new software development projects. It is not as if the software industry is brand new and we have never been through a software development project before. Besides, today many thousands of people have amassed great experience working on software development projects—people who certainly have learned something from all their experiences. Furthermore, there are far better project management and software development tools than ever before.

So what is happening? What is wrong with this picture? Why do so many problems continue to face most software development projects?

What makes this situation even more curious is that most of the problems that plague software development projects are the same ones that affected projects last year, the year before that—and 20 years before that!

For some insight to the answer, picture this.

> You have worked for a company for 10 years. The company began building software products at the time you were hired. Today there are over a dozen software development projects in progress. If you were to calculate how many software projects your company has started over the past 10 years, you would count over 100—including a number of projects that were never completed.

Now let's look at two possible paths this scenario can take.

Path A. The leadership in your company made a very wise business decision (unfortunately a rare occurrence in the software industry) just after the first project 10 years ago. The decision was every software project would have a mandatory postproject review immediately after it is completed or canceled. Furthermore, the members of every new project must review the findings of the most recent postproject reviews and they must implement recommendations from these findings or justify any findings that they want to ignore.

There was some flak at first. Teams would protest, "We don't have time to perform postproject reviews, nor do we have time to always be updating our processes. We are trying to build and deliver products as fast and as inexpensively as we can in this highly competitive industry. We need full freedom to do whatever feels right on each project." Still, management insisted and the reviews were done.

(So you can follow me on this, I will briefly define a postproject review so there is no doubt about the meaning I attach. A **postproject review** occurs when representatives from across a completed or canceled project meet to discuss what went right, what went wrong, and what could have been improved about the project. These conclusions are then carried forward to subsequent projects so that all future projects can benefit from both the good and the not-so-good experiences of the completed project.)

Path B. Management has taken the approach that postproject reviews, although generally recognized as having potential merit, are an optional activity to perform when a project completes. As the company head explained, "If we can find the time, it would be a nice thing to do." If a project is canceled, there is the view that "No postproject review should occur. Enough time and expense have already been wasted. Let's not waste any more."

The outcome from these two paths? The Path A company has demonstrated that completed projects offer a lot of valuable lessons that can be applied to reduce the risk of new projects—as well as reduce expenses, increase productivity, and . . . well, you get the picture. Ten years after the first software development project, the current projects still experience problems that could have been avoided, but these problems are much less frequent and much lower impact than 10 years ago. In fact, the company has gained a reputation in the industry, one that does it right the first time and is almost always the lowest-cost, highest-quality producer. Furthermore, from conducting postproject reviews on canceled projects, the company has learned most about how *not* to run a project. The cancellation rate of projects (those projects over which the company has control) is running at about 5 percent and continuing to improve each year.

The Path B company is often viewed as being all over the floor. Optional postproject reviews are performed on about 10 percent of the completed projects, but the findings rarely are used to benefit new projects. Most projects continue to experience the same major problems that plagued past projects. Well-run projects are uncommon. The few good-running projects there are are that way predominately because of the discipline brought to them by the project heads. When the project heads are reassigned or leave the company, the projects almost always deteriorate. This occurs because there are no processes and culture in place to sustain the project heads' positive momentum. The cancellation rate of projects over which the company has control continues to run about the same each year—35 percent.

The predominant message here is:

 Choosing Path B means that the leaders and members of most projects will continue to not learn either from past mistakes or from past successes—and that the cost will be high.

Success or failure of a project is a people thing—not a tool thing or a technology thing or any other "thing." Projects are led by people, not technology. Although technology can help, such as with state-of-the-art project management and software development tools, it is the *leadership* of a project that makes all the difference.

And you know what makes this all so curious? The knowledge of why projects typically get into trouble is not a secret, although many people don't want to listen. Oh, they hear! They just don't listen. More than ever, companies are laying off workers or going belly up because of the unprecedented competition. Who is winning? In part, the companies that are effectively training their leaders are winning. They are training them to recognize a major problem before it hits them in the eye—and training them to solve that problem quickly so that it does not spread like a festering wound and put the project at risk of failing or not living up to its potential.

By the way, don't think that just because you finally shipped your product that you are successful. Not by a long shot. Some projects would have been better off being scrapped to reduce losses and redeploy the precious resources of people and money. Many an organization suffered serious "wounds" or went under because of heavy maintenance costs and low customer satisfaction.

So where does this new edition of *Managing Software Development Projects: Formula for Success* come into the picture? This book serves both as a 2" × 4" and as the medicine to help you. The 2 × 4 is to get your attention by helping you see the most common problems that plague software development projects. Once you recognize the problems, you are in a much better position to do something about them. And the medicine? The medicine parts of the book are the solutions that are offered to help you avoid or recover from these major project problems.

I often am reminded of a letter I received from a reader. The words that have stuck with me—words that I have heard from countless others—are "I have directed all the project coordinators and managers in my organization to acquire and study your book to help them better learn the application of sound project management techniques. The value of project management is a 'hard sell' and *I frequently use your book as a source of strength and reinforcement to myself that there is value to what we are trying to accomplish."*

The medicine part is also the encouragement you find in this book to learn from past experiences, follow your convictions, and demonstrate the integrity and courage to take charge and strive to stay in control.

Since the first edition of this book was published in 1990, I have received a large amount of feedback that has helped me make the second edition even better than the first. I am always learning, but with over 20 years of front-line software engineering experience as a manager, project lead, instructor, and consultant—and with the knowledge, feedback, and encouragement I have received from many accomplished souls in the software industry—I am confident that this book can help you avoid many of the mistakes I and countless others have made. The first time we err, we can arguably call it a "mistake," but if we continue to repeat the same error time and again, is it really still a "mistake"? I don't think so. Why? Because we all have choices to make. If we know better yet choose a destructive path—for whatever "noble" reason—we are being negligent as professionals. As professionals, we need to search continuously for ways to advance our skills and the art of managing software development projects so that we and the companies that we work for can be successful.

Knowledge about project management usually is acquired through the on-the-job classroom—a miserably inefficient way to learn such high-stakes lessons. Some managers, project leaders, and other project members, for a multitude of reasons, will never learn as long as this job environment continues to be defect-riddled from one project to the next. This book is intended to be the next best thing to instant experience.

Whether you are a manager, project leader, or project member, this book has timely and useful information to help you today on your current project and to prepare you for tomorrow's projects. Read on to learn how you can begin to apply this information immediately so it will work for you.

Identify the Problem—and the Solution

People cannot effectively control what they do not understand. Therefore, the first goal of this book is to identify the most common problems found in software development projects. From your own varied experiences, you might have one or more major problems that you would add to the list. However, the problems I have chosen also will most likely strike home. Interestingly, these problems have not changed appreciably over the years, nor do I expect them to change significantly soon.

You might expect many of the problems mentioned in this chapter to be apparent quickly to a project's members. However, most of these problems will infect a project slowly rather than suddenly and recognizably appearing one day. Moreover, projects in trouble often appear to be under control at any given time. Therefore, being able to recognize problems is an important first step. Since readers of this book have diverse backgrounds, I have tried to define problems as broadly and generically as I can so that they will be easily recognizable to the widest possible audience.

After a problem is identified, the next step is to understand what to do to recover from the problem—and then do it. Here again I have attempted to be as specific as possible for such a broad audience. I have defined the recovery approach at a level of detail that will allow readers to understand how to apply the "fix" to their own projects. However, I do not provide 100 percent of the detail to, say, write a product specifications document or a test plan document. Since detailed activities and processes vary widely from company to company and from project to project, I intentionally have restrained from providing the "gnat's eyelash" level of detail. To do so would presume that the very detailed level of information I present would or could be adaptable to all projects. Instead, as an aid, I have included a bibliography at the end of the book. The bibliography refers you to sources that provide an assortment of detailed approaches—should you desire additional information. Also, each reference identifies the chapter(s) with which it is associated.

I believe the greatest value of this book is that it introduces the reader to the big ticket project problems and recommends a recovery or avoidance approach for each problem. But it does not get bogged down in so much detail that the reader is over-taxed with reading material. *Managing Software Development Projects: Formula for Success* moves to the heart of problems in quick fashion.

Book Layout

Figure I.1 shows the physical layout of the book's 14 chapters, bibliography, and glossary. Each chapter discusses a major problem area for software development projects. The following brief sections describe the major problem that each chapter covers. As you read these chapters, you will find that they also identify numerous lesser problems that are related to the chapter's major problem theme.

Chapter 1 Defining a Software Development Process

Many software development organizations do not fully embrace a defined, repeatable, and predictable software development process. The consequence of this behavior usually is a significantly increased risk to the project in predicting and controlling the critical factors of schedule, cost, function, and quality. This chapter shows you the steps you can follow to define, document, and implement the software development process that works best for you. The chapter also presents a simple, abbreviated software development process that is used to convey many of the concepts and terms that will be referenced in subsequent chapters.

Chapter 2 Discipline: The Glue that Holds It All Together

The single greatest factor that can make or break a software development project is the degree of discipline exercised by the project's leadership. This chapter discusses the need for discipline and explains how to recognize and develop a disciplined organization. It also presents the attributes of the successful leader.

Chapter 3 Communicating in Harmony

The inability of people to communicate effectively with one another is one of the most common obstacles to overcome in a software development project. This chapter

Figure I.1   Book layout.

describes behaviors you can adopt to improve communications between you and others. Recognizing the dignity and value of each individual are central to the success of an enterprise.

Chapter 4   Project Schedule Planning: Getting in Control

Creating an unachievable project schedule plan can have a domino effect that eventually topples a project, as one scheduled activity after another fails to be completed as planned. The most important plan of a project—the heartbeat of a project—is the project schedule plan. This chapter describes the basic concepts that need to be understood before an effective project schedule plan can be developed. It then presents a series of steps that you can follow in developing a project schedule plan for your project.

Chapter 5   *Project Tracking: Staying in Control*

Often project status is tracked too little and too late to be truly effective. The primary reason for project tracking is to identify potential problems *before* they happen. This chapter describes the practical application of basic project tracking and problem management concepts. It then presents a series of steps that you can follow to track effectively a project and manage the resolution of problems encountered along the way.

Chapter 6   *Planning for Quality*

Because many people believe that the quality of a product is not really definable, measurable, or attainable, often too little attention is focused on the quality of a product early in the software development process. This chapter dispels these myths and explains how to define quality, measure quality, plan for a quality software development process to *do it right the first time*, drive toward an expected level of quality, fine-tune the quality process along the way, and recognize and encourage the achievement of quality goals.

Chapter 7   *Managing Priorities Effectively*

There are always problems in a software development project that are crucial to solve—but don't get the urgent attention they deserve. This chapter shows you how to identify and work the most important problems—the *priorities*—on a project. It explains why working intelligently has a lot more going for it than just working hard. Project success doesn't just happen. For the most part, it is predictable, controllable, and implementable.

Chapter 8   *Product Requirements: Understanding the Customer's Problem to Solve*

Understanding your customer's requirements—*problems* and *needs* they want solved—is one of the most ignored activities of the software development process. Can you afford to spend hundreds of thousands of dollars—even millions—developing a product that does not satisfy the problems and needs of its intended user? This chapter discusses the most common requirements-related problems and identifies the topics that a well thought out product requirements document should address.

Chapter 9   Product Objectives: Providing Direction for the Solution

Incomplete and unapproved product objectives can result in several major restarts for the project and an aftermath of throwaway work, slipped schedules, increased costs, poor communications across the project, and frustrated participants. This chapter describes how to set the product's direction early in the software development process. It also identifies the topics that a well-planned product objectives document should address.

Chapter 10   Product Specifications: Defining the Final Product

Creeping function is the act of continually adding function enhancements to a product throughout the software development process. Each unplanned change in the product's function can bring the project a step closer to failing. This chapter shows you how to describe, in detail, the total product early in the development process. It also explains how to define and implement an orderly process to follow when a function change must be made to the product later. This chapter identifies the topics that a comprehensive product specifications document should address.

Chapter 11   Product Ease of Use

The competitive edge for many products today is the degree of user friendliness that they offer. However, this ease-of-use attribute is more often an afterthought in the software development process rather than an activity that receives early attention. This chapter reveals the major activities in the software development process where attention to usability can have the greatest positive impact on the product under development. The chapter also introduces techniques that can be used to define, plan, test, and measure the new product's ease of use.

Chapter 12   Development Testing: Strengthening the Weak Link

This chapter exposes the weak link in the software development process, called *development testing* (also called *unit* and *function test*). The chapter explains how to anticipate and plan for development testing and how you can monitor progress during this important but elusive period.

Chapter 13   Vendor Relationships

A large number of problems can occur when working with vendors and subcontractors. These problems often are especially frustrating to a project's leadership because of the belief that a company can exercise little control over its vendors and subcontractors. This myth has been fueled by poor planning and follow-through. This chapter addresses the most common vendor- and subcontractor-related problems facing software development projects and discusses actions that you can take to get and remain in control.

Chapter 14   Postproject Review: Understanding the Past to Improve the Future

We are forever hopeful that the next software project will proceed infinitely smoother than the last. We know that we wouldn't be so dumb as to make the same mistakes again. But history has shown that we *will* make many of the same mistakes that were made last time, and the time before that, and before that. This chapter shows you how to learn from your past mistakes through the use of a *postproject review* and demonstrates how to apply this knowledge to a current or new project. Two other beneficial reviews are also described: *project review* and *product certification review.*

Chapter Layout

Each chapter focuses on a specific major problem encountered in software development projects. Each chapter is designed to stand on its own. This format allows you to zero in and concentrate on the problems and, consequently, the chapters that most interest you.

Each chapter is laid out in the same manner, illustrated in Figure I.2. A chapter opens with a brief summary of a problem and introduces you to what lies ahead. One or more true-to-life stories—*project tales*—then follow to illustrate how the problem typically can appear within a project. For chapters that relate to processes or activities, the project tales also show how the problem gradually takes root within a project and can grow out of control.

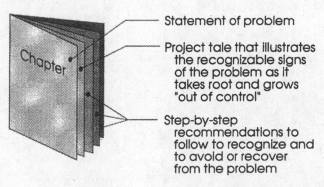

Figure I.2   Chapter layout.

The project tales do not necessarily describe actual projects. They have been created as instructional aids to help you understand and recognize the warning signals that typically accompany the intrusion of these problems into a software development project. The remainder of each chapter offers step-by-step recommendations to follow in your own project. These steps will explain how you can avoid or recover from the topic problem.

Many lessons are revealed throughout each chapter, but the key lessons are designated as "Lesson:" and identified with a pen-in-hand icon. This technique helps you to focus quickly on the most notable points to be made.

Once you have read an entire chapter, you may find it helpful to revisit the project tales and to anticipate how each problem could be confronted through each phase of the story. These project tales also can be valuable as case studies for group discussion. You may even want to add your own case studies.

Before you skip to later chapters, you might find it helpful to read Chapter 1. This chapter defines many of the concepts and terms that will be referenced in subsequent chapters. A glossary of terms at the end of the book provides a quick reference.

1

Defining a Software Development Process

Many software development organizations do not fully embrace a defined, repeatable, and predictable software development process. Without a disciplined process, they usually face a significantly increased risk in predicting and controlling the critical factors of schedule, cost, function, and quality. So why, then, do many organizations operate without an acceptable software development process?

In some cases the organization may have currently defined processes, but those processes are ineffective for one or more of the following reasons:

- Not comprehensive enough: They do not already define all of the activities that apply to all new projects.
- Overly complex: They require too much time and skill to comprehend and apply.
- Not flexible: They are not easily tailored to meet the unique needs of new projects.
- Not "owned": There is weak or no buy-in from the project's members.
- Not understood: The project's members have not been trained sufficiently.
- Not continuously improved: Lessons learned from past projects are not used to improve the current processes.
- Not enforced: The guidelines are there, but the project leadership lacks the discipline to enforce them.

Even worse is the situation where a software development process is not followed because a process has never been defined and documented fully. Having no software development process, or not following a defined process, is indicative of an organization that, albeit perhaps unintentionally, lacks the vision and discipline to become or maintain a world-class position in the fiercely competitive software industry. Even governments and standards organizations recognize the need for industries to have defined and continuously improving processes to help ensure that their customers' best interests are being served. A software development process offers a framework from which to plan a new project, avoid repeating the mistakes of past projects and improve on things that went well.

This chapter:

- Shows you the steps you can take to define, document, and implement the software development process that works best for you, and

- Presents a simple, abbreviated software development process that is used to convey many of the concepts and terms that will be referenced in subsequent chapters.

Before we start defining a software development process, however, let's examine a scenario that demonstrates the problems that can emerge when an organization invests little time and energy in defining and following a well thought out and documented software development process.

A Project Tale

Most people experienced in software development projects have a good sense for the importance of following a well-defined and documented software development process. They can recall many examples of problems that they encountered, first-hand, when the processes being followed by their projects were ill-defined and lessons learned from preceding projects were mostly ignored. Yet many projects continue to operate contrary to proven wisdom and experience.

The following short tale is of a project that had all the "right" intentions, but followed a common path of neglect when it came to defining and documenting a software development process. As you read through this tale, ask yourself if you have seen any of these problems on your past projects. Moreover, do some of these problems offer painful reminders of process-related problems on your current project?

> The organization has been in operation for several years, during which time numerous products have been developed and delivered to customers. An observant person within the organization would know that all projects had overrun their schedules and budgets, some by a small bit, but most by more significant amounts. Furthermore, all projects experienced quality problems that were perceived to be of a magnitude and volume that were higher than necessary and certainly higher than desired. However, in spite of the schedule, budget, and quality problems that always seem to plague the projects, the overall organization continues to grow and the products continue to sell—for now—even if not as well as expected.

At any given time, several projects are under development. It should be noted that no comprehensive software development process is defined and documented for use across the organization. Each project either defines its own process from scratch, or partially follows the process used by a recent project. Let's take a closer look at one of the several projects under way and see what it might reveal. Eenie, meenie, minie, mo . . . let's look at project TKO.

Mark Tyson has been selected to lead project TKO. Because there is no comprehensive software development process to use as a starting point to tailor to his project, he spends more time than expected defining a process for his project to follow. Tyson is very busy juggling the performance of several of his activities at once and, very pressed for time, can define only a bare-bones "process" for the project. The software development process he defines lists all the activities that must be performed during the project. Unfortunately, Tyson does not have time to document what he means by each of his activities. For example, only he knows what he really expects a product specifications to contain, or what the difference between high- and low-level design is, or what is meant by unit test, and so on. Tyson is not overly concerned about the lack of a documented process and feels he can communicate this information verbally or with brief notes to his team at the appropriate times.

As expected, Tyson has little trouble obtaining the buy-in from the project members of the process he has defined. Why? Because no one really knows what the intended scope of each activity is; therefore, each person feels empowered to interpret the activities in a manner than suits his or her own self-interests. The first occurrence for self-interpretation comes when schedules and budgets are to be estimated. To perform this planning, all project members must interpret what they think Tyson meant by the scope of each activity and plan against that interpretation accordingly. Frankly, many members are not as interested in what Tyson had intended as the scope of each activity as they are in what they believe should be done; therefore, it is "open season" on interpreting the scope of each activity.

When Tyson defined the process, he focused on listing all the activities to be performed. In addition to not documenting the full scope of what each activity meant, he neglected to document the entry and exit conditions that must be satisfied before an activity could begin or before one could be considered complete. Consequently, as project TKO progresses, Tyson is beginning to see activities "complete" before their time.

For example, major process-related problems come to light when the product specifications are distributed for approval. Tyson had intended for all high-level design to be completed and any problems discovered during the inspections of the high-level design to be corrected and reflected in the specifications, if appropriate. Unfortunately, the owner of the specifications thought they were complete even though the high-level design was not complete and the specifications appropriately updated. Also, Tyson had expected all the user "externals," such as screen interfaces and messages, to be reflected in the specifications. They weren't. The product's functions were described only in narrative, not in terms of what the user would see. When Tyson discovered these "problems" with the product specifications, he directed that the specifications be updated and redistributed for approval. As the head of the project, he could make this happen; however, there was the price to pay of slipped schedules, increased project costs, and some disgruntled team members.

Process-related problems continue to appear. For example, many project members had not planned to conduct inspections of their high- or low-level designs or of their code. Consequently, when Tyson realized that people were declaring their design and code complete without having performed these inspections, he insisted that people go back and perform the inspections. Because many project members had not originally planned for this, their follow-on activities were going to start later than planned. Eventually Tyson backed off of his demand and allowed some design and code to enter testing uninspected. This decision resulted in lower-quality code entering the testing stages.

Another example of the many process-related problems that were surfacing: Tyson had expected that the test plans for function test, component test, and system test would include a detailed matrix of all functions to be tested against the test scripts to be written. Instead, the test plans did not include this technical information at all; they only defined the administrative process to be used in running the tests and reporting status on the problems found. Although this information is important, Tyson wanted the test plans to include test script coverage to make sure that the testing to be performed was analyzed carefully and approved by several people. He believed in a checks-and-balances approach to help ensure that no tests to be performed were overlooked. However, because of growing schedule and cost problems, Tyson accepted the "incomplete" test plans and increasingly turned more to "hope" that things would work out okay, rather than rely on careful planning and follow-through.

As process-related problems continued to plague the project, Tyson became more and more upset that project members were not checking in with him to make sure that they interpreted the scope of the process activities correctly. Furthermore, many project members, after understanding what Tyson meant for the scope of an activity, would not formally request permission to deviate if they disagreed with his intent. After all, many rationalized, Tyson mostly described the scope of an activity verbally. Without a written description of the scope of an activity, a lot of leeway and interpretation was left to the person performing the activity. Consequently, project members often just deviated and did not inform anyone in advance. This made Tyson feel that he was not in control of the project . . . and he wasn't.

On many occasions, project members would tell Tyson that now that they had completed an activity, they could offer useful "tips" to future potential users of his process, tips that they had learned mostly by trial and error. In fact, the project members believed that had they been told some of these tips earlier, they could have improved the schedule and quality of the activity they performed. Unfortunately, Tyson did not bother to log these tips because he viewed his "process" was a one-time-only deal and, therefore, believed that there was not much to be learned that could be passed on to future projects.

Process-related problems continued without letup. Increasingly, Tyson could not find the time to recover from these problems and still come anywhere near meeting the original schedules, budget, and quality projections. He began to hope that he could shorten the duration and scope of many of the activities that had not yet started. Of course, this was wishful thinking. In fact, many of the downstream activities required *more* time to help recover from the lower product quality being produced.

Most of the project's members felt that only Tyson owned the project's software development process. Little ownership for the process was felt across the project. In fact, the worst periods during the project were when Tyson was on vacation or out of town on business. " 'Process-hell' would break loose," one project member accurately declared as discipline for the process waned.

After the project was completed, it was determined that the schedules had slipped by 50 percent, costs had overrun by 70 percent, and the impact to supporting the resulting lower-quality product was an increase of 100 percent in maintenance costs. No analyses of lower customer satisfaction and lost product sales were done.

A postproject review revealed that most of the process-related problems encountered had been experienced on past projects. Moreover, an examination of the postproject review reports from past projects showed that their process-related recommendations still had not been implemented across the organization. "Will we ever learn?" someone was overheard mumbling. "If we want to be able to reasonably predict the schedule, costs, and quality outcomes of applying a software development process, then we need to define that process fully at the start and continue to improve it over time to make it better." Another person quipped, "You don't need a defined and documented software development process to predict the outcome of a project. I have had sufficient experience in this organization to easily predict the outcome of a project that has *no* process: longer schedules, higher costs, and lower product quality."

It doesn't require a trained project management observer to see the folly in allowing projects to begin with a weakly defined and documented software development process. Although the organization in this tale was defined as "growing and their products continue to sell," the clock is ticking away as competitors increasingly learn the lessons that project TKO seemed doomed to repeat. What makes this tale—and the lessons in this book—more important than ever is that companies can go out of business much faster today than during years past. No organization or company can afford to not wholeheartedly adopt basic and sound project management practices.

What Is Meant by a "Process"?

Let's briefly examine what is meant by the term *process* before we jump into the steps that can be followed in defining a software development process. A **process** can be defined simply as a systematic approach that is performed to achieve a specific purpose. In the context of a software development process, a process is defined as an ordered set of activities that, after completed, results in a software "product" that is delivered to a customer.

Each **activity,** of the many activities that comprise a software development process, has definable input and definable output as shown by the simple activity model in Figure 1.1. The input to an activity, also called **entry conditions,** defines the conditions that must be satisfied before the activity can begin. Similarly, the output of an activity, called **exit conditions,** defines the conditions that must be satisfied before the activity can be considered completed. Each activity can be further described by **implementation conditions;** these are a procedure or set of steps that explains "what" must be done, "how" it will be done, and even "ways" to accomplish it.

An example of an activity is "performing a test" (for example, system test). The entry conditions might be:

- A completed and approved test plan is available.
- All test scripts are written.
- The prerequisite hardware and software are installed.
- Product code which has successfully exited the prior activity (i.e., code, inspection, unit test, etc.)

The implementation condition might be:

- Follow the approved test plan, such as running the test scripts, providing weekly status reports of both the problems being identified and the progress being made, and so on.

The exit conditions might be:

- All test scripts have run successfully.
- All problems have been resolved.

 Lesson: A software development process should be made up of a comprehensive set of activities from which the members of a new project can select the right set.

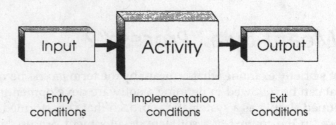

Figure 1.1 Activity model.

A software development process should be defined to a level that can satisfy the needs of a typical new project in an organization as well as be tailorable to meet the needs of the less conventional projects that an organization also experiences. This means that the process should be made up of a comprehensive set of activities from which the members of a new project can select a subset that will best serve the unique needs of that project.

 Lesson: A software development process must be examined routinely for improvement.

A well-defined software development process serves as a roadmap to help ensure that a predictable outcome will be achieved. Lessons learned from past usage should be adopted as routine improvements to the process so that future projects are more productive and are more likely to achieve their goals.

 Lesson: A software development process must never require a user to perform a task that is not useful to the product or project.

A process should not be overly complex or bureaucratic. In fact, the simpler a process is, the better. A process should not require the user to perform an activity or a task within an activity that does not serve some useful purpose. Users of a process need to understand that the process is there to serve them and to help them be more successful in their business. The process is not there to bind them to senseless rules that inhibit them from being the best competitors that they can be.

 Lesson: A software development process must have a simple, expedient method to allow its users to suggest improvements and to deviate.

Even a well-defined software development process is subject to a never-ending progression of changes to improve its usefulness. Because a process must be reexamined constantly for improvements, there needs to be an easy method that users can follow to recommend changes to the process or to, on occasion, to deviate from the defined process. Users of the process must understand clearly how to initiate such changes.

Another point to consider when defining a software development process: registering or certifying your process. If you believe there will ever be a desire or need to register or certify your software development process with an accredited registration body, then now is the time to understand the conditions that you must meet and ensure that the software development process you define is fully compliant. For example, if you have an interest in becoming registered to the ISO 9001 international standard, it will be far less expensive and time consuming to plan to meet those conditions as the software development process is initially being defined now rather than altering the process later.

The Steps to Defining a Software Development Process

You can follow eight steps to define and implement a software development process in your organization. These steps are shown in Figure 1.2. As you examine each step, think about the software development process you currently have defined in your organization. Do these steps reveal ideas that you can apply immediately to improve the definition or implementation of your process?

 Lesson: Defining the right software development process for your organization will have a profound impact on controlling the schedules, costs, and quality of a project.

If you do not yet have a well-defined software development process, then visualize the application of each step in creating the process that best suits your organization. Defining the right software development process for your organization is one of the most important tasks an organization can undertake. Why? Because the right software development process will have a profound impact on controlling the schedules, costs, and quality of a project.

1 Identify the software model.

2 Identify the activities.

3 Identify the relationships among activities.

4 Document other useful information on each activity.

5 Document how to tailor the process.

6 Document how to improve the process.

7 Obtain buy-in of the process.

8 Continually use and improve the process.

Figure 1.2   Steps to defining a software development process.

Step 1.   Identify the Software Model

The first step in defining a software development process is deciding the **software process model** that best fits the needs of your organization. There are numerous models and variations of models from which to choose. The bibliography at the end of this book lists publications that offer a good start in researching which software process model(s) is best for you; however, several models will be introduced briefly here to help you understand the role that a software process model plays in defining your desired software development process. The models introduced are:

- Code-and-fix
- Waterfall
- Incremental
- Iterative

Many definitions exist for these models; however, the definitions offered here are intended to be simple yet informative. Most models are derived, at least in part, from one or more of these basic models.

Code-and-Fix Model

The code-and-fix model, shown in Figure 1.3, is the oldest and simplest of all the models. Little advance planning is performed, and the user of this model quickly begins the coding stage of the product to be developed. Typically some amount of coding is completed, then the evolving product is tested and the problems discovered are corrected. Then more coding occurs, more testing, more problems are corrected, and the coding and testing cycle continues until the product has been fully developed and is delivered to the customer.

This model is most suited for very small and simple projects. Because advance planning is usually lacking and an informal development style usually accompanies the implementation of this model, the quality of the overall product that is delivered to the customer often is lower than the quality resulting from the implementation of other models. Furthermore, the code often is difficult to maintain because the product's design was not carefully planned and documented.

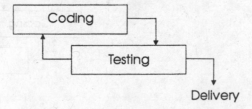

Figure 1.3   Code-and-fix model.

Waterfall Model

Figure 1.4 shows a simple representation of the waterfall model. The name is derived from the appearance of the model; that is, as one stage is completed, the project's activities focus on the next stage, so there is a downward flow, as shown by the solid arrows from one activity to the next. The dotted arrows show feedback loops that are activated when there is a need to revisit an earlier stage to redefine, redesign, recode, or whatever. Even though the figure shows the feedback arrows pointing only to the immediately preceding stage, they can return to any stage.

The waterfall model generally is suited for medium to large projects with well-defined requirements. This model relies heavily on each stage being completed the first time through and operates best when the change activity, although it might be pervasive, does not result in major changes to the definition and design of the product.

Incremental Model

The incremental model is shown in Figure 1.5. While this model is quite similar to the waterfall model, here the product is developed incrementally—in pieces. The figure shows that the requirements, definition, and high-level design are completed and documented. Then the product is developed further in pieces according to a master building plan. After each piece is low-level designed, coded, and tested, it enters into the system test where it is further integrated and tested. The figure represents a common view of the incremental model; however, the development of the pieces could, in fact, begin as early as the definition stage.

A popular advantage of the incremental model is that the pieces of the product can be developed largely in parallel to one another. Thus development activities overlap, which has the benefit of potentially reducing the technical risk of product

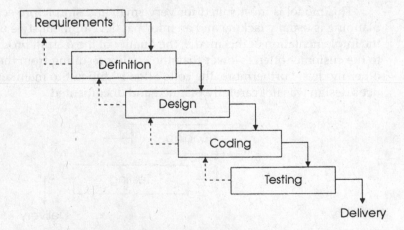

Figure 1.4   Waterfall model.

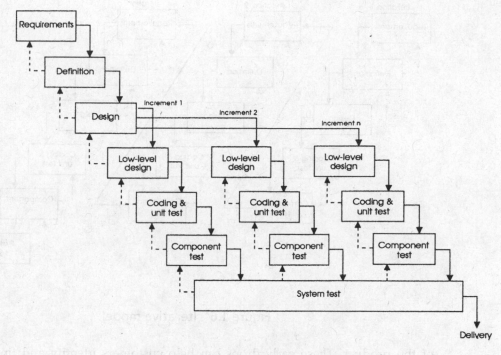

Figure 1.5   Incremental model.

disaster by demonstrating operational code earlier in the development cycle. It also allows the increments, or *drops*, to be made available for early users of the product. Note that as the number of activities in a project that are performed in parallel increases, the greater the complexity in managing the project.

Iterative Model

The iterative model, represented in Figure 1.6, sometimes is confused with the incremental model. Remember, the incremental model can be used when there is a desire to develop, in increments, a product that has known requirements and definition. In contrast, the iterative model typically is used to develop a product that has not been fully defined. The model is used to develop a product to the extent that the requirements and definition are known. As the requirements become better understood and the product is further defined, then the next iteration of the product is developed. Each iteration forms the base for the next iteration. Although the figure shows each iteration beginning with the requirements being revisited, the iterations can begin with the definition or design stages.

The iterative model is particularly suited for use when the requirements and product definition are not well understood and there is a need to begin development more quickly and create a very early version that will demonstrate the look and feel

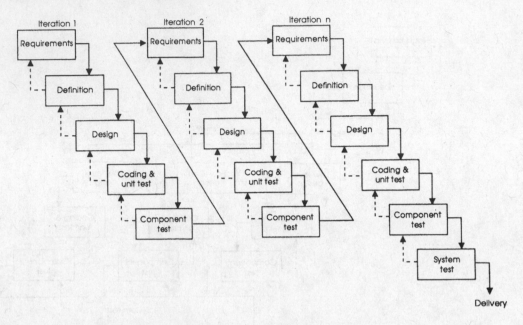

Figure 1.6   Iterative model.

of the product. These early drops can help customers identify and fine-tune the requirements and corresponding product definition for which they are searching.

The iterative model shares many of the advantages of the incremental model but has the distinct benefit of adapting to changing product requirements. The iterative model also introduces additional process complexity and potentially longer product cycles.

Choosing a Model

Don't feel trapped into choosing one of the four common models that were just introduced. There are literally dozens of other models or variations of standard models from which you can choose (including cleanroom, spiral). Instead, view these models as examples of the flexibility you have to choose an existing model or create a unique one that works best for your organization.

Key factors to consider as you search for the right model include:

- Product complexity
- Project size
- Degree that product requirements are documented and understood
- Need for early availability of product function
- Need for customer involvement during development
- Single or multiple customers

- Available software development and project management tools
- Required quality level of product
- Experience and skills of project members, including management
- Physical proximity of project members to one another
- Number of locations and companies involved
- Number of integrated products to be developed
- Maturity of product technology
- Magnitude of anticipated changes during development
- Staffing profile

 Lesson: An organization should strive to have as few software process models as possible.

Although it is acceptable, even beneficial, for an organization to select more than one software process model, every attempt should be made to limit the number of software process models an organization adopts. Project members will be most effective and productive using a model that they understand and have experienced. Familiarity with an acceptable model will aid significantly in the continual successful implementation of that model.

Step 2. Identify the Activities

After the software process model has been selected, the next step is to identify the primary activities that need to be implemented to satisfy it. The list of activities should be comprehensive because the members of new projects will pick and choose activities from this list as they tailor the software development process to meet the unique needs of a new project.

A sample abbreviated list follows. A description of each activity in this short list is presented later in this chapter.

- Requirements
- Objectives
- Specifications
- High-level design
- Publication content plans
- Test plans
- Low-level design
- Code
- Unit and function test

- Component test
- First-draft publications
- System test
- Second-draft publications
- Regression test
- Package
- Delivery

After the list is complete, write a description for each activity in the list. For example, descriptions for the objectives and specifications might be:

Product Objectives

Description: The **product objectives** describe the solution to the problem or set of problems described in the requirements. This document defines, at a high level, a product that will satisfy a marketing opportunity and focuses on the perceived needs of the targeted customer. The objectives document also will provide the underlying direction to be followed by the project as functional and design trade-offs are made throughout the development of the product. Direction for both the programming and publication pieces of the product are addressed.

Product Specifications

Description: The **product specifications** describe, in detail, the externals of the product; that is, they describe what the product will look like to the user. Every function, command, screen, prompt, and other user interface item must be documented so that all participants in the development of the product know the product they are to build, document, test, and support. The product objectives provide the direction and basis needed to develop the product specifications.

Step 3.   Identify the Relationships Among Activities

With the activities listed and described, now define the relationship between related activities. This can be achieved by listing the entry and exit conditions for each activity. If an activity (called B) cannot begin until another activity (called A) has been completed, then the completion of activity A would be stated as an entry condition to activity B.

Let's look again at the earlier example for the objectives and the specifications.

Product Objectives

Entry conditions: The requirements are distributed for review or approval.

Exit conditions: The requirements are approved; the objectives are approved and all problems are resolved.

Product Specifications

Entry conditions: The objectives are distributed for review or approval.

Exit conditions: The objectives are approved; the specifications are approved and all problems are resolved.

Step 4. Document Other Useful Information on Each Activity

As the software development process is being defined, the architects of the process will need a method to record tips and other useful information about the intended use of each activity. As members of new projects attempt to follow the software development process and tailor it to meet their unique project needs, they will need to review this information. One way to record this information is simply to add a new section to be documented for each activity. The section can be called *notes*. Let's look at an example of how the notes section can be defined by revisiting the running example that addresses the objectives and specifications activities.

Project Objectives

Notes: The objectives can be started after a draft of the requirements is available; however, the objectives must not be approved before the requirements have been approved. This will ensure that the requirements are understood fully before the approvers of the objectives can declare that the objectives are indeed satisfying the perceived needs of the targeted audience.

The objectives, after being approved, can be changed only through the designated change control process.

Project Specifications

Notes: The specifications can be started after a draft of the objectives is available; however, the specifications must not be approved before the objectives have been approved. This will ensure that all major problems with the functional direction of the product are resolved before the detailed definition of the product is completed and approved via the specifications.

The high-level design should be completed before the specifications are considered finished. This helps to ensure that any high-level design considerations that could impact the externals of the product are reflected properly in the specifications.

The specifications, after being approved, can be changed only through the designated change control process.

Later in the chapter you will find an abbreviated list of activities that define a software development process. This is the same list shown in Step 2. Each activity presented contains the four sections described in Steps 2, 3, and 4: Description, Entry conditions, Exit conditions, and Notes.

Step 5.   Document How to Tailor the Process

Following Steps 1 through 4 will result in a documented software development process. This process can be defined further by creating a procedure for each activity that describes, in more detail, what must be done, how it will be done, and ways it can be accomplished. A procedure can be a stand-alone document typically anywhere from one to 10 pages in length. A procedure, for example, can describe the steps to be followed in writing and approving the specifications. A formatted template also can be defined as a starting point for people about to write specifications.

 Lesson: Rules in tailoring a software development process must be documented and easy to understand.

No two software development projects are exactly alike, even in the same organization. For this reason, the software development process used across an organization must be able to be tailored to meet the unique needs of new projects. The users of the process need to have clear direction as to what liberties they can take in tailoring the process. Don't assume that people will feel empowered to tailor the process. Furthermore, without tailoring rules, some users of the process might tailor out activities that no project should sacrifice (such as specifications and some testing activities). Although a software development process might be comprehensive enough to meet the needs of projects of over 100,000 lines of code, be prepared to answer the question "What liberties can the members of a much smaller project take in tailoring the process?"

Items that need to be addressed when tailoring rules are documented follow.

- Which activities can be eliminated and which cannot?

Clearly designate the activities that are required and those that are optional. If any activities are denoted as optional, yet in most cases they are expected to be performed, then describe the conditions under which they can be optional.

Don't hesitate to require critical activities. For example, specifications always must be written for a project; otherwise, how will anyone truly know what is to be developed, tested, and documented? Moreover, how can an ill-defined product be supported successfully after it has been delivered to a customer?

- Which activities can be combined and which cannot?

For example, say there are four code tests: unit test, function test, component test, and system test. Is it acceptable to combine one or more of the tests in an effort to be more productive? What if two other tests were defined in the software development process: performance test and usability test? Must these tests be performed independently, or can they be merged with, say, component test and system test?

More examples: If the objectives and the specifications are both required documents, then can they be combined into a single document? Must low-level design always be done? Or can a programmer proceed directly to coding from completing high-level design? Can user publications be distributed for review only once, or must an updated second version also be made available for review?

- Is it okay to add new activities?

Baited question. Of course it is. Moreover, it is important to ensure that all the members of an organization understand that they must take ownership of the software development process that results after all tailoring has been done. If the defined process has deficiencies (and they all do in the intensely dynamic software industry), then project members must feel responsible for "making it right" for their project.

- Who must approve the proposed tailoring?

Must all members of a project reach a consensus on the tailoring proposed? Must anyone outside of the project approve the tailoring proposal, such as an assurance group or management?

Typical projects require at least several project documents to be created (such as specifications, test plans), and, for very large projects, sometimes dozens of different project documents may be required. Use past-project documents as the basis for creating new project documents. Some documents may require only moderate changes from project to project. Identify these documents within your organization and capitalize on them. Using past-project documents as starting points for the creation of new project documents can be a great productivity technique.

 Lesson: At least two complete examples showing how to tailor the software development process should be available.

It is recommended that at least two complete examples of tailoring the software development process are made available for users of the process. Examples are powerful teaching tools and also can improve productivity. The first example should be representative of a typical project within the organization. This example will be heavily copied as a starting point for most projects. The second example is for a very small project. The small-project example is important because it shows users of the process just how flexible the process can be to meet their needs. It also helps to ensure that very small projects do not incur unnecessary overhead and "bureaucracy" in using the process.

 Lesson: It is better to re-create a software development process from a better-fitting software process model than to try to force a project to use an ill-fitting software development process.

When the software development process is being tailored to a new project, and it is decided that the software process model upon which the software development process was built is not the best model for the new project, then what should you do? The most productive approach is to start over at Step 1. However, the steps should go much faster than the first time through because many of the activities already defined for the original software development process will apply directly or with only minor adjustments to the new software development process. Re-creating a software development process from a better-fitting software model is far better than trying to force a project to use an ill-fitting software development process.

Step 6.   Document How to Improve the Process

Now that the software development process is defined and rules on tailoring the process are documented, there needs to be a well thought out method to ensure that the software development process can be improved continually. Three cases for addressing changes need to be addressed.

1. Change requests

Change requests are suggestions for making changes to the process. As project members use the software development process, they often will identify areas for improvement. These change requests need to be collected and addressed relatively quickly. Why quickly? For two reasons: so that the documented software development process can be updated (improved) on a real-time basis so that current and new projects can benefit from these suggestions, and also to demonstrate to the organization's members that the leadership is serious about these improvements and that suggestions are not only welcomed, but they are encouraged and appreciated.

2. Deviation requests

Deviation requests are requests to deviate *one time only* from some aspect of the software development process. Deviation requests are submitted while a project is in progress. These requests require a very speedy response because the decision to grant or deny them can have a significant impact on the schedule and cost of a project. As discussed later, deviation requests are evaluated carefully to determine if the software development process also should be modified.

3. "Postproject review" change requests

When a project has just completed and the product has begun its packaging and delivery-to-the-customer stages, the project's membership (or a representation thereof) should meet to perform a postproject review. Any recommendations for changing the software development process should be submitted and considered relatively quickly, for the reasons stated earlier.

"But," you ask, "where do these change requests and deviation requests get submitted and how do they get acted upon?" An organization can adopt many approaches to address changes to the process. The approach chosen has a lot to do with the size of the organization, whether the members are in close proximity to one another or geographically dispersed, the process maturity level of the organization, and so on. However, let's examine an approach that can be effective in almost any work environment.

A *software development process team,* **process team,** is formed. The process team is made up of members who, collectively, represent all areas from across the organization. This team has total responsibility for defining, documenting, simplifying, improving, and managing the implementation of the software development process.

 Lesson: The overall responsibility for the software development process needs to be distributed across a representative set of people as evenly and as fairly as possible.

Each process team member "owns"—that is, is responsible for—some piece of the process. For example, each activity or major subject defined in the software development process (such as specifications, code, component test, tailoring rules) is assigned to a team member. A team member, also referred to as a *process owner,* can own more than one activity or major subject area, but the overall responsibility for the software development process needs to be distributed as evenly and as fairly across the team as possible. It is important that everyone on the process team personally feels ownership for some aspect of the software development process. The process owner has the prime responsibility for being the advocate for his or her activity or subject area.

So how do change requests and deviation requests get acted upon? Let's first take the case of change requests as shown in Figure 1.7. A change request can be written by any user of the software development process. The change request is submitted to the process team and is routed to the appropriate process owner. (The originator can send the request directly to the process owner if he or she is known.) The process owner proposes the action to be taken on the request and then sends the request and the proposed action to the process team members.

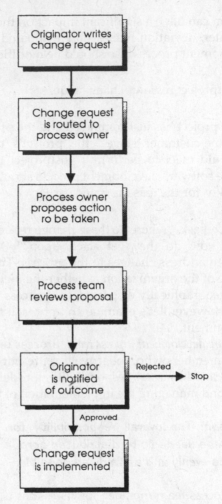

Figure 1.7   Change request.

The process team members can approve, disapprove, or abstain from taking a position. If a consensus is not reached, then the process owner works with the process team members either to reach a consensus or to not approve the change request. The process owner then notifies the originator as to the outcome of the change request. If the request is rejected, the originator can *escalate* the decision to a predefined management path where the change request can be reevaluated. Usually, however, it is expected that the originator will accept the process team's position.

If the change request is approved, then the process owner has the responsibility to ensure that the change is implemented in a timely manner. After the change has been written up satisfactorily in the software development process documentation, it must be approved again by the process team members to ensure that the implementation is understood, correct, and complete. After the documentation has been approved, the members of the organization must be educated on the change so that it is adopted across the organization immediately.

Let's now examine an approach that can be used for deviation requests. Figure 1.8 shows a project member writing a deviation request. The request is then reviewed by the leader of the project. Why the project leader? Because it is important that a deviation is first agreed to by the person with the overall responsibility for the project. If the project leader supports the deviation request, it is routed to the process owner just as a change request is routed.

The process owner is fully empowered to approve or reject the deviation request. If the deviation is rejected, the deviation request process usually stops. However, the project leader can escalate the deviation request to a predefined management path, just as we defined for change requests. If the deviation is granted, either by the process owner or because of an escalation to management, then no further effort is required and the one-time-only deviation is a done deal.

Although random change requests, deviation requests, and change requests resulting from postproject reviews offer good feedback as to the applicability of the software development process in meeting the needs of the organization, other actions

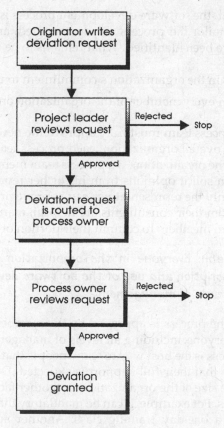

Figure 1.8   Deviation request.

can be performed as well. For example, a survey can be conducted periodically to gain further insight. Also, management can talk to members of the organization periodically, individually or in small groups.

 Lesson: Mostly nonmanagement personnel should own and operate the software development process.

Just what is management's role in defining and implementing the software development process? It is strongly suggested that *nonmanagers* predominantly own and operate the process. This is because it is mostly nonmanagement that must use the process; therefore, nonmanagement must feel the ownership for the definition and application of the process. Although management, particularly at the top, must be supportive of enforcing the software development process, the front-line troops must feel the true ownership of the process and act accordingly.

Step 7. Obtain Buy-in of the Process

At this point, the software development process is fully defined, helpful instructions on how to tailor the process are documented, and the methods of improving the process have been identified. What remains to be done? Two things:

1. Obtain the organization's commitment to use the process.
2. Train every member of the organization on the proper use of the process.

The process team must fully approve the newly defined process. As representatives of the overall organization, each process team member is approving for his or her area of the organization. If a process team member is hesitant to approve, then the member can solicit opinions from his or her represented area. Keep in mind, however, that only the representatives can approve or disapprove the process. Although opinions from their constituents are helpful, management has fully empowered the process team members to commit their portion of the organization.

 Lesson: Everyone in the organization must be educated on the description and use of the software development process, including all levels of management.

After the process is approved by the members of the process team, it is time to educate everyone, including all levels of management, on the new process. The education process is the best way to show people that the process is committed and to let them know that their full support is expected. Depending on the complexity of the process, the size of the organization, and other factors, the education can take on different forms. For example, it can be mandatory that everyone in the organization participate in a one-day training class. Another approach is to spend one-half day introducing most members of the organization to the new process and reserving the full-day training class for the people who have the greatest need to understand the full implementation of the process (team leaders, project leaders, project planners). As new members are added to the overall organization, don't forget to plan for their training so they can understand what is expected of them as they use the software development process.

Step 8.   Continually Use and Improve the Process

 Lesson: Management has the ultimate responsibility to insist that each new project complies fully with the approved software development process.

Now that the software development process is defined, documented, and approved, the last step is to *use it*. Sound trite? This is where many organizations fall apart. They don't practice what they preach. They don't insist that all members of new projects embrace the approved software development process. The responsibility rests with the leadership of each new project. This leadership typically is made up of both management and nonmanagement personnel. However, management has the ultimate responsibility to *insist* that each new project complies with the approved software development process.

Notice that the steps to defining the software development process included one (Step 6) on how to improve the process. It is important that the notion of improving the process is well understood *before* the process is approved. Because no process is perfect in its original design, and because rapidly changing business needs will continue to challenge the process to be improved, it is essential that all members of an organization understand that the process *always* will be undergoing change—that the process belongs to the members of the organization and that it is intended to serve them, not the other way around.

Sample Software Development Process

 Lesson: Every organization has a legitimate need for a uniquely defined software development process.

This section presents an example of a software development process. The example represents an abbreviated process and is made up of the same software development activities that were shown earlier in Step 2. Why abbreviated? Because every organization will have its own uniquely defined software development process to accommodate its particular needs. It would not be possible to define a comprehensive software development process here that would have direct applicability to all organizations. However, by presenting a simple and abbreviated process, two primary objectives are served:

1. The framework of how a software development process can be defined is demonstrated, and

2. The fundamental set of concepts and terms that will be referenced in subsequent chapters can be introduced.

For purposes of illustration, the waterfall model is used as the model from which to define the software development process presented here and referenced throughout the book. The waterfall model is selected because (1) most models are derived to some degree from it, (2) it is one of the simplest models to understand, and (3) most readers already have some familiarity with it.

Figure 1.9 shows the set of activities that will be defined in the abbreviated software development process, presented within the framework of the waterfall model. They range from defining the customer requirements for the product to be developed to performing the final regression test just prior to packaging the product and delivering it to a customer.

Notice that the figure shows the relative relationship among the activities. This figure is intended to help you get a better "feel" for when each activity might start and end in relationship to other activities. It is impractical to provide a figure that accurately shows the start and end, the duration, and the relationship of each activity to another for every type of project. Therefore, Figure 1.9 should be viewed as an example or high-level approximation of these relationships for a so-called typical project.

Notice, also, that no durations are specified for the activities shown in the figure. The durations depend on the characteristics of the project, such as the number of people participating in the project, their experience and skill level, the total lines of code or function to be developed, the technical complexity of the product, the availability of both product- and project-related tools, and other factors.

Not all project activities are shown in the abbreviated software development process. Only the more fundamental activities that, conceptually, make up the foundation of a sound software development process are identified. Several additional activities, however, will be introduced in later chapters.

The remainder of this chapter describes the activities that comprise our sample, abbreviated software development process as depicted in Figure 1.9. As with any rapidly growing and changing industry, it is important to define a common terminology in order to impart knowledge and share ideas. The terminology chosen in the figure, and throughout this book, is an attempt to reach and benefit the broadest audience possible. You will find it helpful to review this material before proceeding to the chapters that follow.

Each activity presented contains the four sections described in Steps 2, 3, and 4: Description, Entry conditions, Exit conditions, and Notes. The purpose for each section is restated here.

- *Description:* A brief description of the activity.

Details, such as specific outlines of plans and documents, and what each section of a plan or document might contain, are omitted and are beyond the scope of this

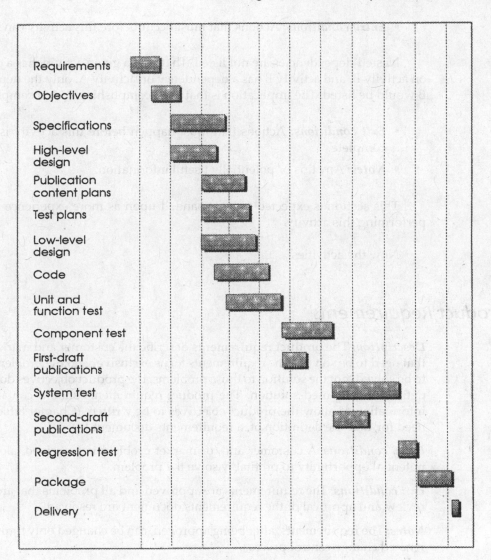

Figure 1.9   Overview of a software development process.

section. However, in the development of a software development process, it is recommended that a procedure be documented that describes the "what" and "how" for the each activity. In the long run, documented procedures can save the members of an organization valuable time from "reinventing the wheel" each time a new project is undertaken, especially when templates for plans are provided as starting points. Procedures also can help ensure that necessary conformity and completeness is achieved for each activity and can be used to train new project members. Procedures also establish a baseline from which to improve the implementation of an activity continuously.

> • *Entry conditions:* Actions that must occur before this activity can begin.

Nested dependencies are not listed. That is, if a given activity has a dependency on activity B, and activity B has a dependency on activity A, only the dependency on B would be listed. The implication is that by accomplishing B, A is completed.

> • *Exit conditions:* Actions that must happen before this activity is considered complete.
> • *Notes:* Any tips or potentially useful information.

This section is expected to be expanded upon as more experience is gained in performing this activity.

Now the activities . . .

Product Requirements

Description: The **product requirements** describe the customer and market problems that need to be solved. The requirements focus exclusively on the problems that need to be solved, not the solution to those problems; the product objectives document will define the proposed solution. The product requirements should contain sufficient information to allow the product objectives to be written. (Chapter 8 focuses on the need for, and the definition of, a requirements document.)

Entry conditions: A customer and/or market problem is perceived, along with the potential opportunity to profitably solve the problem.

Exit conditions: The requirements are approved and all problems that arose from the review and approval of the requirements document are resolved.

Notes: The requirements, after being approved, can be changed only through the designated change control process.

Product Objectives

Description: The **product objectives** describe the solution to the problem or set of problems described in the requirements. This document defines, at a high level, a product that will satisfy a marketing opportunity and focuses on the perceived needs of the targeted customer. The objectives document also will provide the underlying direction to be followed by the project members as functional and design trade-offs are made throughout the development of the product. Direction for both the programming and publication pieces of the product is addressed. (Chapter 9 further describes product objectives.)

Entry conditions: The requirements are distributed for review or approval.

Exit conditions: The requirements are approved; the objectives are approved and all problems that arose from the review of the objectives are resolved.

Notes: The objectives can be started after a draft of the requirements is available; however, the objectives must not be approved before the requirements have been approved. This will ensure that the requirements are understood fully before agreeing that the objectives are indeed satisfying the perceived needs of the targeted audience.

The objectives document is considerably smaller than the product specifications document to be described, perhaps only 10 percent the size.

The objectives, after being approved, can be changed only through the designated change control process.

Product Specifications

Description: The **product specifications** describe, in detail, the externals of the product; that is, they describe what the product will look like to the user. Every function, command, screen, prompt, and other user interface items must be documented so that all participants in the development of the product know the product they are to build, document, test, and support. The product objectives provide the direction and basis needed to develop the product specifications. (Product specifications are the major theme of Chapter 10.)

Entry conditions: The objectives are distributed for review or approval.

Exit conditions: The objectives are approved; the specifications are approved and all problems that arose from the review of the specifications are resolved.

Notes: The specifications can be started after a draft of the objectives is available; however, the specifications must not be approved before the objectives have been approved. This will ensure that all major problems with the functional direction of the product are resolved before the detailed definition of the product is completed and approved via the specifications.

The high-level design should be completed before the specifications are considered finished. This helps to ensure that any high-level design considerations that could impact the externals of the product are reflected properly in the specifications.

The specifications, after being approved, can be changed only through the designated change control process.

High-level Design

Description: **High-level design** is the level of design required to understand how the components (major pieces) of the product technically work (1) with one another, (2) with the surrounding hardware and software environment with which they must operate, and (3) internally. This design identifies the components that make up the product, defines the functional mission for each component, defines the interface across these components and externally to the operating environment, and defines, at a high level, the internal design of each component.

Entry conditions: High-level design begins shortly after the objectives document is started. At this point, as the components of the product are described in terms of how they work with one another and with the hardware and software environment with which they must operate, the high-level design can be defined as preliminary high-level design or "architecture." The architecture is part of the information addressed in the objectives.

Exit conditions: The high-level design is completed and problems found are resolved.

Notes: The high-level design should begin shortly after the product objectives have been started. However, the high-level design should be understood reasonably before the product objectives are completed. This overlap between the development of the product objectives and the preliminary high-level design will prevent the product objectives from defining a product that could not be built technically in a satisfactory manner. There must be confidence that a high-level design supports the product objectives before the objectives are completed.

The high-level design should be completed, and the final draft of the product specifications document correspondingly updated, before the specifications are distributed for approval. If the high-level design is completed after the specifications are approved, excessive change-control activity against the approved specifications document might occur. (The relationship of the high-level design to the product objectives and to the product specifications is a topic of discussion in Chapter 10.)

Publication Content Plans

Description: The **publication content plan**s describe the content and design of each publication to be included in the product. Content plans include the table of contents for each publication and the basic content and structure of each chapter.

Entry conditions: The product specifications are distributed for review or approval.

Exit conditions: The product specifications are approved; the publication content plans are approved and all problems are resolved.

Notes: The writing of the content plans cannot begin until the product specifications activity has been started. Otherwise, there would be too little product externals data available to plan the publications to a chapter level. Similarly, the content plans cannot be completed until after the product specifications have been completed.

The publication content plans are especially important for two reasons, centering around the importance of providing information to the user in an expedient, easy-to-use, and understandable fashion. First, most products require the user to reference the publications that accompany the product. Without a good set of publications, the product will have far less chances for success.

The second reason for the importance of the publication content plans is in support of an industry direction. This direction is to provide publications-related information on-line for the product's users and to make the use of products more intuitive. On-line information—that is, the ability to access information directly from a computer workstation rather than through documents—and intuitive person-machine interfaces both require careful, advance planning. The publications content plans are vehicles to help define this direction early in the development of the product.

Test Plans

Description: **Test plan**s are documents that describe the *who, what, when, where,* and *how* for a designated test. A test plan is written for each test activity, such as unit test, function test, component test, and system test.

Entry conditions: The product specifications are distributed for review or approval.

Exit conditions: The product specifications are approved; the subject test plan is approved and all problems are resolved.

Notes: Test plans cannot be started until after the product specifications have been started. Also, the test plans cannot be finished until after the product specifications have been completed. Otherwise, the test plans would be incomplete, because the externals of the product would not yet be fully known and documented.

Approval for a unit test plan might be simply a team leader verifying its completion; whereas, approval for a function test plan might require several people verifying its contents to ensure a thorough and satisfactory test will be conducted. (Chapter 12 offers more information about unit and function test plans.)

Low-level Design

Description: **Low-level design** represents two levels of design. The first level is the design required to understand how modules within each component will work technically with one another. (A component typically is made up of one or more modules.) This design identifies the modules that make up each component, the functional mission for each module, and the interface across these modules. This is an *intra* component, *inter*module design. (In some development shops, this level of design is called *high-level design*, and should not to be confused with the same term introduced earlier and used throughout this book which refers to *inter*component design.)

The next level of design deals with the internal design of each module of a component. This design identifies each programming decision path and may be documented by using a design language, graphic flows, and so on, or simply by writing English narratives.

Entry conditions: The high-level design has been completed for the component or portion of a component for which low-level design is to be started.

Exit conditions: The low-level design is completed and problems found are resolved.

Notes: There is no requirement to complete all high-level design before low-level design can be started. Notice from Figure 1.9 that some overlap of low-level design and high-level design is typical. Once the high-level design has been completed for a component or a major portion of a component, the low-level design can begin on the modules for that portion.

Code

Description: The code activity is the act of writing instructions that are immediately computer recognizable or can be assembled or compiled to form computer-recognizable instructions.

Entry conditions: The low-level design has been completed for the modules to be coded.

Exit conditions: All code is written, compiled without errors, and problems found are resolved.

Notes: There is no requirement to complete all low-level design before coding can be started. Coding can begin on those areas of components—that is, modules—that have already been designed to a low level. Consequently, as shown in Figure 1.9, a large overlap can occur within a project between the coding activity and the low-level design activity.

Unit and Function Test

Description: The **unit test** is the first time that the code is executed. The unit test primarily refers to the isolated testing of each logic flowpath of code within each module. The **function test** is the testing of each of the product's functions through one or more modules. In both cases, **artificial testing environments** (called **scaffolding** or **stubbing**) may be necessary since other modules of the product may not be far enough along in their development to be included in the testing.

Entry conditions: Coding is completed for those modules to be unit tested and the corresponding unit test plans are completed.

Exit conditions: All unit and function testing has completed as defined in the exit conditions specified in the unit and function test plans.

Notes: Because there is no requirement to finish all coding before unit testing can begin, an overlap is shown (Figure 1.9) between the coding activity and the unit and function test activities. That is, once a module has been coded and its corresponding unit test plan is complete, it can begin to be unit tested. Once all the modules required to test a function have been unit tested and the corresponding function test plan is complete, function testing can begin. The relative time period for unit and function testing shown in Figure 1.9 represents the period when testing occurs. The test scripts to be used must, of course, be defined and written before this test period begins, or at least before those test scripts are required. (Chapter 12 discusses unit and function testing.)

Unit test typically is performed by the same person who designed and coded the module to be tested. Function test typically is performed by the development group that coded and unit tested the modules, not by an independent test group. It is typically during function test that all of the product's modules are placed under **change control** for the first time. This term refers to a method designed to strictly control further changes to a module. Change control is managed best by a group or individuals who did not develop the code.

Component Test

Description: **Component test** is the first test of a product in which all or some of the components are tested together. Typically, no artificial testing environment (scaffolding) is required. All the product's externals should be tested. The tests are developed primarily by studying the product specifications. Occasionally, the design documentation also is studied to gain more insight into areas to be tested.

Entry conditions: The entry conditions defined in the component test plan are met; these conditions typically include the successful completion of the unit and function tests for components to be tested.

Exit conditions: The component test exit conditions defined in the component test plan are met.

Notes: Figure 1.9 shows that component testing does not begin until all of the unit and function tests have been completed successfully. Some project managers may choose to integrate unit- or function-tested code into the component test in pre-planned drops, or stages. The relative time period for component testing shown in Figure 1.9 represents the period when testing occurs. All the test scripts to be exercised during component testing should be defined and written prior to the start of the component test, or at least before those test scripts are required to be exercised.

Component test typically is an independent test that is performed best by people other than those who developed the code. When a product is tested by an independent test group, the objectivity of the test usually increases.

First-draft Publications

Description: First-draft publications are the first drafts of the product's publications that are available for review by groups within the project. The product's publications are primarily the documentation that the user will receive with the product and also are called *user documentation.* However, the product's publications also can include technical manuals that explain to users how to solve problems they discover.

Entry conditions: The corresponding publication content plan is distributed for review.

Exit conditions: The corresponding content plan is approved; the first draft of the publication is fully reviewed and responses are returned to the writers for appropriate action.

Notes: The first-draft publications should be available at or near the start of component testing—both for review by the project's personnel and for use by the testing organization. This draft should be essentially complete and accurate. Comments should be returned to the writers by the middle of the component test. This will help ensure that updates will be available for the second draft of the publications, to be distributed at the start of system testing. (The second draft typically is the final draft of the publications. As the final draft, the second draft of the publications is the draft distributed for approval.)

The duration shown in Figure 1.9 covers only the period when the first draft is distributed for review. The actual writing of the first draft can begin once the corresponding publication content plans have been completed.

System Test

Description: **System test** generally tests the major functions of the product, along with some error situations. This testing is performed strictly by exercising the externals defined at a user level in the product objectives and the product specifications. Functions and interfaces internal to the product are not tested directly. These internals are tested only indirectly by exercising the externally documented functions. Typically there is no reliance on scaffolding code because it is expected that all the product's function and code are available.

During system test, the product also is tested in a *total systems environment* with other software and hardware product combinations that are supported by the product. For example, if the product being developed is an application that must run on several different display screens and printers, then it is advisable to test the new product with all of the stated hardware. Sometimes, however, a reasonable subset may be acceptable and, in fact, the only practical approach. Likewise with software products. If the new product also must operate in harmony with other applications, or even with different release levels of an operating system, then these product combinations also would be tested during the system test.

Entry conditions: The entry conditions defined in the system test plan are met; these conditions typically include the successful completion of component test (or some designated subset).

Exit conditions: The system test exit conditions defined in the system test plan are met.

Notes: System test typically does not begin until component test has been completed. The product is expected to be approaching a customer-delivery quality level when this test begins. However, some project managers may choose to integrate component-tested code into the system test in preplanned drops, or stages. The relative time for system test shown in Figure 1.9 represents the period when testing occurs. All the test scripts to be exercised during system test should be defined and written prior to the start of the system test, or at least before those test scripts are required for testing.

System test typically is an independent test that is performed best by programmers who did not develop the code. A portion of system test also is best performed by test subjects who represent typical users for the product conducted in a real customer environment.

Second-draft Publications

Description: Second-draft publications are the second drafts of the publications. For most products, the second draft will be the final draft that is distributed for review and approval.

Entry conditions: The second draft can begin to be updated after responses are received from the reviewers of the first draft.

Exit conditions: The second draft is reviewed fully and all problems identified are resolved, resulting in approval of the product's publications.

Notes: The second draft should be available at the beginning of system test—both for review and for use in the final testing of the product. Comments should be returned to the writers by the middle of system testing so that final changes can be made before the publications are printed. The final print of the publications should not be started, however, until all product testing has been completed. If product testing continues, a strong possibility exists that a problem will surface, requiring a change to the publications as part of the problem resolution.

As with the first draft, the duration shown in Figure 1.9 covers only the period when the draft is distributed for review. The activities associated with the second draft actually begin immediately after the comments are available from reviewers of the first draft, and end when the final publications are ready for the final print.

Regression Test

Description: **Regression test** is the final test of the product. This test typically is comprised of a carefully selected set of test scripts that are run against the final level of code and supported hardware. These test scripts are run as a final verification that the product's code is indeed functioning as it should. The test scripts for regression test typically consist of selected test scripts from both component test and system test. Regression testing should not begin until system test has completed.

Entry conditions: The entry conditions defined in the regression test plan are met; these conditions include the successful completion of system test.

Exit conditions: The regression test exit conditions defined in the regression test plan are met.

Notes: If a problem is found during regression test, the problem is corrected and, with few exceptions, the entire set of regression test scripts is rerun. Restarting the regression test from the beginning provides verification that the problem did indeed get fixed and that the fix did not cause a new problem.

Regression test can be defined as the end of system test rather than as a separate test with a separate test plan. Wherever it is defined, however, it is very important that the concept behind regression test be adopted. It is very costly to package and deliver products to customers that have obvious defects that could have been found and corrected during regression test, not only financially but also to the image of the product and the company behind it. This is where the adage of an ounce of prevention is worth a pound of cure fully applies.

Regression test typically is an independent test that is performed best by programmers who did not develop the code.

Packaging

Description: The **packaging** activity involves collecting the pieces of the product, such as the code and publications, and preparing them for delivery to a customer. The product's programs are placed on media (diskettes, CD, or magnetic tape), and the product's publications are formally printed or otherwise prepared in the desired format. Then the pieces are packaged in their final wrap and readied for delivery.

Entry conditions: The product is developed and tested completely; that is, regression test is completed according to the exit conditions defined in the regression test plan and the publications are approved and all necessary updates have been applied.

Exit conditions: The product is packaged and ready for delivery to a customer.

Notes: After the product has been packaged, a test should be made to ensure that the product will be acceptable to customers. For example, the code and publications should be unpackaged, just as a customer is expected to do. The code then should be installed and exercised briefly to ensure its readiness. The product's publications should be used for the installation and to perform some of the product's function.

Delivery

Description: **Delivery** is the point at which the packaged product is distributed to a customer. The customer may be the product's user, a distributor, or a third party who will repackage the product in some fashion for eventual resale.

Entry conditions: The product is fully packaged and ready for delivery to a customer.

Exit conditions: The product is delivered to a customer.

Notes: For illustrative purposes, Figure 1.9 shows a relatively small span of time for delivering the product. Of course, the time period for delivering the product to many customers actually can be spread over many months or years.

Now that you are acquainted with a starter set of concepts and terms, you are ready to gain maximum benefit from the chapters that follow. New terms will be defined as they are introduced. The primary goal is to keep you ready to understand and learn. I hope you will find that this book works for you.

2

Discipline: The Glue That Holds It All Together

All leaders want to run a tight ship, but not at the expense of their project personnel's creativity, sense of commitment and ownership, and willingness to take risks. If a leader is too strict or rigid, a level of bureaucracy can evolve that actually has a stifling affect on employee productivity and motivation. On the other hand, if a leader is too permissive, a project can be robbed of the crucial management support and order that is so vital in maintaining a well-run, consistently productive organization. Somewhere, between these extremes of rigidity and permissiveness, is a desirable balance that offers the most in achieving and maintaining a healthy organization. Within this scale, where would you position your leadership abilities?

 Lesson: The single greatest factor that can make or break a software development project is the degree of discipline that the project's leadership exercises.

Briefly stated, **discipline** is the act of encouraging a desired pattern of behavior. Discipline is the glue that holds it all together. Most projects that do not meet their schedule, budget, quality, or function fail because the level of discipline exhibited across the organization is deficient.

This chapter discusses the important subjects of:

- The need for discipline
- How to recognize the disciplined organization
- How to establish and maintain discipline
- Attributes of the successful leader

This chapter is primarily, but not exclusively, for the leaders in a project. These leaders might direct a team of two or an organization of 1,000 and include technical, administrative, financial, and project leaders. Project leaders include both managers and nonmanagers. This chapter also should be of interest to those aspiring to be leaders.

Project Tales

The short scenarios presented in this section illustrate situations to be avoided. They demonstrate situations where discipline is weak, misguided, or missing. Can you recognize the problems? Have you seen them before?

A new department has been created in a busy and expanding development organization. At the first department meeting, the manager, Ralph Nettle, looks over his employees and sets some ground rules for the operation of the department. Weeks later those at the meeting recall that Nettle's most notable statement was: "Do as I say, not as I do."

In the meeting, Nettle announces that he will meet with employees individually to determine their role and degree of progress in the current project. He arranges to meet with each person for 30 minutes over the better part of two days. The first meeting takes 40 minutes; the next, one hour. At the end of two days, six employees have yet to be seen. He reschedules them for the next day but finds time to meet with only one. He apologizes to the other five and reschedules again—and again. Two weeks later he has met with everyone. During each meeting Nettle has committed to get personally involved with each employee on specific problem areas. He sets dates to get back with each of them. After one month has passed, only 25 percent of his commitments have been fulfilled.

This department manager, Matt Holstein, feels really in tune with what's going on in the project. He has been a manager for just under one year. However, Holstein is no newcomer to software development projects. He has held several leadership roles on past projects. He feels he has learned the "right" way to do things and wants the best possible performance from his department. To obtain this goal, he feels he must take an active role in all primary decisions and many lesser ones. He believes that no one in his department can do most tasks as well as he can. He also feels that no one seems to be as self-motivated as he believes they should be. If this department was a separate company, and he was to leave, he just knows that the company would fold. He acknowledges there are people in his department who have potential, and he is determined to bring that potential to the surface.

As a manager, Holstein feels he is a natural leader and can guide his department to excellence in everything it does. To this end, he has defined himself as the focal point for all activities. He initiates and performs most planning exercises. he thoroughly reviews all his department's documents and deliverables before he will allow them to be distributed outside his department. He also, and just as thoroughly, reviews all documents generated by other departments that are for his department's review. He consolidates any comments from within his department and personally creates the response memo for his signature. He not only attends the more important meetings within his department, he runs them. Almost nothing happens within his department without his personal participation.

With all the care and attention he gives to his employees' assignments, Holstein cannot understand why everybody else seems unwilling or unable to make decisions on their own. He notices he is usually the only one working overtime. He does not look forward to being out of the office because, when he returns, he is sure there will be too much work to catch up on and, possibly, from which to recover.

A new project has just started. The staffing occurred almost immediately, with programmers transferred from other projects. The new project is small by some standards, with 20 programmers. The project leader, Erin Springer, sees an opportunity to achieve great things with this newly assembled talented crew and proceeds to declare the schedules that must be met. These schedules are over a one-year period. The project members quickly recognize the difficulty in achieving such aggressive schedules. The generally held view is that aggressive schedules are good business as long as they are *achievable*. An attempt is made to put more realistic schedules in place but Springer holds firm. She states that the schedules have been committed to higher management and, therefore, must happen. Not much is known about Springer's past leadership experiences. In an attempt to be fair, the project members give her the benefit of the doubt and hope she has an "ace up her sleeve." A month passes and the new schedule is one week behind. The next month sees another week lost. At this rate, the project will be late by 25 percent of the schedule's length, yet Springer is unwilling to adjust the schedule. She attempts to compensate by mandating overtime and adding people to the project. Four months into the project, progress is more than one month behind schedule. Hope is rapidly fading that an ace will appear.

The project is four months old, with at least two years to go. The number of people involved in the project has grown rapidly. Several of the earlier people to come on board have been given the more critical lead roles. These people do not appear to be particularly experienced, skilled, or gifted, but they are recognized as being loyal to June Pritchard, the project head. The project is proving to be a challenge in many ways, not the least of which are its technical complexity and sheer size. As is to be expected with any project of this magnitude, daily problems arise and compete for attention. The people Pritchard has assigned to take the critical lead roles are having difficulty extinguishing fires as fast as they flare up. Small problems fester through neglect and grow into serious problems. Many decisions are made and then remade days or weeks later, causing much rework and consternation among the employees affected. Communication across the project is suffering severely. Commitments are being made without consulting the people who must carry them out. Many believe that the people assigned to the project's more critical lead roles are not qualified. Pritchard discounts this notion. She asserts that the project leadership is as it should be. Her view is that the major problem lies in the large number of relatively inexperienced, uncommitted, and unmotivated employees throughout the organization.

Michelle Barret, a hardworking employee, feels frustrated. She graduated as class valedictorian from a prominent university and went on to earn, with honors, a master's degree in computer science and a minor in business. She has worked for one company since finishing college four years ago. At that time, it was her belief that two types of successful companies exist: those that hire their lead people from other companies, and those that grow and groom their leaders from within. She favored working for a company that placed a premium on developing its own people. She felt that this type of company would best prepare her for an executive position.

Barret's views about successful companies have not changed, but her views about her own company have. The lead people in this organization have done little to coach, counsel, or inspire her or any other of the project personnel. She actually feels the opposite happens. People are reprimanded publicly for taking on risks that fail. Those who complete their assignments on schedule and with superior quality are all but ignored. It is next to impossible to receive any personal recognition for a job well done. Barret regularly observes the project leaders she works with reacting to people and situations without listening to the facts. Inconsistent decisions are commonplace. Advancement is significantly slower than is generally expected within companies in the same industry. Today Barret has, with personal regret, submitted her resignation.

These scenarios depict situations that hurt the people involved, the project, and the company. Yet action can be taken to avoid replays of these stories and numerous others like them.

The remainder of this chapter offers some ways to recognize and maintain a properly disciplined organization and to understand the numerous benefits of such an organization. Also presented are the attributes that are characteristic of successful leaders—*self-disciplined* leaders. After you have read this chapter, you might find it useful to revisit the scenarios to identify their problems—and to determine how they could have been avoided.

The Need for Discipline

Discipline is the soul of an army. It makes small numbers formidable, procures success to the weak, and esteem to all.

—*George Washington*

 Lesson: All people want and need to know the acceptable pattern of behavior that is expected of them.

Everyone wants discipline. Everyone wants to work in an environment where people know what to expect. Again, discipline is the glue that holds a project together. It is *the* tool for managing change—and change is essential for progress. The processes and methodologies employed within a project cannot be sustained without the necessary, underlying discipline. A project needs discipline to achieve the desired level of accomplishment for each of its major parameters. These major project parameters are listed in Figure 2.1.

The following sections offer insight on the impact that discipline can have on these major project parameters.

Employee Morale

 Lesson: Projects run their best when employee morale is high.

While great human achievements typically are not accomplished on morale alone, history seems to show that strong morale has added to the effectiveness of many great achievers. Obviously high employee morale offers great value to a project. Good morale can have a positive affect on every major project parameter. However, discipline from the project's leadership is essential for achieving high morale within an organization.

For example, project members want and need to:

- Know what their mission is
- Understand their assignments
- Understand how they are measured against their performance
- Know that they will be recognized and rewarded for their achievements
- Know what to expect from their leaders
- Believe that project leaders make a genuine effort to understand their people and maintain good, two-way communications
- Believe that project leaders will make the best decisions for the success of the project

■ Employee morale
■ Productivity
■ Quality
■ Schedules
■ Cost

Figure 2.1   Major project parameters.

When project leaders exhibit discipline in insisting on an environment that satisfies these wants and needs from the project's personnel, then almost anything can be accomplished. Significant accomplishment, however, is impossible when the project's management fails to exercise the necessary level of discipline that is needed to create and sustain such an environment—an environment that *encourages* high employee morale.

Productivity

 Lesson: Employee productivity is at its highest when employees know what to do, how to do it—and do it!

Employee productivity is at its best when project processes are defined, measurable, and enforced—and project members are educated about their roles. Discipline within the project is required to make these things happen. Consider an example.

In every software development process, the product passes through phases as it is being developed. Some typical phases are:

- Product definition
- Product design
- Code

Each of the project's phases can, in turn, be defined in more detail. For example, "product specifications" falls within the phase "product definition." The product specifications activity could be divided into five smaller activities:

- Product specifications preparation
- Product specifications review
- Product specifications update
- Product specifications approval
- Product specifications refresh

Each of these activities can be defined further in terms of entry, implementation, and exit conditions. (See Chapter 4 for more on phases, activities, and process conditions.)

After the project's processes to be followed are defined to a level at which the participants can measure their adherence, the project members then must be properly trained and educated to understand those processes fully. Finally, those processes must be fully supported and enforced by the project leaders. To make all this happen, the project's leadership must demonstrate discipline.

Quality

 Lesson: Quality will suffer without deliberate discipline.

Quality is another major project parameter that will suffer without discipline. It seems that many people have their own definition of quality. (See Chapter 6 for more on planning for quality.) Regardless of the definition used, however, there is always a great need to define and follow processes that will yield the desired product quality. While quality often is associated with the "worker bee" in the trenches doing the designing, coding, or testing, the project's leadership must first exhibit the discipline that leads to a quality-producing work environment. There is a real temptation to sacrifice quality first—whenever a project falls behind schedule. But quality actually should be the last parameter to be sacrificed, if ever. Sheer discipline from the project's leadership is required to avoid the let's-lower-the-quality trap. The following saying holds true for too many projects—perhaps even yours:

We never have enough time to do it right, but we always find time to do it over.

Schedules

 Lesson: The need for continuous discipline is perhaps most evident when managing a project's schedules.

This saying leads into the next reason for discipline—schedules. How many projects do you know about that actually finished under the same schedule they began? For those projects that changed their schedules, how much of a contributing factor was the lack of project discipline by the project leaders?

Earlier it was mentioned that change is essential to progress. When a project's schedules are defined and approved early in the software development process, many assumptions and dependencies are identified. As time passes and some activities complete and many more begin, the project personnel who participated in the creation and approval of the schedules become more knowledgeable. For example, a certain document that was estimated to take four weeks to write might now require six weeks because the expected dependencies were late or because the effort simply was underestimated.

What is happening is that *change* is being introduced into the project equation. In order to maintain the overall schedules, the discipline required to manage this ongoing change must be alive and active. Software development projects are not static. They are extremely lively and in constant need of attention. Discipline from project leaders is vital to maintain the overall, committed project schedules.

Cost

Cost is another major project parameter at the mercy of discipline. Budgets are affected by such factors as the number of programmers involved, the number of computer workstations available, the tools employed, office space, furniture, and so on. The list can be extensive. Even the timing chosen by a project's leaders to begin moving people from one project into another can be quite costly. The opportunity to spend beyond the budget can be too tempting. "Borrowing from Peter to pay Paul" only defers pain into the future. Rationalizing a multitude of ways to recover costs can become easy. Of course, when recovery plans are implemented later, many turn out to have looked better on paper. Here again, discipline by project leaders is essential—essential in routinely controlling budgets so costs can be contained.

 Lesson: A great deal of discipline is required to manage the constant change that is common to all software development projects.

All of the major project parameters—employee morale, productivity, quality, schedules, and cost—influence each other to some degree. For example, if morale is low, then quality and productivity will suffer. This will cause schedules to be extended, which, in turn, will increase costs. But no matter which parameters are used to show this domino effect, any parameter that "goes south" can pull the overall project with it. Again, the management of change is critical to the success of the project. And critical to the management of change is the discipline required to hold all parameters of a project together.

Recognizing the Disciplined Organization

Have you ever noticed that some organizations seem to be more successful than others? That the energy level of the people involved seems to be higher? That these people generally seem to have better attitudes about themselves and the work they are doing? That more things just seem to go right? Also, have you noticed that these organizations seem to be able to attract the most interest from employees in sister organizations who desire to join?

 Lesson: The better managed projects manage discipline better.

What is so unique about these seemingly "magnetic" organizations that attract good fortune at most turns? The general answer is that they are managed better. The specific answer is *discipline* exercised by project leaders in both *what* they do and *how* they do it. Discipline comes in many flavors, but only the discipline that supports the project's mission is desirable. This is the discipline that supports the pattern of productive behavior needed in and wanted by project personnel. This is the discipline that should be encouraged. This is called positive discipline. Positive discipline is what this chapter is all about.

Before venturing further into this topic, it can help to take a brief look at negative discipline. Remember, discipline is the act of encouraging a desired pattern of behavior. If the leader of a group trains the group's members to follow a certain pattern of behavior, and that behavior is not productive to achieving the group's mission, then the discipline exercised is negative discipline. As an example, consider an organization that needs its employees to take more risk in accepting responsibility. Now consider a leader within that organization who continually punishes each risk taker who meets with failure. This leader would be displaying negative discipline because the discipline works against the project's mission. The scenarios at the beginning of this chapter provide additional examples of negative discipline.

Implementing Discipline

Now consider positive discipline once again, focusing on the discipline that project leaders demonstrate in both *what* they do and *how* they do it. Figure 2.2 shows the four essential traits that are the *what* of the well-disciplined organization. This is a good point to examine these traits closer and discuss *how* they need to be addressed.

Trait One: Set Realistic Goals

Every organization needs goals. How else can success be measured? Goals must be:

- Simply stated
- Understood by all
- Measurable

Figure 2.2   Traits of the well-disciplined organization.

Lesson: Discipline begins by setting realistic goals.

To "do good" is not a goal. To build a defect-free product is a goal. However, to expect a defect-free product might not be realistic. If your product will have 1 million lines of code, and your measure of success is to prove that it is 100 percent defect-free, then you will likely go out of business. Why? Because the tremendous cost to develop 1 million lines of code that is defect-free would likely extend schedules and raise the product price to a point that would reduce its competitiveness significantly. However, if your goal is to deliver this product with no more than one defect for every 10,000 lines of code, and technology is within reach to make this happen, then your goal is realistic. (In this example, assume that the customer accepts this defect rate. Also assume that the frequency and effect of the defects discovered by the customer are manageable—for instance, the defect is encountered only once during the start of leap year and will not lead to disaster.)

How do goals (that are theoretically achievable) happen? They happen when the project's leadership establishes and maintains a productive environment. The leaders must make it easy for people to do their jobs and must create a work environment that sets people up for success, not failure. In creating a productive environment, project leaders should strive to:

- Provide the necessary training, processes, and tools
- Offer a sense of accomplishment
- Foster teamwork
- Encourage risk-taking

Now take a closer look at these elements.

Provide training, processes, and tools. A goal is not realistic if the people expected to make it happen have not been trained properly, processes have not been defined and implemented, and the necessary tools have not been made available. The project's leadership is responsible for making these things happen. In the 1-million-lines-of-code program example, project personnel will not know if they have achieved the acceptable defect rate unless a rigorous software development process has been defined and implemented to track and measure product defects carefully.

Offer a sense of accomplishment. People achieve their best when they are "stretched"—when their skills are used and their potential is tapped. When these things happen, people sense they are valued as members of the team. Project leaders should not hold back in providing people with assignments that are challenging but achievable. A project's goals are closer to being realistic when the project's members are happy about their work.

Foster teamwork. Fostering teamwork involves encouraging the participation of *all* project members. Great human achievements are possible when people work as a team. Whether the project is to harness the great energy of the atom, to walk on the moon, or to build a large complex software program, teamwork draws on individual accomplishments. These individual accomplishments are collected in a fashion that allows greatness to be achieved at a level far beyond the abilities of any one person. Everyone has something to offer to a team. The more participation is encouraged, the greater the likelihood that the project's goals will be met.

Encourage risk-taking. Taking risks is the difference between *doing* the unthinkable and only *dreaming* about it. Establishing a risk-supportive environment can allow the imagined to become reality. It may be *the* ingredient that allows the estimated 1-million-lines-of-code program to be done with 25 percent less code. Or it may simply make the difference between delivering a product on schedule or much later. An environment that encourages risk and rewards success but does not penalize failure is an organization to be reckoned with. The movers of tomorrow are taking risks today.

Trait Two: Obtain Commitments

The last section, "Trait One: Set Realistic Goals," stresses that a well-disciplined organization defines realistic project goals in a manner that is simply stated, is understood by all, and is measurable. Furthermore, all project players understand their individual assignments and roles in making the bigger picture happen. A second trait of a well-disciplined organization is the obtainment of commitments from *each* person in the organization.

 Lesson: Everyone must feel personally committed for discipline to have its greatest impact.

A committed plan does not exist until *everyone* has made a personal commitment. This means from the very top gun to the troops in the trenches, managers and nonmanagers alike. People will take more pride in their work when they have a personally committed stake, when they sense they have responsibility and accountability. No greater tool exists for motivating people to do their job than getting their personal commitment to making it happen. Giving people the opportunity to participate in developing product content, processes, and schedules is not only beneficial, it is a must.

Trait Three: Track Progress Against Plans

At this point, the organization has a realistic project plan (trait one) to which all members of the project have committed (trait two). So far, so good. The third trait is the tracking of each activity against the plan. (Techniques for tracking plans are discussed in detail in Chapter 5.)

 Lesson: It is not enough to plan your work; discipline requires that you also ensure that you are working your plan.

Remember that discipline is the act of encouraging a desired pattern of behavior. Now that a plan for the project is in place, how can the project's leadership be sure that the plan is being followed continually? More important, how will the leadership know when problems arise and where resources should be redeployed to help solve problems and protect the planned schedules? Discipline is required to track the plan on a regular and frequent basis. Tracking the plan also involves recording new problems and ensuring that current problems are being solved satisfactorily.

> Scenario: Consider the plight of a person walking through a desert. Without sophisticated navigation tools, it is highly improbable that this person could walk a straight line through the desert. (For this example, assume it is physically possible to track to a straight route, free of obstacles.) In this analogy, the start and end points of the person's journey represent the start and end points of a project. The straight line, which is the shortest route through the desert, is symbolic of the shortest project schedules possible. Now picture this person veering a little more off course each week. For any given week, the deviation doesn't represent a major alteration of the final destination. However, as the weeks pass, these minor off-course excursions collectively could spell disaster. That is, the final destination would not be reached anywhere near the planned date. If, however, this person's direction could be reset each week, problems could be addressed close to the time they occur, so that the final destination's targeted arrival date has a much higher chance of being achieved.

The desert example is simplistic but nevertheless provides insight into the need to track against a project plan at frequent, regular intervals. Often just the act of tracking the plan is a form of preventive maintenance. People are more apt to meet a checkpoint if they are being tracked regularly and frequently than if they are tracked infrequently.

Trait Four: Enforce Commitments

You may want to read this section twice. The reason is simple: If everything mentioned up to now has been done—setting realistic goals, obtaining commitments, tracking progress against plans—but this final, fourth trait of the well-disciplined organization is not made to happen, then all bets are off. Enforcing commitments is an absolute must. This is not a strong arm tactic. Rather, the enforcement of commitments represents a statement of support from the project's leadership to the project's participants.

Most software development projects will encounter several severe problems along the way. (A severe problem is defined here as one that potentially can cause a delay in the final delivery of the product.) Moreover, many severe problems are not totally solvable by the specific group that is experiencing the problem. An example is the team that falls behind schedule in writing test scripts. The people are all working overtime but still may not be able to complete the activity on schedule. The person leading this team has no other resource to add to this effort. The project's leadership, however, can choose to redeploy people from other areas of the project to shore up the development activity of the test scripts.

Therefore, one useful approach project leaders can employ to ensure that commitments are met is *management of priorities*. Priorities requiring attention often will vary from week to week. As a result, management of priorities requires discipline to ensure that the proper activities are getting the needed resources and focus. Often it is more fun and easier to deal with some problems ahead of others. However, this temptation should be resisted. Instead, it is better to understand problems and take action on resolving them according to priorities that best serve the organization. (See Chapter 7.)

Another important action to take in enforcing commitments can be called "making it happen now." This is a tightly held philosophy of leaders who have a reputation for getting things done. Whereas management of priorities ensures that resources within the organization are being diverted dynamically for the good of the total plan, "making things happen now" is the act of dealing swiftly with problems before they fester and grow out (or further out) of control. This is considered to be a strong positive act of support for the people in the organization.

 Lesson: People need to be rewarded regularly for demonstrating the desired behavior.

Reward those who meet or beat their commitments. Whether the reward is expressed privately or publicly, stated on paper, made with money, or made through some other means, it is important to provide feedback to individuals and to the organization. Let people know when their behavior contributes to the project's goals.

 Lesson: Everyone looks to the project's leadership to provide a work environment that encourages success.

By the same token, proceed cautiously before reprimanding failure. Be firm but fair. Maintain a sense of justice and fair treatment. Most people don't fail intentionally. Could it be that the project's leadership did not provide the proper work environment to facilitate the employee's success? If it is clear that a person is performing unsatisfactorily, don't ignore this. Help the person to develop an acceptable level of performance. If, after a reasonable energy expenditure, the person still is not showing the needed improvement, then find a job that fits this person's skills or remove him or her from the company. *Do not do nothing.* All eyes are on the project's leadership to take proper action before the situation deteriorates further.

Attributes of the Successful Leader

> *Leadership is action, not position.*
> —*Donald H. McGannon, American broadcasting executive*

This section is devoted to the role of the leader and contains what I believe to be among the most important leadership philosophies, or tenets, that have been shared with me over the years or that I have shared with others. These leadership tenets have worked for me and I have seen them work for others. Being a leader carries a lot of responsibility, but it also can be a lonely, stressful job if you allow the role to control you rather than you taking charge of your own emotions.

Earlier sections have discussed the need for discipline within the organization and have explained how to recognize a disciplined organization. Now is a good point to focus candidly on *self-discipline* for the leader. First, consider some definitions of a leader. A leader:

- Is the principal player within a team, the human "glue" that holds the team together
- Inspires and guides a team toward a common goal
- Exhibits integrity
- Is a continual source of energy
- Encourages desired behavior from others
- Sets an example for others
- Is accountable
- Achieves results

 Lesson: The importance of leadership in creating and nurturing a successful organization cannot be overstated.

This is certainly not an exhaustive list of what being a leader is all about. However, it is sufficiently complete to point out the importance of a leader in creating and nurturing a successful organization.

Figure 2.3 lists the attributes of the successful leader. Let's take a closer look at each of these attributes.

The Ability to Create and Nurture a Vision

As a leader, it is important to create and nurture a vision—a far-reaching purpose—that you can share with your entire team and that the team can think about all day long, all week long, all project long. This vision will translate into the team purpose. Having a purpose has a powerful effect on the positive outcome of the team's mission. Not only does a purpose channel the energies of the team into a single focus, it helps to ensure that the trade-offs and compromises made along the way fully support the vision.

Note, however, that creating a vision requires you to know where you want to go. This is essential if you plan to lead others to that destination. Only then can you be sure that the journey followed will result in victory. Great accomplishments are made possible by great visions.

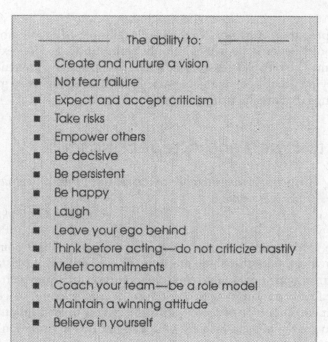

The ability to:

- Create and nurture a vision
- Not fear failure
- Expect and accept criticism
- Take risks
- Empower others
- Be decisive
- Be persistent
- Be happy
- Laugh
- Leave your ego behind
- Think before acting—do not criticize hastily
- Meet commitments
- Coach your team—be a role model
- Maintain a winning attitude
- Believe in yourself

Figure 2.3 Attributes of the successful leader.

The Ability to Not Fear Failure

Failure is, in a sense, the highway to success, inasmuch as every discovery of what is false leads us to seek earnestly after what is true.

—John Keats, English poet

We all fail at things—all the time. It is natural and expected. It is the way we learn. You could not walk the first time you tried. Or talk. Or type. Or ride a bike. Or play that video game. And so on. When we were very young, we simply got up, dusted ourselves off, and tried again and again until we mastered our goal. But something happened to some of us as we "matured." We began to fear failing and therefore shunned opportunities that we believed increased our chances for failing.

What a shame. You see, life is full of paradoxes. The person who is no stranger to failure is often the person who is *most likely to succeed*. Every failure offers a lesson and from every lesson comes strength. If you learn from each failure, you get a little stronger. And after a while, you can even amaze yourself at the progress you have made.

Of course, all this is made more possible if you don't fear failure. Fear can perpetuate failure and encourages you to "quit." Think of those around you who fear failure. Most likely they are not leaders, are content with complacency, and seek so-called safety by maintaining the status quo wherever they may be. They literally withdraw from many of life's opportunities.

Now look at those whose failures seem to be visible, yet from each fall they rise to prepare for the next challenge. If failure means growth and opportunity, then it should never be feared. The only real failures are the experiences we don't learn from. The most successful leaders have learned to view failures as the positive force they are, that is, as the necessary steps in enabling us to grow and to achieve those things that are important to us.

The Ability to Expect and Accept Criticism

Criticism is something we can avoid easily—by saying nothing, doing nothing, and being nothing.

—Aristotle, Greek philosopher and scientist

If you expect criticism, you will seldom be disappointed when you receive it. However, note that there are two types of criticism: *constructive* and *destructive*. Of course, you should welcome constructive criticism, which is well-meaning and useful feedback. Constructive criticism should leave you feeling that you have been helped. This type of feedback can help you to learn about yourself and the impact you are having as a result of your actions. It is information you can use to help make choices for yourself and to help you grow in the direction of your personal goals.

Destructive criticism is input you receive that might be maliciously rooted and offers little, if any, real value for your learning and growth. However, what often may appear to be destructive criticism might, in fact, just be an unfortunate and ineffective attempt to offer some useful information—but from a person who does not know how best to communicate the information. Be aware that some well-intended criticism might come your way awkwardly masked in destructive garb.

You will always find those who disapprove of your behavior or your decisions. Even the people you love, and who love you, will, at times, disapprove of your actions. When people criticize you, remember it is only their opinion. If you allow the absence of their approval to immobilize you, then you are allowing others to control you. You are, in effect, saying that what other people think about you is more important than what you think about yourself. Instead, you should ask yourself if there is something to be learned from the criticism. If there is, then, by all means, learn! If there is nothing to be learned, then forget the experience and go about fulfilling your dreams.

The Ability to Take Risks

Great deeds are usually wrought at great risks.

—Herodotus, Greek historian

Risk—that simple yet mighty four-letter word. The willingness to take risks is what changed the perception of a flat world to round, gave humans wings to fly, and gives people the ability to understand their own capabilities. If you want to achieve the extraordinary, you *must* take risks. Risk-taking can occur on a small scale, such as driving a new route home from work, speaking out when you disagree with an issue, or volunteering to take on an additional assignment. If you practice becoming comfortable with smaller risks, you will find yourself much more prepared to recognize a larger risk and much more willing to take it on.

If you increasingly take on more risk, you will find an unexpected benefit—the recognition that your level of energy and enthusiasm grow in proportion to the risk that you take. Often assignments that are the riskiest are later viewed as the assignments that were the most enjoyable, memorable, and career-building. There is nothing wrong with gradually expanding your risk-taking abilities. Only you can decide what your limitations are and what level of risk is suitable for you. The leaders of tomorrow are taking risks today.

The Ability to Empower Others

> *No man will make a great leader who wants to do it all himself, or to get all the credit for doing it.*
> —*Andrew Carnegie, American industrialist and philanthropist*

It is common for new leaders not to give up some of their "power" by empowering others—to give them full responsibility and accountability for key tasks. The reasons include a belief that they can do the job better or faster than another or even the fear of giving others too much work. Another reason: They allow society's work ethic—being independent and self-reliant—to interfere with their duties as a leader of others. Resist these attitudes and transfer some of your tasks, your key tasks.

A successful leader knows he or she achieves goals through the dedication, skill, and efforts of others. You must learn to trust and work with others in ways that allows them to grow and achieve their dreams. After all, you appreciated the opportunities that others gave you to learn. Give others their chance as well. It is good for you and good for your team members. It frees you to lead and frees them to learn. Everybody will win.

The Ability to be Decisive

> *Once the WHAT is decided, the HOW always follows. We must not make the HOW an excuse for not facing and accepting the WHAT.*
> —*Pearl S. Buck, American novelist*

Your organization will react to your actions. When you delay in making crucial decisions, you also are delaying the time that will be needed to implement those decisions. Many organizations have the capacity to increase their productivity and effectiveness. By putting off decision making, you are not driving your organization efficiently. If you delay your own decision making, you also are preventing the next tier of decisions from being made. This *decision queue* can build to a point where progress within the organization is seriously impacted. The result is an uncontrollable sluggishness that spreads throughout the organization and that only the project leader can correct.

It is better to make decisions early—when their pain and cost to the organization are relatively minor, yet when their long-term impact can have a major positive effect. Some decisions will, in hindsight, prove to be less than the best. However, if you wait until absolutely no risk remains before taking a position on a problem, then you will lose all competitiveness.

The Ability to Be Persistent

> *Great works are performed not by strength, but by perseverance.*
> *—Dr. Samuel Johnson, English poet, critic, essayist, and lexicographer*

Perseverance is a universal characteristic of successful leaders. This attribute can propel a so-called common person to achieve uncommon feats. Perseverance pushes a chemist to try that 10,000th mixture that finally succeeds, an athlete to achieve an Olympic-class victory, an artist to create a masterpiece, and the medical biologist to locate a disease-causing gene. Perhaps, however, the most inspiring effect of perseverance can be seen in a person who overcomes a major physical handicap and goes on to accomplish a feat that would be difficult for even a fully functioning person to achieve.

Intellectual and physical capabilities vary widely among people. However, it is encouraging to know that we all have the innate ability to exercise perseverance and determination in achieving those goals that are important to us. Being persistent can make all the difference between dreaming and seeing the dream blossom into reality. Act as if it is impossible for you to fail. You can achieve nearly anything you set out to make happen if you are persistent in following your dreams.

The Ability to Be Happy

> *Everything you need to be totally fulfilled you already have . . .*
> *—Dr. Wayne Dyer, American psychologist and author*

Be happy. Feel good about yourself. Being happy is the cornerstone of your continued effectiveness. Don't *strive* to be happy. Don't set goals and then tell yourself that once those goals are reached you will be happy. Putting off happiness until some external event occurs will guarantee that your happiness will continue to be elusive.

You have everything you need today to be happy. You don't need a promotion, award, new car, vacation, retirement, or whatever, to be happy. Happiness is an attitude. It is something that comes from within—not from external events or things. It is an acceptance of what is. It is something that no one can take away from you. You can lose all your material possessions and still be happy.

This does not mean you should stop working for self-improvement or improvement to your family, job, company, world, or whatever is important to you. It means that you must not allow external forces to control you to the point at which your actual happiness is no longer within your own control. However you define success for yourself, you will improve your likelihood of attaining your goals significantly if you recognize and exercise your ability to be and remain happy.

The Ability to Laugh

> *It is my belief, you cannot deal with the most serious things in the world unless you understand the most amusing.*
>
> —*Sir Winston Churchill*

Consider this scenario: A meeting has just been called to settle a dispute between two parties. As people are assembling in the meeting room, an uncomfortable silence is felt. Everyone has arrived and the meeting is about to start. There is an instability in the air, a feeling of tension that one wrong word or action could ignite into an emotional explosion. The first words are spoken and strike everyone in the meeting with the same response—a round of heavy uncontrollable laughter fills the room.

Can you relate to this scenario? Most of us can. That well-timed bit of humor was sorely needed. All too often we take the moment much too seriously. We fail to loosen up and find the humor in ourselves and our situation. How terribly depressing for an organization to resist expressing the lighter side of the daily problems we face. As a leader, support a healthy dose of humor in the organization. Displaying a sense of humor also helps you to remain cool under pressure and to keep problems in perspective.

Caution: Don't use sarcasm in your humor. While many people may view your comment as amusing, it may leave others feeling uncomfortable and unsettled. Sarcasm also can hurt the trust you have developed with others. People appreciate benevolent humor better than sarcastic humor. If you have a hard time initiating this welcomed variety of humor, then at least show appreciation when others are amusing. While humor has been shown to preserve the health of people, it also adds value to the health of the total organization.

The Ability to Leave Your Ego Behind

We all have an ego. For some, the ego can cause a paralysis, inhibiting their quest for growth and opportunity. Here is another paradox: Often the person who insists on attention is the one least likely to receive the type or amount of attention desired. An overactive ego does not help win the recognition, admiration, and approval that the egotist seeks. Instead, it has a repelling effect that encourages others to want to limit their association with the egotist. Furthermore, it leads others to question the real value and substance that exist behind all the verbal arm waving.

An oversized ego also can interfere with recognizing others for their contributions. And it can bias decisions being made, favoring who is right rather than what is right. You probably have seen leaders with large egos. Having an exaggerated ego doesn't mean you will never get to be a leader. It means that fewer people will trust you or want to work for and with you. It means that you will make your job harder and less effective than it needs to be. An unbridled ego is a haunting liability. The less approval you demand from others, the more you are likely to receive.

The Ability to Think Before Acting—Do Not Criticize Hastily

Resist the temptation to criticize hastily. When you suspect poor work, ask questions and carefully listen to the answers. Once a wrong or regrettable word is spoken, it cannot be taken back. After you understand the reason behind a problem, attack the problem, not the person.

Give others the same courtesy that you would like for yourself. Take this opportunity to not only help someone resolve a problem, but to help him or her benefit from the experience. Also, work at increasing the bond and trust between you and the project member. If you demonstrate constructive behavior and resist attacking the person, you may find yourself with a more loyal and dedicated project member. (Chapter 3 offers additional ideas on communication skills.)

The Ability to Meet Commitments

When you make a commitment, it is a personal statement about yourself. It is a statement that says that you can be depended on, that you will do everything within your abilities to honor the pledge that you have given another.

The success of any organization depends on its ability to meet its commitments. As the saying goes, a chain is only as strong as its weakest link. The project structure, represented as a chain, can break quickly when one or more commitments are broken.

Make no commitments lightly. Commit only to that which you believe you can achieve. To commit unconditionally to more is to be distrustful, for if your commitment is weak, so too are those commitments that depend on you. Pull your own weight and do as you say you will.

When you meet your commitments, you will be recognized as a greater value to the organization. You also may find that you will be given the option to assume greater responsibilities as well as be exposed to increased opportunities. People will prefer to have you on their team or will want to be on your team. You also will find that you will be given greater freedom to manage your activities as you choose.

The Ability to Coach Your Team—Be a Role Model

We all learn the easiest and fastest by observing others—by having an example to mimic. As a leader, others look to you—and rightly so—for that example. They look to you for strength, for wisdom, for caring, for attention. They also look to you for your honesty with being human and having human frailties. For example, the integrity that you demonstrate when you make a mistake, admit it, recover, and continue on can have a profound positive impact on those around you.

Teach what you have learned. Impart your knowledge and experience. Prepare others to take on more responsibility. You know what you want from your leaders; work to provide the same to your subordinates and peers, and even back up to your leaders. Work continuously to build a stronger organization this month than the one that existed last month. When you come across a problem, fix the problem—then fix the process that caused the problem. The greatest leader is the one who leads by example. Practice what you expect from others. Show you care, offer your support, be there to make it happen.

The Ability to Maintain a Winning Attitude

> *The quality of work is affected as much by one's attitude as by one's skill.*
> —*Anonymous*

Attitude is the disposition, manner, or approach that you bring to everything you do. One of the most admired traits you can have is a good attitude, or positive attitude. A positive attitude actually can bring pleasure to performance of a tedious or difficult task. A positive attitude can make a long day seem short and even can improve the productivity and quality of the work being performed. People who consistently maintain positive attitudes tend to have higher energy levels than those who are less positive. These people look for something positive—and they find it—in every chore they tackle. You have probably observed a situation where two people are being considered for the same assignment and the person chosen is the one who appears to have somewhat less experience or knowledge. Yet this person was chosen because of his or her positive attitude.

As a revealing anonymous quote states: "A pessimist finds difficulty in every opportunity; an optimist finds opportunity in every difficulty." People can take great liberties in choosing how to think. A glass of water can be half filled or half empty. How a person thinks does not change the fact that the glass has 50 percent of its capacity *used up* by water. But how a person chooses to think does have an affect on the efficiency with which a task is completed and on the enjoyment the person derives from accomplishing that task.

As a leader, you want the people whom you are leading to demonstrate good attitudes in every endeavor that you assign them. People who exhibit these upbeat attitudes are considerably easier to manage and more enjoyable to be around than less positive people. In order for a winning attitude to permeate your team, you must demonstrate and encourage that characteristic. As a leader, the manner in which you approach your work is also the manner most likely to be adopted by those who work under, alongside, and above you. Adopt a winning attitude in the tasks that you undertake, and you also will create winning people and winning products in the process.

The Ability to Believe in Yourself

> *Always bear in mind that your own resolution to succeed is more important than any one thing.*
>
> *—Abraham Lincoln*

The most successful leaders have learned *to believe* in their ability to make something happen—to follow their dreams and transform those dreams into reality. They draw from an inner strength that they have chosen to acknowledge is there to work for them. An inner strength that no one can take away—unless they allow it. You *must* believe in yourself if you expect to be and remain a successful leader, and if you expect others to believe in you. In fact, the belief in one's own capabilities magnifies the contribution from all the other attributes that we have discussed.

If you believe you can—you will. If you believe you can't—you won't. These pearls of wisdom have been around at least as long as recorded history. They are as true and as real as the mountains and oceans themselves. And the great news is that no one has a monopoly on these words. They apply to you as much as they do anyone.

 Lesson: You are what you perceive yourself to be. Your vision of yourself becomes your reality.

You deserve to be what you choose to be and work at becoming—regardless of your age, race, sex, religion, current wealth, whatever. You are what you perceive yourself to be. Your vision of yourself becomes your reality. As a leader, you must believe in your ability to get the job done, to achieve the desired results. If people took on only those jobs where they knew all the answers and had no chance for conflict or failure, there would be no leaders. A successful leader knows that no one person holds the answer to every problem, but with the proper balance of time, energy, and talent, no problem escapes being solved.

It is almost always true that our greatest obstacle to becoming what we truly want is ourselves. If it is truly important to you, then never, never, *never* give up. As Henry David Thoreau, American writer, philosopher, and naturalist, said:

> *If one advances confidently in the direction of his dreams and endeavors to live the life he has imagined, he will meet with a success unexpected in common hours.*

I believe that everyone has the capability to be a successful leader. Everyone! There is room for many more leaders, millions more. Although some are more effective than others, or rise to greater heights, this does not diminish the great opportunities for turning your visions into realities. All the attributes can be learned if you choose to learn them.

Checking the Organization's Pulse

If you follow this chapter's advice up to this point, how can you tell if it is working for you and your organization? The external signs should be quite evident. For example, the status of the project plan would be known at regular and frequent intervals, schedules should be tracking to plan, and any exceptions would have recovery plans. Problems would be logged, assigned an owner, and target dates for closure committed. But what about the internal signs? What do the individual project members really feel about their organization and how it is being run?

Managers can use many methods to test the effectiveness of the discipline exercised across a project. Some of these methods are listed in Figure 2.4. Let's take a closer look at each method listed.

Random walks through work areas have the greatest immediate payback because listening to project members' spontaneous opinions offers the best opportunity to learn. These walks can build a closer and more trusting working relationship between managers and nonmanagers. Understanding problems at the point where pain is felt the most also adds valuable insight into providing the support needed. These walks are most effective if they can take place for at least 30 to 60 minutes each day at least two to three times per week. Surveying the members less frequently is still, however, a valuable method for gaining insight into the way a project is running, but it will be more difficult to maintain a personal bond with project members.

Scheduling chats with project members for 30 to 60 minutes per person is also a useful way to get feedback. These *one-on-one interviews* can be scheduled once or twice a week with a different person from a different group each time. The person can be given up to a week's notice. The meeting should be set at a convenient time for the invited member. The actual interview should first focus on any questions or thoughts that the member wants to pursue. Then the manager might ask a few general questions of the project member.

Roundtables are a productive way to meet the most people in the least amount of time. Roundtables typically involve a gathering of five to 15 people from across the organization. These sessions may occur once every one or two weeks and may last up

- Random walks through work areas
- Scheduled one-on-one interviews
- Scheduled group roundtables
- Formal opinion surveys
- Quality improvement teams

Figure 2.4   Methods to check the organization's pulse.

to two hours. Such meetings are not not only informative tools for the manager, they also are team-building techniques for roundtable members.

Formal opinion surveys typically are administered on paper or through a computer workstation. The anonymous survey may ask a few or many questions, most of which would be answered by rating the participant's views from "very satisfied" to "very unsatisfied." This is an effective tool for medium- to long-range planning.

Quality improvement teams are another effective way to understand the problems that can stifle parts or all of an organization. These teams are described in the "Quality Improvement Teams" section of Chapter 6. Quality improvement teams are mentioned here due to their considerable benefit in encouraging participation of project members from across the organization. These teams can candidly assess any discipline-related problems that may exist and can offer creative recommendations that have the added benefit of being sponsored from the bottom up rather than from the top down.

The Desire for Discipline

 Lesson: As a project leader, your actions always will speak louder than your words.

You must want discipline in order to make it happen. Discipline cannot and will not happen without your support. If you say you want discipline, but your actions tell another story, the entire organization will read you like a book. Vague policies and permissive attitudes convey the impression that unproductive (destructive) behavior is acceptable.

 Lesson: As a manager, you are accountable for the well-being of your organization; it cannot be delegated.

You hold the keys to building a poor, ordinary, or extraordinary organization. You are the boss. You can initiate change whenever and wherever you want. Most problems are not as large as they appear. What is large is the fear or hesitancy to deal with problems head-on—when they first appear. This is not to say that all problems are easy to solve or can be solved in a short time. Problems that compete for resources or time need to be prioritized according to the needs of the organization. Then these priorities need to be managed with the urgency they deserve.

 Lesson: Discipline—the glue that holds it altogether.

Discipline is an everyday thing. It is not occasional. Discipline is the glue that holds it all together. Everyone wants positive discipline. Exercising discipline has great value to each project participant, to the organization as a whole, and to the products that are developed by the organization. Everyone wins. Can you afford to have your project fail, to be less than it needs to be? Be a winner!

3

Communicating in Harmony

In software development projects, the inability of people to communicate effectively with one another represents one of the most common obstacles to the achievement of high product quality and high productivity. This obstacle might manifest itself as poor communications among employees, between management and their employees, or among management. Communication problems are common topics of complaint within most projects. Everyone knows what they do not like, but few really act to do something about perceived problems.

 Lesson: The dignity and value bestowed upon and felt by each individual is central to the overall success of an enterprise.

Lack of communication is a problem area that technology has done little to improve, an area where nature has left its mark so ingrained that the term *human nature* often is used to excuse uncommunicative behavior. It is an area that has particularly frustrated many project leaders and managers. Rapid advancements in technology have not reduced the need for people to communicate and get along. To the contrary, the need for effective communications among people is at a greater premium than ever before. Critical to the success of an organization—particularly the long-term success—is the dignity and value that each individual feels from the organization.

Improving communications among project players offers substantial morale, productivity, quality, and, therefore, cost benefits to a project. Once communications problems surface, the process to follow to bring the problems under control is:

- Understand the cause of the problems.

- Put corrective action into place.
- Enforce an ongoing communicative work environment.

But the real goal should be to *prevent* the problems from developing. The approach lies in encouraging behavior that focuses upon this simple yet powerful statement: *Respect the individual.*

This chapter describes such behaviors—behaviors that you can adopt immediately to improve the communications between you and others. Of course, even more exciting and beneficial would be the impact of these behaviors being practiced by *all* members of an organization, the results of which can be a positive and constructive environment that would be the envy of any project.

Project Tales

Demonstrating respect for others is the cornerstone for improving communications among people. The following collection of scenarios illustrates how poor communications are fostered and tolerated. How many of the situations portrayed in these scenarios have you encountered? Can you spot the problems? As you read through these scenarios, keep in mind the words of Harold Nicholson, British statesman and author: "We are all inclined to judge ourselves by our ideals; others by their acts."

Sophie Berger, a programmer working in the test area, has been assigned to review the drafts of the product's publications as they become available. Berger has agreed to review each chapter as it is completed by Mark Hood, the writer. This review process was requested by Hood's manager and approved by Berger's manager. It is intended to aid in obtaining an early assessment of the progress being made on the publications. The review process also will provide Hood with the opportunity to work more closely with a programmer (in this case, Berger) in those areas in which Hood requires assistance.

Berger has more than five years experience in software development. Hood, on the other hand, has just completed his first year. He has been obtaining his information primarily from the "final" product specifications, which, incidentally, happen to be incomplete. Hood also has, on many occasions, requested additional information from the programmers who have written the product specifications. These programmers frequently have stated that they do not have the time to brief him on the specifications. Unfortunately, however, several of the chapters reviewed by Berger require major revisions in some sections because Hood, with the best of intentions, made invalid assumptions. Berger seems quick to tell her peers, "The 'pubs' people don't know diddly-squat about this product. I could write these chapters faster than the time it takes to teach this writer what he needs to know." Berger has influenced her peers to the point that they agree with her wholeheartedly.

Nobody seems to know what is happening in this project, except maybe a handful of lead development programmers. These programmers seem to remain inaccessible to anyone whom they do not have any direct responsibility for or commitment to. These lead developers meet on a regular basis with their respective teams. The goals at these meetings are to exchange status, to conduct design reviews, and, in general, to plan their next one to four weeks. The peripheral groups (writers, testers, quality assurance people, schedulers, tools people, and so on) have asked if they can attend or send a representative to these regularly scheduled meetings. The reply is almost always "No, we don't have any information to share at this point." When no other groups are around, the developers chatter among themselves, saying "The other groups sure have cushy jobs. You never see them working after hours. They just sit around and complain that things aren't just like they think they should be." The management from the development shop and the other shops have not made any serious attempts at discussing and remedying the situation.

The management in this company recognizes the value of receiving an independent assessment of the progress for products being developed. Managers also acknowledge the benefit of an independent group working closely with product development groups to help guide the developers, as efficiently as possible, through their processes. For these reasons, management declares the creation of a **quality assurance group.** Furthermore, to help maintain objectivity, no quality assurer will report directly to the leadership of the project whose products he or she is assuring.

To higher management, the quality assurance mission is understood and welcomed. The troops in the trenches, on the other hand, see quality assurance as adding little value. As one developer quips to another, "Nonconcurred! I spent weeks writing my section of the product specifications and one assurer nonconcurs just because of a few TBDs [to be determineds] that I had in the document! I said I would complete those sections just as soon as I have some free time. Now I have to finish the sections by next week. I was hoping to do some coding first. How can I meet my commitments when I keep getting sidetracked? I thought quality assurance was here to help us, not slow us down!"

A manager, Bill Foley, has just called his department together for a meeting. These meetings occur infrequently. There are several topics to be discussed, some timely and some that have been accumulating over time. Foley is known for being outspoken and saying what is on his mind. Some department members have been annoyed over the poor communications and working relationships that appear to be rampant on this project. The mission of Foley's department is to design and code product enhancements. The department members are currently "under the gun" and are working an average of 30 percent overtime. Someone asks Foley if the department will be hiring anyone to help with the workload. Foley replies, "The budget does not permit any additional employees on this project. What we ought to do is reduce or disband some of the test, publications, and support departments. I never see any of them here on weekends or after hours. I really can't see the value that they are adding to the project. It seems all they do is slow us down."

There are nearly 200 people assigned to this software development project. Many processes have been defined and implemented to better control critical activities within the project. One such critical activity is the library control and build procedures. These procedures are used to ensure that all modules being developed and tested are properly identified, added to a library of modules residing on a set of computer disks, and access-controlled through a checkout scheme that allows orderly modifications to be made to the library modules. The build group is responsible for ensuring the smooth operation of this activity. The build group also is responsible for building **driver**s for the development and test organizations. (A driver is a collection of modules that are linked to form a workable "product" that can be tested and evaluated.)

The product being developed is considered to be complex and resides across several different types of computer systems. When new modules are ready to be added to the library, a long list of information about each module must be collected from the development organization. These data are essential to compiling and linking these modules with other modules. Whenever the development group delivers modules, it seems that some valuable information about them is overlooked. These missing data cause the build group to waste scores of person-hours trying to debug new drivers that must contain these modules. To correct this loss of productivity, the build group initiates a meeting with the developers to create a comprehensive checklist that development can use each time new modules are added to the library. The build group must rely on special knowledge and skills that the developers possess regarding the modules and the environments in which the modules must operate.

The first real use of the checklist arrives and the build group, for once, feels good about the data the developers deliver to them. Unfortunately, the build group spends an unexpected two full days and several people trying to build a driver with the new modules. Frustrated, they ask the developers to participate with the debugging. The developers quickly locate the problem and blame the build team for not asking the right questions on the checklist. A member of the build team snaps, "But we had asked you to make sure that all the needed data was being requested."

A developer responds, "Do we have to do all of your work for you? We are up to our ears developing a product. The least you can do is handle the operations of the library control system!"

Later one developer says to another, "I know 10 times more about building libraries than that entire build team. I see problems with their procedures that they don't even realize exist. When are they going to get their act together?"

This project developed and issued a quality plan. It was approved by all. The plan defined, among other things, how the code was to be designed, coded, unit and function tested, inspected, and formally tested. The developers then issued their unit and function test plans. These plans also were approved by all. Development followed the plans to the letter. Then the developers delivered their code, on schedule, to the independent test group for additional testing.

Several of the programmers in the test area are now upset with the "low quality" of the code that the development programmers delivered to the testers. It is taking the testers longer than they had anticipated to run their bucket of test scripts successfully. The feeling of these testers, and of other testers who have come under their influence, is that the developers must not be very proud of their work, seem to lack any real dedication, and, in general, appear not to know much about what they are doing. Although the testers are constantly grumbling, there has been no formal communication with the developers on this matter. The developers are not aware of the severity of the quality problem as perceived by the testers. The testers are not aware that the developers are beaming with pride in delivering "high-quality" complex code, following the approved process, and on a very aggressive schedule.

Every software development project member has at least one similar war story. And each member has added, at one time or another, his or her share to the communications problems that can plague a project. Most project members don't cause such problems on purpose. They just don't think. They have their own problems to deal with and expect others to solve their own as well. Seldom do people make plans to anticipate and, therefore, head off communications problems before they grow out of control. The good news is that most problems can be dealt with effectively, many before they have a chance to fester. This chapter describes methods to deal with these communications problems directly.

Respect the Individual

 Lesson: There is no better advice for working alongside others than to treat others as you would like to be treated yourself.

If you are looking for that special phrase or set of words to carry along with you after you have read this chapter, this is it: *Respect the individual.* Similar pearls of wisdom have been uttered throughout history, such as this one by Confucius—"What you do not want done to yourself, do not do to others"—or this one from the New Testament—"Do unto others as you would have them do unto you." Don't be blinded by the simplicity of these words. There is gold here.

 Lesson: Understanding ways to improve communications is the first step; practicing—practicing—practicing the Golden Rule is the key step.

To help relate these words to your job and your work environment, Figure 3.1 lists actions that you can initiate to improve the communications between you and those with whom you work. Each item listed is discussed in a section that follows. You probably will be able to identify with many of these actions. You also may find much of the guidance offered to be common sense; however, don't be satisfied with merely understanding the messages that these actions are intended to convey. Understanding is just the first step. You must then work to break old habits and develop new habits that support the messages you wish to impart to your peers, superiors, and subordinates. Practice these guidelines and you will see, firsthand, the positive impact they can have in your daily environment. Practicing the Golden Rule is not a sacrifice but an *investment.* Not only can it benefit an entire organization, but it comes back to benefit you as well. People learn to treat you as they observe you treating them.

When You Are Wrong, Admit It

 Lesson: Admitting when you are wrong can change the mood from one of confrontation to one of cooperation.

There will be times when you are wrong. You will know when this happens. So will the person you wronged. Being stubborn at this time only serves to build walls between people. Don't cling to the work ethic that says admitting fault or apologizing is a sign of weakness. You gain respect when you are wrong and have the courage and integrity to admit it. Immediately, tensions ease. The face of a situation changes from *you and me* (confrontational) to *us* (cooperative). Also, the experience begins to be productive because one or both parties are now open to learning rather than defending.

- When you are wrong, admit it.
- Exercise tolerance.
- Meet people.
- Be quick to assist.
- Ask others for assistance.
- Use tact—put your comments in the correct perspective.
- Keep others informed—do not surprise.
- Close problems.
- Show appreciation.
- Be a good listener.
- Greet people—remember their names.
- Consider compromise.
- Be willing to break with tradition.
- Know what to expect from others.

Figure 3.1   Actions to improve communications.

Exercise Tolerance

 Lesson: The tolerance that you extend to others also will teach others to be tolerant when it is called for by your actions.

A typical situation calling for tolerance involves a person who is learning. It could be a new employee, an employee in a new assignment, or an employee learning something in an existing assignment. It could be a peer, a subordinate, or your boss. It could be you.

Recall a few of those times when you unintentionally "screwed up." (We all have—and will again!) Remember how you felt when you were met with zero tolerance for your mistake? Now recall your grateful response from an instance when tolerance was extended to you. You can have a similar, positive affect on others who are in a learning position or just happened to make a mistake.

Meet People

 Lesson: Interactive communications is still the best there is.

It is far easier to criticize behind someone's back rather than face to face—especially when you have never met the face! Go out of your way to meet the people on whom you are dependent or who are dependent on you. Talk to them. Invite them to your meetings, ask to attend theirs. Call them on the phone instead of sending a note. Your goal should be to initiate communication that is immediately interactive. Communicating through memos and third parties lacks a dimension of rapport that must be available in order to build a close, working relationship.

Next time you call a meeting, ask yourself who else could benefit by attending. Then extend an invitation. You will find this to be an inexpensive yet productive investment, not only in building preferred relationships but also in improving morale and productivity within a project.

Be Quick to Assist

 Lesson: As members of a project willingly share their knowledge and experiences, the collective strength of the project increases.

Help others along when you can. Encourage a team atmosphere, which is more fun and more productive than working alone. However, be careful not to do the work of someone else. You have your own work by which you are being measured. If you do somebody else's work, you might miss your commitments. Also, if you do the work of others, you are encouraging them to be dependent on you. Instead, teach them self-reliance. Help them to "get going." Suggest things they can do to learn, such as participating in a class, looking at examples, or reading a special book or article.

Regardless of the size of a group, it is typical to have one or more people whom others know will show them the way when they are in need of help. These helpers are frequently the most respected and admired members of a team. Set an example of helpfulness. Let others know what they can expect from you, and live up to that expectation.

Ask Others for Assistance

 Lesson: Tapping into the potential of another leaves you both to gain from the experience.

Everyone has something of value to add to a project. This fact cannot be overemphasized. Tap into the resources available from those around you. Ask for assistance in reviewing a test plan, a publications chapter, a memo, an idea, or whatever. You might be surprised, not only when your request is accepted, but also when you receive the response that transforms your piece of good output into excellent output.

Of course, the person whom you asked for assistance also will feel pretty good. Not only do others learn from you, but people want to belong, they want to contribute. Offer them that chance and you could find yourself discovering valuable assets and friends. You cannot beat this "win-win" combination.

Use Tact—Put Your Comments in the Correct Perspective

Tact is the art of making a point without making an enemy.
   —Howard W. Newton, American advertising executive

Use tact in defining the problems of others. Put yourself in the other person's shoes. Ask yourself, "How would I react if someone were to approach me in this manner about this problem?" If your answer is not positive, then search for an alternate approach. Finding problems should be viewed as a positive contribution to an organization. Only the perception of your approach to communicating the problem can turn the situation negative. Keep emotion out of the discussion. Focus on the facts at hand. Show people that you are willing to work with them where appropriate, that you are attempting to add value to the product or process.

 Lesson: The message you send may not be heard as loud as the manner with which you send the message.

Consider an example: If your assignment includes evaluating output from another department or organization, then, before you respond with problems or issues, carefully consider your remarks. The output you are reviewing could be a product specifications document, a test plan, or a publications draft. If you are about to dispute one or more items, find a way to state your case tactfully. Finding legitimate, serious problems is a great help. But if problems are minor, don't blow them out of proportion. If you feel you should list relatively small problems, make sure they are listed separately from major issues. Concentrate your energies on meaningful problems. Ask a friend or a peer whose opinion you value to assess both the problems you are about to catalog and the wording you have chosen. If you believe that your statements will be misunderstood or you are not sure how they will be received, then share them with the owner of the output you reviewed or call a small informal meeting to discuss them. This is professional courtesy. You might find that you had false assumptions about an issue, or you might even be able to resolve an issue immediately.

You lose the desired and rightful impact of your positions when you frequently overplay or emotionalize your response to someone. Your responses can add value to a project's mission. Your responses and those of others should all be encouraged. Exercise caution: Present your positions so that their real value can be appreciated and recognized. Give others the same respect as you would wish them to give you in similar circumstances.

Keep Others Informed—Do Not Surprise

 Lesson: Strive not to surprise others with bad news.

Most people like to be surprised—at a surprise party or some other situation where the surprise is affectionately intended. However, most people do not like to be surprised in their work environment, especially bosses. Why? Surprising others represents a way of broadcasting that they are not in control or that something they are doing is not acceptable to you. The reference here is to bad news, which is what most work-related surprises are all about. If you are surprising someone with good news, there is little chance of harm—either to you or that person. But surprise someone with bad news and that person may remember the stunt for what can seem like an eternity.

Bad news does happen. But *how* bad news is delivered can make all the difference. Avoid revealing bad news to the principal party in a public setting. You should disclose such news in as private a setting as possible. Put yourself in this person's shoes and decide how you would want to receive the news. A concerned, sensitive approach to revealing bad news can even leave the recipient with a greater respect for your kindness and judgment. You also might find that you will receive more support and less criticism when the news is made public.

 Lesson: Bad news is like garbage; the longer you delay in acting upon that news, the greater the potential for stink.

If you have surprising news, usually it is beneficial to reveal that news as early as possible. Delaying bad news usually will only amplify the negative reaction of others when the news is finally revealed. The goal is to put the bad news behind you quickly, learn from the experience, and channel your energies toward making further progress. Surprises do not always have to have an unhappy ending. Remember, with a thoughtful approach, not only are you saving face for others, *your* face will look better too.

Close Problems

 Lesson: Lingering problems between people or groups have a negative effect on communications.

A common communications problem between people or groups is the "unresolved problem." People need order and predictability in their work environments. They also need to feel that progress is being made. Communications can break down or come to a halt if there is an open problem between two people or groups that is not making satisfactory headway toward being resolved.

When you hear repeated phrases similar to those listed in Figure 3.2, they can be signals that a problem exists that is not receiving the necessary attention to be closed in a timely manner. To ensure that an important problem receives the necessary attention, log the problem in an accessible database, then ensure that it is assigned an owner, given a target close date, and tracked routinely. (See Chapter 5 for more on tracking problems.) If the problem is yours to resolve, meet your commitments in closing it promptly and completely. (See Chapter 2, "The Ability to Meet Your Commitments" section.)

Show Appreciation

 Lesson: One of the most important sentences that you can speak: "Thank you."

> ■ "We'll see what happens."
> ■ "I will get back to you."
> ■ "I don't know what I am going to do."
> ■ "Let's work on that later."
> ■ "I haven't got around to that yet."
> ■ "I haven't forgotten about it, but . . . "

Figure 3.2   Indications that a problem may not be receiving the necessary attention.

"Thank you." These two short words go a long way. When people do something for you, show your appreciation. It will give them a more gratified feeling of acceptance. They probably also will be more willing to help you again. If you can give praise where others also can hear, the sincerity and benefit of your appreciation grows geometrically by the size of the gathering. The more ears that hear, the stronger the echo of appreciation will sound.

Recall those times when you did something kind or unusual, whether it was for someone in particular or just an outcome of your assignment. Then remember how you felt when the expected "thank you" did not materialize. Now remember how you felt when a "thank you" eventually *was* expressed, especially if it was not anticipated. Share that feeling with others.

Be a Good Listener

 Lesson: Listening provides great benefit to both parties.

Communication is a two-way process. To be an effective communicator, you must be able to send *and* receive information. Listening is the fundamental act of receiving information. Listening requires a certain level of concentration. A person who sends information (the speaker) rarely has a problem concentrating. This person often is deeply immersed in thought. However, the person receiving, or listening, can be distracted by other, pressing thoughts. The listener could be focusing on what was said two minutes earlier and mentally structuring a response, or the listener could be counting the seconds until he or she can escape, or the listener simply could be daydreaming. Whatever the distraction, two-way communication will not be effective unless the listener provides total attention to the speaker.

Many useful techniques are available to help a listener concentrate and retain information. One of the more popular techniques is to ask the speaker questions about the subject matter being related. Another frequently used technique is to restate the speaker's message. Both of these approaches flatter the speaker by demonstrating an attentive listener. But the person who listens gains much more than the speaker's approval. The listener gains knowledge. It is from this knowledge that a listener can learn, grow, and add value to a project. The next time someone has something to say to you, give it your undivided attention and witness the results for yourself.

Greet People—Remember Their Names

 Lesson: Acknowledging others—especially by name—is a powerful way to embrace others and to feel embraced.

Remember when you were passing a senior manager in a hallway and you were greeted not only with "Good morning!" but you also were acknowledged by name?

It helped to perk up your day and made you feel appreciated, important, and accepted. All this from a two- to three-second greeting.

Now, recall how you felt on another, similar occasion, with a different senior manager who passed you and not only said nothing but ignored you altogether. To make matters worse, you and the manager rode in an elevator, in silence, for a full 30 seconds. Ouch!

These two simple but common examples demonstrate the power of acknowledging another person. The positive effect of a greeting is magnified when you address the person by name. You do not have to be a senior manager in order to brighten someone up. That someone can be a peer, a subordinate, or even someone who is in a higher job position. We *all* like the feeling of being recognized, of being accepted, no matter how low or high our job status. We also tend to work a little harder, do a little more, for someone who demonstrates this act of respect.

Consider Compromise

 Lesson: A compromised solution is often the best overall solution.

It is not unusual for two parties to disagree on an issue. Furthermore, it is not only conceivable but probable that neither has the best or "right" solution. In these cases, compromise can be the best approach to reaching a superior resolution.

In the software development world (as in most other endeavors), compromise is essential to ensure the best overall balance of function, schedules, and cost. It is a sign of strength, not weakness, for one to weigh carefully all aspects of an issue and be willing to "back off" the less important aspects of a problem so that the most important aspects are satisfied.

Be Willing to Break with Tradition

 Lesson: Don't allow past habits to impede positive progress.

Sometimes communications problems arise and, worse, begin to fester because of some aspect of tradition; that is, "that's how we have always dealt with that situation." It is easy for us to succumb to old habits and adopt the traditional view of things. Figure 3.3 lists examples that might sound familiar.

We live in a rapidly changing world. All of us must be open—more than ever—to new ideas and new ways of thinking. Just because an organization or group has a history or pattern of doing things a certain way is not sufficient reason to believe that that is the way those things must always be done or should be done. Keep an open mind when communicating with others. Strive to do what makes the most sense overall rather than what you did last time.

- "We have never invited them to our meetings. Why begin now?
- "There weren't product requirements on the past several projects. Why do them now?"
- "We have never put that kind of information in the product specifications before! Why should we now?"
- "But didn't the publications writers take on that task last time?"
- "But the testers have always performed that task. Why should I?"
- "I don't ever recall team leaders performing that task. Why change things now?"

Figure 3.3   Past habits can impede positive progress.

Know What to Expect from Others

 Lesson: Project members must understand the role of others if an effective team is to emerge.

Some of the most common communications problems among people, departments, or organizations are misunderstandings that arise from expectations about the responsibilities of others. That is, people expect certain things from those on whom they rely in some manner. Unless these expectations, or dependencies, are clearly documented, approved, and measurable, it is folly to expect that they will occur.

It is so easy to assume that other people or groups will know what you expect from them. The fallacy here is that no one can ever know what you expect unless you communicate your expectations. And you cannot know what others expect unless they offer to share it or unless you ask. When two parties agree to communicate their expectations of each other, it is important for these expectations to be documented, approved, and measurable. Documentation can reduce the chance that misunderstandings will arise later. Approval ensures that all involved parties understand the conditions of an agreement and commit to support these conditions. Measurability is needed to track the execution of an agreement, to ensure it is being implemented correctly. Knowing what to expect from others is such an important topic that some examples are provided next. Each example is divided into *problem*, *scenario*, and *solution*.

Problem   Development's expectation of the role of those who have been invited to a design inspection meeting does not match the expectations of the invited. (Note: An inspection involves a group of people, typically peers, who gather to examine an activity with the goal of identifying and removing defects and problems. See Chapter 6 for more about inspections.)

Scenario   When the development group is planning an inspection of its design, several groups from outside the immediate development area are invited. These groups typically include publications, test, performance analysis, product support, quality assurance, and even other development areas. The developers expect the invited groups to evaluate the design technically. What often happens, however, is that most of the design inspection period is consumed by educating invited group members in the way this portion of the product works, rather than discovering design defects. It irritates developers to get so little benefit on their investment of time spent preparing for and conducting the design review. Ill feelings also are exhibited by many of the invited guests, who see these design inspections as one of the few opportunities to acquire much-needed education about the product.

Solution   There should be a small inspections-related document that not only defines the what, who, how, when, and where of the inspection process, but also states the objectives of the inspection process as they relate to each of the invited groups. This document should be reviewed and approved by all the attending groups *before* the first inspection occurs. Once everyone knows what to expect from one another, then the same meeting described in the scenario can be viewed as a successful meeting—where all groups walk away as winners.

Problem   Testers frequently are asking developers to fix "problems" in the code, which later turn out not to be problems. The developers expect only valid problems to be reported to them.

Scenario   Once the code has been developed and is in the hands of the independent test group, all types of problems will be reported to the developers for them to fix. Many of these problems will not be actual code defects and therefore will be rejected for one or more reasons. Some examples of invalid problems include:

- User error
- Duplication of a problem already reported
- Not reproducible
- Suggestion—function not intended in this release

Perhaps as many as one out of every two problems reported turns out not to be a problem at all. For a developer who must investigate every problem reported against his or her code, this can lead to a great deal of wasted effort—and annoyance.

Solution   The developers should call a meeting and invite the testers. The objective is to limit the number of problems that are logged and eventually rejected. Guidelines for the testers to follow should be created. An example: The telephone numbers of certain developers are made available to the testers to allow questions to be asked. This will help testers establish the validity of each problem before it is logged. Also, subsequent meetings should be called to examine the problem statistics to ensure that the number of rejects being logged continues to decrease. It should be agreed that the developers and testers will work together to improve their mutual productivity—should additional action be required.

Problem   The publications writers expected the product specifications to be complete for use in writing the product publications, but the specifications were not "complete."

Scenario   The first draft of the publications is being written. These publications will become part of the final product. The writers are having a very difficult time acquiring the necessary information about the product. Most of the data were expected to be included in the product specifications. The only option remaining to obtain the necessary information is to go to the developers and ask them dozens of questions, answers to which are to be found only in their heads. This option, however, is exercised infrequently. Not only would such questioning be unbearably time consuming for the writers, but the developers would object to spending any appreciable time doing this.

The first drafts of the product publications are finally made available for review. Later the responses from reviewers show that the publications have some serious omissions and that numerous assumptions made by the writers are not correct. The writers are peeved at the developers for not providing the necessary data when it was originally required. The developers are peeved at the writers for not getting "up to speed" more quickly on the product and for consuming as much of the developers' precious time as they did.

Solution   The writers should have made their expectations known to the developers at the *beginning* of the software development process. Doing so would have been easy. The writers should have documented what information they expected from the product specifications. They also should have documented the need for occasional consulting from the developers and the nature of the consulting. The developers may want to designate one or two developers as the focal point for the writers, rather than allow all the developers to be interrupted from their assignments. These requirements should then have been approved by the development shop. Then the two parties would know what to expect. If the product specifications become available and do not meet the agreement, then the publications shop must not approve them until they are updated to the agreed-upon level. The point to be made here is that, once a *document of understanding* has been agreed upon by these two groups, it is relatively easy to address and resolve any conflicts that may arise.

Management Tools

 Lesson: In the final analysis, management has the authority and is accountable for ensuring that the needed communications exists across a project.

In the end, management is accountable for creating, encouraging, and enforcing a healthy communications atmosphere across a project. Of course, the efforts from nonmanagement personnel are vital, but management sets the tone. Examples of actions that can be taken by management to foster the desired communications are listed in Figure 3.4.

Nonmanagers look to managers to correct both intra- and interdepartment communications problems before they become serious. Most problems will be apparent to the astute manager. Some will be difficult to uncover. It is the manager's responsibility to maintain an open two-way channel of communication with employees, with peer management, and with senior management. This communications link should keep the manager aware of serious, or potentially serious, problems that occur. All eyes will be on the manager. The worst thing that could happen is for the manager to take no action. This will be viewed as condoning the problem, and this can cause a decline in morale among the project players. (See "Checking the Organization's Pulse" in Chapter 2 for more ideas on how project leaders can maintain an open channel of communications within a project.)

Project members want to be kept informed. Usually the amount of information that members expect will be more than they need to perform their assignments. Department meetings are a great way to communicate information in a fairly small and informal setting. They encourage camaraderie among the department members and stimulate the flow of good, open communications. The frequency of department meetings really depends on the type of department, but consider having one each week. At least schedule meetings for the same time each week, and if something interferes with that time slot, it is okay to skip a week now and then. It would be helpful if *all* departments within an organization or project reserve the same half-day for such meetings. (A given department meeting typically would last one hour or less.) This *united* approach will help to ensure the availability of this time period each week. The department manager should keep the meeting flowing with useful, interesting, or entertaining information. If the manager allows meetings to linger past their usefulness, the participants will begin to look for ways to avoid the meetings— and rightfully so.

Area meetings, where two or more departments get together, also can be a good communications tool. However, area meetings should be held less frequently than

- ■ Catch communications problems early; don't allow them to fester.
- ■ Ensure a level of information flow, throughout the project, that is viewed as at least adequate from a frequency, quantity, and quality basis.
- ■ Treat everyone equally; be fair but firm.
- ■ Do things that are fun.

Figure 3.4   Actions to foster good communications.

department meetings. Area meetings should share the accomplishments of all project groups that are participating in the meeting. They also are a good place to recognize those employees who have accomplished something special or unique.

Another useful technique is to invite selected nonmanagement leaders and aspiring employees to attend management meetings where the project is tracked. The nonmanagers will gain insight from their attendance, insight that they might be able to utilize in their assignments and share with others. Nonmanagers also will become more visible to the management team.

Management must do its best to treat all employees the same. No biases should be allowed to exist. In addition to fairness, management should develop a reputation for being firm and for acting swiftly, which will foster confidence in the management team. Employees want an action-oriented management team. Inaction will breed complacency and contempt for the organization.

Encourage hard work, but make sure that a healthy dose of fun is included. Many ideas are available to foster enjoyment. Some examples include providing unique entertainment at selected meetings, sponsoring seminars, and having picnics with softball or volleyball challenges. A particularly beneficial, creative idea is a *skills-enrichment day*—a day set aside to allow project participants to listen to speakers who are experts in various technology areas and self-improvement topics.

We Are All in This Together

> *Coming together is a beginning,*
> *Keeping together is progress,*
> *Working together is success.*
> *—Anonymous*

Reams of material have been written on the subject of interpersonal communications. This chapter is intended to expose you to some of the more common communications problems encountered in software development projects. You probably have recognized that many of these problems are common to any group of people, in practically any field of endeavor, who are assembled to achieve something.

You also might have recognized that the recommended way to eliminate or at least control these problems requires actions that many would view as common sense. If sense were so common, communications problems would not be so pervasive. A concerted effort is required on everyone's part to fix these problems. Management, in particular, must build and then maintain a work environment that supports effective, interpersonal communications.

Demonstrating respect for others is essential for improving communications among people. When project players understand that "we are all in this together" and that it is through harmony with one another that achievements are reached, then they have risen above providing the adequate to producing the best.

4

Project Schedule Planning: Getting in Control

The schedules created for a software development project can make or break the project, the product, and the people. The attention and forethought applied to this critical scheduling activity of developing the **project schedule plan** can mean the difference between:

- Management in control and management in panic
- High product quality and poor product quality
- A full-function product and a limited-function product
- High employee morale and low employee morale
- High employee productivity and low employee productivity
- On-time (or early) delivery and late (or no) delivery
- Competitive product costs and uncompetitive product costs
- Successful market entry and unsuccessful market entry
- Customer satisfaction and customer dissatisfaction
- Marketing strength and marketing weakness
- Timely next release and late (if at all) next release
- Product success and product failure

 Lesson: The most important plan of a project is the project schedule plan.

Simply put, the project scheduling activity can make the difference between profit and loss. The heartbeat of the entire software development process—and the single most important plan of a project—is the project schedule plan. It defines the roadmap of activities that affect virtually every member of a project and is the keystone for communications across a project.

If the schedules defined by the project schedule plan are unreasonable, then the expected progress on the project soon will become blocked. This blockage will cause project challenges to emerge, challenges that would otherwise be unnecessary, challenges that now must be met in order to deal with the obstructions. The failure of a major activity to be completed on schedule eventually will impact the schedules of subsequent project activities. This domino effect could continue until the project topples.

If you want to minimize potential rework on a project and meet the project's schedules, costs, and quality, a generous amount of care and attention must be given to the development of the project schedule plan. Experience suggests that a well thought out plan, in concert with a sound tracking and problem management process (see Chapter 5) can save both costs and cycle time for a project.

   Lesson: The project schedule plan is all about getting in control.

As Plato said, "The beginning is the most important part of the work." This rings true for two key areas of a project: defining what you are going to build and developing the overall plan to build it. Defining what you are going to build is embodied across the product requirements, product objectives, and product specifications—areas of focus for later chapters. Developing the project schedule plan to build the product is the primary theme of this chapter.

This chapter:

- Describes the basic concepts that need to be understood before an effective project schedule plan can be developed, and

- Presents a series of steps you can follow in developing a project schedule plan for your project.

A Project Tale

The following scenario illustrates how an unrealistic project schedule plan can snowball into a major mess. Doing a poor job developing a project schedule plan is akin to scheduling a project for failure.

During the first month of the project, an unofficial, rough scheduling estimate allows for a 12- to 18-month product development cycle. A month later, after the product requirements have been written and approved, a preliminary schedule is developed that suggests a 12-month duration. Everyone in touch with the project knows that this 12-month schedule is quite optimistic; however, no one is overly concerned because the schedule is only preliminary. A final schedule with all the necessary detail is forthcoming.

In the meantime, the product objectives are completed and all the participating groups agree on the direction the product should take. The writing of the product specifications has begun. The high-level design is also beginning. There is an overall good feeling about the project. Staffing of people with the required skills is under way. Coming on board are programmers, for both developing and testing the product, publications writers, and support personnel.

Everyone understands that this project is extremely important to the company. Everyone also understands that the product must be delivered to customers as soon as possible. Two factors are offered as major reasons for supporting an early customer delivery. The first reason is to bring in revenue in the next fiscal year, which starts in one month (and, therefore, ends in 13 months). The second reason is to help ensure that several key customers choose this product over competitive products. No one doubts that the product must be delivered as soon as possible.

The project planners commit to having detailed project schedules in place within the next two weeks. One planner remarks, "The detailed schedules really could be available within just one week. This project is a lot like others that I have planned, and there really isn't much to laying out the schedules." The planners decide not to include the technical people in the project scheduling activities. The rationale is "Leave the technical people alone as much as possible so they can get some 'real' work done."

A draft of the detailed schedules is ready in three days, when it is reviewed by a few members of the management team. Everyone agrees that the schedules are aggressive, but they also believe that this is the "right" schedule plan if the product is to hit the marketplace on time. Some minor changes are made and a final draft is produced. The planners survey most of the technical leaders about the schedules. Some technical leaders express opinions that the schedules are too aggressive and could be met only "if the wind is at our backs and no surprises occur, of which both are unlikely events." Also, there is concern that the projected staffing might be too aggressive to be achieved, or, if staffing levels are achieved, the skill level of the new people might be lower than required. If the project is staffed with people with a lower skill level than anticipated, more time will be necessary to bring these people "up to speed." The reply from the planning department is "Don't worry about staffing. That is our turf and we are working on it."

Some of the technical leaders feel that vacations and holidays have not been planned into the proposed schedule sufficiently, especially since some people have accrued excess vacation days from the previous aggressive project. The response is "Overtime was not planned. Therefore, overtime acts as a buffer should it be needed. Besides, there are many months before the end of the year when major holiday and vacation periods could occur. We should be in pretty good shape by then."

Another concern is that the expected programmer productivity rate is on the high end of the range rather than in the middle or on the low side. The response from planners is that most of the technical leaders are seasoned veterans whose high skills skewed the productivity rate higher. The planners add, "If this project is to be successful, we will have to achieve the higher productivity rate." A few other concerns are raised, but are essentially shrugged off. However, to address (appease) the concerns of the technical people, schedules are lengthened by two weeks. While this does not significantly satisfy them, it does help to reduce some of the tension that is building. The technical leaders rationalize, "The product will be done when it's done, so why make a big deal of it now? Anyway, nearly every project seems to follow this pattern. So what's new?"

The planners grumble, "It's too bad the lead technical people don't have more business savvy and realize that, to make it big in this business, you have to take big risks. That's why the technical people don't run the business. We will just have to drive the organization to achieve this schedule."

There seems to be an unsettled feeling across the project, something of a standoff. No mutual meeting of the minds ever took place where each side could work through the concerns of the other side. (In fact, there should not be a notion of "sides." Instead, the business and technical objectives should be shared by all. A we-are-in-this-together spirit should be the prevailing goal.) The general conclusion is that perceived standoffs like this have never stopped forward progress before. This is "business as usual."

The product specifications are written, then reviewed. There are more review comments than expected. The reason appears to be that the specifications were not quite finished (nor was the high-level design), but in the interest of maintaining project schedules, the product specifications were distributed on time. The planners are happy. The technical people are not happy, but recognize the importance of meeting schedules. The product specifications are updated to address the review comments and then redistributed for everyone's use. More comments are generated from the updated specifications. The most recent comments are all but ignored. It seems that the schedules did not allow for a second review of the product specifications. It was expected (and hoped) that the review cycle could be shortened to a single, three-week review period, rather than two, two-week review periods with a document update period in between.

Since more time is required to perform the single update of the product specifications than has been planned, the high-level design is slipping farther behind schedule. The developers are working overtime in an attempt to finish the high-level design as soon as possible. Furthermore, one of every two design inspections is failing. The schedule had allowed for design inspections but not for recovery time for inspections that failed. Even with the overtime that people are working, the schedule is slipping slowly and frustratingly. High-level design is finally completed yet is two weeks behind schedule. The perception is "Not too bad," especially when the two weeks that were added to the project are taken into account.

As low-level design, coding, test plans, and publication content plans are being developed, a disturbing realization takes hold. The product specifications are still not sufficiently complete. The prevailing thought is that they would have been complete if they had been through two review cycles, with a document update period in between. Unfortunately, it is too late to turn the clock back. All developers do their best to update their personal copy of the specifications as they proceed with their low-level design and coding. However, there is no time for them formally to update and redistribute the product specifications to other groups within the project. Now the testers and the publications writers begin to fall behind their schedules. Many options are offered, but only one will really solve the problem: The developers must update and redistribute the product specifications. They do just that.

Several weeks pass. The product specifications have been updated and distributed throughout the project. The low-level design has been completed. The coding, unit testing, and function testing, however, are farther behind schedule. Also, the testers and writers discover that they are not able to recover all their lost time. They perceive that the real critical path of the project lies not with them but with the developers—in getting the code ready to enter the first phase of the formal test period. It seems that, when the schedules originally were developed, no one thought to include the writing of the unit test and function test plans. In the interest of protecting schedules, the unit test is abandoned and the function test is now the focus of activity.

The project is now six weeks behind the planned schedule. If any additional slips occur, the project will not be able to bring in revenue for the next fiscal year, as planned. (The two-week buffer, plus starting one month before the fiscal year began, accounts for the six-week leeway.) In response, the code is declared ready for the first independent test phase—the component test. Plans are put in place to complete the function test in parallel with the component test.

A medium disaster develops. Two groups, the developers and the testers, are performing tests on the same code and at the same time. Many of the same bugs (defects) are being discovered by both groups. To make matters worse, the developers' response time in fixing the bugs found by the testers is much longer than desirable. The reason: The developers are busy trying to complete their own function testing. To "fix" this problem, the developers are instructed to correct bugs according to priorities set by the testers. The project leadership stresses the importance of containing the duration of the component test to its original plan. However, in spite of this mandate, the component test takes four weeks longer than planned. The code that the developers delivered was just too "buggy."

The schedule is now 10 weeks longer than was originally planned. The developers have been working a heavy dose of overtime for many months. People are weary, frustrated, and edgy. The major holiday and vacation period has arrived, but few are able to take any appreciable time off. The most repeated phrase is "I don't want to go through this again!" The second most repeated phrase is "But it will happen again. It always is the same way. We never seem to learn from our mistakes!"

If this scenario were to run its course, the project would be nearly four months late. This would cause the product cost to come in significantly higher than planned. Even though the "planned" project schedules were apparently too aggressive to begin with, the expected, and missed, delivery date promised to the project leadership, marketing, customers, and other interested groups can only cause disappointment. Disappointment, however, may be too kind a word, since the plans that outside groups have made based on the product's expected delivery date will need to undergo serious modification.

Other negative "fallout" also will be felt. Some expected customer sales will have disappeared, the next release will be available much later than planned (if at all), and a sometimes irreversible toll on the personal lives of the project team might have occurred. Whether the blame for lateness rests with the planners, the project technical people, or should be shared by both is not a point for debate here. The point is, the more a project schedule plan is thought out and mutually agreed to by all the key participants as being aggressive but *achievable,* then the greater the likelihood that *everyone* will win as the plan is executed successfully.

A project schedule plan should guide the project on a successful journey toward delivery of the product on time, within cost, with the expected quality, and without demoralizing the project's personnel. Three primary ingredients are necessary for developing an effective project schedule plan. The plan must:

- Be well thought out
- Have the commitment of the participants
- Be aggressive yet achievable

Many factors contribute to the successful implementation of these primary ingredients. Before focusing on the actual series of steps to follow in developing a project schedule plan, the first order of business is to understand the essential concepts that must be applied when developing a project schedule plan. These concepts are presented in the forthcoming sections. Afterward, the steps to developing a project schedule plan are described.

When to Start the Project Schedule Plan

 Lesson: While waiting for the needed information to develop the full project schedule plan, a near-term schedule plan should be established.

For a new project, broad, project-oriented schedules should be identified within weeks of the project's conception. Although these schedules will be preliminary, they will set the pace and level of expectation for the project until better schedules can be developed. A *near-term* set of schedules, however, should be available almost immediately. The near-term schedule plan should address the activities that must be worked within the next four to six weeks.

The development of the full project schedule plan cannot be started seriously until after the product objectives have been completed and are available for review. The information in the product objectives becomes the basis from which a project schedule plan can be developed. The project schedule plan should be completed a short time after the high-level design and product specifications are approved. After the high-level design and product specifications activities have been completed, there should be sufficient understanding of the product to support a definition of a full set of schedules. (More on this in the upcoming section, "Initial and Final Project Schedule Plans.")

 Lesson: The progress being achieved on a project cannot be measured unless a plan first has been established against which progress can be measured.

Cyril Northcote Parkinson, British historian and author, once wrote that "Work expands so as to fill the time available for its completion." Schedules are critical to maintaining a healthy productivity rate for the members of a project, whether for a small group of people or for a large organization. It is difficult to measure progress unless there is a plan to track against. Resist waiting until all imaginable details about the product content and the project plans are known before working the full project schedule plan. Each person has a **variable productivity potential.** Analogous to a variable resistor, a person has considerable flexibility to vary his or her productivity to match the needs of the task at hand. Aggressive but achievable schedules will help to harness the energies of project personnel so that an acceptable level of progress can be achieved throughout the duration of the project. Also, a "busy" person is much more content than a partially busy or idle person.

Top-Down and Bottom-Up Planning

 Lesson: A top-down plan is developed without the participation of all project members and, therefore, should not be construed as a committed plan.

Project schedule plans come in two varieties: **top-down** and **bottom-up.** A top-down plan typically is developed by one person (or a small subset of people on a project). The top-down plan lists the more significant activities of a project and suggests a set of schedules that might be achieved for it. A top-down plan does not involve the participation of all project members and, consequently, should not be conveyed to management as a committed schedule, but only as a target schedule. Top-down plans are strictly estimating techniques to help people get a better feel for the size, cost, and complexity of a project. Top-down planning is an essential business exercise and should be viewed as such, but with the understanding that the resulting schedules are typically high risk.

In contrast to a top-down plan, a bottom-up plan is developed with the participation of virtually all members of a project. All activities are identified (not just the significant ones), along with the activity owners, the activity durations, and the dependencies among the activities. A bottom-up plan, if final, is *the* plan that should be committed to management. This chapter focuses on creating the bottom-up project schedule plan.

All participants in the product development cycle must feel ownership for their piece of the total project schedule. Only then will an individual's optimal productivity be possible. You might have observed instances where an individual did not feel ownership of the schedules for his or her activities. When the going gets tough, this individual might not put the extra effort forward. This hurts not only the individual but the project as well. Personal commitment from each participant is a must. Bottom-up planning helps to ensure the personal commitment from every member of a project.

Initial and Final Project Schedule Plans

Is there any value in creating both an initial project schedule plan and a final project schedule plan? Yes. A bottom-up project schedule plan usually is best developed in two stages: the initial project schedule plan and the final project schedule plan.

 Lesson: Never commit to a detailed schedule to build something unless the something is well defined.

As shown in Figure 4.1, the initial project schedule plan, hereafter called the *IPSP*, can be created after the product objectives have been written fully and are available for review. The IPSP should not be considered complete until the product objectives are approved. However, the IPSP, although a bottom-up plan, should not be committed to management. Why? Because it is based on product objectives and not on the more definitive product specifications. You should never commit to a detailed schedule to build something when, in fact, the *something* is not defined.

The final project schedule plan (*FPSP*), as shown in Figure 4.1, can be started after the product specifications have been written fully and are available for review. However, the FPSP should not be considered complete and approved until the product specifications are approved. This is important because the product being built must be well defined before an FPSP can be considered complete and credible. The FPSP is the plan to commit to management.

 Lesson: Project members need a plan to follow in order to achieve their greatest productivity.

You might ask, "Why bother to even create an IPSP? Why not just wait for the product specifications to be available and then build the FPSP?" The reason is simple. If a project does not have a plan in place, even a relatively basic bottom-up plan, then precious time will be lost in getting to the FPSP. Why? Because everyone will be working hard on something, but not necessarily the *right* something. The members of a project need plans not only to ensure the right activities are being acted upon first but also to help the project members pace themselves.

 Lesson: For every day that a project delays in completing a plan, one-half day of poorly invested time is lost from the project that can never be regained.

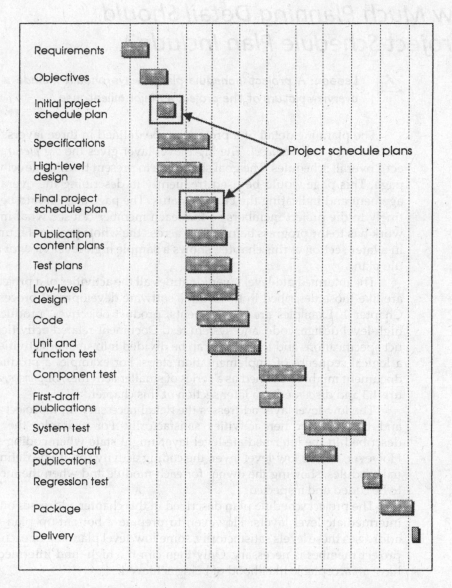

Figure 4.1   Initial and final project schedule plans.

Experience suggests that, once a project schedule plan is able to be developed, for every day that a project delays in completing the plan, at least one-half day is lost from the overall project cycle time. This is time that can never be recovered. If you delay by two calendar months in completing the plan, for example, you will have lost at least one calendar month of time from the project. People need a plan against which to pace their speed and priorities in order to achieve the most efficiency.

How Much Planning Detail Should a Project Schedule Plan Include?

 Lesson: A project schedule plan always should include a one-page overview picture of the project's major milestones.

The planning detail of a project can be defined in three layers: *high level, intermediate level,* and *low level.* The high-level layer gives the *big picture* view of a project's overall schedules. The goal should be to present the high-level view on a single page. This page would be used frequently in describing the overall plan to management and indicating the current status. The page also should be presented routinely to the project members so that each member can see what impact his or her work has to the progress being made across the whole project. Figure 4.6, discussed in a later section of this chapter, shows a sample high-level view of a project schedule plan.

The intermediate-level layer identifies all the activities of a project. The activities are like those described in the sample software development process introduced in Chapter 1. Examples are requirements, product objectives, product specifications, high-level design, code, and system test. Document-related activities, such as product specifications and test plans, can be divided into smaller activities that represent a logical sequence of implementation steps. For example, a product specifications document might be defined as a series of smaller activities, or *phases,* as shown in Figure 4.3 and discussed in a later section of this chapter.

The low-level layer addresses the detail necessary for a project member to plan and track his or her activities satisfactorily. For example, the coding activity described in the intermediate-level layer might state when coding starts and ends. However, for the low-level layer, the coding activity should be defined into individual modules, showing the owner for each module and when the module is planned to be coded and inspected.

The project schedule plan described in this chapter addresses only the high- and intermediate-level layers. However, to prepare a bottom-up plan that sufficiently addresses these levels satisfactorily, some low-level planning of each activity by each project member is necessary. Only then can the high- and intermediate-level plans have an acceptable likelihood of being achieved.

Types of Activity Relationships

Figure 4.2 shows the three basic activity relationships and three variations per relationship that most projects require and most project management tools recognize. This means that at least nine variations of activity relationships are possible. These three basic activity relationships and their corresponding variations are briefly described here. A fourth is acknowledged.

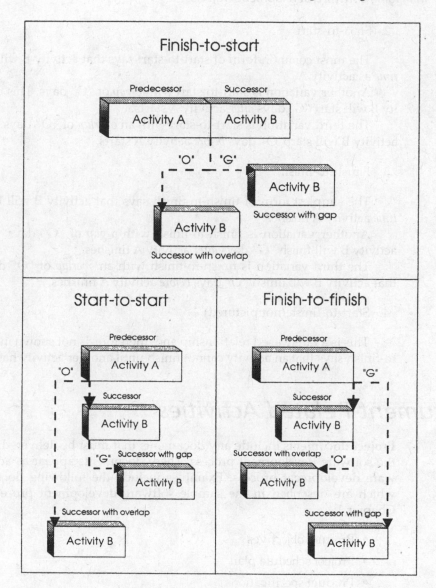

Figure 4.2   Activity relationships.

1. Finish-to-start

This is the most common relationship. In its simplest form, finish-to-start says that activity B will start *after* activity A finishes.

Another variation is finish-to-start with a *gap* of "G" days. This means that activity B will start "G" days *after* activity A finishes.

The third variation is finish-to-start with an *overlap* of "O" days. This means that activity B will start "O" days *before* activity A finishes.

2. Start-to-start

The most common form of start-to-start says that activity B will start *at the same time* as activity A.

Another variation is start-to-start with a *gap* of "G" days. This means that activity B will start "G" days *after* activity A starts.

The third variation is start-to-start with an *overlap* of "O" days. This means that activity B will start "O" days *before* activity A starts.

3. Finish-to-finish

The simplest form of finish-to-finish says that activity B will finish *at the same time* activity A finishes.

Another variation is finish-to-finish with a *gap* of "G" days. This means that activity B will finish "G" days *after* activity A finishes.

The third variation is finish-to-finish with an *overlap* of "O" days. This means that activity B will finish "O" days *before* activity A finishes.

4. Start-to-finish (not pictured)

This is a rarely used relationship and, therefore, is not shown in Figure 4.2. Start-to-finish says that an activity cannot finish until another activity has started.

Document-Related Activities

Project documents include any documents that must be delivered at some point in the software development process. These documents appear as activities in a software development process. Examples include the following documents, some of which are described in the sample software development process introduced in Chapter 1:

- Product objectives
- Project schedule plan
- Product specifications
- Contracts with vendors
- Process and methodology documents
- Design documents
- Publication content plans
- Test plans
- Publication drafts

 Lesson: Document-related activities should be expanded into a series of smaller activities.

Document-related activities should be expanded into smaller, more discrete activities when developing the project schedule plan. For ease of illustration, these discrete activities are referred to as document implementation *phases*. Figure 4.3 illustrates the development of a document in a logical sequence of implementation phases: *preparation, review, update, approval,* and *refresh.* Let's briefly look at each of these five phases.

1. Preparation

This is usually the longest of the phases and can vary anywhere from one week for very small, simple documents to many weeks for large, complex documents.

2. Review

This phase begins when the document is distributed for examination. This phase is typically one to four weeks in duration, depending on the document type and size and on the proximity of the reviewers. (Do they work in the same building? Same city? Same country?) Test plans might take two weeks, product specifications four weeks. You should make certain that each document is distributed to all parties who must approve or review it. This is the time to ensure that the distribution list of people is complete and that no required people or organizations are overlooked.

 Lesson: Review-level documents should be complete.

Documents distributed for review should be essentially complete—no sections should be missing or significantly deficient. The goal is for all information to be avail-

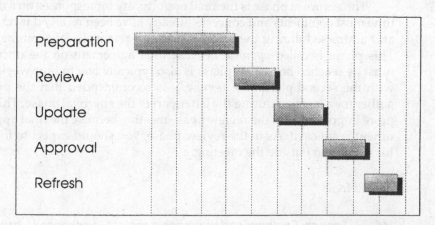

Figure 4.3   Implementation phases of a document.

able, complete, and accurate. This allows a better review to occur. Furthermore, the next time the document is distributed for comments, the reviewers will need to review only the areas that were updated based on earlier comments. This means that surprises, such as a flurry of new and major comments, will be less likely to occur.

It is recommended that a meeting of the primary reviewers be called during the latter part of the review phase. A face-to-face meeting is an excellent way to allow all participants to voice their concerns to one another and to identify and log as many problems as can be identified. You should not expect to resolve many problems in this type of meeting. In fact, the primary purpose for the meeting is to record problems, not resolve them. Spending more than one to two minutes to resolve a problem is usually detrimental to the progress of the meeting. Problems that require more time to resolve should be logged and then solved outside the meeting.

3. Update

 Lesson: Some form of highlighting should be used when updating documents.

This phase is used to modify a document in response to comments from reviewers. The update phase sets aside time to react to comments and concerns that, once addressed, will ensure a better product or project. This phase may be from one to six weeks in duration, depending not only on the size and type of document but also on the quantity and complexity of the problems identified and the comments made. Any updates made to a document should be highlighted in some fashion, such as the use of **change bars** in the margins. This will allow the reviewers to locate quickly the most recent changes to the document.

4. Approval

The approval phase is the final opportunity for responses on a document. By this time most comments and concerns already have been received from the review phase and addressed during the update phase, so relatively few comments are expected. This phase is called *approval* because final agreement on the document's contents must be reached here. This phase is also typically one to four weeks in duration. As with the second phase, the review, it is recommended that the primary reviewers gather for a meeting during the latter part of the approval phase. This meeting is even more important than the review phase meeting because the final approval of the document is solicited. As in the review phase, you should expect to log some problems for resolution outside the meeting.

5. Refresh

 Lesson: Communication across a project is enhanced when the refresh phase is applied to project documents.

The last phase is used to record any changes to the document that have occurred during the approval phase. The document is then distributed for informational purposes only; no more comments are expected or solicited. This phase could be as short as one day (to issue a memo describing any agreed-upon changes) or as long as several weeks (to update changes in a large document). Again, if changes are made in the document, then some form of unique change bars should be used.

Lesson: Critical or complex documents typically require all five phases to be implemented.

Some documents might need only the preparation, approval, and refresh phases. These documents are typically small in size, cause little controversy, and would require little change from a first review. Documents that typically require all five phases are those that are considered critical or complex project documents—such as product specifications, test plans, and product publications drafts. To omit the review and update phases for documents that are considered primary is usually a grave mistake. Do not attempt to shorten the product development cycle in these areas.

Lesson: The owner of a document should insist on a thorough review phase.

For documents that have both a review and an approval phase, you should be aware that there is a tendency for the review phase draft to receive a less thorough review than you might expect. The reason: Reviewers will attempt to manage their own time as effectively as they can. Knowing that another draft will be forthcoming during the approval phase, they frequently will put off a thorough review until a document is at its best. While this type of procrastination might make sense for reviewers, it is inefficient for the document and the project as a whole. The owner of the document has a responsibility to ensure that reviewers participate throughout the document review cycle.

Although the five phases described here are probably adequate for most documents, you might choose to identify other phases for some documents. For example, separate phases related to customer validation or inspection might be added.

Overlapping Activities

Allowing activities that have a relationship to one another to overlap rather than be performed in series can be either good or bad, depending on the kinds of activities and the amount of overlap involved. For example, the high-level design of a product must be done before the low-level design. However, it is possible, and frequently recommended, to allow some low-level design to begin before all the product's high-level design has been completed. This is okay, providing that all of the high-level design that can impact the specific area to be low-level designed has been completed. In this fairly clean example, no revisions or duplicate workloads are anticipated.

There are cases where overlapping two activities can be harmful. In the project tale presented earlier in this chapter, overlapping the function test and the component test was *not* okay, and resulted in lower productivity for both activities and a project that was certainly difficult to manage. An approach that would be acceptable, however, is to allow the component test to begin only on those functions that have already been function tested. Then two groups wouldn't duplicate their time by finding the same bugs. A caution to note here is that, if the same developers who must fix the bugs discovered in the component test are still function testing other code, then a productivity "impact" will occur as their time is shared across two goals.

 Lesson: Avoid allowing activities to overlap if the activities have any dependencies on one another, either directly or indirectly.

When you examine activities that might benefit from being overlapped, it should be readily apparent whether the overlap is acceptable. The key is to look for dependencies among the activities. You should avoid scheduling two activities to overlap if one can be impacted by the other; in other words, if one has a dependency on the other. Whenever an impact occurs, someone or something must wait for someone else or something else. This cuts into productivity, which is directly related to scheduling.

Another example from an earlier scenario involves the publications writers who were waiting for the product specifications to be completed. It is not possible to write product publications at the same time the product is being defined in the product specifications. The writers need the product specifications to define the subject matter for the publications.

Consider the following negative by-product, which can result when one person is waiting for another person: Sharon Williams is waiting for Ann Smith to complete an activity. There is a tendency for Williams to try one of two things. Either Williams will slow down Smith further, by asking questions and gathering data, or Williams will make assumptions. These assumptions might not all prove correct, and, consequently, revisions will be necessary later.

 Lesson: The complexity of managing a project increases as the number of overlapping activities increases.

Overlapping activities that will not impact one another can have a positive impact on overall schedules. For instance, management should consider overlapping activities when a schedule needs to be refined to shorten its total length. However, bear in mind that the complexity involved in managing schedules increases as the total number of overlapping activities increases. Also, be certain that the people and machine resources required to implement each of the overlapping activities are not tightly shared between the activities. If you do plan to share these resources, and allow little or no room for contingency, then you are risking a situation in which one or both activities will not be completed on time. If one activity falls behind schedule, the resources to complete the other activity are impacted immediately. This situation places an undesirable competition for resource attention upon both activities.

Estimating the Duration of an Activity

Estimating the duration of an activity is perhaps the most difficult task in developing the project schedule plan. It is difficult because often you are estimating how long it will take to do something that you have not done before. Oh, sure, you have designed or coded or tested or written documentation before, but to the exact characteristics of this project? Probably not. Most new activities to be performed are unique enough to make estimating their duration something other than an exact science. Let's look at some things to consider that can help in estimating activity durations.

- Use a work breakdown structure.

 Lesson: When estimating the duration of an activity, break the activity into smaller work pieces and account for the duration of each work piece.

The more the estimated work is divided into smaller pieces, the better your estimate will be. For example, say you must prepare a product specifications document for review and you guesstimate it will take two months to write. If you spend a little more time to break up the activity into more discrete activities and then estimate the time to perform each of the discrete activities, your estimate will be more credible than the first approach. Specifically, you might decide that there will be 12 chapters and three people will each write four chapters. Then the three people will review each other's work for completeness, accuracy, and consistency and make any necessary changes. Then the product specifications will be distributed outside the three-person team for review. It is much easier to estimate the time to perform discrete activities that last one week or less than to estimate activities that last several weeks or months.

It is important to note that the planning performed here on the product specifications would fall under the category of low-level planning as discussed earlier. It is not recommended that the low-level activities be added to the intermediate-level project schedule plan. Doing so would only increase the complexity of the plan and unnecessarily make it more difficult to grasp and work with. Instead, the durations of the discrete activities should be tallied and the resulting value used in the project schedule plan for the activity called "product specifications prepared."

 Lesson: For best estimating results, break an activity into work pieces of approximately one week's duration.

The breaking of *big* activities into smaller and smaller activities defines the **work breakdown structure** (WBS). Every activity can be pared down to smaller discrete activities. For the most part, the intermediate-level activities that should make up the project schedule plan should be defined already in your organization's software development process. This is one level of the WBS. Each of these activities, in turn, can be broken into smaller pieces. And so on. If you own an activity, you probably will want to create the WBS to the level of detail that makes sense to best support your overall estimate. It is recommended that the WBS be defined to multiple discrete activities lasting one week (or less).

- Use historical data.

Use historical data, if available, from past similar projects to help in estimating activity durations. For example, determine the productivity for performing high-level design, low-level design, coding, unit test, writing test scripts, writing a page of a user's manual, getting a design change request (DCR) approved, fixing and verifying a bug found in test, and so on.

- Include contingency buffer.

In general, all activities should have contingency buffer built into them. There is a tendency to estimate the time required to complete an activity as if there will be absolutely no interruptions. The buffer ensures there is time to complete the activity and perform other activities or interruptions that are often overlooked. If a comprehensive list of ground rules (see the final bullet) has been accounted for, the buffer might be minimal or perhaps not be necessary. (For more on the subjects of buffers, see "Planned Contingency Buffers" later in this chapter.)

- Solicit others as a sounding board.

Use others as a sounding board to help add credibility to your estimates. Any problems identified while scrubbing your estimates can save many headaches later as you are implementing your activities and held accountable for meeting your estimates.

- Develop a set of ground rules from which to estimate.

 Lesson: A project should have a common set of ground rules from which everyone plans.

When the project members are assembled to develop their pieces of a total project schedule plan, it is important that everyone begin the journey on the same footing. That is, a common set of assumptions, or *ground rules*, needs to be developed. (These ground rules typically are developed by the project schedule coordinator as part of Step 3 of developing a project schedule plan and are delivered to the project members in Step 4. These steps are described in "The Steps to Developing a Project Schedule Plan" later in this chapter.)

Examples of items that might appear on the list of ground rules include:

- No overtime
- First shift only
- Account for vacation and holidays
- State activity durations in workdays (not weeks)
- Account for skill level of team members
- Account for education/training needs
- Account for participation in design and code inspections
- Account for participation in reviewing project documents
- Account for participation in project meetings, such as team/project tracking meetings
- Account for identifying, recording, and displaying various quality- and process-related measurements
- Account for travel time
- Account for availability of hardware, tools, and the like that are required
- Account for realistic projections of personnel staffing
- Base estimates to design, code, and test on productivity rates of . . . ; explain any deviations
- Include an *X* percent contingency buffer in each activity
- Account for ongoing support of products that have already been delivered to customers
- List any special assumptions made that are in addition to those in the ground rules

Critical Path

 Lesson: To shorten a project's duration, focus on what can be done to those activities that make up the critical path.

You should know the activities that make up the **critical path** of the project schedule plan. The critical path is the sequence of activities that, collectively, define the starting and ending dates for the project. The path of these activities has no slack time (excess time) in accomplishing the schedule. Said another way, if you were to reduce the total project's duration, the activities in the critical path are the initial ones upon which to focus. Furthermore, if you are to achieve your committed schedules, it is the activities on the critical path that typically need the most immediate attention.

Typically 20 percent or fewer of all a project's activities are on the critical path. Activities (including documents) commonly in the critical path are the product requirements, product objectives, product specifications, high-level design, low-level design, code, unit test, function test, component test, system test, and packaging and stocking the product for delivery to customers. These activities are described in the sample software development process defined in Chapter 1. Keep in mind that the activities in the critical path can be different in your project depending on many factors, such as the software development process you employ and the characteristics of the product you are building.

You might ask, "That's a lot of activities. What activities are missing from this list?" A lot. Some examples are: a "quality plan," build and integration plan, various test plans, writing test scripts for the various tests, publication content plans, writing the product publications drafts, and many other activities. However, it is important to note that these activities can be in a project's critical path, although typically they are not.

Figure 4.4 shows a simple example of a critical path in a primitive network. The example depicts six activities and their corresponding dependencies and durations. The critical path is the serial flow of activities A-B-D-F. To shorten the critical path by one day, the day must be removed from among the A, B, D, and F activities. Activities C and E each have slack time of 2 days.

Note that, if activity D were reduced to seven days, a new critical path would emerge: A-E-F. This is because activity E now would end one day after the combined serial durations of activities B and D. A project might easily have 200 or more activities defined in its network. Reducing the critical path on most projects is not a trivial exercise and can, in fact, be downright arduous.

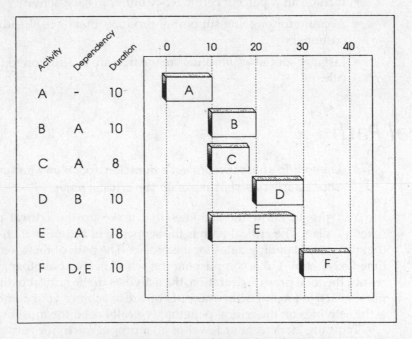

Figure 4.4   Example of critical path A-B-D-F.

Resources

A common trap experienced while developing a project schedule plan is not fully understanding the staffing resources that will be applied to the project. Listed here are some items for consideration. Have you accounted for such items as:

- Staffing ramp-up and staffing roll-off?
- Up-front investment to ensure completed product requirements (if not done by now)?
- Prototyping?
- Training or the learning curve that might be necessary for a person or group of people before they can be fully productive?
- Other education (nonproject related but career or professional related)?
- Matching the skills of the people assigned to the skills required of the activities?
- Supporting project processes, such as those involved in defect removal and correction and tracking project progress?
- Identifying, recording, and displaying quality and process-related measurements?
- Vacations and holidays?
- Interference from activities outside the new project, such as resolving problems in products that have been delivered to customers already?
- Those project members who are performing multiple activities in parallel and, according to the information from the project management tool, do not have sufficient calendar time to complete all their activities?

Accounting for staffing resources when creating a project schedule plan can add considerable complexity. Here are some thoughts to consider to help make this task more manageable.

 Lesson: First build a schedule-constrained plan, then transition to a resource-constrained plan.

A project schedule plan can be thought of as a collection of many team plans. When creating a team plan, it is recommended that you begin with a **schedule-constrained plan,** not a **resource-constrained plan.** For example, initially construct a team plan without focusing on staffing resources. That is, first identify the activities, their owners, and their dependencies. Then add a rough cut at what the duration for each activity might be. Next, debug the plan by making sure that all the activities are linked with one another properly.

After the team plan is thought to be constructed properly, carefully factor in the impact of staffing on each activity. Naturally, the duration of some activities will change as the focus now shifts from building a schedule-constrained team plan to a resource-constrained team plan.

 Lesson: Staffing is not just accounting for "heads," it is accounting for heads with the right skills.

Before committing to a plan, teams must understand their available resources and make sure that the duration of each of their activities is achievable based on the skills of the people available. In effect, this is saying that the burden of resource planning rests primarily with the team plans, not with the project schedule plan.

After the team plans are considered complete, the data used in their construction need to be rolled up into the project schedule plan. However, a note of caution here. If you choose to include the roll-up of resource data with each activity, do so for the primary purpose of recording all the resource requirements in one place. Do not do it to manage resources across the project. Why? Because the added complexity of attempting to manage the resource of each activity at the project schedule plan level requires far more discipline, skill, and accounting techniques than most projects can offer. Besides, rolling up the resource with the expectation of managing it at the project schedule plan level is not necessary to plan and manage a project successfully.

Planned Contingency Buffers

A **buffer** is a designated period built into a schedule to serve as extra time or contingency to help absorb delays that might occur unexpectedly. There are three buffer categories for a project schedule plan:

- Planned contingency buffers
- Overtime, shifts, and temporary personnel buffers
- Holiday and vacation buffers

This section will discuss planned *contingency buffers*. The remaining categories are discussed in the two sections that follow.

 Lesson: Every project schedule plan should include contingency buffer.

Every project schedule plan should have some contingency buffer built into it. This buffer plan should not involve holidays, vacations, and overtime. If the project schedule plan is built for things going "right," they won't. Ante up the buffer now—other than holidays, vacations, and overtime—to avoid making the regrettable mistake of having to live through an "oversight" for possibly the duration of a project.

Typically, every project activity should have some buffer built into it. For example, when planning for a system test, recognize that the test scripts must be run more than once. The first time they are run, defects in the product code or in the test scripts themselves will be found. Once corrected, the tests can advance further, but more defects likely will be discovered. Many algorithms are available for determining the duration of major activities, such as for a system test. However, any generalized algorithms are subject to debate, and this is not a point of discussion here. If you believe it takes one week to run all the system test scripts, assuming everything runs with no problems, and it is your belief that the system test will be an equivalent length of four such runs, then you have identified four weeks of work. Whatever algorithm you employ, however, attempt to factor in an additional 10 to 20 percent buffer. This holds true for most activities, including the writing of product specifications, designing the product, coding the product, and writing the product publications drafts.

Adding a 10 to 20 percent buffer is not an excuse to create a schedule that is not aggressive. The goals are for every schedule to be aggressive and to meet every schedule commitment. If you have estimated the time to complete an activity by assuming that you will be uninterrupted for many days or weeks at a time, think again. Many things go on around us that can interfere, such as meetings, training, outside appointments, reviewing documentation, participating in inspections, and others.

 Lesson: Distribute contingency buffer across all the activities of a project.

An often-made mistake is to place the whole buffer period at the tail end of a project. Instead, the buffer should be appropriately distributed across all the activities of the project—particularly those activities along the critical path—if the project schedule plan is expected to hold together. This distributed placement of a buffer significantly increases the likelihood that people will meet their intermediate project schedules. It also will help to reduce a buildup of frustration that results when a project continually cannot complete major activities as planned. This frustration not only has a negative effect on morale, but it also robs the project of valuable productivity that can never be recovered. Occasionally, the "luxury" of a buffer will not be possible for some project activities. When this happens, activities that fall somewhere before and after the no-buffer activities must have an ample buffer to compensate.

 Lesson: Preserve weekends as one form of contingency buffer.

When feasible, always begin multiweek activities on Mondays and end them on Fridays. This paces the organization to complete an activity by Friday, but, if more time is needed, the weekend can act as a minibuffer. If activities are scheduled to end on Mondays, there is a tendency to either plan a working weekend or to think you can accomplish more than you actually can on that one day. When a weekend is planned, it no longer serves as a real buffer.

Overtime, Shifts, and Temporary Personnel Buffers

 Lesson: Never plan for overtime; it will happen anyway.

Overtime is a natural buffer to help protect imperfect project schedule plans. If overtime is planned, even more overtime will be needed—a trap to avoid. The greatest cause of **burnout** is excessive overtime. Burnout is a condition that typically results when a person works long hours across many days and takes an insufficient amount of time away from the workplace for rest and relaxation. Burnout results in a person making more mistakes, being less productive, and frequently being more irritable to coworkers. Again, excessive overtime is the greatest cause of burnout. You want to avoid both.

The advice offered in this section is generalized. There are specific exceptions, of course. For example, if a project lasts only one month, then perhaps all three areas—holidays, vacations, and overtime—must be factored into the schedule plan. In this case, however, the employee can be given time off immediately after the month's activities are completed. For very long projects, it should be easier to honor the goal of not planning the use of holidays, vacations, and overtime in the project schedule plan.

Assigning people to work split shifts can be an effective way to manage limited resources within a project. For example, if the project is entering system test and there are a limited number of machines available to use for testing, then people might have to work split or separate shifts. One test team can work from 8 A.M. to 4 P.M. while another test team can work from 2 P.M. to 10 P.M. The two-hour overlap is useful to ensure continuity between the two test teams. When projects resort to working shifts, the greatest difficulty is to ensure that all necessary personnel are also available to support the longer work day. In the example just cited, developers must be available to fix problems that testers find. Also, the people who support the machines must be available to ensure that the machines remain operable.

The use of temporary personnel can be another effective way to buffer schedules. These additional people can come from within or from outside a company. However, several pitfalls can reduce the effectiveness of this option:

- Failure to plan ahead
- Failure to plan for training time
- Loss of skills
- Additional need for management and communications overhead

 Lesson: Be prepared to cope with the loss of knowledge and skills when temporary personnel leave a project.

It is not realistic to expect that the number of people with the precise skills needed will be available for transfer to your project on short notice. You must anticipate the need for temporary personnel if you expect to obtain skilled people when they are required. Even if you find skilled people to help, they still will require some time to get "up to speed." Therefore, factor in this training curve when you set the start date for temporary recruits. A caution, assume the temporary personnel are just that, temporary. Do not forget that, when the temporary personnel leave, they take with them knowledge and skills that you may need later in the project or on a subsequent project.

Finally, remember that more people, even though temporary, will require additional time to manage and lead. Communications, already a major obstacle in software development projects (see Chapter 3), also will require additional time and attention from the project leadership.

Holiday and Vacation Buffers

Do not plan to work holidays. There are two reasons for this. The first is that everyone needs some time off, whether to spend with family members, friends, or just to be alone. In the heat of trying to maintain schedules, this oasis of holiday time can be therapeutic physically, mentally, and emotionally. Having said that, the second reason for not planning to work holidays is that these days represent the very last buffer to reach for. An example is in order.

> The product being developed has already been announced to the public. The delivery date for the product also has been announced. A customer has placed a very large order and is expecting special delivery on the same day the product becomes available. For whatever reason, the project has since fallen behind schedule. A company commitment has been made to the customer. The customer has made an appreciable financial outlay in people and materials in order to be ready for the product the first day it is available.

Now what happens? Every reasonable attempt must be made to honor the commitment to the customer. Unless there is extenuating personal hardship, the employee should be asked to work a holiday. This example is an extreme case. While it is not likely to happen often, it will occur. Note that this example applies to a recovery schedule plan, not to the original project schedule plan.

 Lesson: Make sure to account for holidays and vacations when developing a project schedule plan.

A project schedule plan should be developed with the preferred vacation days of each participant in mind. Hardship cases, especially, must be recognized and planned for. Once a project schedule plan begins to take shape and mismatches are being negotiated, vacations, with the approval of the vacation owner, are likely targets of movement. Most employees will be flexible with their vacation days. For example, there are times throughout a project development cycle when a given person is most busy and least busy. It is strongly preferred that a person plan his or her vacation during a least-busy period. This **vacation factor** is a useful tool when arranging schedules.

The Second Opinion

Having an outside person or group review the proposed project schedule plan before it becomes committed is a beneficial exercise. Someone who is not emotionally attached to the project can offer insights that might otherwise be missed. This individual also might provide you with the encouragement to go in the direction you had felt, deep down, was the right way but were too reluctant to mention or pursue.

 Lesson: Obtaining a second opinion on a project schedule plan can be an invaluable, yet relatively inexpensive, exercise.

The cost, in terms of time and money, to get a second opinion will be much less than one might expect. Experience suggests that a seasoned, software project management "consultant" reviewing a project schedule plan for a week or less will discover better than 80 percent of the potential problem areas. The additional time and dollar cost for this second opinion can be insignificant compared with the potential savings of time and expense throughout the project.

A word of caution: If you don't expect to listen or react to the advice from the second opinion source, don't bother to solicit a second opinion. More harm can result in ignoring what might prove to be good advice than in not getting any outside advice at all. The harm can come from two directions. The first is from the person(s) who was designated to provide the second opinion. A lot of work might have gone into the analysis, and that person could feel that his or her time was wasted. The second source of harm is from your subordinates, peers, and project leadership. If you turn down what is viewed to be good advice, and the project later suffers for literally months, then your credibility as a decision maker can be impaired. However, if the person providing the second opinion offers poor advice, you obviously are better off by not adopting that advice.

Identifying Milestones

A project can be divided into major pieces. When one of these pieces has completed, a significant accomplishment, or milestone, for the project has been reached. Examples of milestones are listed in Figure 4.5.

There are two major reasons for identifying milestones in a project schedule plan. The first reason is to avoid losing sight of the big picture. A project may have several hundred distinguishable work activities. The owners of these activities are concentrating on their particular tree in the project forest. It is important to see the total picture and to put accomplishments into perspective. A particular work activity might be well behind its committed schedule, yet its delayed completion might have little or no real impact on the bigger picture. Of course, the opposite also can be true, and almost always seems to be. A manageable way to view the total picture must be achieved so that problems and their consequences can be understood and dealt with in an effective manner.

- Product requirements approved
- Product objectives approved
- Product specifications approved
- High-level design completed
- Low-level design completed
- Code completed
- Unit and function test completed
- Component test completed
- System test completed
- Product packaged and available

Figure 4.5   Examples of project milestones.

The second major reason for identifying milestones is to report status to higher management. This is an effective way to relate progress. Higher management usually will not have the interest or time to become mired in project details. More data can always be prepared for presentation if needed.

All project schedule plans should have major milestones. Figure 4.6 shows a sample high-level project schedule plan with major milestones. Recall that the planning detail of a project can be defined in three layers: high level, intermediate level, and low level. Figure 4.6 shows the high-level layer. This layer provides the big picture view, the *overview,* of a project's overall project schedule plan and is expected to focus mostly on a project's major milestones. A goal is to present the overview on a single page or chart. Let's examine Figure 4.6 for a moment.

- The overview includes a GANTT chart showing the major milestones depicted as *checkpoints* C1 through C8. These checkpoints represent the list of milestones presented earlier in this section, but with some modification. C3 in the figure, "product definition," is meant to include both the product specifications and the high-level design. Also, low-level design and code have been combined into a single major milestone. The checkpoints are listed in the order that they are to be completed. The checkpoints are actually the *end* dates for each of the periods shown.

- The *start* and *end* dates shown are for illustrative purposes. They help to show the relative time spent in each checkpoint. (Only workday, not weekend, dates are used; holidays have been ignored.)

- The overview not only provides a helpful picture of the time spent in each checkpoint but gives the viewer a perspective of the overlap, if any, that exists between checkpoints. For example, the product objectives period can be started shortly before the product requirements period has completed. Another exam-

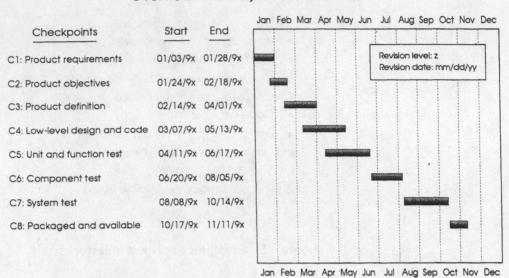

Figure 4.6   Sample high-level project schedule plan.

ple is the overlap that can be seen between the C3 period (product definition) and the C4 period (low-level design and code).

- The small box in the upper right-hand corner of the bar chart box can be used to notify viewers of both the revision level and revision date of the chart. This information is important for determining the currency of the information being presented.

Figure 4.6 shows eight major milestones, or checkpoints. Of course, you might choose to define your project differently so that you have more, less, or simply different milestones.

Chapter 5 shows how this chart can be updated to reflect the current progress against a project schedule plan.

Activity Responsibility Matrix

The activity responsibility matrix is developed along with the project schedule plan. This matrix lists the project's activities and identifies the owner, approvers, and reviewers of each activity. Figure 4.7 shows a sample portion of an activity responsibility matrix. The activities shown in the sample matrix are described in the software development process presented in Chapter 1. When the software development process in being defined for an organization, it is a good idea also to define a corresponding activity responsibility matrix that can be used as a starting point for defining the matrix for each project.

Activity	Planning	Development	Test	Publications	Usability	Assurance	...
Requirements	O	A	R	R	R	R	...
Objectives	O	A	A	A	A	R	...
Specifications	A	O	A	A	A	R	...
High-level design	A	O	R	R	R	R	...
Publication content plans	A	A	A	O	A	R	...
Unit test plan		O	R			R	...
Function test plan		O	A			A	...
Component test plan	A	A	O	A	A	A	...
System test plan	A	A	O	A	A	A	...
Low-level design		O			R	R	...
Code		O				R	...
Unit test		O	R			R	...
Function test		O	A			R	...
Component test		A	O			A	...
First-draft publications	R	R	R	O	R	R	...
System test	A	A	O	A	A	A	...
Second-draft publications	A	A	A	O	A	A	...
Regression test		A	O	A		A	...
...	...	...	...	...	...	...	...

Figure 4.7   Sample activity responsibility matrix.

Looking again at Figure 4.7, the column headings of Planning, Development, Test, and so on represent some of the unique skill groups found within a "typical" organization. For purposes of illustration, it is not important to understand the definition of these particular skill groups fully, although you probably have a good idea. What is important, however, is to note that there are three letters that can appear in these columns: O, A, and R. The O designates the owner (performer) of the activity; the A designates the approver of the activity; and the R designates the reviewer of the activity. The use of these letters in the matrix is for illustrative purposes only and is not meant to signify who the owner, approvers, or reviewers must be for each activity shown.

 Lesson: The activity responsibility matrix is a great tool for clarifying project areas of responsibility and helping project members anticipate workloads.

Later in this chapter, the steps to developing a project schedule plan will be presented. Several of these steps refer to an activity responsibility matrix. Although the activity responsibility matrix is not, necessarily, a mandatory part of building a project schedule plan, it is strongly recommended that each project subscribe to such a matrix. An activity responsibility matrix greatly helps in determining who must approve or review documents and other activities and also helps affected project members to anticipate workloads. For this reason, the activity responsibility matrix is included as part of developing a project schedule plan.

Project Checklist

One of the items that results when developing a project schedule plan is a **project checklist.** The primary purpose of a project checklist is for use in project tracking meetings when gathering project status and anticipating problems. The project checklist is derived from the project schedule plan.

A project schedule plan contains a sizable amount of data about the project's plan. These data include the identification of the items listed in Figure 4.8.

The project checklist, however, usually contains a subset of the information found in the project schedule plan. As discussed earlier, the planning detail of a project can be defined in three layers: high level, intermediate level, and low level. The project checklist is an example of representing the intermediate-level layer and is one of the exhibits most often used in the routine tracking of a project. Therefore, it needs to present only the necessary data as simply as possible. The project checklist used in tracking usually is generated by the project management tool used to develop the project schedule plan. The project checklist typically identifies the:

- Project's activities
- Person responsible for each activity
- Predecessor activities (dependencies) of each activity

- Project's activities
- Person responsible for each activity
- Duration of each activity
- Predecessor activities (dependencies) of each activity
- Successor activities of each activity
- Resource required to accomplish each activity
- Planned start and end dates of each activity (typically generated by a planning tool)

Figure 4.8   Information included in a project schedule plan.

- Planned start and end dates of each activity
- Actual start and end dates of each activity

 Lesson: Customize a project checklist to show only those activities for which a specific project member or project team is responsible.

Tailoring a project checklist to include only the activities of a specific project member or of a specific project team results in a **customized project checklist**. The customized project checklist is a key exhibit in project tracking meetings against which project progress of a person or team is tracked. Let's examine the sample customized project checklist shown in Figure 4.9. The following notes will help in understanding some areas of this checklist.

- Each activity is numbered to allow the predecessor activities (dependencies) to be identified more easily. The nonsequential order of the numbers listed indicates the relative interspersed position these activities might have in comparison to all the activities identified in the full project checklist. The specific number chosen to identify an activity is not important; however, it is helpful for an activity to be easily identified by a number.

    Knowing which activities are on the project's critical path is important. This knowledge helps to raise the level of focus on those activities that can result in missing the project's major milestone dates if their planned dates slip. A *C* appears next to the *Id#* of those activities that are on the critical path.

Id#	Activity	Depend.	Respon. Person	Planned		Actual	
				Start	End	Start	End
210	CTP preparation	51s	Berry	04/04	05/13		
211	CTP review	210	Berry	05/16	05/27		
212	CTP update	53, 211	Berry	05/30	06/10		
213	CTP approval	212	Berry	06/13	06/17		
214	CTP refresh	213	Berry	06/20	06/24		
220	STP preparation	51s	Berry	05/23	07/01		
221	STP review	220	Berry	07/04	07/15		
222	STP update	53, 221	Berry	07/18	07/29		
223	STP approval	222	Berry	08/01	08/05		
230C	Component test	213, 321s	Berry	06/20	08/05		
224	STP refresh	223	Berry	08/08	08/12		
240C	System test	223, 230, 323s	Berry	08/08	09/30		
250C	Regression test	240	Berry	10/03	10/14		

Figure 4.9 Sample customized project checklist.

- The activities shown are for illustrative purposes only. They help show what the relationship might be among some testing-related activities and several other project activities. The terms *CTP* and *STP* represent the activities of component test plan and system test plan, respectively.

  The regression test activity does not show a plan being prepared and approved before regression test occurs. In this simple example, the regression test plan activities could be added, or one might assume that the system test plan addressed the planning needs for the regression test activity.

  Although there are several ways to order the activities listed in a customized project checklist, such as by activity identification number (*Id#*), *Planned Start* date, or *Planned End* date, this checklist has the activities ordered by *Planned End* date.

- It is useful to show the dependencies of each activity in a project checklist. This helps in recognizing the impact that a given activity might have on later activities that are dependent on the successful outcome of the earlier activity. For example, notice that the activity denoted by Id# 211 is dependent on the successful completion of Id# 210.

  The dependencies column lists some numbers that are followed by an *s*. This character defines a specific relationship. If no character is shown, there is a *finish-to-start* relationship between the activity and its predecessor activity. The *s* means that there is a *start-to-start* relationship between the activity and the predecessor activity. An *f* would mean that there is a *finish-to-finish* relationship. You are free to choose any notation that suits your needs.

  Dependency numbers that are not shown in the *Id#* field of this table represent activities that are not owned by the *Responsible Person* (Berry) of this customized project checklist. These numbers and what they might represent are: 51s—product specifications preparation, 321s—first-draft publications review, and 323s—second-draft publications approval.

- The *Actual Start* and *Actual End* columns are reserved for recording the actual dates that the activity starts and ends.

- Although not shown, a comment column could be added to record information that might be useful, such as why a certain date was missed or why a new dependency was added.

Chapter 5 displays this chart and shows how it can be updated to reflect the current progress against the plan.

Project management tools typically allow project checklists to be generated automatically from a project schedule plan. Therefore, manual creation of these lists usually is not necessary.

The Steps to Developing a Project Schedule Plan

This section describes a series of steps you can follow in developing the initial project schedule plan. Developing the final project schedule plan and reworking it (if necessary) are discussed at the end of these steps. Among the benefits that can result from applying the step-by-step approach defined here are the items listed in Figure 4.10.

Figure 4.11 shows an overview of the 12 steps that describe the project schedule planning process. (*PSP* is the acronym for the project schedule plan.) Each step is described by five fields:

- *Description:* A description of the items to be performed.
- *Entry Conditions:* Actions that must occur before this step can begin.
- *Exit Conditions:* Actions that must happen before this step is considered complete.
- *Duration:* The range of time, rounded to hours or days, that this step typically might require. The actual number of days can vary widely from project to project and is dependent on a number of factors, including the size and complexity of the project, whether it is a single- or multilocation project, the skill level of the person coordinating the schedule planning activities, and the software engineering maturity level of the organization. The duration values shown assume that the project members responsible for participating in a given step are dedicating most, if not all, of their time in completing their tasks for that step. For illustrative purposes, the range of days estimated is intended to apply to projects that fall within the size range from 10 to 200 members.
- *Notes:* Any potentially useful information.

The following steps apply to developing a project schedule plan for any size project: small, medium, or large. However, for small projects, ones with only a handful of participants, some steps might be reduced in effort or even combined with other steps. The decision to tailor, expand, or adopt these steps belongs to the product manager and his or her designated project schedule coordinator.

- ■ Ensuring that each project member has committed to his or her portion of the project schedules

- ■ Ensuring that the project schedules have been communicated to, and reviewed by, all project members

- ■ Ensuring that the project schedules are developed and presented in a manner that facilitates tracking the project

- ■ Providing a baseline project schedule planning process for continual process improvement

Figure 4.10   Benefits of using the project schedule planning process.

1	Assign project schedule coordinator.
2	Identify tools to use.
3	Prepare for project schedule planning meeting.
4	Kick off project schedule planning meeting.
5	Complete assignments.
6	Scrub data from each submitter.
7	Construct PSP using tool.
8	Review results with each submitter.
9	Conduct full review of PSP.
10	Update PSP in tool.
11	Approve PSP.
12	Distribute approved PSP to project members.

Figure 4.11   Steps in building a project schedule plan (PSP).

Step 1.   Assign Project Schedule Coordinator

Description: The product manager assigns a person to be the **project schedule coordinator,** hereafter referred to as the *PSC*. The PSC is fully responsible for coordinating all the activities necessary in creating a bottom-up project schedule plan and resulting project checklist.

The PSC performs a critical role within a project. The effectiveness demonstrated by the PSC in leading the effort of creating an approved project schedule plan can have a profound impact on the project members for the duration of the project. For this reason, both the PSC and the product manager should carefully understand the role of the PSC and the corresponding empowerment that accompanies the assignment. Examples of levels of empowerment that should be considered within the domain of the PSC assignment are described throughout this chapter.

Entry Conditions: A project is started.

Exit Conditions: A person is assigned as the PSC.

Duration: One day. In practice, this step might take only a hour or so to nominate a person and receive his or her acceptance of the assignment. Or several days might be required to search for potential candidates and interview and select the best candidate. However, one day has been chosen as a goal for completing this step.

Notes: Although the PSC can be either a manager or a nonmanager, it is recommended that this person be a nonmanager. Consequently, the steps in developing a project schedule plan are defined in a manner that assumes this to be the case. The manager, participating in several of the steps, serves as a check and balance to ensure that the plan developed is satisfactory and that all issues are appropriately resolved. If the PSC is also a manager, the steps still apply but management approval of the project schedule plan should be made by a manager who is at least one level higher than the PSC.

 Lesson: On most projects, the role of the PSC is a full-time position; therefore, it is recommended that management empower a nonmanager to perform this role.

A project requires some level of plan almost immediately after its conception so that the project members have a documented roadmap of the activities to be performed, who owns what activities, the dependencies of each activity, and when they are scheduled to begin and complete. Ultimately, a project schedule plan should be created and approved. However, this is not realistic until at least the product objectives are available for review. Therefore, until the product objectives are available and the initial project schedule plan is completed, preliminary plans addressing the activities to be performed over the coming several weeks or months are necessary. The PSC can develop these plans.

Step 2.   *Identify Tools to Use*

Description: The PSC identifies one or more project planning or project management tools to be used to aid in the development of the project schedule plan and the project checklist.

Entry Conditions: A person is assigned as the PSC.

Exit Conditions: The tool is selected.

Duration: Zero to five days. If your organization already has defined the set of tools to use for new projects, then a duration of zero days might apply. If a project is starting from scratch in identifying a project management tool, then even five days might not be enough; however, the range of zero to five days has been chosen as a goal.

Notes: Before beginning the steps in developing the initial project schedule plan, having already created a top-down plan can be helpful. (This is a tip for next time if you have already passed this point on your current project.) The top-down plan allows the product manager to take a high-level look at the scope of the product-development effort well before an initial project schedule plan is developed. The use of a project-estimator tool can be a big help, not only in adding some credibility to the rough schedule that becomes the top-down plan, but also in "sanity checking" the results from the initial and final project schedule plans. (See Step 8 for another opportunity to use a project-estimator tool.)

If time is needed to install and learn the chosen tool, the installation and training for the PSC (or a designated tools person) is expected to occur between Steps 2 and 7.

Using a tool is strongly recommended for projects of more than a few people. Even for projects of a few people, a tool can be helpful. The steps presented here assume a tool is used; however, the steps apply even if no tools are utilized. In that case, perform the relevant schedule build process step mechanically when using a tool is mentioned.

Step 3. Prepare for Project Schedule Planning Meeting

Description: The PSC prepares for the *project schedule planning meeting*. The actions to be performed include:

- Scheduling the meeting and distributing the meeting notice
- Describing what is to be built
- Creating a starter set of project activities
- Defining the ground rules
- Reviewing past postproject reviews
- Collecting other useful information

The PSC determines who must be invited to attend the project schedule planning meeting. If the project membership is small, say five to 15 persons, all members might be invited. For larger projects, the people invited to the meeting might be just the team leaders or persons performing "independent roles" who need to represent themselves. Management and assurance should be included in the list of invitees. The meeting room should be large enough to accommodate the expected participants and have walls that would allow charts to be displayed of planning-related information brought to or gathered at the meeting. The meeting invitation should be distributed with sufficient lead-time notice for the meeting. The PSC should ensure that the meeting has the full support of the product manager and that the invited participants are keenly aware of the priority of this meeting compared to their other duties.

The PSC (or a designee) describes, at a somewhat high level, what is to be built. That is, a simple, easy-to-understand description of the product to be built is constructed, preferably in pictorial form. The information used to describe the product typically is extracted from the product objectives document. It is important that the attendees at the kickoff meeting (Step 4) clearly grasp the big picture of "what are we really building." This knowledge is essential for the meeting members to discuss, in a productive manner, the development process to be followed that will eventually evolve into a project schedule plan.

The PSC identifies a starting set of activities, in a list, that must be worked throughout the development cycle. This list will be scrubbed during the upcoming meeting, and activities likely will be added and deleted. For most organizations, it is hoped that a software development process has already been defined and documented (see Chapter 1) and that this documented process is used as a starting point in identifying these activities. The list of activities can be the beginning of the project checklist. The PSC should attempt to assign an owner to each activity. During the meeting in Step 4, the names assigned as owners will be validated or changed.

The PSC defines the ground rules to be followed in developing the initial project schedule plan. This helps to ensure that the schedules developed by each project member are created under the same criteria (no overtime, first shift only, includes time for vacations, and so on). For a sample list of ground rules, "Estimating the Duration of an Activity" earlier in this chapter.

This is the perfect time to look at lessons learned from past projects. If your organization has performed postproject reviews on past projects, then examine the lessons learned. The goal should be for this implementation of the project schedule planning process to avoid repeating past mistakes.

The PSC should assemble any other information that can help in developing the project schedule plan. This information should be made available at the kickoff meeting. For example, any appropriate historical schedule-related database information (prior project experiences) should be made available for reference. Other tips (written) should be provided to help in developing schedule data. An example: Performers of an activity who depend on a document from an earlier activity should state if their activity can begin with a review draft of the document versus an approval draft or the approved copy.

Entry Conditions: The tool is selected.

Exit Conditions: The PSC is fully prepared for the project schedule planning meeting, and the meeting notice is distributed.

Duration: Five to 10 days. If you have already been through an implementation of this project schedule planning process for a project similar to the one you are now planning, or if you are planning for a very small project, this step might be performed in fewer than five days.

Notes: As you can see from the subjects addressed in this step, careful and thoughtful planning here can have a major positive impact on the efficiency experienced in the upcoming steps. The scope of the project is well thought out in this step.

Step 4. *Kickoff Project Schedule Planning Meeting*

Description: After the product objectives are available for review, the PSC calls a meeting of the designated project members (see Step 3), including management and assurance. This meeting kicks off the official start of the project schedule planning activities.

During this meeting, the owners of every activity identified in the starter list of activities are agreed upon. Additional activities discovered at the meeting also have owners assigned to them. Each owner is then assigned to perform the following actions after the meeting has ended.

- Identify, to an appropriate level of detail, all the activities to be performed during the life of the project; the detail should be to a level that helps to ensure that the activity durations (see next bullet) are realistic.

- Define the duration of each activity using the ground rules developed in Step 3; no start or end dates are required. (The list of ground rules should be reviewed for completeness.)

- Identify the dependencies (predecessor activities) of each activity.

- List the assumptions related to each activity; this should include the projected productivity rates (with the supporting methodology and projected defects), people and machine resources required, as well as the associated skills required; this also should include assumptions on tools, programming languages, prototyping, reuse, design and code inspection process, metrics to be collected, causal analysis considerations, and others as necessary.

The PSC identifies the sequence of visits to activity owners to gather the necessary schedule input (Step 6). The order should be in sequence of critical-path activities such as those owned by planning, development, and test, followed by support-related activities such as those owned by publications, usability, and assurance. Typically, the PSC will interface directly with a project's team leaders. The team leaders, in turn, will work with the members of their team in developing their portion of the project schedule plan. For small projects, the PSC might work directly with all project members.

The PSC requests that anyone who has the responsibility for a project activity also must propose who the approvers and reviewers related to that activity should be. This assignment is made easier if a generic activity responsibility matrix was produced as part of defining a software development process. (See "Activity Responsibility Matrix" earlier in this chapter.) This matrix will define the recommended approvers and reviewers of the activities that make up the software development process.

Soon after the project schedule planning meeting has ended, the PSC should ensure that complete minutes of the meeting are written and distributed. The minutes contain information that the project members will need or find helpful in fulfilling their assignments.

Entry Conditions: The meeting notice is distributed and the PSC is fully prepared to kick off the project schedule planning meeting.

Exit Conditions: The meeting attendees reach an understanding of the project schedule planning process to be implemented and understand their role in the upcoming steps. Any problems not resolved are logged, assigned owners, and assigned target close dates for resolution.

Duration: Two to three days. The meeting, in most cases, should occur within a one day period. However, another one or two days might be necessary to document and distribute the meeting minutes.

Notes: In addition to the initial product objectives being available, it is recommended that the initial quality plan (see Chapter 6) also be available before kicking off the project schedule planning meeting. The reason? Information in the quality plan (such as defect prevention and customer satisfaction goals) can affect the development process to be followed and the productivity of the project members. This is important information to work with as the project plan is being developed.

   If a project is estimated to last longer than 12 months, the product manager and the PSC might decide to focus predominantly over the next six to nine months. The planning for the remaining months should still occur but might be at a somewhat higher level of detail and, therefore, include additional buffer contingency. After six months or so have passed (pick a major milestone), then the next six to nine months of the schedule is worked at a lower level of detail. And so on. Special care must be exercised in estimating the schedule for projects longer than a year. As long as complete product specifications are available and approved, management will ask for, and rightfully expect, a commitment on the overall schedules.

Step 5. Complete Assignments

  Lesson: A new project must recognize planning a project as a high-priority activity.

Description: The project participants perform their assignments from the kickoff meeting. If questions or problems should arise during this step, they must be brought to the attention of the PSC immediately. It is not advisable to proceed based on shaky assumptions. Furthermore, all project members participating in this scheduling exercise must recognize what their priorities are. That is, many project members will have other work assignments (some on different projects), and must be told what the priority of this scheduling activity is compared to their other duties. Typically, planning a project should take precedence over virtually all other activities of the new project. This is necessary to ensure that each member is not just working hard, but working smart—working on the various project activities in the optimal sequence.

Entry Conditions: The project schedule planning meeting has been completed successfully.

Exit Conditions: The project participants have completed their assignments and are ready to submit their planning data to the PSC.

Duration: One to five days.

Notes: The PSC should be on call during this step to help project members with any assignment-related questions they might have.

One approach that might be considered in developing the various portions of the project schedule plan is a process called the *yellow sticky process*. Briefly, the yellow sticky process is a simple but effective technique that can be used in building a visual representation of portions of a project schedule plan or of the entire plan. The process involves the use of Post-it brand notes. (Post-it is a trademark of the 3M Company.) Each individual slip represents a project activity. These slips are connected together to construct a network of activities that represent the plan of a single team or of an entire project. (See the bibliography entry authored by Dennis Miller to obtain more information on the yellow sticky process.)

The yellow sticky process can work well, especially with small teams. If the PSC feels it is needed, the yellow sticky process, or some variation, could be introduced in Step 4.

Step 6. Scrub Data from Each Submitter

Description: The PSC gathers the data from the owner of each activity according to the sequence defined at the kickoff meeting. During these one-on-one meetings, the PSC asks a number of questions to help ensure the completeness of the submitted information. Sample questions might be:

- Explain why each activity has the dependency it does.
- Is a given activity dependent on each of its predecessor activities fully completing, or can some predecessor activities complete only partially in order to satisfy the dependency?
- What rationale was used to support the duration defined for each activity?
- Are the people resources adequate? Are they onboard? Do the people have the skills necessary? If not, has education/training been accounted for?
- Has resource balancing across all activities been accounted for, both project- and nonproject-related?
- Was each of the items in the ground rules addressed appropriately?
- Where are the critical paths? How might the risk for completing these paths be reduced?
- What additional resources or events would allow the critical paths to be shortened without increasing the risk to the project?
- Is there sufficient detail behind each activity to track its progress against the plan on at least a weekly basis?

All questions must be resolved satisfactorily or logged to be worked later. Any news that might be useful to owners of other activities is recorded and shared with them at the first convenient or necessary moment, as appropriate. It is very likely that the PSC will revisit each activity owner at least once while performing Step 6. It is important to note that the PSC is fast becoming a valuable repository of information that must find its way to project members in a timely manner. The PSC can address this by distributing project "notes" or conducting minimeetings.

It is suggested that the PSC reserve a meeting place to work with all the project members submitting data. This formalizes the data-gathering process and conditions the project members to view the project schedule planning process as the critical project effort that it is.

Entry Conditions: The project participants are ready to submit their planning data to the PSC.

Exit Conditions: All the planning data to be loaded into the project planning tool have been scrubbed for problems, and the problems have been corrected appropriately.

Duration: Two to five days.

Notes: An alternative to scrubbing data from each submitter, one on one, is to assemble the designated project members in a room and manually construct the project schedule plan along the walls following the yellow sticky process. The full plan is developed, real time, as each member adds activities and scrubs each other's data. The benefits of this approach include:

- Immediately resolving conflicts between owners of activities.
- Using the full contingent of skills and experiences from the meeting members to help discover and resolve problems.
- Building synergy among the project members.
- Helping to increase the overall buy-in of the project schedule plan.

Another benefit of this approach might be a reduction of the overall time it takes to perform Steps 7 through 10. Why? Because experience suggests that this approach might result in fewer problems discovered in transferring the proposed project schedule plan to a tool (Step 7), resulting in fewer conflicts to resolve later with the corresponding owners of the activities (Step 8), fewer problems to discover during the full project review (Step 9), and, therefore, fewer updates to be applied to the tool (Step 10).

It is important to note that there is no substitute for well thought out, methodical planning. Either the one-on-one or the yellow sticky process can provide good results. If the latter approach is adopted for this step, ensure that an appropriate set of questions, like the sample questions introduced at the beginning of this step, is used against the information being used to construct a network manually.

On the subject of people communication, when working with input from remote locations, there is always the danger of miscommunication. In most cases, communicating with personnel at remote locations via telephone, workstations, teleconference, fax transmissions, and video-conferencing, to name some of the more popular techniques, might be acceptable. However, at some point, in-person communications is strongly recommended. The critical steps for in-person communications are this step and Step 9.

Step 7. Construct Project Schedule Plan Using Tool

Description: With the necessary preliminary scheduling information available, the PSC is now ready to load these data into a project planning tool, as mentioned in Step 2. This is not as simple a task as one might think. The data must be entered carefully and accurately. Even a small error in stating the correct dependency of an activity can have a profound impact on the overall schedule that the tool generates.

The PSC also assembles all the project's activity information that was gathered and creates an activity responsibility matrix that identifies the owners, approvers, and reviewers for every activity.

Entry Conditions: All the planning data to be loaded into the project planning tool have been scrubbed for problems, and the problems have been corrected.

Exit Conditions: The planning data have been loaded into the project planning tool, and an initial pass at the project schedule plan has been generated.

Duration: One to five days.

Notes: Steps 6, 7, and 8 could, in large part, be performed as a single step. How? The PSC could be entering the submitted information into a project planning tool *real time* (as it is being received). Many of the conflicts that surface can be addressed immediately, resolved, and the tool updated *on the spot*. Some conflicts, however, might not be able to be resolved immediately, especially if another person must be consulted first.

Another approach is to perform Steps 6, 7, and 8 in an iterative fashion; that is, as the PSC is gathering information from one person, the information received from a prior person can be entered into a planning tool by a helper to the PSC. The helper can alert the PSC to conflicts as they are discovered, and the PSC can work to have those conflicts resolved as soon as possible. In this way, the project schedule plan continues to evolve as plan data become available.

Step 8. Review Results with Each Submitter

Description: The tool generates the schedule dates based on all the activities, durations, dependencies, and resources that were provided. The probability is high that the resulting schedule is longer than what was either expected or is considered acceptable. The PSC analyzes the tool's results and works to massage the data to smooth out the schedule so it is aggressive but achievable, paying particular attention to the activities on the critical path. The PSC does not have the authority to change schedule commitments made by the owners of the activities. Only the activity owners can do that. Therefore, the PSC must work with the activity owners, as required, to reach an acceptable project schedule plan.

It is important that all the designated project members working with the PSC review this level of the project schedule plan, even if the PSC perceives that there are no conflicts to be resolved. This is the first time that actual dates are tagged to each activity. Each member must review these dates to ensure they do not conflict with other activities already scheduled or committed, including activities that may be part of other projects that some members are also working. The schedule actually might become extended further due to such conflicts.

The PSC also reviews the activity responsibility matrix with the owner, approvers, and reviewers of each activity and reaches agreement on the full list of approvers and reviewers.

After reviewing the project schedule plan with the designated project members, the PSC schedules a meeting of all project participants and distributes, with the meeting notice, a copy of the project schedule plan and the activity responsibility matrix. The invitees can study the latest plan before the meeting begins (Step 9).

Entry Conditions: An initial pass of the project schedule plan has been generated.

Exit Conditions: All the designated project members have seen the generated project schedule plan and have addressed any resulting problems, including the challenge of reducing the overall duration of the schedule. The notice for the upcoming "all-hands" meeting has been distributed.

Duration: Two to six days.

Notes: Unless specified otherwise, the day an activity is scheduled to complete means that it will be completed *at the end of the day.* Never show an activity starting the same day that its predecessor activity is completing if the later activity really requires the earlier activity to complete fully.

Upon viewing a project schedule plan that lasts longer than expected or acceptable, a common response is to perform more activities in parallel with one another. Be careful. Although this technique, given ample resources, can have a positive affect in shortening the overall schedule, it can result in increased project risk because more activities might now reside in the project's critical path. Also, be aware that some activities should not be overlapped. (See the "Overlapping Activities" section, earlier in this chapter.)

If you ran an estimator tool earlier (see Step 2), you might consider rerunning it to help develop the top-down plan now that more accurate input data are available for the total lines of code, function points, or whatever input parameters were required. The new results from the estimator tool should be compared to the results shown from the initial project schedule plan. This comparison can be used as another means in helping to sanity check the likelihood of achieving the overall initial project schedule plan.

See Step 7 for examples of how Step 8 might be combined or performed iteratively with Steps 6 and 7.

Step 9.   *Conduct Full Review of Project Schedule Plan*

Description: The PSC calls a meeting of all project members, including management and assurance (or some other independent person or group), and conducts a review of the total initial proposal. At this point, most problems should have been resolved within the previous steps. If problems remain, consideration should be made to inform, before the meeting, those affected so that they might offer proposed solutions at the onset of the meeting.

This might be the first time that many project members have seen a complete project schedule plan. The critical path activities should be clearly visible and receive special attention and scrutiny. With all the eyes looking over the proposed project schedule plan, it is expected that new problems will surface. The identification of problems should always be welcomed so they are made known, logged, and tracked to closure. Many problems will need to be resolved before the proposed project schedule plan can be accepted. However, some problems probably will not affect the project schedule plan and can be worked separately. The activity responsibility matrix is reviewed at this time also.

After the review meeting, the project members will have a good sense of the complete project schedule plan, their personal commitments, and how the plan will require every activity to complete successfully in order for the total schedule to be achieved as committed. All members and interested parties should approve their area and perspective of the project schedule plan. If problems discovered at the meeting need to be corrected in the project schedule plan before a member approves, that should be okay. However, all members, with the possible exception of the product manager and assurance, should approve the plan before Step 11 (Approve project schedule plan) occurs. The product manager and assurance might want to wait until all plan updates have been made and approved by those affected.

The PSC should ensure that complete minutes of the meeting are written and distributed as soon after the review meeting as possible.

Entry Conditions: Designated project members have reviewed their areas of the plan individually and have received an updated copy of the project schedule plan that includes their changes.

Exit Conditions: The review meeting has completed satisfactorily, open problems have been logged for subsequent action, and meeting minutes are distributed.

Duration: One to two days. The meeting, in most cases, should occur within one day. However, another day might be necessary to document and distribute the meeting minutes.

Notes: If this project is especially critical (and it seems most projects are—by whatever definition you decide), you might consider inviting a consultant to this review. The consultant would act as an unbiased party who would look specifically for problems and high-risk areas in the proposed schedule. These high-risk areas should be monitored for however long they exist in the project. (See Chapter 5, "Project High-Risk Areas" section, for ideas on tracking project high-risk areas. See "The Second Opinion" section earlier in this chapter for more on obtaining another opinion.)

Step 10. Update Project Schedule Plan in Tool

Description: The PSC updates the data in the tool with changes identified from the review meeting. The tool then is used to generate the proposed initial project schedule plan and the resulting initial project checklist. As before, the PSC must work with activity owners before changing their activity commitments. The activity responsibility matrix also is updated as needed.

Entry Conditions: The review meeting has completed satisfactorily and changes, if any, to the project schedule plan are identified.

Exit Conditions: The proposed project schedule plan is generated by the project planning tool.

Duration: One to three days.

Notes: This step is important so that a complete project schedule plan can be presented to the product manager for approval.

Step 11. Approve Project Schedule Plan

Description: The PSC brings the proposed initial project schedule plan, the resulting initial project checklist, and the activity responsibility matrix to the product manager for management approval. Because the product manager is expected to have attended the project schedule planning meeting (Step 4) and the full review (Step 9), approving the schedule should go relatively smoothly. It is expected that assurance has approved the plan by this step and has advised the product manager accordingly.

Entry Conditions: The proposed project schedule plan is ready for management approval.

Exit Conditions: The product manager approves the proposed project schedule plan.

Duration: One day.

Notes: After the project schedule plan is approved, it is baselined—that is, becomes the baseline—and placed under a change control process.

Step 12. Distribute Approved PSP to Project Members

Description: The PSC distributes the approved initial project schedule plan, the initial project checklist, and the activity responsibility matrix to the project members. The distributed package should include:

- A one-page overview (the big picture) of the project schedule; see "Identifying Milestones" section earlier in this chapter.
- The initial project schedule plan containing a complete listing of all the project's activities (with schedules and durations); for project leaders only.
- The initial project checklist containing the approved schedule for all the project's activities.
- A customized project checklist containing only the list of activities that the receiver of the package (or the receiver's team) owns, in a format that will be

used during the project tracking meetings; see "Project Checklist" section earlier in this chapter; for project leaders and project members that own one or more project activities only.

- A copy of the activity responsibility matrix; for project leaders and affected personnel only.

Entry Conditions: The product manager approves the proposed initial project schedule plan.

Exit Conditions: The appropriate packages have been distributed to the members of the project.

Duration: One day.

Notes: After Step 12 has been completed, the initial project schedule plan and initial project checklist will be ready to be tracked on a regular (recommended weekly) basis. See Chapter 5 for information on tracking a project.

Remember, the initial project schedule plan should not be committed to management. Although it might be a reasonable plan and was developed using the best information available, it is used primarily to plan and track progress until the product specifications are available and the final project schedule plan can be developed.

Developing the Final Project Schedule Plan

After the final product specifications are available for approval and the final quality plan is approved, the final project schedule plan and the final project checklist can be developed. Steps 3 through 12 should be revisited as necessary. The final project schedule plan, once approved, is the plan to commit to management.

Depending on a number of factors, the time required to develop the final project schedule plan can vary widely, typically from five to 20 days. These factors include the level of completeness and accuracy of the product objectives and the completeness and accuracy of the initial project schedule plan. Also, if buffer contingency was used effectively, there may be little or no change in the dates of major milestones.

Reworking the Final Project Schedule Plan

It should be noted that typically various activities are added to the approved final project schedule plan as they become apparent. For example, many plans (publication content plans, component test plan, and the like) are written and approved after the final project schedule plan has been approved. These new plans often will contain activities or special-event dates that need to be added to the final project schedule plan to ensure they receive the tracking visibility they require.

Routine changes to the project schedule plan should occur through the change control process chosen. For a recommended approach, see Chapter 5. If events occur that require the approved "final" project schedule plan to undergo significant change, then Steps 3 through 12 should be invoked again as necessary. Examples of events that might cause the final project schedule plan to change substantially include major changes in product requirements, changes in the ground rules used when planning the project, or tracking data that demonstrates that the project's schedules are eroding.

 Lesson: As plan dates change, always keep the original dates visible.

Throughout the course of the project, whenever plan dates are changed, the original dates on the project checklist should not be overlaid. A new line should be added for each planned date changed to show history of revision.

As the members of a project execute their approved project schedule plan, only rarely is a project significantly ahead of schedule. Unfortunately, it is not so rare for a project to be significantly behind schedule—particularly if the product being built is the first of a series of products or incorporates new technology. No one wants to report bad news up the management chain. Consequently, a tendency might exist to hang on to the original, even though unachievable, schedules longer than is best for the product or the people who are building the product.

 Lesson: Never change a project schedule plan if you believe the project's members have a prayer's chance of recovering.

There are two major reasons for *not* changing the project schedule plan when a project has fallen behind schedule. The first reason focuses on people. As long as the people within the project feel commited to the schedules, and as long as there is a prayer's chance of recovery, then frequently the productivity of the organization will rise to the occasion. Creativity and breakthroughs often peak during these times of stretching an organization to its performance limits. Also, incidentally, there is an element of art in recognizing the balance between what is achievable and what is not achievable. Years of experience can help to fine-tune this art for some.

The second major reason for *not* changing the project schedule plan is an inability to see clearly how the schedule plan should be changed. Just because a schedule is "in the ditch" doesn't mean that arbitrarily moving the schedules one week, one month, or even six months will necessarily solve the underlying problems.

Never change a project schedule plan unless you believe the four items listed in Figure 4.12 to be true. Once you believe these four items to be true, then you must sell higher management, or whomever must be sold, that the plan must change. Here is where the project technical leadership and the project management have a joint responsibility to fix a bad situation. They have a responsibility to the people on the project, to higher management, to their company, and to themselves. Some things cannot and should not be delegated.

 Lesson: Limit the times a project schedule plan is reset; for example, reset a plan no more than once for a project with a duration of 12 months or less.

- The original plan is no longer achievable.

- The problems causing the schedule slip are understood and reasonable solutions are known.

- The proposed project schedule plan change is achievable.

- The proposed project schedule plan has the commitment of the people who must make it happen.

Figure 4.12 Conditions to be met before a project schedule plan should be replaced.

When you contemplate major changes to a project schedule plan that has a duration of one year or less, plan to make the major changes only once. Do not attempt to change a plan every two or three months. Each time a plan is reset, a cost to the overall productivity within a project is incurred. It takes time to evaluate new schedules and, once they are adopted, to reset the project's pace to these newer schedules. The project's members' long-range attitude also pays for changes. There is a strong tendency for people to become accustomed to the culture and ways that they have been exposed to day after day and month after month. When project schedules are readjusted frequently, everyone receives the message that this is acceptable behavior. This, in turn, conditions the project personnel to expect a pardon when their own schedules become uncomfortably aggressive. After all, if you thought it was acceptable behavior, wouldn't you opt to move back the schedules for your own activities rather than increase your working hours each week? (Although some people would not, I believe most people would.)

For projects lasting a year or longer, you should expect some major adjustments to be required as a project evolves and progresses. Making major changes every nine to 12 months will not be unusual. Again, avoid making major changes every two or three months.

Aggressive But Achievable

Some unknown wit once wrote that "The longest distance between two points is the shortcut." Defining an aggressive project schedule plan is good business. The higher the productivity of the participants, the shorter the overall project schedule and the lower the project expense. The lower the project expense, the lower the cost of the product to the customer. The lower the customer cost, the higher the volume of sales. The higher the volume of sales, the more profitable and successful the product.

 Lesson: The best project schedule plan is aggressive but achievable.

But the shortcut often is defined as an aggressive but *unachievable* project schedule plan—which translates into bad business. Everyone—project participants, the customer, higher management, the company—suffers when plans that have no reasonable chance of succeeding are set in place. All project schedule plans should be aggressive, but they also must be achievable. Project schedule plans can have levels of risk, but again, they must be achievable.

 Lesson: Although every project member is responsible for his or her own actions, a project's leaders bear the greatest responsibility for ensuring a well-planned project.

Making some mistakes when developing a project schedule plan usually is acceptable, although not welcomed. Making the same mistakes twice is less acceptable. Making the same mistakes project after project is inexcusable. The project leaders, whether managers, planners, or technical leaders, are responsible for learning from past mistakes and for looking after the welfare of the project, its people, the company, and, of course, the customer. Listen to your subordinates and peers. Trust your instincts. Follow your hunches. Work together as a team to develop the right project schedule plan. Not everyone's advice will be worth implementing, but listening and sorting will benefit everyone.

The first line of defense (offense?) is the project schedule coordinator, who has the responsibility of ensuring that everyone appropriately participates in the development of the project schedule plan. The project members are the next line of defense to ensure the best, *right* project schedule plan is put in place. They do this by ensuring that their piece of the plan is well thought out and realistic. They do this again after the full plan is available for review. The final line of defense is the product manager. If the project schedule coordinator and the project members have done their job, the product manager's task here is relatively easy. However, veteran product managers know the value of personally investing the time in understanding the project schedule plan in some detail.

 Lesson: Remember that, once you commit to a project schedule plan, you will be living through it—day by day, month by month.

Building a project schedule plan that is aggressive, but reasonable and achievable, may appear to yield a longer schedule plan than one that is too aggressive but is reset several times. However, it costs time and dollars to reset schedules and to address the problems that an unthoughtful schedule helped to cause. There is no better schedule than the one that is a balance of aggressiveness and achievability. If you must work through a project schedule plan that is months, or even years, in length, doesn't it make sense to plan these months carefully? After all, you will be living through each one of them.

5

Project Tracking: Staying in Control

A software development project is like a living organism. To survive, all of its vital parts must function in harmony. If one of the parts fails to perform its mission, dependent parts also will begin to fail soon. Like a row of dominoes, the problem, if left unchecked, can topple the whole organism. Survival is not enough, however. The objective is to strive for a *healthy* survival. Getting a product out the door late, with poor quality, or with a higher cost is far from a healthy survival.

 Lesson: Project tracking is all about staying in control.

Project tracking is about ensuring that the project's vital parts all function in harmony. It is about finding problems and fixing them—quickly and absolutely. It is about discovering problems early and deliberately controlling the outcome so that only minimal damage will occur and the project will be successful. To help ensure a successful software development project, it is essential for the project's participants to remain in control. The project's leadership must be in control of the overall project, and each member of the project must be in control of his or her area of responsibility.

The two primary problems in tracking projects are that (1) problems usually are discovered later than necessary, and (2) the needed action to recover is slow in coming or sometimes nonexistent. As Frederick P. Brooks, Jr., so aptly said in his book *The Mythical Man-Month*, "How does a project get to be a year late? . . . One day at a time." Project participants often fail to stay on top—in control—of recognizing and correcting problems.

 Lesson: The number-one reason for project tracking meetings is to identify potential problems before they happen.

Plans are good only until their point of execution. To an objective bystander, it would make no sense to plan your work and then *not* work your plan. You might hear the same words from a project's leadership. Unfortunately, the necessary action required to enforce the words is not always apparent. To be able to say that a project has a successful tracking and problem-management process, two elements are needed. The tracking process must be able to:

1. Identify potential problems before they happen.
2. Put recovery plans in place before unrecoverable harm occurs.

Many factors come into play in creating a tracking and problem-management process that can satisfy these two criteria. This chapter discusses those factors by:

- Describing the practical application of basic project tracking and problem management concepts, and
- Presenting a series of steps you can follow in tracking a project and managing the resolution of problems encountered along the way.

A Project Tale

The following scenario provides an example of how an otherwise well-planned project gets into trouble one day at a time.

The project appears to be off to a good start. The product requirements and the product objectives are written and approved. The product specifications are in the process of being written. The high-level design has started. Special attention was paid to developing the project schedule plan. All the project's activities are defined, their dependencies identified, and their durations accepted. Now that an approved project schedule plan is in place, it is just a matter of managing according to the plan.

The "top dog" on the project, Ralph Macho, is a project head who believes in taking charge. His motto is "Let's not talk about it, let's do it!" It is generally believed that this assertive style probably gave birth to this project. Not many people on the project really know what to expect from Macho. He is a relative newcomer to the organization. The general view, however, is positive.

The word is out that this project is very important and *must* be a success. (Sound familiar?) Macho declares that the project must be tracked closely. The first status meeting is called. All the project leaders are instructed to attend. They each display the status of their activities on transparencies so others can follow them. The morning meeting was scheduled to be three hours long. Four hours have passed and less than half the project leaders have made their presentations. During the first four hours, several problems are discovered that span across departments. The owners of those problems are told, "Go fix them." After eight tedious hours, the meeting ends. About a third of the project leaders have still not reported their status, but Macho needs to end the meeting due to a prior commitment. He states that he wants to see the status reports that have not been presented and will arrange a time tomorrow.

The project leaders attending the "three-hour" day-long meeting have mixed feelings about the event. They feel they learned a lot about what the other departments are doing. In some cases, problems were revealed in their own area. But the general feeling is that the benefits gained do not compensate for being tied up a full eight hours. Many project leaders had to miss meetings they had scheduled for later in the day.

The next morning, meeting notices are sent to the project leaders that have yet to present their status reports to Macho. The new meeting is scheduled for two hours that afternoon. A few minutes before the meeting is to start, Macho's secretary says he is "running late" and the meeting may be delayed by 30 minutes. It begins 90 minutes later and ends, once again, before everyone can present their status. Macho is quick to say "We will have to catch the remaining presentations at some other time." This doesn't sit well with those project leaders who have yet to present their status reports, but they understand that these things happen.

The next project status meeting is scheduled to last four hours for the following week. Just moments before the meeting is to start, it is reset for two days later. Macho's secretary announces that changes had to be made to his calendar. When the meeting finally starts, it is quickly apparent that the people attending are not all the same as last time. About 60 percent of the project leaders are present, but 30 percent sent representatives and 10 percent are not represented at all. The representatives do not all know the problems presented in previous meetings, so they are unable to discuss them. There is an attempt to resolve some problems in the meeting, but the representatives are mostly unwilling to make commitments without their project leader's consent. To make matters worse, the project leaders had different "memories" regarding the action that was to be taken on several of the problems raised from the previous meeting. No minutes were recorded for that meeting. Each person had only his or her own notes. This time a summary of the problems to be acted upon are surveyed at the end of the meeting. The four-hour meeting lasts six hours.

The next few project status meetings follow a similar pattern. The scheduled time on the calendar is changed at the last moment. One meeting did not even take place because Macho was called out of town. Over time, fewer and fewer project leaders attend, with more and more representatives attending. The meetings continue to run longer than scheduled. Differences in opinions about the problems that have been identified at prior meetings and about their assigned owners continue to increase. The meeting attendees are having less and less success at getting commitments on work items from others in the meetings. Many of the dependencies and work items are beginning to be implemented later than required, and the project schedules are slowly eroding.

A few project leaders get together and decide there must be a better way to track project status and get problems logged and tracked to completion. They list a half-dozen primary problems that exist with the current project status meetings.

They also list recommendations to address these problems. They manage, with some difficulty, to be scheduled on Macho's calendar for a one-hour discussion. After two days of getting bumped from the project head's calendar, they finally meet with him. He appreciates their input and recognizes that some of these problems probably should be addressed. However, he asks, "Why can't all the project leaders solve these problems on their own initiative? To get anywhere in a business you have got to take it upon yourself to make things happen."

Reluctantly he agrees to adopt several of the recommendations. He assigns a person to conduct meetings when he is not available. This person also will issue minutes of each meeting and will make sure that all problems are recorded. The project leaders feel somewhat relieved that some improvements will be made and somewhat distressed that they had to sell so hard to get these improvements.

The project status meetings are now held at the same time each week. Macho rarely finds the time to attend, although he promises to be there "next time." Communication across the organization is improving, but the actual resolution of problems is not. Dependencies between organizations continue to be missed more frequently. Most project leaders are not attending meetings. Each department's activities, as well as its dependencies on other departments, are being driven almost exclusively by the skills and motivations of each project leader. Some project leaders are not leading to the extent necessary, but the lack of leadership is not entirely intentional. Some just don't know how. It was agreed from the beginning that quick closure on higher-priority problems may require an escalation to get the needed focus. (An escalation occurs when a person cannot get another person or organization to address a problem satisfactorily. The problem remains open until a mutually agreed to solution is arrived at. This sometimes requires forcing higher-level project leaders from different organizations to meet until the problem is addressed and closed.)

The big problem here is that many of the escalations find their way to the project head's office. They may sit there for a week or longer, waiting for Macho's availability. Occasionally more homework must be done and a follow-up meeting needs to be scheduled. It takes too long to get some problems resolved. Everyone knows this. Consequently, there is a tendency to not start the escalation process as quickly as a problem may require. There is a general feeling that things are out of control, that the *system* necessary to monitor project progress efficiently and to enforce corrective action just does not exist.

The project is falling farther behind schedule. Because project status is not always reported accurately and completely, some activities that were thought to be on schedule one week ago are being reported, just one week later, to be *more* than one week behind schedule. Some groups are working considerable overtime, while others seem to be taking it all in stride. No one seems to be leading the organization. The question "Who's in charge?" is asked often. The usual answer is that it probably is the project head—when he's available. An underlying tone can be heard: "Oh, well, if our project head is not more interested, then we will just have to do the best we each know how and hope that things will improve." (Anytime there is an "oh, well" atmosphere, you can bet that a lot of commitment will be missing, along with its sidekick, productivity.) The lack of serious commitment by

Macho to enforce the tracking process and ensure that problems are being identified early and resolved early is obvious to everyone. Morale is slowly eroding across the organization. Fingerpointing for scapegoats is becoming all too frequent. Everyone now agrees that the project will miss its product delivery date. To make matters worse, no one can agree on how deeply the project is "in the ditch."

How will this scenario end? How much damage has been done to project schedules? The events in this scenario, if left unchecked, only can get worse. A few project leaders do care enough to try to right the wrongs. However, even these determined project leaders can get frustrated and begin to perform under their potential, or eventually they even may seek to work for other organizations or other companies. The sad part is that this negative situation is curable. Not just patchable, but really curable. The remaining sections of this chapter offer guidelines for avoiding the traps shown in this scenario as well as for avoiding other related, and common, pitfalls.

What Should Be Tracked?

Obviously, a man's judgment cannot be better than the information on which he has based it.
—*Arthur Hays Sulzberger, American newspaper publisher*

Before we list the items that should be tracked, let's take a look again at the primary objectives for tracking:

1. Identify potential problems before they occur.
2. Put recovery plans in place before unrecoverable harm occurs.

Notice that the focus is on identifying and resolving problems. This means that there are two general categories of information to be tracked:

- Plans for project activities
- Known problems

Project activity plans are tracked so that potential problems can be identified as early as possible. Once problems are identified, they are tracked individually to ensure they are resolved. "But," you might ask, "what exactly should be the subjects of focus at project tracking meetings?" The major subject areas for presentation and analysis at project tracking meetings are listed in Figure 5.1. These subject areas are so key that each will be discussed in a separate section that follows. However, before proceeding to these sections, three key terms used throughout this chapter must first be introduced: project tracking team, project tracking team meeting, and project tracking team leader.

The **project tracking team,** or *PTT*, is a group of project members who routinely meet to present their progress and problems. On a small project, every project mem-

- Project high-risk areas
- Overview of project progress
- Progress of project activities
- Progress of action items
- Project outlook

Figure 5.1   Topics to be tracked.

ber might participate. On a larger project, a subset of members attend who, collectively, can represent all the activities of the project. When the PTT members get together, it is called a **project tracking team meeting,** or *PTT meeting*. The primary purpose of PTT meetings is to serve as a communications forum for the project members to accomplish the three items listed in Figure 5.2.

The **project tracking team leader,** or *PTT leader*, is the person chosen to lead the PTT. The PTT leader is fully responsible for coordinating all the activities necessary in creating and using a successful tracking and problem-management process for use throughout the project's development cycle. The project schedule coordinator (PSC), described in Chapter 4, and responsible for developing the project schedule plan, might be chosen to act as PTT leader. (More can be found on the role of the PTT leader later in "The Steps in Tracking a Project Schedule Plan" section.)

Project High-Risk Areas

 Lesson: If a project's high-risk areas are not being identified and tracked routinely, then the project is not being tracked sufficiently.

The project's **high-risk areas** are collected in a list. This list represents the project's most critical problems to solve. (These problems also are called **high-priority**

- Discover potential project problems before they occur.
- Ensure recovery plans are put in place before unrecoverable harm occurs.
- Provide and receive basic project status and communications.

Figure 5.2   Primary reasons for project tracking meetings.

problems, as explained in Chapter 7.) These problems are currently impacting a major project milestone or, based on "current course and speed," are expected to do so. Of all the problems identified within a development project, these are the problems that require the most immediate attention for resolving. (Figure 5.4, described in the next section, shows a sample overview of a project schedule plan that includes the major project milestones of checkpoints.)

The list of high-risk areas typically is prepared and presented by the PTT leader at the regularly scheduled PTT meetings, although assurance (or an equivalent "outside" person with a close, but independent, view of the project) might perform this activity. Another approach is for the PTT leader to conduct a brainstorming session among several of the project leaders. (Brainstorming is a problem-solving technique whereby a group of people collectively pool their knowledge and experiences to focus on a problem or subject.) The PTT leader is usually the preferred person to present this type of information because he or she is expected to be in a position to have the best insight into the major problems impacting, or having the potential to impact, the project.

 Lesson: Do not attempt to work concurrently more critical project problems than your project's personnel can effectively deal with.

Every attempt should be made to restrict the list of high-risk areas to a single sheet. This helps to ensure that the more critical project problems receive the necessary focus and greatly helps the PTT members and the project's leadership not to be overwhelmed by many more problems than an organization can rally around effectively at any one time. Each problem should be defined by a corresponding **action item** as a means of assigning an owner to resolve the problem and for tracking its progress and eventual closure. (Action items are described in the "Progress of Action Items" section that follows.)

It is recommended that the list of high-risk areas be presented as one of the first exhibits at each PTT meeting. This will help sensitize the PTT members to focus especially on the problem areas on the list as they listen to, and analyze, the presentations of activities that are related to the problems. This sets the focus on the areas that are perceived to require the most leadership involvement. Figure 5.3 shows a sample list of high-risk areas for a fictitious project called TKO. Let's take a closer look at the figure.

The fields shown serve the following purposes:

- *Item:* A project high-risk area. The items are listed chronologically according to the date they are opened as action items. The list could, however, be ordered according to priority. That is, even though all the problems are important, they could be arranged according to their overall impact to the successful outcome of the project. Be aware, however, that the order might change from week to week.

    If more information on an item is desired, the action item should be referenced rather than adding more text to the data already included in the list of high-risk areas.

- *Owner:* The person who has accepted ownership for resolving the problem.

Project TKO High-Risk Areas: 04/15/9x				
Item	Owner	Date opened	Target close date	AI#
1. Product requirements have not been validated with a subset of potential customers.	Madison	02/18	(03/22) 04/18	12
2. Implementation schedules for component ABC are exposed because the vendor contract has not been signed.	Kaptsan	04/01	04/15	37
3. Committed availability date of hardware equipment required to support unit and function test is one month later than required.	Miller	04/01	(04/11) 04/18	38
4. Project staffing is behind plan. Development of the publications and the test scripts for both component test and system test are exposed.	Short	04/01	04/29	39
5. Project costs are exceeding plan by 10% and growing against the plan by 1-2% per week.	Casey	04/08	04/22	41
6. Low-level design scheduled completion date is exposed due to unexpected design rework resulting from inspections.	Yamato	04/11	(04/18) 04/25	44

Figure 5.3   Sample format for high-risk areas.

- *Date opened:* The date the action item was opened.
- *Target close date:* The date the owner believes he or she can resolve and close the problem. If the date is later than what is needed to protect the integrity of the project's schedules, the owner must negotiate with affected members of the project and settle on an acceptable target close date.

 Lesson: Whenever a planned date is reset, add the new date, but leave the "old" date visible.

Note that more than one target close date appears for some of the items. Each time the target close date is changed, it is recorded under the last date committed. It is recommended that whenever a planned date is changed, the original date not be overlaid. This technique allows revision history to be shown.

- *AI#:* The number assigned to the item when it is logged as an action item. Assigning an action item number requires an action item to be opened for each high-risk area. This forces a disciplined approach to logging and tracking each high-risk area.

Don't forget to update the chart's date (see the chart's title box) to coincide with its presentation at each PTT meeting.

 Lesson: The longtime presence of a high-risk area on the chart usually indicates that the critical problem is not receiving the attention required.

Problems should not be listed on a chart over a long period of time. If they are, it is typically a sign that the project, or some aspect of it, is in a rut and that the critical project problems are not being resolved in a timely manner.

Overview of Project Progress

After the project's high-risk areas have been presented and discussed, the next logical exhibit to present at each PTT meeting is an overview—the big picture—that shows where the project's progress is in relation to where it was planned to be. The high-level layer of the project schedule plan is an appropriate visual to use. This overview typically is presented by the PTT leader as a single chart. The overview chart also serves as a common communications artifact to higher management who wish to be kept informed of the overall progress and status of a project. Figure 5.4 shows a sample overview chart for a project.

This chart was introduced in Chapter 4 and has been updated to show the progress that project TKO has made as of a specified date (04/15/9x). Note the following changes:

- The vertical dotted line in the GANTT chart, called a *time line*, depicts the progress that was expected (originally planned) to be made as of the last update of the chart (04/15/9x). The dark bars show the plan. (A GANTT chart displays the durations of activities relative to other activities.)

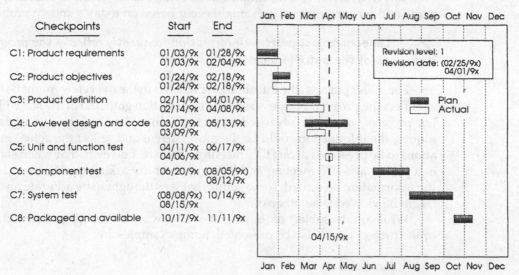

Figure 5.4   Progress of sample high-level project schedule plan.

- The actual progress is shown in the GANTT as white bars placed just under the corresponding dark bars.

- The *Start* and *End* columns now show, immediately under the planned dates, any actual dates that have occurred. If a planned date is shown in parentheses, as depicted for the *End* date of checkpoint C6 and the *Start* date of checkpoint C7, then the date immediately underneath is the new planned date. The corresponding dark bars are updated.

- Each time a planned date is changed, the revision level and revision date for the chart should change also. The original date of the chart is shown as 02/25/9x and the first (and only) revision occurred on 04/01/9x.

If this chart was taken at face value, one would conclude:

- Work on checkpoint C1 started as planned and completed one week later than planned.

- Work on C2 started and ended as planned.

- Work on C3 started as planned and completed one week later than planned.

- Work on C4 started two days later than planned and is currently about one week behind plan.

- Work on C5 started five days ahead of plan and, judging from the GANTT, is running a few days ahead of plan.

Of course, this chart does not show many other project factors that must be taken into account, such as progress in staffing, acquiring equipment, resolving technical problems, staying within budget, tracking within the quality goals, and others. However, this chart serves as a communications vehicle to talk to the overall progress being made and where future impacts might occur based on today's known problems.

 Lesson: Project overview information frequently reflects the progress as of the last PTT meeting.

For many projects, the information depicted in the overview might be "old," that is, reflect the project's progress as of the information gathered at the *last* PTT meeting. For projects with more advanced project schedule plan tracking and updating techniques, the information could be the most current and reflect the actual information about to be presented at *this* PTT meeting. (Beware, however, that when status finally is reported at a PTT meeting and PTT members are asking questions and analyzing the information presented, some status that was thought to be accurate and complete might be viewed to be otherwise.)

While on the subject of looking at overview status for the project, other aspects of the project might also be presented. Some examples are:

- Financials

This status might focus on a comparison between the actual expenses incurred to date and the planned expenses.

• Resources

This status focuses on the comparison between the actual staffing on board and the planned staffing. Nonhuman resources also might be discussed. Some projects include the subject of resources as a subset of the "financials."

• Quality

This status can cover a wide range of quality-related aspects of a project. Most common is the area of defect prevention and discovery. For example, a graph might show the comparison between the expected discovery rates of defects throughout the development stages (high-level design, low-level design, code) to the actual discoveries.

Some project leaders prefer to discuss nontechnical items, such as "financials" in a different meeting from the technical-related schedules. No matter. The important point is that nontechnical items also should be tracked on a routine basis. However, it is recommended that as many project members as possible become exposed to these subjects. Only then can everyone be more conscious of their role in helping to control some of these project parameters, such as containing expenses.

Progress of Project Activities

The project schedule plan (PSP) is the "blueprint" behind the tracking of the project. The PSP is represented in the form of a project checklist to facilitate tracking the project's activities. The project checklist is the key exhibit in the PTT meeting against which project progress is tracked. The PTT leader (or a designee) distributes, to each PTT member, a portion of the project checklist that has been customized to list his or her activities. This handout, updated and distributed several days before each PTT meeting, is typically a single page.

During the PTT meeting, each PTT member presents his or her customized project checklist and compares the actual progress against the planned start and end dates. Figure 5.5 shows a sample customized project checklist.

Let's examine, for a moment, this sample customized project checklist. This chart was introduced in Chapter 4 and has been updated to show the progress that "Berry" has achieved. Note the following items:

• Dates now appear in the *Actual Start* and *End* columns, signifying the progress that has been made in starting and completing some activities. Notice that when an activity ends later than planned (as in Id# 210), it has a negative effect on the start of any activities (as in Id# 211) that depend on its successful completion.

Id#	Activity	Depend.	Respon. Person	Planned		Actual	
				Start	End	Start	End
210	CTP preparation	51s	Berry	04/04	05/13	04/04	05/16
211	CTP review	210	Berry	05/16	05/27	05/17	05/27
212	CTP update	53, 211	Berry	05/30	06/10	05/30	06/14
213	CTP approval	212	Berry	06/13	06/17	06/15	06/22
214	CTP refresh	213	Berry	06/20	06/24	06/23	06/27
220	STP preparation	51s	Berry	05/23	07/01	05/23	07/01
221	STP review	220	Berry	07/04	07/15	07/04	
222	STP update	53, 221	Berry	07/18	07/29		
223	STP approval	222	Berry	08/01	08/05		
230C	Component test	213, 321s	Berry	06/20	(08/05) 08/10	06/23	
224	STP refresh	223	Berry	08/08	08/12		
240C	System test	223, 323s	Berry	(08/08) 08/11	09/30		
250C	Regression test	240	Berry	10/03	10/14		

Figure 5.5   Sample customized project checklist.

- Two activities had one of their planned dates changed: Id# 230C and Id# 240C. The original dates are in parentheses (to preserve a history of changes), and the new planned dates are shown immediately below the dates they replace.

How would this chart be used in a PTT meeting? The owner would receive the chart from the PTT leader several days before the next meeting. Any activity that started or ended since the last PTT meeting would be added, by the owner, to the chart in the *Actual Start* and *End* columns. The owner then presents the chart at the next PTT meeting. Also presented are any appropriate charts to show the progress made in activities that are under way. (More on supporting charts in a moment.) At the end of the PTT meeting, the PTT leader collects all the charts presented. Several days before the next PTT meeting, the PTT leader updates the customized project checklist with the information presented at the last PTT meeting and distributes the updated chart to the owner. The cycle repeats until all the activities have ended successfully.

Project management tools typically allow project checklists to be generated automatically from a project schedule plan. Therefore, manual creation of these lists usually is not necessary.

 Lesson: If a project activity is multiple weeks in duration, then a supporting chart should be presented to back up the PTT member's claim of actual progress made against the plan.

In most cases, it is expected that each PTT member also will present one or more additional charts that show a reasonable level of detailed status to support his or her claim of actual progress made against the plan. These additional charts should be graphical presentations whenever possible. The graphical nature of the charts allows the PTT members to see the actual status more quickly.

Figures 5.6 and 5.7, depicted in the section that follows, show two sample graphical charts to illustrate this point. These charts display progress against an approved plan. This allows everyone quickly to understand the expectation (the plan) and to compare the current status (actual progress) against the expectation. Although the PTT leader typically will collect these charts after they are presented, the owner of the charts controls their contents. This contrasts to the customized pages of the project checklist, all of which are controlled by the PTT leader.

It is recommended that the future outlook for each activity also be presented. This activity-oriented outlook typically might project out 30 days or so. A PTT member with several activities to present might display a single chart that briefly states the outlook for each activity currently under way or approaching the planned start date. Remember, the first purpose for PTT meetings is to identify potential problems *before* they become problems. This proactive view will require activity owners to think about the outlook for each of their activities.

Sample Graph Charts

A PTT member presents status at the PTT meeting for the activities listed in his or her customized project checklist. The charts in this section demonstrate the level of information that should be presented to support the PTT member's perspective of progress made to date.

If too little information is presented, the other PTT members will have insufficient data from which to judge the true progress being made on an activity. If too much information is presented, not only is valuable meeting time wasted, but *information overload* might make it more difficult quickly to assess the progress being made. The PTT members need to see the big picture, but from a simple perspective that builds the picture from its parts. The *picture* referred to here should show the current progress (actual progress) compared against the expected progress (the plan) on a week-by-week basis. Let's look at some sample charts.

Figure 5.6 shows the plan to prepare the first-draft publications. The plan allows for 10 weeks to write the drafts. Notice that the plan follows an *S-shape* curve. This curve is common for planning many types of endeavors. It suggests that progress usually is slow at the start of a task, builds to a peak, and then slows again during the more difficult phase of completing the task.

The scale at the left of the chart shows percent of work complete. You might ask, "How can we really be sure of the accuracy of completeness, when we haven't ever written these publications before?" Obviously, there is some art form here, but there is also some science. For example, if there are approved publication content plans (see the sample software development process presented in Chapter 1), then we have a good idea of the number of manuals to be written, their table of contents, chapter-by-chapter layout, and the estimated page count. From experience, we can project roughly how long it takes to prepare drafts based on their page count, the

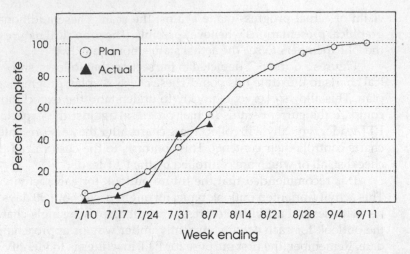

Figure 5.6   Progress in preparing the first-draft publications.

skills of the writers assigned, and so on. The plan that might be derived is summarized in Figure 5.6.

Because PTT meetings are recommended each week, the chart shows the plan by week. Notice that the progress is recorded at the end of each week. Actually, you can decide the day of the week to capture the progress; however, it is recommended that the data be within one to two days of the PTT meeting so the status is reasonably current.

In the sample chart, the actual progress is tracking within two to three days of plan. Whenever a plan is behind, the owner should state what the recovery plan is to get back on plan by the following week (or as soon as possible). A recovery plan should be prepared for situations where the committed planned end date is in jeopardy.

Let's look at another chart: Figure 5.7. This chart shows the plan, by week, to code and inspect the product (or component, or increment, or whatever is being built). The entry in the customized project checklist might say simply the planned start date is 3/30 (the start of a week) and the planned end date is 6/5. This chart shows the progress expected over the 10 weeks planned for this activity. As you can see, one can grasp the progress being made reasonably quickly by viewing a graph chart such as this one. Rather than the owner of this activity saying that he or she is "about on schedule," we can get a fairly comfortable feeling just how much "about" actually is.

Obviously, there are also some problems with a chart like this. For example, all modules are not the same exact size and complexity. In fact, the simpler modules often are written and inspected first. This is another reason why the S-shape curve is so reliable for use in planning; it helps to compensate for easier work being accomplished first and the harder work later. Anyway, even if the activity was precisely on schedule, it doesn't mean that it's going to be a cakewalk. (As an aside, it is suggested that the project's standards define the approximate size for a typical module. Not

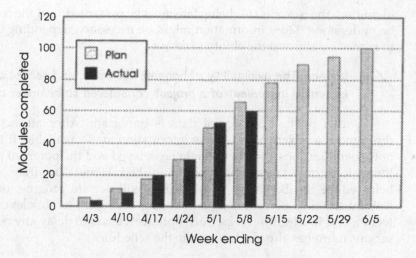

Figure 5.7   Coding progress.

only would this help in laying out the design and planning the coding, but it can have a profound impact on the maintainability of the modules.)

The first sample chart is called a *line chart*; the other chart is called a *bar chart*. These charts could have displayed their data in either manner, or they could have used some other pictorial method. The method used is not as important as the need for the activity owner and the PTT members quickly to grasp the progress being made against the plan. Also be aware that the content and format of the charts presented at the PTT meetings are likely to evolve over weeks or months. This gradual maturing of the charts will continue until the chart owners and PTT members feel the project information that they need is readily available and interpretable.

Looking at both sample charts, you can see that the low-level detail of what's going on is usually not necessary for display in a PTT meeting. For example, consider a case in which a team leader is interested in tracking the progress of the coding for his team. The team leader will want to understand how many modules are being coded, the planned start and finish dates of each module, and the status of actual progress compared with planned progress. Additionally, the team leader will want to know the programmers, by name, who are ahead of and behind schedule. For those behind schedule, the team leader will want to know why the work is overdue and what plan is in place to pull the activity back on schedule. Those ahead of schedule might be able to assist those behind schedule. The status information the team leader must work with is considerably detailed but is necessary to manage the team's commitments effectively.

Now consider the detail to be tracked at a project level for the same activity: coding. At this level the forest is more important than the individual trees. The project leadership is more interested in the total number of modules to be coded within the project, when that coding must begin and finish, and the actual progress of coding compared with the plan. Little detail about coding activities is required if the coding is on schedule. However, if coding is behind schedule, the teams that are late must be identified, the reason(s) for being late must be presented, and the recovery plan must be understood. More information might be necessary, depending on the severity of the schedule slip and the ability to recover.

 Lesson: The availability of honest, accurate, and realistic data is an essential ingredient of a project considered to be under control.

A final point: Accuracy of data is important. After all, actions are decided throughout a project based on the information made available. If the information is not reliable, actions to recover might be delayed and the potential positive impact of the actions, once taken, might be diminished. Honest, accurate, realistic data also help reduce the likelihood that someone will declare progress on a 10-week-long activity to be 95 percent complete during the ninth, tenth, eleventh, twelfth, thirteenth, and fourteenth weeks. Such optimism tends to delay any needed action until serious harm has already occurred to the schedules.

Progress of Action Items

 Lesson: Every project member should be able to log a problem at any time, regardless of where the project resides in the development cycle.

All projects should have a method whereby project problems can be logged and tracked regardless of where in the development cycle the project resides (definition, design, implementation, test, delivery). These problems are referred to as action items in this chapter. Project members should be able to log action items at any time of any day, or at PTT meetings where action items are tracked.

Several days before each PTT meeting, the PTT leader (or a designee) distributes to the assigned owners action items that have been logged but remain unresolved. During the PTT meeting, each PTT member presents status on the action items that he or she owns. Before an action item can be closed, the person who opened the action item must agree that the problem it represents has been resolved.

Although new action items can be raised at any time during the PTT meeting, it is suggested that they not be discussed until after the progress of unresolved action items has been presented. This technique helps to maintain order and progress in the meeting. Each new action item logged during the meeting should have a person assigned and, if possible, a target close date committed before the meeting adjourns.

Figures 5.8 and 5.9, depicted in the section that follows, show sample forms that can be used to log and track action items.

Sample Forms for Tracking Action Items

This section shows sample forms that can be used initially to log, and then to track, an action item until it is successfully closed. These forms depict the type of data needed to log and track a problem sufficiently. Let's examine the fields on these forms.

Figure 5.8 is a sample form that can be used to log a project-level problem as an action item. The fields shown serve the following purposes.

- *Opened by.* The name of the person opening the problem.
- *Date opened.* The date the problem is opened.
- *Problem title.* A one-line abbreviated description of the problem.
- *Required close date.* The date by which the person opening the problem requires (or believes) the problem should be closed.
- *Suggested assigned person.* The name of the person believed to be the right individual to be assigned to solve the problem. Although a problem may require more than one person to solve fully, it is recommended that only one person be assigned as the owner of each problem. The owner is accountable for working with all the necessary parties and to provide routine status on the progress being made until the problem is closed successfully.
- *Scheduled activities impacted.* Project activities that are now, or might become, impacted by the problem.
- *Description of problem.* A full description of the problem, in sufficient detail so that it is well understood.

Figure 5.9 is a sample form that can be used to track an action item until it is closed successfully. An example problem is shown to illustrate the use of the form. Let's examine the fields.

```
┌─────────────────────────────────────────────────────────────┐
│                                                              │
│              ┌──────────────────────────────┐                │
│              │  Action Item Reporting Form   │                │
│              └──────────────────────────────┘                │
│                                                              │
│   Opened by ----------------------->  _____ │
│   Date opened ---------------------->  _____ │
│   Problem title -------------------->  _____ │
│   Required close date -------------->  _____ │
│   Suggested assigned person ------->  _____ │
│   Scheduled activities impacted -->  _____ │
│   Description of problem ----------->  _____ │
│                                        _____ │
│                                        _____ │
│                                        _____ │
│                                                              │
└─────────────────────────────────────────────────────────────┘
```

Figure 5.8   Action item reporting form.

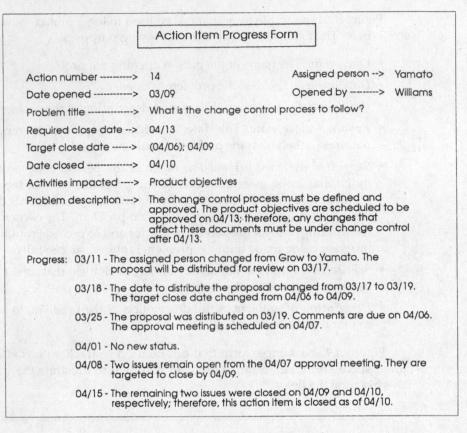

Figure 5.9   Action item progress form.

- *Action number.* Each action item is assigned an identification number to facilitate tracking it.

- *Assigned person.* The name shown here is the person who has accepted ownership of the action item. The name usually will be the same name suggested on the original Action Item Reporting Form.

- *Date opened.* The date the problem is opened. (Taken from the Action Item Reporting Form.)

- *Opened by.* The name of the person opening the problem. (Taken from the Action Item Reporting Form.)

- *Problem title.* A one-line abbreviated description of the problem. (Taken from the Action Item Reporting Form.)

- *Required close date.* The date by which the person opening the problem requires (or believes) the problem should be closed. (Taken from the Action Item Reporting Form.)

- *Target close date.* The date the owner believes he or she can close the problem. If this date is later than the required close date, negotiations must occur between the person who opened the action item, other people impacted by the problem, and the owner of the action item. All involved parties must agree to work with the date that is accepted to appear here. Note that two dates appear in the example. The first date was changed and the project is now tracking to the second date. It is recommended that whenever a planned date is changed, the original date not be overlaid.

- *Date closed.* The date the action item is closed. The person who opened the action item must agree that the problem has been resolved successfully before the action item can be closed.

- *Activities impacted.* Project activities that are now, or might become, impacted by the problem. (Taken from the Action Item Reporting Form.)

- *Problem description.* A full description of the problem. (Taken from the Action Item Reporting Form.)

- *Progress.* Each time the PTT meeting occurs (weekly is shown here), progress on the action item is reported by the owner of the action item. If an action item does not need to be closed for a long period of time (many weeks) and the PTT leader believes the risk is minimal, status might be presented less frequently than at each PTT meeting. For example, reporting status might be suspended until, say, two or three weeks before the action item is committed to be closed.

After an action item has been submitted on an Action Item Reporting Form, the PTT leader (or a designated person) logs the new action item into the tool used for tracking action items. From this point on, the Action Item Progress Form is used. The PTT leader lists the date of the next PTT meeting under the progress field and sends the Action Item Progress Form to the owner. The owner updates the area to the right of the date with the latest status. The resulting chart then is presented at the PTT meeting on the designated date. At the end of the PTT meeting, the PTT leader collects the Action Item Progress Form from the owner and updates the tracking tool with the latest status that was just presented.

The cycle repeats with the updated progress form being sent to the owner for use at the next PTT meeting. This continues until the action item is reported closed at a PTT meeting. These steps can vary depending on the tracking tool used and the ability of the action item's owner to access the tracking tool data base.

Project Outlook

After the project status has been presented, it is helpful to predict the project's progress during the coming 30 days (or whatever length of time feels right for your project). The outlook is project-oriented, not activity-oriented as discussed in an earlier section. This information might be presented by assurance but could be handled by the PTT leader. In either case, both parties should work together so as not to be surprised by the information and the conclusions that were drawn.

The project outlook chart(s) should be prepared before the PTT meeting. However, because the latest status is presented during the PTT meeting, an attempt should be made to adjust, *real time,* the project outlook as new information becomes available throughout the meeting.

It is recommended that the project's outlook include the assignment of a *risk value* that attempts to gauge the likelihood that the project will achieve at least the following major milestones:

- Next major milestone
- Public announcement date
- Product delivery date

Definitions of risk values that can be assigned vary widely in practice. An example of one approach that might be used is the assignment of any one of three risk values: low, medium, and high.

- Low

A condition where the risk consequence would have insignificant impact on planned schedules, function, costs, and quality; and/or the probability of occurrence is sufficiently low as to cause no concern. Normal monitoring and control is required to ensure continued low-risk status.

- Medium

A condition where the risk consequence would have a noticeable and disturbing impact on planned schedules, function, costs, or quality; and/or the probability of occurrence is high enough to be of concern. The level of risk requires:

—Close control of all contributing factors.

—Establishment of a recovery plan.

—Efforts to identify a contingency plan.

- High

A condition where a high probability of occurrence and/or the consequence would have significant impact on the overall project (schedules, function, costs, or quality). The level of risk requires:

—Close control of each high-risk area.

—Close control of each contributing factor.

—Establishment of a recovery plan.

—Identification of the contingency plan and the factors that, when reached, will trigger its implementation.

 Lesson: Assigning a risk value to a project has little significance if the project has no committed project schedule plan against which to evaluate.

The assignment of a risk value is a method of predicting, based on historical and current data, the likelihood that the project schedule plan will be achieved for certain upcoming major milestones. If a project has no approved project schedule plan, assigning a risk value has little or no significance; if you don't know where you are supposed to be, then how can you possibly gauge your likelihood of getting there?

When Should Tracking Occur?

 Lesson: PTT meetings should be conducted weekly to achieve optimal productivity against the approved project schedule plan.

It is strongly recommended that the PTT meeting occur weekly throughout the full project life cycle. Meeting more frequently can cause unnecessary and undesired overhead that can interfere with the overall productivity of both the PTT members and all the project's members. Meeting less frequently than once a week often will allow problems to fester unchecked for longer than the project can bear.

PTT meetings should be conducted on the same day, the same time, and the same place. Participants who are required at tracking meetings are usually very busy. They need to be able to plan their time and manage their calendars. Regularly scheduled tracking meetings allow participants to plan their other activities and to prepare for the meetings. Part of the preparation involves gathering the necessary status information for their own area's work activities and also might involve negotiating problem resolutions with other groups.

 Lesson: PTT meetings serve as the primary driving force of a project.

Another important reason for regularly scheduled tracking meetings is people's need to pace themselves for effective productivity. Most people work more intelligently and with more conviction when they are being measured against their commitments. Infrequent or irregular tracking typically results in occasional spurts of improved productivity. When people's progress is tracked at frequent and predictable intervals, they are conditioned to maintain a fairly constant and predictably high level of productivity. Furthermore, this action helps to drive a critically needed level of discipline into an organization. In fact, the PTT meeting, and its derivative actions, serves as the primary driving force behind the project.

It is suggested that PTT meetings occur on Tuesday, Wednesday, or Thursday of each week. Mondays are avoided to allow the PTT members sufficient time to gather status and update the appropriate charts for the PTT meeting. This also allows project members who worked the weekend to include reporting on their weekend progress more easily.

Fridays should be avoided for two primary reasons. One reason is that many people like to take Fridays off to create long weekends. Also, many holidays fall on Friday. The Friday disruption means that the PTT meeting members might begin to view the PTT meeting as an "optional" event, which it is *definitely not*. The other reason why Fridays should be avoided is that a PTT meeting is very likely to cause certain problems to require immediate attention. You guessed it: Friday afternoon is a bad time to get news that will interfere with a person's planned personal weekend time.

 Lesson: PTT meetings are most effective if conducted on a Tuesday or a Wednesday—and the following day is reserved for work meetings and escalation meetings.

The author favors Wednesday as the preferred day for the PTT meeting. It is strategically placed in a week and allows ample time both to prepare for the meeting and to recover from its aftermath. Furthermore, it is recommended that all-day Thursday be left open on the calendars of all the project's members. Thursday is reserved for work meetings and for escalation meetings (discussed in an upcoming section) for the problems identified as needing immediate attention in the PTT meeting. By reserving the day after the PTT meeting, the problems are assured of getting attention immediately. Use of the day after the PTT meeting for this purpose helps to avoid problems lingering from week to week and helps to force a structured method upon a project to ensure that these project-level problems get the attention they deserve and require.

Should PTT meetings occur during mornings or afternoons? Most people seem to favor mornings because there is a belief that most people are more alert in the morning than they are in the afternoon. Also, there is a belief that afternoon PTT meetings are more likely to have to compete with other events for the full attention of the PTT members. The notion is that, if the meeting is conducted in the afternoon, then PTT members are more likely to come to it late, or leave early, or skip it altogether due to other demands on their limited time, demands that appear to increase as the day progresses.

Who Should Attend Tracking Meetings?

The PTT leader identifies the areas of the project that must be represented at PTT meetings. The PTT leader might even recommend the specific people from those areas which should be represented in the PTT. The members chosen should be approved by their managers.

If the project membership is small, say five to 10 persons, all project members might participate on the PTT. For somewhat larger projects, say 10 to 25 persons, the lead person in each group (planning, development, test, publications, assurance, and others) might be the appropriate representative at the PTT meeting. For projects larger than 25 members, PTT members might be team leaders (even if more than one per group) and persons performing independent roles who need to represent themselves (the sole person interfacing to a vendor group, for example). Collectively, the project members chosen to attend the PTT meeting must be able to represent the status of all the project's activities and action items.

 Lesson: In the interests of encouraging accountability at the lower levels of an organization, PTT members typically should not include management personnel.

Due to the popular and vital concept of empowerment and moving the authority to the point of responsibility, management personnel typically should not be members of the PTT. However, managers will find the PTT meetings to be the best source of project status and often might choose to attend. An optimal number of full PTT members (versus occasional guests) seems to be in the realm of 10 or fewer people; however, larger meetings are possible and, in fact, are necessary for larger projects.

 Lesson: PTT members must be able to represent their areas adequately.

A project leader is usually the best person to attend tracking meetings. However, there are times when some things must be delegated. In these cases, project leaders should work with their representatives to give them the authority and support they need. It is essential that PTT members be able to represent their area adequately by fielding expected questions, negotiating solutions to problems, and making commitments for their area. There will be a serious, negative impact on the success of the PTT meeting if PTT members weakly represent their areas.

The Tracking Meeting Agenda

In the section "What Should be Tracked?" the major subjects of focus at tracking meetings were discussed and listed in Figure 5.1. They are repeated here for convenience. The PTT meeting agenda is centered around these major subjects.

- Project high-risk areas
- Overview of project progress
- Progress of project activities
- Progress of action items
- Project outlook

 Lesson: A well-planned PTT meeting agenda can have a significant positive impact on the control maintained, not just for the meeting but for the project as well.

The following guidelines will help you develop an effective meeting agenda. Figure 5.10 shows a sample PTT meeting agenda format that will help to demonstrate these guidelines. After the guidelines are presented, the sample agenda in the figure will be examined closely.

- Each item to be presented should have a person's name assigned (versus no name or an organizational or functional name).

This technique helps to drive ownership and accountability upon those persons responsible for coming to the meeting fully prepared. It also helps to avoid: "What? I didn't know you expected me to present that!"

Time	Item	Presenter
	PTT Meeting Agenda: 04/15/9x	
8:00	Project high-risk areas	Turner
8:15	Overview of project progress	Turner
	Progress of project activities	
8:20	Change control	Yamato
8:30	Low-level design and code	Grow
8:40	Unit and function test	Miller
8:45	Component test	Berry
8:50	System test	Berry
8:55	Publications	Vandegrift
9:05	Performance	Vila
9:10	Usability	Smith
9:15	Progress of action items	
	41	Casey
	37	Kaptsan
	5, 12, 19	Madison
	38	Miller
	39	Short
	27, 44	Yamato
9:30	New action items	All
9:45	30-day outlook	Rosenman
9:50	Plan work/escalation meetings	Turner, all
10.00	Adjourn	

Figure 5.10 Sample project agenda format.

- Each item and presenter in an agenda should have a time limit stated.

For example, the "project high-risk areas" might be presented in 15 minutes. (If this appears too long, remember that these are the most critical project problems in the project. The PTT members need to comprehend fully the impact (potential or otherwise) that these yet unresolved problems have on the project.)

The time limit for presenting progress for a given project activity will, of course, vary widely for each activity. However, if each person is given somewhere between five and 10 minutes to present the status for all his or her activities, this might be adequate. Depending on the activity and its complexity, either five or 10 minutes is chosen. By contrast, the time to present each action item might be one to two minutes.

- The order of subject areas should follow some logical pattern.

For example, when the "progress of project activities" is being presented, the sequence of activities might be in the order that the project is proceeding; that is, present progress on the high-level design before the low-level design, the low-level design before the coding, and so on.

Furthermore, if an iterative development process is being followed, present progress on the first iterative piece before addressing the second piece, and so on.

Sound obvious? Maybe, but this technique of logical sequencing is not always followed. The discipline with which the PTT meeting is planned and executed will have a marked impact on the discipline exercised throughout the project.

The sequence of presenters can be adjusted for logical reasons, but it should be predictable and planned. For a case in which a person from outside the project has something to report each week, but has no need to sit through the entire meeting, this person could present at the beginning of the meeting and then leave.

- The PTT meeting agenda should be available several days before the meeting.

PTT members need time to prepare for the meeting. Also, they need to be certain of the areas that they are responsible for addressing. The PTT meeting agenda helps the PTT members know what is expected of them.

Armed with these guidelines, let's examine the sample project agenda format in Figure 5.10.

- Project high-risk areas and overview of project progress.

Notice the same person is presenting both items. This would imply that "Turner" is the PTT leader.

- Progress of project activities

Because low-level design is the first development activity presented, this means that the product requirements, product objectives, product specifications, and high-level design have completed and are now under change control. The inclusion of "change control" in the agenda means that someone (Yamato) must address the current status of requirements/function/design changes being proposed for the project. Although there are many names used to describe these change requests, some projects call them: requirements change requests (RCRs), design change requests (DCRs), or simply change requests (CRs).

Notice that the development activities appear in the list in the order they are performed in the development cycle—until "publications" appears. The activities centered around publications, performance and usability relate across many areas of the development cycle and, therefore, usually are presented after the so-called development activities.

 Lesson: The progress of activities performed by vendors and subcontractors should be tracked just as routinely as that of other members of a project.

Activities can be added, merged, or deleted from this list. This depends on the size and scope of your project. For example, if a vendor is performing the low-level design, the progress for that activity must be presented. It could be presented under low-level design or as a separate activity referred to simply as "vendor" or "component ABC." No allowances for skipping status should be made for vendors or subcontractors. Their activities should be tracked on the same regular basis as if it were being performed under the direct control and proximity of the product manager.

- Progress of action items

Notice that start times are not shown for each presenter. This is because one to two minutes usually should be sufficient for presenting status for an action item. Setting time increments to this level of accuracy adds no value to the meeting agenda.

A typical way to decide the order of presenting the action items is by alphabetical order of the action item owner's last name. If a person owns more than one action item, then his or her action items might be presented in chronological order as shown in the agenda.

- New action items

Anyone with a new action item can log it now. It is expected that each new action item will have a person assigned to own it and, if possible, a target close date committed before this portion of the PTT meeting ends.

- 30-day outlook

Because the name (Rosenman) is different from the name on the "project high-risk areas" and "overview of project progress" items (Turner), it might be assumed that assurance (or a person with an equivalent perspective) is presenting this item. However, the PTT leader is an alternative choice to address this item.

- Plan work/escalation meetings

The PTT leader spends the last moments of the meeting declaring what project activities and action items require special attention over the next two to three days. For best results and proactive project control, the meetings to address these special project areas should be scheduled now, preferably for the following day. These meetings become priorities within the project.

Scheduling the Tracking Meeting

The meeting room should be large enough to accommodate the expected participants and be comfortable enough for the PTT members to spend the designated length of time. Ensure the necessary accessories are in the room, such as projector (with backup lamp bulb), wall boards to write on, flip-chart paper and holder, blank transparencies, markers, Scotch tape, and so on.

 Lesson: Schedule the PTT meeting room for 30 minutes longer than the planned meeting.

Reserve the room for the planned duration of the PTT meeting, plus another half hour. Why? Because sometimes a topic will be so pressing that a few more minutes past the scheduled meeting time is required. Although every attempt should be made to avoid extending the meeting time (after all, it can wreak havoc with everyone's calendar integrity), the extra minutes can be a blessing at times. Don't forget to reserve the meeting room for the same day, time, and place each week for the duration of the project.

You might want to consider arranging the chairs and tables in a manner that might help encourage a participative environment. For example, if only a handful of people are meeting, perhaps they can all sit around a single table where they have ready eye contact with one another. If the meeting has around 20 members, perhaps the tables can be arranged in the shape of a horseshoe. The opening in the "horseshoe" is reserved for the transparency projector and writing boards. This arrangement allows everyone to have direct eye contact with every other person.

The meeting invitation should be distributed with sufficient lead-time notice and should be distributed on a routine schedule. The PTT leader should ensure that the meeting has the full support of the product manager and that the invited participants are keenly aware of the high priority of this meeting as compared with their other duties.

Tracking Meeting Ground Rules

 Lesson: A simple set of PTT ground rules will establish expectations.

A short, simple set of *PTT meeting ground rules* will help PTT members to understand what is expected of them at the meeting. These ground rules should fit on a single sheet of paper and be displayed at meetings when needed. An example of a set of ground rules is:

- Come on time.

Not five or 10 minutes late.

- Come prepared.

Not just in your head, but also with the media (transparencies, diskettes for computer screen projections) from which you will report your status and which you will provide to the PTT leader after you have presented.

- If behind on an activity, then address:

—Why the activity is late.

—What other areas are/might become impacted.

—What recovery plan will be/is in place.

—Whether you need help.

 Lesson: It is in the best interests of the project and its members for a project member to seek help when needed.

Many project members avoid asking for help. The most effective projects encourage its members to request help when it is needed.

• Time-consuming problems are to be resolved outside of the meeting.

If a problem can be resolved within two minutes, do it. Why? Because there is a unique opportunity with the breadth of groups and skills represented at the meeting to resolve some problems easily. However, if more than two minutes is required, log the problem for resolution outside the meeting.

• "Raise hand" if the meeting is perceived to be off course.

This can be a helpful mechanism for PTT members to employ in reminding the PTT leader and others that the meeting seems to be on an unproductive tangent. The PTT leader can then decide to move on or complete the discussion. This form of empowerment helps to keep meetings in check.

• Encouraged: Open and candid status reports and discussion.

This is essential for a successful, productive meeting. There is a tendency for presenters to make their status appear more positive than it is. Participants should feel encouraged to present complete and accurate status, even if the news is negative. The project's health is in far better shape if the project's members are cognizant of the project's problems. Problems can only be resolved if they are visible and being worked.

Don't be fooled by the simplicity and obvious subjects in this example set of ground rules. These are problems that commonly plague PTT meetings (as well as most other types of meetings).

 Lesson: A project's leadership must fully support the PTT meetings and related events if a project is to be as successful as possible.

There is no point in tracking a project if the project's leadership (including the PTT leader) will not enforce the ground rules. PTT members must recognize the critical importance of their role in PTT meetings in helping to ensure successful tracking meetings. Furthermore, the project leadership must support the PTT members' need to have time to gather, prepare, and present status, and to work on resolving problems. The PTT members must have a clear understanding of the priority that this task has relative to their other duties.

The entire organization wants to be successful. Everyone looks to the project leadership to provide the environment necessary to attain this success. The disciplined tracking of a project helps to create an environment for success.

Recovery Plans

 Lesson: Recovery plans are for fixing a problem quickly and limiting the damage that can result.

An effective tracking process doesn't just discover problems, but also ensures that recovery plans are implemented and tracked before the problems have a chance to cause lasting damage to the project. The first rule of thumb is to protect the overall integrity of the project schedule plan. The goal of recovery plans is to fix the problem quickly and limit the damage to the smallest area. For example, an activity might be completed late by one week, but if the successor activities can maintain their completion dates and the next major milestone date is preserved, the recovery plan will probably be viewed as successful.

Recovery plans should be put in place when a problem arises with an activity that has the perceived likelihood of causing unacceptable harm to some aspect of the project. This is not a time to ignore the problem or to delay in making a decision to begin the recovery. As Thomas J. Watson, Jr. had been known to say: "Better to do something—even the wrong thing—than to do nothing at all."

Recovery plans should address the following items:

- Identify the owner of the recovery plan.

- Identify the sequence of activities that must occur to complete the resolution.

- Determine the dates when each activity of the plan will be started and completed, and identify the dependencies of each activity.

- Ensure that the appropriate people or groups approve the plan. This includes those groups who have a dependency on the successful implementation of the plan.

The best recovery plans don't just show how the activity in trouble recovers; they show how damage is contained for those activities dependent on the troubled activity. Also, recovery plans should be included as items tracked in the PTT meeting and should be presented when the relevant activity is being reviewed.

The Role of Escalations

An **issue** is a problem that, if not resolved, is believed to have a significant harmful effect on the outcome of the project. The effect can, for example, relate to such things as schedules, cost, resources, quality or customer satisfaction.

When two affected parties are unable to agree on the resolution of an issue, and a sincere attempt to negotiate a resolution has occurred, then higher levels of the project's leadership must be called upon to help resolve the issue. This is called an **escalation.**

Typically the next higher level of project leadership, from both sides of the issue, are called together to understand the issue. Then, through consensus, it is hoped that the problem will be finally and mutually resolved.

If the problem is still not resolved, the next levels of the project leadership are called upon. Eventually the two organizational chains will come together at the same boss. Then, the buck finally stops and the decision is made. Most escalations do not go this high. Moreover, experience has shown that the most agreeable solutions are those reached at the lower levels. There are different approaches to conducting an escalation. Be certain that you understand the approach to be followed in your organization.

 Lesson: Escalations can be the proper and healthy course of action to follow in resolving an issue.

To some, *escalate* is a dirty word because they either don't understand its purpose or the project leadership has a reputation of punishing one or both of the parties involved. Escalating an issue must be viewed as a healthy form of doing business. Emotions must be removed from the escalation process. The solution must be the right one for the business, not for a given person. Project leaders who might punish one or both parties for allowing an escalation to reach them should reconsider. There are many times when both parties might be making the *right* business decision from their respective viewpoints. Someone higher in the chain must make a decision from a different perspective or from a position of additional information. Project members and lower-level project leaders must be encouraged to work things out at their levels. However, escalating, at times, is the proper and healthy course of action to follow.

The following scenario illustrates how some project members might view escalations:

> Dorothy Casey, a project leader of a development organization, called a meeting of about 10 persons who were all outside of her direct authority. These people represented several different organizations, all of which provide some form of service to her organization. Casey viewed the meeting as a way to understand the status of several work activities in progress. In one case, a group had missed its commitments three times in as many weeks. Casey was growing uneasy because her shop needed support that it was not getting.
>
> She looked at Barney Sullivan, who represented the group that was consistently making and then missing the commitments, and asked what he had planned as his next action. Sullivan said he was dependent on a person in another department and that person kept missing the commitment. Sullivan also said that "the person is very busy and was doing the best that he can." Casey asked Sullivan if he had escalated (as he had said he would). He had not. When Casey asked why not, Sullivan said, "I need to work with this person and we have a good working relationship now. I don't want to upset that."

Casey replied, "Have I ever escalated you over an issue?" The replying nod was a yes, followed by, "Two or three times." Casey continued, "Are we still working together and managing to negotiate and do what's right for the business?"

Sullivan said, "Yes, but that's different—" then stopped, realizing that it wasn't any different. Sullivan got the point. The project leader got the commitment for the final time.

Frequently, you can actually help people by escalating an issue *over their heads* and, assuming you win, have their priorities officially redirected. The issue may have been something that they wanted to do all along, but they did not feel they had the authority to alter their current priorities.

 Lesson: Escalations should be initiated within two working days of the need being identified.

When two parties cannot agree on an important issue, escalations should be set up quickly. If the issue is truly important, a decision must be reached so that everyone can get on with their business. As a guideline, escalations should be initiated *within two working days* of being identified. Immediately, the next levels of project leadership (or whoever gets involved in your organization) must reserve time on their calendars for the escalation meeting. Although an advance notice of two work days might not always be enough time to get an appointment on some calendars, management must support the expedient resolution of escalated issues.

 Lesson: When an escalation is underway, do not stop working the plan-of-record.

Some guidelines to help address the important area of escalations are:

- Escalate only after a sincere attempt has been made to resolve the issue.
- The dissenter is responsible for escalating the issue.
- Initiate an escalation *within two working days* of knowing the problem is unresolvable at its current level.
- Escalate the problem, not the person.
- Always inform your management prior to initiating an escalation; you will need their support.
- Always inform involved parties before beginning the escalation; the goal is *no surprises*.
- When an escalation is being pursued, do not stop working the plan-of-record.

Remember, issues are serious problems that can bring projects to their knees if left unattended. Issues deserve the highest priority attention within a project. This point cannot be overstated.

The Steps in Tracking a Project Schedule Plan

This section describes a series of steps you can follow to track a project and perform on-going problem management. Figure 5.11 shows an overview of the steps that describe the project tracking and problem management process. These steps apply to tracking a project of any size: small, medium, or large; however, for small projects, ones with only a handful of participants, some steps might be reduced in effort because it might be acceptable to require less tracking-related, formal documentation and to increase the reliance on informal avenues of communications. The decision to tailor, expand, or adopt these steps belongs to the product manager and his or her designated PTT leader.

Each step is described by five fields:

- *Description:* A description of the items to be performed.
- *Entry Conditions:* Actions that must occur before this step can begin.
- *Exit Conditions:* Actions that must happen before this step is considered complete.
- *Duration:* The range of time, rounded to hours or days, that this step might typically require.
- *Notes:* Any potentially useful information.

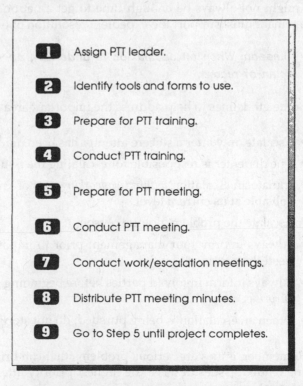

Figure 5.11   Steps in tracking a project.

Step 1. Assign Project Tracking Team Leader

Description: The product manager assigns a person to be the PTT leader. As defined earlier, the PTT leader is fully responsible for coordinating all the activities necessary in creating and using a successful tracking and problem-management process for use throughout the project's development cycle. The project schedule coordinator (PSC), described in Chapter 4, and responsible for developing the project schedule plan, might be the person chosen by the product manager to act as PTT leader.

The PTT leader performs an essential and critical role within a project. The effectiveness demonstrated by the PTT leader can have a direct impact on the discipline and professionalism exhibited throughout the project and the successful execution of the project schedule plan. For this reason, both the PTT leader and the product manager should carefully understand the role of the PTT leader and the corresponding empowerment that accompanies the assignment. Examples of levels of empowerment that should be considered within the domain of the PTT leader assignment are described throughout this chapter. However, two areas of special note that require agreement of the product manager—making changes to the approved project schedule plan and resolving escalations—are presented in the Notes fields of Steps 7 and 8.

Entry Conditions: A project is started.

Exit Conditions: A person is assigned as the PTT leader.

Duration: One day. In practice, this step might take only an hour or so to nominate a person and receive his or her acceptance of the assignment. Or several days might be required to search for potential candidates and interview and select the best one. However, one day has been chosen as a goal for completing this step.

Notes: A project requires tracking almost immediately after its conception. A goal, however, is to define a project plan, as soon as possible, so that the project members have a documented roadmap of the activities to be performed, who owns what activities, the dependencies of each activity, and when they are scheduled to begin and complete. Ultimately, a project schedule plan (defined in Chapter 4) should be created and approved. However, this is not realistic until at least the product objectives are available for review. Therefore, until the product objectives are available and the initial project schedule plan is completed, preliminary plans addressing the activities to be performed over the coming several weeks or months are necessary. These plans can be developed by either the PSC or the PTT leader.

 Lesson: PTT meetings are most effective when an approved project schedule plan is available from which to track.

The tracking and problem-management process described in these steps applies to projects in any stage of development: just starting, midway, or nearly complete; however, the examples and tips provided are based on the assumption that a project schedule plan has been developed, approved, and is being tracked.

Step 2. Identify Tools and Forms to Use

Description: The PTT leader identifies one or more tools to be used to aid in tracking the progress being made against the project schedule plan and in tracking the identification, progress, and closure of the project-level problems (referred to as action items). Usually the project management tool used in tracking the project schedule plan is also the same tool that was used in developing the plan; however, often this tool cannot easily handle tracking action items.

If any special forms or computer screen panels are needed to aid in the tracking, they are created as part of this step. Some tracking tools require you to define special user-oriented forms or panels. However, you may decide to create your own forms and use them in concert with a chosen tool or create your own methodology rather than using the one promoted by an off-the-shelf tool. Naturally, you will want to choose the most productive approach that meets your needs. The important point of this step is to decide *now* the environment and method that will be used in tracking the progress of your project schedule plan and to manage the resolution of project problems. The earlier "Progress of Action Items" section shows an example set of forms that can be used to log and track project problems. These forms will be referenced in subsequent steps.

Entry Conditions: A person is assigned as the PTT leader.

Exit Conditions: The tools and forms are selected or created.

Duration: Zero to five days. Some organizations might have already defined the set of tools and forms to use for new projects. In this case, a duration of zero days might be possible. If a project is starting from scratch in identifying tools and forms, then even five days might not be enough. However, the range of zero to five days has been chosen as a goal.

Notes: If time is needed to install and learn the chosen tool, the installation and training for the PTT leader (or designated tools person) is expected to occur during this step and Step 3.

A project's tracking and problem management process is usually the most efficient and effective if automated through the use of computerized tools. However, for projects that are considered in the early stages of adopting a sound, disciplined tracking and problem-management process, you should not feel compelled to automate everything the first time through. It is better to focus initially on defining and adopting a process and work at getting it accepted and installed throughout a project. After some experience with the process, you might then choose to focus on increasing the use of automated tools as part of improving your process.

Step 3. Prepare for PTT Training

Description: The first PTT meeting serves as a training session for all the PTT members. This training session teaches them how future PTT meetings will be conducted and what their roles and responsibilities are before, during, and after the meetings.

The purpose of this step is for the PTT leader to prepare for the PTT training meeting. The actions to be performed, material to be prepared, and items to consider include the following topics. All but the last two items have been discussed in earlier sections of the same name.

- What should be tracked?
- When should tracking occur?
- Who should attend tracking meetings?
- The tracking meeting agenda
- Scheduling the tracking meeting
- Tracking meeting ground rules
- Recovery plans
- The role of escalations
- Reviewing lessons learned from past projects
- Installing and learning the selected tools and forms

This is the perfect time to understand project tracking-related lessons that can be learned from past projects. It is hoped that **postproject reviews** (discussed in Chapter 14) have been conducted on some past projects. These reviews offer an excellent opportunity to learn what went right and what went wrong on earlier projects. The goal should be for this implementation of the project tracking process to avoid repeating past mistakes.

The tools need to be in place and operational before the next step, "Conduct PTT Training." This also means that the tracking-related forms need to be defined and ready for use.

Entry Conditions: The tools and forms are selected or created.

Exit Conditions: The PTT leader is fully prepared for the PTT training meeting and the meeting notice is distributed.

Duration: Five to 10 days. If you have already been through an implementation of this tracking process, this step, for some projects, might be performed in less than five days.

Notes: None.

Step 4.   Conduct PTT Training

Description: The PTT training meeting is conducted by the PTT leader. It is expected that some of the materials that the PTT leader prepared for this meeting will be modified as a result of feedback from the PTT members. Also, the membership of the PTT meeting, as well as the day, time, or location of the meeting, might undergo change. It is good to have everyone concentrating on the training rather than actually presenting status. This way, when they present their status in the next PTT meeting based on the guidelines established in this meeting, they will be better prepared to have a productive meeting.

Entry Conditions: The PTT leader has completed the preparation for the PTT training meeting.

Exit Conditions: The PTT members reach a consensus on the tracking and problem management process to be followed and the meeting ends. Any tracking process-related problems not resolved are logged, assigned owners, and assigned target close dates for resolution.

Duration: Two hours.

Notes: The participants in the PTT training meeting also should include project members who will serve as backups when PTT members are unable to attend a meeting. Also, the PTT leader should ensure that any future new members to the PTT meeting receive proper training.

Step 5. *Prepare for PTT Meeting*

Description: The PTT leader and the PTT members prepare for the PTT meeting. The actions to be performed include:

- The PTT leader, using the feedback from the PTT training meeting, updates the affected material so that all changes have been included and distributes the minutes from the PTT training meeting (one-time activity).
- The PTT leader schedules the first "real" PTT meeting and distributes the meeting notice (one-time activity).
- The PTT leader prepares for the PTT meeting.
- The PTT members prepare for the PTT meeting.

The first two items listed are one-time-only activities. They apply if this step was entered directly from Step 4, Conduct PTT Training. The last two items, however, are routine exercises that the PTT leader and PTT members must perform before each PTT meeting.

Entry Conditions: The minutes from the last PTT meeting have been distributed, or if this step was entered from Step 4, the PTT Training has successfully completed.

Exit Conditions: The PTT leader and the PTT members are fully prepared for the upcoming PTT meeting. If this step was entered directly from Step 4, the PTT leader also has (1) updated the affected material and distributed the minutes of the PTT training meeting, and (2) distributed the PTT meeting notice.

Duration: One to two days. It is difficult to predict how long it will take the PTT leader or each PTT member to prepare for the PTT meeting. The time might vary widely, from an hour to more than two days, from meeting to meeting depending on the project activities and action items being worked. However, the time range of one to two days is expected to apply in most cases.

If this step was entered directly from Step 4, the PTT leader will need additional time to write and distribute the minutes from the PTT training meeting. Also, the PTT leader and the PTT members might require more time to prepare for the PTT meeting because this will be their first application of the format and guidelines agreed to at the PTT training meeting.

Notes: None.

Step 6. Conduct PTT Meeting

Description: The PTT leader conducts the PTT meeting. The sequence of items presented at the meeting follows the outline in the PTT meeting agenda described in the section entitled "The Tracking Meeting Agenda." The PTT leader must exert discipline in keeping the meeting on course and within its time constraints. An efficiently run meeting will send a clear signal to the meeting participants that their full participation is required and appreciated.

As a ground rule, when a problem requires more than two minutes to resolve (or whatever time limit your team has agreed upon), its solution should not be attempted at the meeting. If an attempt is made to resolve a problem within the agreed-upon time, and the time has elapsed, the problem should be logged as an action item (if not already done) and taken outside the meeting for resolution.

Although each presenter typically presents his or her progress or item while standing in front of the group alongside a transparency projector, other approaches might be tried to save time. For example, the PTT leader (or some designee) can manipulate the transparencies while the presenter remains seated and speaks from his or her seat. Another example is employing electronic means to automatically present preloaded presentations. These techniques might save a minute or so each time a new presenter must walk to the projector area, wait for the last speaker to clear his or her material, and set up the new material.

Entry Conditions: The PTT leader has distributed the minutes and updated material from the last PTT meeting at least three work days before the next PTT meeting.

Exit Conditions: The PTT leader adjourns the PTT meeting.

Duration: 30 minutes to four hours. The duration of the meeting will vary depending on a number of factors, including the size and complexity of the project, the number of project activities and action items to discuss, and the experience of the meeting members in presenting and working as a team. As time goes on, it is expected that the meeting time will stabilize and even be reduced. For example, the PTT leader can limit the topics to be presented, such as only allowing activities in the critical path or items in trouble to be reported; however, in the beginning, it is recommended that such shortcuts be avoided.

Notes: Because the effective implementation of this meeting is critical to a project's overall success, it is recommended that PTT members who fail to attend or consistently come late be brought to the attention of their immediate management. This meeting must have everyone's support to be effective.

Consideration should be given to assigning a person, other than the PTT leader, as the recorder of the meeting's minutes. This approach can help free the PTT leader to provide his or her full attention to running the PTT meeting.

Step 7. Conduct Work and Escalation Meetings

Description: Just before the close of each PTT meeting, but after all status has been presented, the PTT leader identifies those project activities and action items that require special attention during the next two to three days. These are problem areas that are missing their commitments or have the strong potential for doing so, and need special help in getting the right people together to understand and resolve the problems appropriately. Some of these problems might be lingering after an earnest, but unsuccessful, attempt by the involved parties to work out any disagreements. In this case, escalation meetings are required to resolve them satisfactorily.

This step ensures that time is set aside to work these types of project problems. The importance of these meetings cannot be overstated. Commonly this is an area that the project leadership (the PTT leader, the team leaders, and the project's management) on many projects fail to manage and control adequately. For best results, it is recommended that the day immediately after the PTT meeting be reserved for these work and escalation meetings. As long as every member of the project reserves this day for this purpose, then the problems can be worked to a satisfactory closure more quickly.

The PTT leader schedules most, if not all, of these meetings. If necessary, the PTT leader will attend and act as a facilitator in helping to ensure the problem is fully understood and an acceptable solution is agreed upon.

Entry Conditions: The PTT meeting has completed and the meeting or escalation has been scheduled.

Exit Conditions: The problem has been resolved satisfactorily (or at least one meeting has occurred on behalf of proceeding toward a resolution).

Duration: 30 minutes to one day. Most problems can be worked or escalated within a one-day allocated period. However, some problems might require much longer. Solving the problem is not always the objective. Sometimes the objective is for the involved parties to agree on a plan of action that can be followed and tracked; the idea is that, after the plan is implemented, the problem is resolved. Any plans that result should be logged appropriately and included for subsequent tracking in the PTT meeting.

Notes: These work and escalation meetings can take place at any time throughout a project. They are not dependent on first being identified at a PTT meeting and subsequently being scheduled for a work or escalation meeting. However, the PTT meeting serves as an orderly and structured process for initiating these meetings.

The PTT leader is the primary agent who works on behalf of the product manager to ensure that the approved project schedule plan is executed successfully. In this vein, consideration should be given to empower the PTT leader to resolve certain types of escalations, such as issues against the product specifications, test plans, machine resources, and function test—documents, resources, and activities under the domain of the product manager. Escalations that might require the involvement and decision of the product manager—such as issues affecting the product's readiness to be announced to the public and its subsequent availability—would be brought to the product manager for resolution; however, even in these cases, it is recommended that the PTT leader offers a recommendation of resolution to the product manager.

Step 8. *Distribute PTT Meeting Minutes*

Description: The PTT leader (or a designee) creates and distributes the minutes of the PTT meeting. These minutes should be distributed within two working days of the PTT meeting because they contain the latest information on the project and the PTT members need them to update their status for the next PTT meeting. The minutes should include:

- Project high-risk areas

- Overview of project progress

- Updated project checklist

Any schedule date changes that were accepted at the PTT meeting are recorded into the project schedule plan (using the chosen project management tool). Each PTT member receives only his or her set of project activities in the form of a customized project checklist; however, some groups, such as assurance and the project's management, receive the entire project checklist. Anyone can request the full package.

- Updated action items

The action items are updated with the marked-up status presented at the PTT meeting. New action items are logged and displayed on an Action Item Progress Form. Each PTT member receives only the action items that he or she has been assigned as the owner; however, some groups, such as assurance and the project's management, receive the entire package of action items. Anyone can request the full package.

- Project outlook
- PTT meeting agenda for the upcoming PTT meeting

Entry Conditions: The PTT meeting is completed.

Exit Conditions: The PTT meeting minutes are distributed.

Duration: Two days.

Notes: The PTT leader maintains the project schedule plan. Once approved, the project schedule plan is baselined, that is, it is placed under change control. As the project schedule plan begins to be tracked, it is suggested that the PTT leader be empowered to decide whether certain proposals will be accepted for changing scheduled dates in the project schedule plan. For example, if the owner of an activity requests to change his or her planned end date to occur one week later, and all affected parties agree to the proposal and are able to contain the slip, the PTT leader would have the authority to accept the date change and update the project schedule plan accordingly; however, if a date change requires a major milestone date to slip, it is suggested that the product manager be called upon to make the decision. In this case, the PTT leader should provide a recommendation to the product manager for his or her consideration.

Step 9.   Go to Step 5 Until Project Completes

Description: The sole purpose of this step is to serve as a pointer back to Step 5 (Prepare for PTT Meeting) or to exit the process if the project has completed.

Entry Conditions: The PTT meeting minutes are distributed.

Exit Conditions: Step 5 is reentered or the tracking process is exited.

Duration: Not applicable.

Notes: It is strongly recommended that the PTT meeting occur weekly throughout most of the project life cycle.

One Day at a Time

Projects fail because they are allowed to. They fail from neglect. Oh, perhaps not intentionally, but through inattention to the basic tracking principles presented in this chapter. The irony about all this is that the principles of sound project tracking already are known. They have been around for many years. It is not a brand-new frontier that has yet to be explored, understood, and tamed. In fact, the likelihood is high that someone in a lead position on your project or in your organization—perhaps you—is well aware of the basic project tracking principles.

So what's the problem? Assuming an approved project schedule plan is in place, too many of us don't spend the time and energy anticipating problems—identifying potential problems before they happen. Then, after the problems are made known, we act too slowly or too weakly in putting recovery plans in place before unrecoverable harm can occur.

The solution? Practice the project tracking principles discussed in this chapter. Ensure a PTT leader is assigned who understands the job and is empowered to make it happen. Ensure that the project's leadership is in full support of the project tracking principles discussed—and that they are committed to enforce them. Teach the PTT and other project members what is expected of them. Then demonstrate the discipline—*one day at a time*—required to stay in control. Nobody said it would be easy or simple. On the contrary, there is a tremendous amount of skill and discipline required. But it *can* be done!

6

Planning for Quality

Quality has become so important to the consumer that if your company does not provide "quality" software products (and services), it will be short-lived. Look around you today for the companies that were on top just 10, five, even one year ago and try to find many of them today.

For almost all of us, our company's survival is increasingly dependent on providing quality products; if we don't, there is always someone out there who is more than willing to oblige. Competition has never been so fierce and prolific—and it continues to accelerate.

"But," you say, "we all know what quality is and we are delivering it the best we can. You can't ask for more." I'm not! Your customers are!

The problem, simply stated, is that many companies, big and small, still do *not* seem to understand what quality is. If they did, they would not be losing ground to their competition and behaving toward their customers the way they do. Unfortunately, quality still means different things to many people. Figure 6.1 lists some examples of definitions of quality—of which *none* addresses the essence of what quality is.

 Lesson: If you want to provide a quality product, you first have to know what quality is.

Quality is *providing a product that satisfies the customer.* Furthermore, quality is definable, measurable, and attainable. This chapter provides you with a better understanding of what quality really is, and will explain:

- How to define quality
- How to measure quality

181

> ■ Quality is the result of doing the best you can.
>
> ■ Quality is a subjective thing that cannot be defined and, therefore, can be viewed differently from one day to the next.
>
> ■ Quality is a bureaucratic thing; that is, it is an attempt by management to tell the real workers in an organization how to do their job with the effect of slowing them down.
>
> ■ Quality is building and delivering a product within cost and on time.
>
> ■ Quality is delivering a product that conforms to the product specifications.

Figure 6.1   Definitions of quality—all unsatisfactory.

- How to plan for a quality software development process to *do it right the first time*
- How to drive toward an expected level of quality
- How to fine-tune the quality process along the way
- How to recognize and encourage the achievement of quality goals

A Project Tale

The bitterness of poor quality lingers long after the sweetness of meeting schedules is forgotten.

Quality addresses both building the *right product* and building the *product right*. This scenario focuses on building the *product right*—an area that most organizations can improve upon radically. Follow this scenario and see if you can spot the problems. These problems collectively undermine any chance of predicting whether the outcome will be a quality product.

The project is three months old. Both the product requirements and the product objectives are written and approved. The writing of the product specifications is under way, as is the high-level design. The project is two-thirds staffed. The schedules are defined, committed, and *aggressive*. In other words, the project is off to a "normal" start.

Various groups within the project—designers, developers, testers, product publications writers, and so on—have met twice now to better define the roles among the groups. The activities that each group must perform have never been defined clearly. Since most of the players have had experience from other projects, many just assume that everyone knows what to expect. Someone in this latest meeting comments to the others that, although most of the people have prior project experience, few people worked on the same project. This individual suggests that his perception of each group's activities within the project might not match the perceptions of others. He concludes that perhaps the precise activities, deliverables, and expectations from each group should be listed to ensure no surprises appear later.

Another person speaks up. "On an ideal project where there is plenty of time to do what's 'right' that would be fine, but I don't have hours to spend on this."

A third person declares: "The checks and balances are obvious. For example, before the test group accepts the code for testing, it will run a set of 'acceptance test scripts' to help ensure that the code meets minimum conditions for entering the test."

A developer in the room, upon hearing this, requests that she be given these test scripts so she can check for those conditions as part of her own tests. The test person agrees to this. The meeting rambles on a bit longer and then adjourns. Many of the participants have an uncomfortable feeling—a haunting feeling—that something's not right. No one seems to communicate this feeling openly. (Could it be that the trusted instincts are raising a red flag?)

Two months pass. The product specifications are now completed and approved. The product's high-level design, however, has several more weeks of inspection activity. Each of the many design inspections has a different person, called a **moderator,** leading and controlling the inspection meeting. For some inspections, people from many different groups have been invited to participate, while conspicuously few are invited to others. Someone who happened to be invited to two separate inspections observed that they were conducted very differently. Each seemed to uncover a similar number of major problems, yet only one of the inspections resulted in the moderator failing the inspection and requesting rework and a reinspection.

The high-level design inspection period finally ends. It is estimated that about 70 percent of the total high-level design was actually inspected. By some, this is considered a notable achievement, even though the goal had originally been set at 100 percent.

The project continues relatively on course into the low-level design activity. Overall, the project schedules have been missed by about two to three weeks, but that is considered "normal." Also considered normal is the pressure that everyone feels not only to prevent the schedules from slipping further but to attempt to regain some of the lost schedule time.

Another month passes and the project is midway into performing low-level design inspections. There is a replay of the inconsistently moderated inspections that were "normal" during the high-level design activity. Also, an estimated 40 percent of the low-level design escapes inspection. At the start of the low-level design activity, a decision was made to forgo inspections of any design developed from the more experienced programmers, as well as the design for the simpler modules of the product, regardless of the experience level of the authoring programmer. Even so, a 60 percent inspection coverage is considered acceptable by the project's leadership. Project schedules slip another week, but it is perceived that the slippage would have been worse had an attempt been made to inspect all of the low-level design as originally intended at the start of the project.

Coding is under way. A small number of programmers have requested inspections for their code. In all cases there is a less-than-expected turnout at the code inspections. Several of the programmers coding some of the more complicated areas of the product were hoping to, as one put it, "invest some time now to prevent a lot of potential rework later." These programmers believe that, as they progress through the design and coding activities, many assumptions are made that relate to the interpretation of the product specifications as well as to the internal design and interfaces of other related areas of the product. These programmers were hoping to verify all assumptions during the code inspections. Unfortunately, they feel that the code inspections did not accomplish their objectives.

Three months later, the code is completed and the unit and function tests are now the primary activities. The project is six weeks behind schedule. Many programmers, in an effort to recover some of the schedule, skip unit test and directly proceed to function test. Several programmers express concern that this omission of a vital test will cause additional problems to be found during function test and beyond. These programmers additionally explain that this test omission may further perpetuate the erosion of schedules. The reason: A problem discovered during function testing of one person's code might in turn affect the progress of many other programmers and testers since the code begins to be integrated during function test.

After some thought, the project head decides, "This is business as usual and is the best way I know to try to recover some of the schedule slip. After all, the final product delivery date has been communicated and committed to higher management." He goes on to say "We will just have to work harder during function test to remove those problems that would have been found during unit test." Testing continues.

Another three months pass. Function test is declared completed. Two weeks have been recovered from the schedules, largely due to the omission of unit test. The project leadership's hopes for recovering more schedule time increases. The function-tested code is delivered to the independent test group. The test group had indicated earlier in the software development process that a set of acceptance test scripts will be run. If the test scripts run successfully, the code will be accepted and independent testing will begin officially. If not accepted, the code must be reworked and the acceptance test rerun. The acceptance test scripts are run—and quickly fail. Someone then remembers that the developers had requested an early look at the acceptance test scripts so they could be pretested. Unfortunately, the request was not part of a formal agreement or part of the exit conditions for function test. Consequently, in the heat of trying to complete function test, the developers felt there was no great need to exercise the tests. With "loose" conditions to start independent testing, the project's leadership declares victory and officially recognizes the start of the independent test period.

The acceptance test scripts continue to be run to ensure that the code is reasonably stable. The test scripts require nearly two weeks of test time before the code begins to show signs of stability. Someone mentions aloud, "I wonder what the 'quality' of the code is? Will we get through the remainder of independent testing smoothly?"

Another person counters, "Your guess is as good as any, but I wouldn't bank on it." No one seems to know what to expect.

Independent testing uncovers a rash of problems. To some, the quantity and type of problems being found seem to be in the realm of reasonableness—based on past experiences. But several others observe that many of these problems could have been discovered during design and code inspections, unit test, and even function test. A tester mutters, "If only there had been a condition that the function test plan must be reviewed and approved before the function test could start."

Another tester replies, "I just wish the design and code inspections had been better defined and enforced."

Midway through independent testing, an analysis of the problems that have been discovered shows that several modules in the product have a higher problem rate than others. A meeting is convened to evaluate what action, if any, should be pursued. The meeting participants represent the project's leadership. The group is divided about the direction to take. One side feels that design and code of the error-prone modules should be inspected and reworked as necessary. The other side feels that most of the problems probably have already been discovered and that any rework of modules would only introduce new problems. The project head makes the final decision: "There will be no reworking of modules. We cannot afford any further delays on this project. Time is money. We have committed to senior management to announce the product next week. Along with that announcement, we will also announce when the product will be available. I don't want any more delays."

One week passes and the product is announced. Three months later, independent testing finally is completed. The product begins to be packaged—*four times*—for delivery. The product had to be recalled from packaging three times to correct newly discovered problems. The original schedule was missed by four months. The product was announced on time but was not shipped on the announced ship date. Instead, a token few were shipped to satisfy the more outspoken customer requests. All of these token shipments had to be replaced with later, repackaged versions.

After another six months, the scenario develops into this.

During the first six months after the product was delivered to customers, an "unexpectedly" large number of problems was reported. The problems seem to be concentrated in several modules, the same modules that were earlier determined to be error-prone. Members of the team assigned to maintain the product find themselves overworked and making trade-offs, just like those before them. The trade-offs are balanced on the side of schedules rather than quality. After all, quality is subjective, isn't it?

Quality Defined

We all have heard a lot about quality in recent years and the subject continues to receive front-page attention. (Who is not interested in quality?) Definitions abound. But what really is quality?

To understand quality, you need several things:

- A customer
- A problem or need to be satisfied
- A product (or service)

If a product performs as needed and expected, and satisfies its customer, then it is said to be a quality product. The key phrase is "satisfies its customer." Let's look at an example.

> The members of a software development shop define a product—via a product specifications document—that they perceive will meet the needs and expectations of a customer. They build the product to conform exactly to the product specifications. The product's costs are within budget and the schedules are all met. The development of the product went unusually smoothly and there were far less problems encountered than on past development projects. The members of the development shop are beaming with pride over their achievement. They deliver the product to the customer, but the customer is not satisfied.

 Lesson: Always strive to see quality through the customer's eyes.

Is the product considered a quality product? No. Because the customer, who is the ultimate judge of whether or not the product is "fit to use," has judged the product to be unacceptable. The message here is that it is not enough to build the product right, the *right product* must be built—and the right product is judged through the customer's eyes.

 Lesson: Quality is centered around satisfying the customer.

The factors that affect the "quality" of a product are all centered around *satisfying the customer*. The product must satisfy the customer's problems and needs, and it must meet the customer's expectations. The expectations cover a broad area such as function, cost, minimal defects, reliability, good level of service, competitiveness, and so on. The key? Satisfy the customer.

Are you surprised to see the customer's cost as a quality variable? Think about this: Customers will purchase and stay with products with which they are the most satisfied—and as consumers, we all know the importance of cost when we make a decision to acquire a product. You cannot have satisfied customers if you don't have customers; therefore, cost plays into the overall quality equation.

Notice that competition is another factor when defining quality—and a constantly moving target, at that. You might have the most popular product today and the most satisfied customers, but if competitive products emerge that markedly reduce your market share, then it can be said that your "quality" is not what it use to be or needs to be. Remember, quality is judged primarily through the customer's eyes; when customers abandon your product for others, your product no longer is satisfying.

 Lesson: Quality applies to the life of a product and covers all aspects of a product.

As you can see, quality is something that applies not just when the product is being built and delivered to a customer initially; quality applies for the life of the product and covers all its aspects. Does this definition of quality leave you feeling that it is elusive and perhaps just too broad a subject to grasp and deal with? Relax. Although building a quality product requires some thoughtful work, it is definable, measurable, and attainable.

There are two primary objectives to meet in the pursuit of building a quality product.

1. Build the right product—a product-related statement.
2. Build the product right—a process-related statement.

The upcoming sections will describe how to obtain these objectives.

Building the Right Product

 Lesson: The customer is the ultimate judge of whether you have built a quality product or not.

There is only one place you can go to know whether you are building the right product: the customer. You can build the neatest "flidget" in all the world, but if customers aren't satisfied with it, it does not pass the test of quality.

So how do you go about building the right product? Using the software development process defined in Chapter 1 as the base, there are four primary actions to take, as shown in Figure 6.2. Each action is discussed.

Action 1.   Product Requirements: Understand the Customer's Problems and Needs

The first action is described in Chapter 8. This action requires you to focus on what the customer really wants and needs to be satisfied. It does not focus on the solution to the customer's problems and needs; that will come later.

1 Product requirements:
Understand the customer's problems and needs.

2 Product objectives:
Define the high-level solution.

3 Product specifications:
Define the detailed solution.

4 Ongoing customer involvement:
Validate customer requirements.

Figure 6.2   Actions in building the "right" product.

Never assume that you understand your customer's problems and needs if you have not worked closely with him or her for this purpose. You will learn a lot from your customers—and your customers will learn a lot by discussing their problems and needs. The result of this action is a product requirements document that describes the problems and needs to be addressed. Moreover, documenting this information greatly helps you to articulate what you think your customers are asking for.

After the product requirements have been written, they must be reviewed by the customer (or a subset of customers if there are many). The product requirements also must be reviewed (and approved) by areas of your organization that will play a key role in developing, distributing, and supporting the eventual product that will satisfy the requirements. Now is the right time, at the very start of the software development process, to force any important issues to surface that might otherwise be overlooked, incorrectly assumed, or discovered late in the project. Another great benefit of creating and obtaining agreement on the product requirements is that the product requirements document will provide a tangible means against which to validate the solution that will be proposed later.

Action 2.   Product Objectives: Define the High-Level Solution

The second action, as shown in Figure 6.2, is to define a high-level solution that satisfies the problems and needs identified in the product requirements document. This action is described in Chapter 9. Armed with knowledge of the problems and needs that the customer must have satisfied, the proposed solution is described in a relatively small document called the product objectives.

As with the product requirements document, the customer reviews the product objectives document to help ensure that the solution being proposed will indeed satisfy him or her. The product objectives also are reviewed (and approved) by those areas of the organization that will participate in building, distributing, and supporting the proposed product.

Action 3.   Product Specifications: Define the Detailed Solution

The third action, to define the proposed product in detail, is described in Chapter 10. By now you should feel good with the ongoing communications between you and your customer (and you and the rest of your organization). To have reached Action 3, both the product requirements and the product objectives have been defined and agreed to. Now you are ready to define the product in detail in the product specifications document.

This is the first time the customer will see the proposed product completely described. He or she should review the document carefully, and problems identified should be resolved. The impacted areas of the organization also must review (and approve) the product specifications document to ensure its contents satisfy their needs.

Some of the important benefits that result from employing the first three actions shown in Figure 6.2 are:

- The customer's problems and needs are reasonably understood by both you and the customer.

- The initial proposed solution has been blessed by the customer, with any identified problems resolved *before* the detailed proposal is fully defined.

- The detailed proposed solution has been blessed by the customer, with any identified problems resolved *well before* most of development and testing of the proposed product has occurred.

As Chapter 11 reveals, by the time that the product specifications have been agreed upon, the prime opportunity for prototyping a portion of the proposed solution should have been exploited. The use of a **prototype,** particularly with customer involvement, provides an additional and powerful tool in helping to ensure that the product to be developed will satisfy the customer.

Action 4.   Ongoing Customer Involvement: Validate Customer Requirements

 Lesson: Expect the product requirements to evolve throughout the software development process.

It is important, *throughout the software development process*, to continue to validate that the proposed product will be satisfactory to the customer after it is completed and ready for delivery. No matter how certain the customer appeared in blessing the product requirements, product objectives, and product specifications, expect the product requirements to evolve. This will happen primarily for three reasons: second thoughts, new technology, and competition. Of course, the longer the development cycle, the larger the volume of requirements changes that are likely to occur.

Second thoughts will surface as the customer has more time to think about the proposed product. Moreover, changing business conditions also can fuel the flames of second thoughts. If you are concerned that involving the customer at strategic points in your software development process will open Pandora's box for a flurry of requirements changes, consider this: Before you begin to involve the customer, document an understanding that says you may not be able to afford accepting requirements changes unless he or she is willing to pay for the extra expense. Of course, if you are building a product for many customers, only the critical requirements changes may be adopted—these are changes that most customers will need before they will perceive the product to be acceptable.

 Lesson: It is always better to know your customer satisfaction problems early than to discover them late—perhaps too late.

If you decide *not* to involve the customer because you fear he or she will only get in the way and slow things down, *beware!* You are far better off knowing what the customer's problems are early in the software development process than to wait until the product is already built and then discover that the customer is not satisfied. Most problems can be corrected at a fraction of their postdelivery cost if they are addressed early in the software development process.

New technology also can be a cause for requirements to change, especially if the new technology can have an immediate positive impact on the operations of an enterprise. And *competition?* Competition is perhaps the greatest thorn for a software development shop. If the competition just announced and made available a product that has all the function of your product (plus more) and at a lower price, you may find your product requirements changing quickly and perhaps radically.

How can a customer become involved during the software development process, other than through the first three actions we have already addressed? There are many ways. Let's look at a few of the more popular approaches.

- Usability testing

Chapter 11 describes a number of activities in which a customer can be included. These activities include usability walkthroughs of the product specifications and again after the product has been low-level designed and coded; usability testing with a prototype; and usability testing with real running code and user publications.

- Participative development

Participative development is including one or more of the customer's employees in the development and/or testing of customer-interested areas of the new product. These areas may be as general as testing the overall operation of the product or as specific as testing the installibility of the product or defining the algorithm for accessing data bases in time-sensitive applications. Knowledge of the customer's operations and even including customerlike databases while testing can be invaluable in helping to ensure the product will satisfy the customer.

- Early delivery drivers

As portions of the product are available for testing, these drivers can be provided to the customer, who can use them for a number of purposes: verifying that the requirements satisfied in the product specifications have been properly addressed in the running code and early user documentation; validating that the original requirements were indeed correct and the product is "fit to use"; providing product testing while also training employees on the new product; and exercising the product distribution and support processes.

- Partnership

By including the customer as a partial or full partner in the development and/or launch of the new product, you are certain to build a product that he or she will view as satisfactory. If the product is intended for many customers, then partnering with one or more will help ensure the product satisfies the wants and needs of the intended customer set.

 Lesson: Make your customer a part of your software development process . . . and beyond.

Remember, quality is viewed through the customer's eyes. To increase significantly the likelihood that the new product will be viewed as a *quality* product, customers must be included in the software development process.

 Lesson: Quality demands continuous attention for the life of the product.

Because quality applies for the life of a product, you also must focus on customer involvement *after* the product has been delivered. It is important to know if the product is operating satisfactorily, if it remains competitive, if the support being offered is satisfactory, and so on. Remember, if you ease up on your attention to ensuring that your product is a quality product—and that it remains that way—your competitors will gladly demonstrate their interest in winning over your customer.

Building the Product Right

As stated earlier, the first pursuit in building a quality product is to *build the right product*. Building the right product is all about understanding the customer's problems to be solved and needs to be addressed. This information is presented in the product requirements document. The product objectives and product specifications documents then are developed to propose a product that will satisfy the product requirements. After the customer has agreed to these documents, a software development organization can feel reasonably assured that the *right* product is defined. Building the right product is a *product-related* focus.

The other objective in the pursuit of building a quality product is to *build that product right;* that is, follow a software development process that offers a way to measure the conformance of the emerging product to the product specifications. The process used also must ensure that the development of the product cannot pass from one phase or activity to the next until certain conditions are met. Building the product right is a *process-related* focus.

Let's look at an example. Before the product passes from the development test phase to the independent test phase, certain exit and entry conditions must be satisfied.

- Development test exit conditions:
  - —All *major* problems have been corrected in the code.
  - —All remaining problems have a committed plan to be resolved.
- Independent test entry conditions:
  - —The test plan for the independent test (component test) has been approved.
  - —The independent test *acceptance test scripts* have run successfully.
  - —All independent testing scripts are written, inspected, debugged to the degree possible, and ready to be run.

If any of these process-related conditions are not satisfied, the product should not progress to the next phase of the software development process until the necessary recoveries are made. Otherwise, problems that were expected to be solved in earlier phases will be passed to succeeding phases and show up as an increase to the planned workload. This situation will invalidate the basic project planning of people, duration of activities, and so on, that went into laying out the project's schedules, resources, and costs. If participants continuously waive the fundamental need for all process conditions to be met, a project's activities will become uncontrolled and its schedules unpredictable.

How do the members of a project define the approach to use in building the product right? A recommended technique is through the use of a quality plan. Read on.

The Quality Plan

> *It is much less expensive to prevent errors than to rework, scrap, or service them.*
> —*Philip B. Crosby, American author, lecturer on quality*

A **quality plan** is a document that can be used to define, track, and measure product quality goals throughout the software development process. It requires the project's leadership consciously to think about quality goals early in the software development process. The quality plan is *the* roadmap for an organization to follow in an attempt to *do it right the first time.* This plan helps to create the projectwide quality culture desirable. The primary focus of the quality plan is process-related; that is, building the product right. However, you can choose also to address the product-related aspect: building the right product.

The quality plan should be written and approved before the product specifications and the high-level design are completed. Figure 6.3 illustrates the optimal point in the software development process for the creation and approval of the quality plan. Because process-related information for the product objectives and the start of

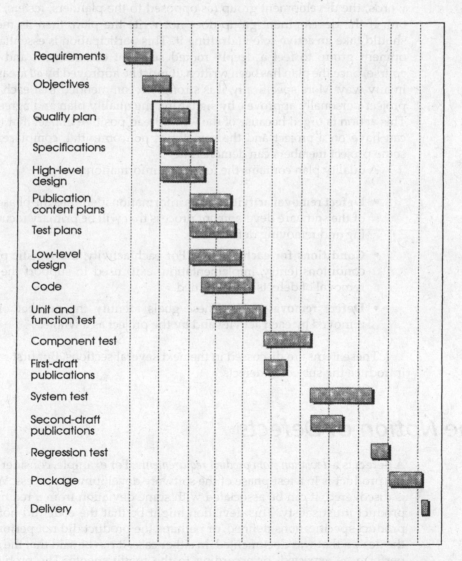

Figure 6.3   The quality plan in the software development process.

the product specifications and high-level design activities must be defined and agreed to *before* the quality plan is approved, these topics can be addressed separately at the start of the project or in a "standard" project document that applies to all projects of an organization.

 Lesson: Each member of a project must express a commitment to the quality plan.

Can any organization write the quality plan? Yes, but the preferred group to write the plan is the one that has the most "skin" in its implementation—in other words, the development group (as opposed to the planners, testers, writers, and so on). If the development group does not write the plan, then its members at least should take an active role in drafting it. This participation is essential for the development group to feel a deeply rooted sense of commitment and ownership. Of course, once the plan has been written, it must be approved by *all* areas that it impacts in any way. More specifically, it is strongly recommended that each member of the project personally approves, by signature, the quality plan and agrees to support it. This action is urged because of the widespread positive impact that the quality plan can have on a project and the sometimes noncommittal, complacent attitude that some project members can demonstrate.

A quality plan contains the following information:

- **Defect removal activities:** This information identifies the phases and activities of the software development process that will be primary focus areas for finding and removing defects.

- **Conditions for each activity:** For each activity, the specific process-oriented conditions (entry, implementation, exit) used to support the discovery and removal of defects are identified.

- **Defect removal goals:** These goals identify the number of defects to be removed by each activity and by the project as a whole.

These items are discussed in the next several sections. But first it is important to introduce the subject of defects.

The Notion of Defects

A **defect** is a *deviation from product requirements*. For example, consider a case in which the product is in a test phase of the software development process. When a problem is discovered, it can be associated with some deviation from a requirement that the product must satisfy. This deviation might be that the code did not operate as the product specifications defined, or perhaps the product did not perform according to the design that was documented. In either case, it can be said that the product did not perform as expected, or according to the requirements. The problem is therefore labeled as a defect.

Two Goals

Two goals of all software development processes are:

1. To remove as many defects as is *reasonably* possible before the product is delivered to a customer.

2. To remove as many of these defects as *early* in the software development process as possible.

As a product is being defined, designed, and coded, the developers inadvertently introduce errors, called defects. Defects discovered and corrected during the software development process obviously will not be found later by a customer. Therefore, the more defects that can be found during the software development process, the fewer defects that will remain in the product when it is delivered to the customer.

Accelerating Costs

 Lesson: It is far less expensive to discover and fix defects early in the software development process than later.

The cost of identifying and correcting a defect early in the software development process is less than the cost of correcting that same problem later in the cycle. In fact, the cost increases with each subsequent development phase or activity that is entered. This message is so important to comprehend, it bears an example.

Visualize that you are involved in the development of an application that performs a very large number of file reads and writes. At an inspection of your low-level design, a defect is discovered in the algorithm that manages the file reads and writes as well as in the allocation of memory required to hold the file records. After the inspection, you:

- Rework the algorithm to correct the defect.
- Verify the solution with several peers.

Say that this took you two full days. Had this defect gone undetected until the code inspection, the rework might have affected several hundred lines of code. The cost could then be a week, required to:

- Rework the algorithm to correct the defect.
- Verify the solution with several peers.
- Recode the affected portion of the program.
- Reinspect the code to ensure the proper coding implementation of the design.

Now suppose this defect had been found during component test. The cost to the project is now much greater. In addition to the week of rework that was required when the defect was discovered in a code inspection, there are now these additional costs:

- Assistance of the tester to re-create the alleged defect.
- Isolation of the exact cause of the defect within the application, possibly requiring several developers to locate the problem.
- Dedicated machine time to support the debugging.
- Blocking of additional test scripts from being run.
- Retest the fix to verify the defect has been corrected.

These activities easily could represent the equivalent of yet another person-week or more of costs to the product. The message?

Find and remove defects *early.*

This is accomplished by defining the process to be followed for each phase or activity of the software development process and by getting all participants to agree to follow that process. If these *process conditions* are met, it can be said that the development of the product followed a *quality process.*

Defect Removal Activities

Figure 6.4 illustrates how the product phases, along with their more significant activities, can be defined. The activities have been selected based on their ability to yield major gains in removing defects. Note that other activities could be examined for the removal of defects (such as writing and reviewing publications, inspecting test scripts, or inspecting the module/link build process). However, the list of activities in the figure includes many of the "heavy hitters" and therefore is sufficient for illustrative purposes. Most of these activities are introduced in Chapter 1. However, three activities need to be clarified further here:

- High-level design inspections
- Low-level design inspections
- Code inspections

These activities share an important element—inspections. An **inspection** typically consists of the following:

A group of peers meets to inspect the design or code of a fellow peer. The data to be inspected (document, design, code) are distributed to the inspection participants a few days before the inspection meeting. This allows them time to study the data and attend the inspection prepared to ask questions and identify suspected

Product phase	Activity (source of defects)
Requirements	Product requirements document
Definition	Product objectives document Product specifications document
Design	High-level design inspection Low-level design inspection
Code	Code inspection
Development test	Unit test plan Unit test Function test plan Function test
Independent test	Component test plan Component test System test plan System test Regression test plan Regression test

Figure 6.4   Activities to be measured.

defects. A moderator controls the meeting and logs all the defects that are identified as well as any questions that cannot be answered immediately. At the end of the meeting, the moderator declares that the inspection has either passed or failed. After the inspection meeting, a report summarizing the defects and questions is prepared and distributed. All unresolved defects and unanswered questions are tracked to ensure that they are resolved satisfactorily. If the inspection failed, a reinspection must occur.

At this point you probably have a general understanding of each of the activities shown in Figure 6.4. If not, you might want to review Chapter 1.

Conditions for Each Activity

Before specific conditions for each activity are identified, the first order of business is to understand the *need* to define the process conditions for each activity. Again, an example of activities to focus upon is illustrated in Figure 6.4.

The activity model shown in Figure 6.5 depicts a way to view an activity. (This model was introduced in Chapter 1, Figure 1.1, and reprinted here for convenience.) In order to perform an activity, there must be input upon which the activity is dependent. For example, the "function test" activity requires the function test plan to be completed and approved before function testing can begin. Those elements that must be in place before an activity can be implemented are called entry conditions.

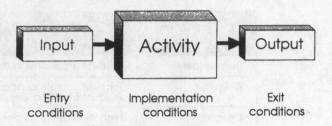

Entry   Implementation   Exit
conditions   conditions   conditions

Figure 6.5   Activity model.

Each activity has implementation conditions. These are process conditions that help define how the activity will be implemented. For example, implementation conditions for the "function test plan" activity include a test plan that must have both a review and an approval phase. Another example: A meeting with all the approvers must be scheduled at the end of the review phase and at the end of the approval phase. Since there are many ways to implement an activity, these implementation conditions serve to bring order and efficiency in completing the activity.

Before an activity can be considered complete, certain things must occur. These are called exit conditions. For example, the "function test" activity requires that all function test scripts have run successfully.

Benefits

After all the entry, implementation, and exit conditions of each activity are defined, they must then be tracked and adhered to. These conditions serve several useful purposes in a product development shop. In particular, they:

- Provide measurement criteria
- Force communications between groups
- Raise the quality consciousness level of the project

 Lesson: Each activity of the software development process should have entry, implementation, and exit conditions defined.

Process measurement criteria often are viewed as being subjective and, therefore, difficult to define and follow. Consequently, some projects may tend not to employ enough staff to address this area of a project. Such projects are more inclined to focus on the traditional, tangible areas of coding (measuring progress by counting the lines of code written) and testing (measuring progress by counting the number of test scripts that have run successfully). However, the larger the project, the greater the need is to focus on the process aspects of *each* activity, not just the traditional ones. The saying "If you don't know where you are going, then how will you know when you arrive?" applies nicely here. By having and applying measurement criteria at the entry and exit points of each activity, a heretofore subjective concept becomes an objective reality that can be measured readily.

 Lesson: The owner of an activity is responsible for ensuring that any dependencies on others are defined and agreed to.

To some, the term *force communications* might sound rather aggressive and unfriendly. However, the truly unfriendly act is *not* communicating. For example, if you are responsible for the implementation of an activity, then you first must make certain that all the entry conditions for your activity have been completed before you can start. If an entry condition is an activity that is owned by another person (or group), then you must communicate that dependency to that person. Then both parties must agree mutually on what exactly is being delivered and on what schedule. This situation conveniently forces groups to communicate early in the software development process and avoids uncomfortable and costly problems later. Now everyone knows precisely what is expected of them, and by whom and when.

Quality is something that everyone wants but many do not know how to achieve. With a clear definition of the activities and their entry and exit conditions, the project members in the trenches get a strong signal from the project's leadership that quality is more than a word. It is defined and it is practiced. When quality is understood, it becomes contagious, and similar measurements are developed for other aspects of a project.

Once the concept of entry, implementation, and exit conditions is accepted, the next step is to apply this concept to each of the project's activities that have been identified for measurement. This preplanning will later facilitate the discovery and removal of defects from each activity.

The following examples are provided only to illustrate the type of entry, implementation, and exit conditions that can be defined for a given activity. The conditions illustrated are not an exhaustive list. You might want to choose different conditions for the activities in your project.

Example 1. The Product Objectives Document

Process conditions for the product objectives document could be:

- Entry conditions:
    - —The project must be funded or management approved.
    - —Product requirements document distributed for review or approval.
- Implementation conditions:
    - —There will be a review draft.
    - —The contents of the review draft will be 90 percent complete before it is distributed for general review.

—The contents of the approval draft will be 100 percent complete and will address all problems logged against the review draft.

—There will be a meeting of the document owner and all approvers at the end of both the review and the approval phases. (The purpose is to reduce miscommunications of problems and to help the owner to better understand the problems reported. Also, these meetings allow many problems to be resolved on the spot.)

—All problems discovered from the review draft and the approval draft must be recorded and tracked to closure. The answers also must be recorded. All approvers should receive the total problem/answer list.

- Exit conditions:

—The approval draft must be approved by the people or organizations that are the recognized approvers.

If these conditions are met, a minimum number of defects will be passed along to the next activity: product specifications. Notice that no mention has been made of the topics that must be addressed in the product objectives document. It is assumed that the topics already are defined in some *standards-related document* within the project or other acceptable approach. (Chapter 9 identifies information that should be addressed in the product objectives document.)

Example 2.   The Product Specifications Document

The second example is the product specifications document. Process conditions for this document are almost identical to those for the objectives document. Exceptions might include these implementation conditions:

- The approval draft cannot be distributed and approved until after the product objectives document is approved.

- The product specifications cannot be approved until 100 percent of the high-level design has been completed.

The percentages used for some of these requirements can be arbitrary, based on variables such as the type and complexity of the product being built. But you will find it constructive and productive to strive for specific percentages as a way to both drive and measure progress.

Example 3.   Low-Level Design Inspections

The third example is for low-level design inspections. Process conditions might be:

- Entry conditions:

—The low-level design for any portion of the product cannot begin unless the corresponding high-level design has completed an inspection successfully.

—An inspection must have a trained moderator.

—The documents to be inspected must be in the following format (. . .) and must address the following items: performance, memory/DASD storage requirements, messages and return codes, and so on.

—The *design package* to be inspected must be distributed for review at least three working days before the inspection.

—If any of the required participants fails to attend the inspection, the inspection is canceled and rescheduled.

- Implementation requirements:

  —During an inspection meeting, the moderator is responsible for:

  Recording all major problems (defects) found.

  Recording all minor problems (defects) found.

  Declaring that the inspection passed or failed. (If an inspection fails, a reinspection is required and must be scheduled.)

- Exit requirements:

  —All major defects discovered must be resolved and the design documentation appropriately updated.

Other activities that would follow similar conditions are high-level design inspections and code inspections. When all the inspections of an activity—in this example, low-level design—have been completed, consideration can be given to issuing a composite inspection report summarizing all the data from the individual inspection reports. This overall picture gives a clear view of the progress made and problems encountered.

If all guidelines for conducting an inspection are not documented already somewhere in the project, they could be listed here in the quality plan.

Example 4.   Component Test

Consider one more example: component test. The process conditions for component test might be:

- Entry conditions:

  —Function test has been completed successfully.

  —Component test's acceptance test scripts have run successfully.

  —All major defects found during function test have been corrected in the code.

—A committed plan must be in place to resolve all minor defects discovered in function test.

—A review draft of each product publication is available.

—The component test plan has been approved.

- Implementation conditions:

    —Weekly test reports must be issued to selected groups. These reports must focus on:

    Planned and *actual* progress for test scripts attempted and run successfully, and number of problems reported.

    Type of problems discovered.

    Severity of problems discovered.

    Response time to fix different severities of problems discovered.

- Exit conditions:

    —All test scripts have been run successfully.

    —All major defects discovered have been corrected in the code.

    —A committed plan to resolve all minor defects discovered in component test is in place.

 Lesson: Defining and enforcing entry, implementation, and exit conditions for each activity helps in tracking the project's progress and in maintaining control.

The process conditions given in these four examples might not be strict enough for some projects or might be too strict for others. Whatever process conditions you choose for the activities of your project, it is important that they be enforced. If the project's leadership is not serious about their enforcement, then do not bother to define them. But a note of caution: If a quality process is not defined for the project, the cost of producing a quality product will most assuredly increase. This increased cost will result from rework due to vague or nonexistent entry, implementation, and exit conditions for project activities. Also, with no defined quality process, knowing when you have achieved a quality product will be more difficult.

Defect Removal Goals

It is better to aim at perfection and miss than it is to aim at imperfection and hit it.
—*Thomas J. Watson, Jr., American past president*
and chairman of IBM Corporation

Including a section on *defect removal goals* in the quality plan is optional. That is, although it is an exercise that offers some benefit, it is not required to ensure the development of a quality product. If all the recommendations discussed up to this point in this chapter are addressed in a quality plan and implemented within the project, a strong foundation will exist for an acceptable quality process. A section on defect removal goals offers a bonus to the already defined quality process. This section offers a methodology for anticipating the number of defects that must be identified and removed from each designated activity in order to deliver a product with a predetermined, preapproved number of undiscovered defects. In other words, to ensure that a product will be judged acceptable by customers, the product owner, working with the customer, can estimate how many undiscovered defects can be delivered with the product. From this number, the maintenance and support costs also can be projected.

A popular method used to describe defects in a product is to reference their number against the lines of code for the product. The notation for this is *defects per thousand lines of code*, abbreviated as *Defects/KLOC* (pronounced *KAY-LOCK*).

Lines of code sometimes is defined to include comments and prologues. However, in this book, any discussion of lines of code does *not* include comments and prologues. The definition for lines of code includes only the instructions and data declarations that require some logic to create. When the code is tested, it is from the lines of code that problems, also called defects, will be discovered. Defects found in comments and prologues, by definition, will not prevent code from running successfully, since compiled code does not generate executable instructions from comments and prologues.

Many papers and books discuss how to predict the total number of defects/ KLOC that a product can be expected to have from "cradle to grave." The works also show how many of the total defects can be expected to be found and corrected in each phase or activity of the software development process. From this algorithm, a prediction can be made for the number of defects that remain in the final product delivered to the customer. The product owner, working with the customer, must decide if this number of defects will be acceptable. The product owner also must decide if this estimated number of defects will yield an acceptable cost to maintain and support the product after it has been delivered. Once the product owner decides on the number of undiscovered defects that are acceptable to ship with the product, the total-defect algorithm then is adjusted to reflect the number of defects that must be removed at each phase or activity of the software development process.

Although some subjectivity is involved in defining any defect algorithm, the algorithm should be based on past project experiences. Project leaders should have confidence in the methodology before they use it as a planning tool.

The product owner must identify three variables before a defect removal plan can be completed. These variables are listed in Figure 6.6 and described in the next sections.

Delivered Defects

As discussed earlier, the product owner, working with the customer, must determine the number of undiscovered defects that he or she views will yield an acceptable

1. Number of undiscovered defects that will be delivered with the product
2. Total number of defects throughout the life of the product
3. Number of defects that will be removed for each designated activity

Figure 6.6 Three variables to identify for a defect removal plan.

level of quality for delivery to the customer. The number of defects remaining in the product can have a direct impact on its market success. The number also will have a direct impact on the costs required to maintain and support the product. Therefore, the product manager is motivated to remove defects throughout the development of the product.

But there is another side to this issue. Each defect removed from the product carries with it a cost. Time and, therefore, real dollars are involved in discovering defects. Examples are preparing a design or code inspection package, reviewing the package, conducting the inspection, following up with an inspection report, and so on. Each discovered problem carries considerable overhead, not only in the actual discovery of the problem, but in the rework and retest activities that must follow. If the requirement is to deliver a product with 100 percent of the defects removed, then the product might not sell. The selling price would have to be prohibitively high to recover the steep development costs. On the other hand, if a product is riddled with defects, customers soon will abandon it—and even if they continue to use it, the maintenance and support costs can eventually sink it.

The product owner must find a balance between product costs and customer satisfaction. One such balance is revealed in the defect quality goal defined. For purposes of illustration, assume this goal is set at .1 defect/KLOC. This means a product that contains 100,000 lines of code is to be delivered with no more than 10 defects. Stated another way, no more than 10 unique defects will ever be reported during the field life of this product. These 10 defects are unknown at the time the product is delivered (with perhaps a few last-minute exceptions). Before a defect removal plan can be completed, the product owner first must identify the estimated number of defects to be delivered with the product.

Total Product Defects

The second variable to identify is the total number of defects that are in the product throughout its life cycle. The life cycle includes both the product development period and the period that the product is in use by the customer. In defining this variable, some homework is required to determine the history of other, similar types of projects. Again, for purposes of illustration, assume the following number of defects: 50 defects/KLOC. This says a product that contains 100,000 lines of code has a total of 5,000 defects that could be discovered throughout its life cycle.

Defects to Be Removed

The third, and last, variable to identify, the number of defects to remove from each designated activity, is really several values—one for each activity. Figure 6.7 provides an example of the number of defects that must be removed from each activity if a product is to be delivered at the defect quality goal of .1 defects/KLOC. The "———" entries for the regression test plan mean that the number of defects expected to be removed is less than .1/KLOC and is therefore insignificant. Figure 6.8 shows more graphically the percentage of defects to be removed from across the product phases. This is only an example and might not be realistic for your project. The number of defects to be removed from each activity would be derived from experience—gained from counting the defects found during similar projects.

If the defect estimates are believed to be reasonable, yet significantly fewer defects were found in a certain activity, then a careful analysis must be made. Perhaps the defect removal process was not very efficient. Or maybe there was incomplete recording of defects. Or maybe the previous activity removed more defects than expected, thus leaving fewer for discovery later. Even the skill level of the programmers can have an affect on both the number of defects that were introduced into the product as well as the number of defects discovered.

Numerous measurement techniques are available for counting defects. For example, defects discovered in a document (such as the product specifications document) might be derived from the following algorithm:

Product phase	Activity (source of defects)	Defects /KLOC	% of total
Requirements	Product requirements document	2.5	5.0
Definition	Product objectives document	3.5	7.0
	Product specifications document	8.5	17.0
Design	High-level design inspection	5.0	10.0
	Low-level design inspection	7.5	15.0
Code	Code inspection	6.4	12.8
Development test	Unit test plan	0.5	1.0
	Unit test	4.5	9.0
	Function test plan	0.5	1.0
	Function test	4.5	9.0
Independent test	Component test plan	0.5	1.0
	Component test	3.5	7.0
	System test plan	0.3	0.6
	System test	2.0	4.0
	Regression test plan	———	———
	Regression test	0.2	0.4
After delivery	Customer-reported problems	0.1	0.2
	Totals	50.0	100.0

Figure 6.7   Defects/KLOC to be removed per activity.

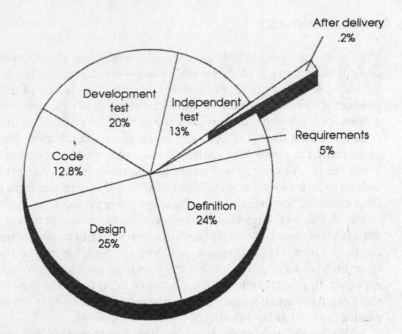

After delivery
.2%

Development
test
20%

Independent
test
13%

Requirements
5%

Code
12.8%

Definition
24%

Design
25%

Figure 6.8   Defects removed from each product phase.

$$\text{Defects/KLOC} = \frac{(\text{major defects} + (\text{medium defects}/3))}{\text{total KLOC for product}}$$

In this formula, major defects are considered to be severe errors or omissions that require entire sections to be written or rewritten. Medium defects are considered to be misleading statements that would cause the reader to draw the wrong conclusion. These statements must be rewritten. If desirable, recommendations and spelling/ grammar items also can be weighted in an algorithm and could be viewed as minor defects; however, avoid spending any appreciable amount of time on trivial defects— this time can take you away from working the more serious problems.

Defects counted from design and code inspections might be only those considered major. Major here means that the design or code implementation is definitely incorrect and would result in a defect being propagated through the software development process.

Any problem found during a test of running code that results in a code change would be counted as a defect. These defects, as well as those found at inspections, would be tracked as:

$$\text{Defects/KLOC} = \frac{\text{problems}}{\text{total KLOC for product}}$$

Again, please note that the values and algorithms used in this section are strictly for illustrative purposes. They might not reflect what is right for your project. A considerable amount of homework must be done to develop a reasonable defect removal model for a product. Once again, it is my view that predicting and then tracking against defect goals is not a requirement for a good quality process. However, the added focus and care involved in removing and counting defects can have a positive influence both on the product and the people developing it. By defining a defect measurement process, the project's leadership can better track where the project has been, where it currently is, and where it is heading.

Quality Improvement Teams

The keynote of progress, we should remember, is not merely doing away with what is bad; it is replacing the best with something better.
—*Edward A. Filene, American retail merchandising pioneer*

The people who make up a project possess a tremendous creative energy that has only to be tapped. It is a frequently accepted assertion that people want to do what is right. All they ask is an environment that gives them the opportunity to participate and that will listen to what they have to offer. Here enters the **quality improvement team.**

Quality improvement teams are called by many different names. Some of the more common labels are *quality circles, quality teams, improvement circles, quality control circles,* and *excellence teams.* The actual name used is not as important as the purpose for the quality improvement team. Simply put, a quality improvement team is *a group of people who meet to solve one or more problems.*

The group usually consists of a small number of participants, say, three to eight, but also can include a larger number of people. In addition to solving one or more problems, the group may meet to identify a list of problems. This list would then be ordered so that the more important problems can be addressed first. The group might meet only once to solve a particular problem, or on a regular basis to take on any problems that come their way. The group might consist of people from the same department or from several departments representing various groups from across a project.

The ground rules for running a team can vary. But one very important ground rule of any quality improvement team is for every team member to be involved. Everyone, without exception, has something to offer. The team leader must allow everyone a chance to be heard and limit criticism to that which is constructive and properly used to support the goals of the team.

 Lesson: To ensure a quality process, it is not enough to fix problems as they are discovered; the process that caused or allowed the problem also must be fixed.

Every organization has its share of problems. How well an organization handles its problems has a direct relationship to its success. For example, when an organization encounters a problem, it should do two things:

1. Fix the problem.
2. Fix the process or thing that caused the problem.

Take a look at two examples.

The communications are considered very poor in this project. Both the test and the product publications people constantly are learning too late about changes that the developers have made to the product specifications. Sometimes the test and publications people are not informed at all. There is a serious concern that the code and product publications will not accurately support one another and that the test scripts will not test all the product functions. As testers and writers discover a new change in product function, they visit the developers to collect the new information. But it is recognized that some process needs to be established to better communicate, and perhaps even control, the changes being made in the product specifications. A quality improvement team is asked to evaluate the problem and recommend a process that will satisfy the project's needs. The final recommendation may be anything from "merge the testers and writers into the development departments that they are supporting" to "define and implement a product specifications change control board."

The product is in its independent test phase. During an analysis of the problems that have been discovered thus far, it was observed that three of the 100 modules that comprise the product have a significantly higher percentage of errors. A quality improvement team is convened to recommend the course of action to be taken. The team identifies several options and then recommends its favorite to the project's leadership. The list of options might include:

- Reinspect the error-prone modules and then redesign, recode, and retest them.
- Leave the modules as they are and predict and anticipate the defects that have yet to be discovered.
- Inspect the test scripts to ensure 100 percent test coverage for the function of these three modules and find the remaining problems that way.
- Pursue some other action.

 Lesson: A quality process can help the project members significantly in meeting their schedule, cost, and quality commitments.

It is almost always the processes within a project that will make the difference between:

- Making or missing schedules
- A productive or a nonproductive project team
- High or low employee morale
- Maintaining or exceeding product costs

Lesson: Quality improvement teams are a great way to endorse and encourage continuous quality improvement within an organization.

The subject of quality improvement teams has been included in this chapter because it has a positive impact on maintaining a quality focus throughout the software development process. Quality improvement teams are great tools for focusing on improving processes within the organization. An added benefit is that people feel more ownership and pride in *change* when they have participated in making it come about. Quality teams also are great tools in focusing on *continuous* improvement, for quality demands nonstop attention.

 Lesson: The project's leadership has the responsibility to lead the charge in ensuring the "quality system" is working.

One last note—this one to the project's leadership. Quality improvements result from project leadership action and support. If the "quality system" is not working, it is your job to lead the charge in fixing it. The easiest way to destroy the desire for quality improvement teams is to ignore the recommendations that you have asked the teams to make. It is not enough to put a recommendation in place. Many acts of change within an organization require ongoing support, tracking, and nurturing to help ensure their success.

Quality Recognition

 Lesson: Subtlety is not a virtue in the world of quality.

If you want to be a winner you must think like a winner. If you want to produce quality then you must think quality. The support and commitment that project leaders demonstrate on quality-related activities have a direct relationship to the employee commitment to quality. Because many people view quality as being largely intangible and subjective, quality must be given an assertive presence—a presence that begins at the highest levels of management. Usually a higher-management commitment is required before any true, sustained progress can be achieved at lower levels. The attitude and behavior an organization demonstrates toward quality is nourished and sustained by the attitude and behavior of higher management.

However, focus for a moment on what project-level leaders can accomplish. The project's leadership must show its commitment and support for quality. Some tried and true approaches are:

- Public recognition
- Quality awards
- Performance evaluations

- Quality day
- Quality plan

Public Recognition

Providing public recognition to a person or a group of people for a noted quality achievement has several benefits. The person(s) receiving the recognition will likely feel a sense of pride for the accomplishment and for the praise from project leaders. This may inspire others to modify their work habits and place a greater emphasis on quality improvement. An added benefit is that the project's leadership demonstrates its commitment to quality.

Quality Awards

Quality awards can be nonmonetary certificates of achievement that a recipient can display on his or her office desk or wall, or a monetary amount can be given, or both. If nonmonetary certificates are the typical tangible form of recognition given, it is suggested that the best of the best be awarded some cash as well. A company can save money and probably even make money when this higher level of attention is paid to quality on the job. Cash awards are not only appreciated but also demonstrate that the project's leadership is willing to share some of the savings with the major contributors. This can be a great incentive. However, when possible, also include the certificate. After the money has been spent, the certificate offers an ongoing reminder of the achievement and, for some, an incentive for the future.

Performance Evaluations

Those who contribute the most should gain the most. Another way to do this is for performance evaluations to give overt note to employees' attention to quality in their everyday duties.

Quality Day

A *quality day*, week, or month is another way to express both project leadership support and commitment. One or more seminars could be scheduled to explain what quality is and how real savings can be accrued from just being persistent and methodical in identifying and removing defects in a project. The more people learn about quality, the more they can plan for achieving progress in their own activities. As Phil Crosby, author of *Quality Without Tears*, has often expressed, "Quality is free." Usually it is less costly to prevent defects or identify and remove them earlier in a software development process than it is to scrap or rework them later.

Quality Plan

I have intentionally ended this section and this chapter with a few more words about the quality plan. There is so much to gain when a project defines its quality goals early and has defined the steps that will be taken to prevent and remove defects. The primary objective is product success, for only then can everyone win. The quality plan is a blueprint for ensuring that the product will be all that it was intended to be. Considering the keen competitiveness that exists in the software arena, can you really afford not to have a quality plan?

7

Managing Priorities Effectively

In every project, there are problems and there are *problems*. Whenever a project's known problems are listed, there are always some that stand out as being urgent. These high-priority problems might change many times throughout the life of the project, but the level of attention they receive will have a major impact on the health of the project. Neglecting these problems for lower-priority problems is like buckling your seat belt at the end of a trip. Some items demand attention first—to ensure a successful journey.

 Lesson: "Drift" occurs on projects whose priorities are not managed well.

If a project's leadership is unable or unwilling to focus the project's resources on solving the most important problems first, then the project and its participants will **drift**—that is, will be diverted from following the most expedient course. Drifting has a serious, negative effect on many areas of the project. These effects include lower productivity, longer schedules, lower morale, lower quality, increased rework, and maybe even the eventual death of the project. The death knell might arrive before the first line of code is written or soon after the final product is delivered to the first customer.

This chapter shows you how to identify and work the most important problems—the priorities—on a project. It explains why working intelligently means a lot more than just working hard. Project success doesn't just happen. For the most part, it is predictable, controllable, and implementable.

A Project Tale

The following scenario describes an example of a project that gets caught up in drift. This drift can cause or accelerate erosion, which can seriously damage the health of a project.

The project is several months into an estimated two-year product development cycle. Many project activities have been started. Among these are the product requirements, product objectives, the product specifications, the project schedule plan, the product design, and even some code. No activities have been completed.

Staffing of project personnel is judged to be 60 percent complete. The project members are uncertain about what, specifically, they are supposed to be accomplishing and when, but this does not stop them from working on tasks they believe must get done anyway. Enthusiasm abounds. Optimism can be seen and felt everywhere.

Two months pass. More activities are started. Seventy percent of staffing has now been completed. The project's leadership is under increased pressure to complete some key activities. The first completed activity is the project schedule plan. Many people feel some relief now that an agreement has been reached on a defined set of schedules. Everyone now knows what activities must be completed and when.

Two more months pass. Almost every activity that has been started is shown to be behind schedule. The code that has been unit and function tested has some serious function and interface problems. The design was not properly inspected, under the excuse that no inspection process has yet been approved. Also, the programmers made assumptions about the contents of the product specifications, but the product specifications have not yet been approved. The approvers of the specifications cannot agree on the full set of product functions, in part because the product objectives also have not been approved. The objectives have been written but have not been approved because the various organizations with approval rights either cannot settle on the precise product to build or fear the current architecture and design assumptions that are being implemented cannot support the full set of product objectives. Furthermore, because a product requirements document has never been completed and approved, it seems impossible for the project's leadership to reach agreement on what the customers' wants and needs really are. It is like a free-for-all where everyone lobbies for what they believe the product should be—and many of the opinions conflict.

The project head declares, "Enough is enough. I want to know the major obstacles to progress in this shop. I want these problems resolved immediately. This logjam must be broken, and broken now."

A list of the major project obstacles is compiled. These problems are then ordered according to priority. An owner is assigned to each of the top 10 problems. The owners are directed to correct their assigned problems by specified dates. Project members feel a mix of apprehension and relief. They are apprehensive about the large number of problems that have been identified and the complexity of some of them. They are relieved because the list appears to be comprehensive and for once the project leaders seem to be working together and gaining some semblance of control.

Another two months pass. The product requirements and product objectives finally are approved. The approval of the product objectives took longer than expected. Because the development organization had already made considerable progress with the product specifications, design, and coding, numerous compromises were made in approving the product objectives. The major challenge was to ensure conformity between the product objectives document and the product specifications document. Unfortunately, the product specifications are now locked in controversy. Agreement cannot be reached on how to resolve several product specifications issues. These issues include the ability to reach agreement on product performance characteristics, the degree of product usability, and some major functional definitions. Those approvers who had been reluctant to approve the product objectives were expecting to have more success in negotiating the content of product specifications. However, because a large portion of the product has already been coded and tested by the development team, it is argued that a functional change at this point would require major rework and further schedule slippages.

Another month passes. The product specifications finally are approved. Significant areas of the code are being reworked to match those changes that were negotiated in the final specifications. The schedules continue to slide. The project's leaders briefly analyze the root causes behind the sliding schedules. The major problems are singled out to be:

- Failure of the project's leadership to resolve major product issues quickly and completely
- Conflicting project priorities, which are further compounded by limited people and equipment resources
- Lack of discipline from the project leaders in meeting their schedule commitments

Some frustration is evident among the project's leadership. One project leader is overheard saying to another, "There just doesn't seem to be enough hours in a day. If only the leadership across this project could reach a consensus on which problems are most important, and if the whole project would unite and support this list of priorities, then the needed project structure and progress would follow."

The decision is made to reset the project schedules and to get a commitment from the project leaders to make the new project schedule plan happen. It is also acknowledged that staffing is significantly behind planned levels. Staffing was expected to be 98 percent complete but is only at 75 percent of expectations. The delay is blamed on the multiple tasks that project leaders have had to focus on and, therefore, the limited time remaining for them to solve other problems. The project leaders are again told to fix this. One project leader confesses to his manager, "Along with all the other problems I am solving, I don't have sufficient time to work on staffing."

The reply is "If you had made recruitment a priority among your work activities, then you would now have the people necessary to deal with many of the problems you are currently experiencing."

The new project schedule plan is finalized and brings a long-awaited sigh of relief from both the project leaders and the project members. Some of the project members voice their concern that the new plan, which is viewed as achievable, might not be attainable with the current project leadership style. Nevertheless, everyone accepts the new plan and is determined to make it work.

Two more months pass. Six weeks of progress have been made. This progress is viewed as being slow yet better than before. The current issues of the day are:

- Staffing delays

- No well-defined usability objectives

- No approved control process for making changes to the product specifications, product objectives, and product requirements documents

- Inconsistent and incomplete design and code inspections

- "Off-spec" product performance characteristics

- Major rework required against the first drafts of the product publications

- No firm commitment for needed hardware equipment

- No routinely scheduled project tracking meetings

As before, these work items, and others, are assigned to individual project leaders to fix. No formal plans for any items are requested, and the items are not tracked over the course of the next month. The project head assumes that, as professionals, the project leaders will complete these work items on a timely basis.

One month later there is a request for status reports on the issues that were delegated a month earlier. Only one issue is considered complete by its assigned owner: commitment for hardware equipment. Unfortunately, the commitment does not satisfy the schedule requirements. The owner of the work item had not pursued this item further because she believed this was the best the hardware people could do. It is discovered that the current issues of the day are almost identical to those of one month earlier and of the month before that.

The project head is furious and requests a personal accounting on each issue. These unresolved issues continue to cause the organization to drift away from its ability to function as an effective, working unit. They also are causing further schedule delays and in some cases are resulting in significant rework time having to be added to the project schedule plan. Confusion abounds over which problems to deal with first, second, and so on. The ongoing mismanagement of priorities being handled across the project continues to erode overall project progress.

The project continues in much the same misguided way until the final product is delivered to customers. Yes, it *is* shipped, although nearly nine months later than the original two-year plan had specified. Unfortunately, it is shipped with some of the same problems that were known from the start, problems in product performance, usability, incomplete and inaccurate publications, and design. All this has left the product on shaky ground for customer acceptance as well as for additional funding required to support the problems that users will find.

What went wrong? Almost everyone on the project could see that the issues—the major project problems—were not receiving the attention they required. Yet everyone had a "valid" excuse: They were too busy to take time to identify and then deal with the most important issues. The claims were that, if the main issues were focused on with the intensity required, then too many other areas of the project would suffer. As one of the newer project leaders put it, "If I had to do it all over on the next project, I would probably do it the same way. It was just an aggressive project."

Don't believe it!

Solve the Most Important Problems First

 Lesson: Project leaders must not be too far removed from the major project problems—or too close.

It is easy to get caught up in the day-to-day flurry of activities, allowing the onslaught of daily problems to consume every inch of each day's mile. When this happens, there is a strong tendency to delegate more and to become farther removed from the endless, revolving list of problems. This situation can lead to a loss of control. If you are a project leader, you cannot afford to be too far removed from major problems and decisions. The farther removed you are, the greater the chances for the project to enter the drift zone. The drift zone is recognizable when the items listed in Figure 7.1 occur.

There is another, although opposite, reaction to the endless emergence of problem after problem. That reaction is actually to get closer to all the problems, to cultivate actively the view that "unless I personally fix these problems, they won't be fixed correctly and a bad situation will get worse." Unfortunately, this approach is also disastrous. The project head or a project leader becomes a critical path to getting problems resolved. Progress will ultimately slow down, not speed up. Displays of ownership from those who should be solving these problems will wane, as will morale, productivity, and schedules.

 Lesson: The project's leadership is responsible for ensuring that the project's most important problems are receiving the attention necessary to solve and close them as soon as possible.

- No one appears to be in control of the project.
- Activities are not completed.
- Wheel spinning and rework become the norm.
- Schedules slide.

Figure 7.1   Symptoms of the "drift zone."

What option is left? Stay abreast of the most important problems and allow those around you to handle all other problems. Frequent and regular project tracking team meetings will keep you as informed about the problems of lesser importance as you need to be. The more important problems can cause the most harm to the project. The project leadership must manage these problems directly or be confident that they are being managed properly by others.

How do you decide which problems to get involved with directly and to what extent you should be involved? Figure 7.2 identifies the four steps to follow. Adherence to these steps will allow you to maintain the control necessary to yield the successful closure of your most critical problems. These steps are discussed in the sections that follow.

Step 1. *Pinpoint Priorities*

At any given point in a medium or large project, there can be literally hundreds of problems that are known and being solved. Most of these are typical, business-as-usual problems. Examples of business-as-usual problems are those found while:

- Reviewing or using the product specifications
- Inspecting the design
- Correcting defects in the code
- Writing and updating the product publications
- Conducting routine project tracking team meetings

The major problems, those problems that inhibit others from doing their job, problems that have a major impact on the well-being of the project, the product, and the people involved, also occur. These are the project's most critical problems to

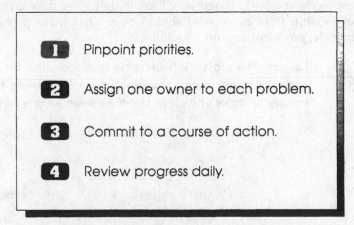

1 Pinpoint priorities.

2 Assign one owner to each problem.

3 Commit to a course of action.

4 Review progress daily.

Figure 7.2   Steps for managing priorities.

solve—the **high-priority problems** (also called the project's high-risk areas as explained in Chapter 5). These problems are currently impacting a major project **milestone** or, based on current progress, are expected to do so. (See "Identifying Milestones" in Chapter 4.) These problems are similar to those revealed in the opening scenario in this chapter.

Examples of high-priority problems are listed in Figure 7.3. This list may vary from project to project, or from one phase of the project to the next.

The first thing to do in managing the most important project problems is to list them. One person can start this list. However, if only one person is assigned to generate it, the list might be limited by his or her relatively narrow viewpoint. A useful approach, introduced in the "Project High-Risk Areas" section of Chapter 5, is to assemble the project leaders and ask each of them to list the top three problems that they recognize. Then compile all the problems on a single list. Using this list as a base, and the synergism from the assembled team, then brainstorm for additional items.

Of course, every problem on the list will not have the same priority within the project. Once the list is considered complete, prioritize it by placing the most important problems—the priorities—at the top. One way to prioritize is to ask each person to select the top three problems from the list. Then, for each item on the list, note the number of votes it received. The top three to five priorities should become apparent quickly.

Usually a project cannot work effectively more than five or so "top" priority problems at once; therefore, focus on only a few at a time. When those are solved, move on to solving the next set of high-priority problems. And so on.

 Lesson: The high-priority problems should be visible daily to all project members who are affected, either directly or indirectly.

- Incomplete and unclear product requirements
- Incomplete and unclear product objectives
- Incomplete and uncommitted project schedule plan
- Inability to meet product performance specifications
- Ineffective change-control process for making changes to the product requirements, product objectives, and product specifications
- Ineffective project-tracking process
- Late staffing of project personnel
- Inadequate hardware equipment delivery commitments
- Untimely closing of contracts with outside companies for deliverables required to complete the project successfully

Figure 7.3   Examples of high-priority problems.

The project head should post these high-priority problems on his or her office blackboard, wall, or in some visible area near or in the office so that they are reinforced throughout each day. All project members who are, in any way, affected by these project priorities should be aware of their importance to the project and know that they are being worked currently. Each high-priority problem is also logged as an action item to become part of the formal project tracking system. (See the "Project High-Risk Areas" section in Chapter 5 for more on action items.)

Other project leaders can follow a similar process for identifying the top important problems within their areas and also can display the list in an easily seen location. However, the top problems across the project area must be publicized for every impacted project leader and project member to see and understand. The project leaders must support these priorities fully when applying their resources. They also must ensure that other activities being implemented do not conflict with these priorities.

Step 2.   Assign One Owner to Each Problem

This section and the next follow the same basic guidelines that were presented in the "Recovery Plans" section of Chapter 5. Only a few words will be added in support of that section.

 Lesson: Assign one person to own both the problem and its solution.

Assign lead people to own high-priority problems. The same person who owns the problem also must own the proposed solution. The notion of *accountability* is key here. Also, only one owner should be assigned for each problem. Often the effectiveness in resolving a problem quickly and efficiently is inhibited when two or more people jointly share responsibility for solving it.

Step 3.   Commit to a Course of Action

The following example illustrates an error that causes many projects to miss the mark:

Ron Clark is assigned to fix a problem. It is an urgent matter that must be corrected within two weeks. This is considered a very short time period, but with the proper attention, it should be able to be closed within that time. What the journey to reach a solution must be is obvious. Therefore, Clark is left to his own devices to close the problem.

One week later, Clark presents the status of the problem resolution. It doesn't appear that the problem can be closed within the remaining week. Perhaps, if more time and a more intelligent effort had been spent on the problem during the first week, it could have been closed within the two-week goal. The project's leadership who review the status information suggest that the approach be reset and ask for a status update at the end of the following week.

At the end of the next week, Clark declares he is still a few days away from closing the problem. Some refinements are suggested to his approach and no additional status meeting is scheduled. It is assumed that the problem will be closed during the following week. No further status meeting is scheduled. The problem will *not* be closed.

 Lesson: If there was ever a problem that requires a plan to ensure it is solved and closed properly, then it is a high-priority problem.

What is missing in the preceding scenario? No detailed plan or course of action was required. An issue that is recognized as one of the hottest in the project and, to boot, must be closed in just two weeks should be a clear signal that each day counts. Therefore, a committed, detailed *plan* must be required from the person assigned to resolve the issue. Do not accept the comeback "With the time it will take me to build a detailed plan, I could have had most of the problem solved." This response only reinforces the need for a detailed plan—if not out of necessity, then for insurance. This plan should spell out not only the events to be completed each day, but also the dependent parties who are required to resolve the issue successfully. The plan should be approved by the project head as well as by those who are performers. All of this preparation helps to ensure that the problem is solved *the first time*.

Do not neglect to seek help from outside the project or even outside the company. These important project problems must not be allowed to linger. Perhaps outside resources of equipment, consultants, or even uniquely skilled people are needed. The cost to procure them can be more than offset by the importance of solving the problem on a timely basis.

Step 4.   Review Progress Daily

 Lesson: As a project leader, always spend more time on solving the most important project problems than on solving the less important problems.

Time is scarce for a project head and his or her project leaders. That is why it must be invested wisely. Project leaders should not spend 80 percent of their time on low-priority project problems and 20 percent on high-priority problems. Eighty percent of a leader's time should be spent on the most important problems. However, there is a strong attraction to work almost exclusively on the lesser problems. Minor problems tend to be easier to solve than major problems, and it is satisfying to see frequent accomplishments. But resist! Deal with important issues first.

Some form of status must be pursued each day on *each* of the high-priority problems. Tracking these problems daily will help ensure that they close as quickly as possible and close appropriately. What is meant by "appropriately"? It is not enough merely to close these high-priority problems; they also must be closed with solutions that really *fix the problem* in an acceptable manner. For example, if a high-priority problem is to obtain hardware with which to perform system test, the problem is not necessarily closed simply by soliciting a commitment for the hardware. The hardware also must be available *in time* for system test to meet their schedule commitments.

 Lesson: High-priority problems require attention every day.

The daily tracking meetings can be formal with the appropriate participation by those involved or simply a five-minute briefing against each established plan. It is not so important as to *how* these high-priority problems are tracked as it is to track the progress *daily*.

The status of a project's most important problems should be shared with everyone at the project's routine project tracking team meetings. The "Project High-Risk Areas" section of Chapter 5 focuses on the presentation and tracking of these major project problems at the weekly project tracking team meetings.

Measure of Success

 Lesson: The high-priority problem list must be reexamined routinely to ensure it always reflects the latest and most important problems.

The top-priority problems in a project likely will change many times throughout the life of the project. This high-priority problem list must be reevaluated at regular intervals. Weekly evaluations are preferred, although twice-weekly evaluations can be best for projects that are starting a list for the first time. Evaluations can be as infrequent as once every two weeks for mature, structured projects that have been managed according to a high-priority problem list for some time. Of course, a meeting is not always required to determine whether a new addition should be made to the list. The project head or designated person such as the project tracking team leader (see Chapter 5 for his or her duties) must exercise authority in changing the problems on the high-priority problem list when the need to do so arises; however, any changes made must be communicated in a clear and timely manner to all those who might be affected. Doing so is essential in maintaining control and a respectable productivity within the project. After a while, the use of the high-priority problem list will be an established activity and focusing on it will become automatic.

 Lesson: A measure of an effectively run project is the swift attention to, and closure of, the high-priority problems.

A good way to measure how effective an organization is at responding to its major problems is to compare the high-priority problem list from one month to the next. If the same items are present, something is wrong and the organization is still suffering from drift. That is, too much time is spent doing rework and too little is spent in working effectively. The organization is drifting from one activity to the next without achieving a clear closure on earlier activities. Or it may be entering the next set of activities before those activities are fully ready.

 Lesson: A well-managed high-priority problem list helps the project members to not lose sight of the forest.

A side benefit in focusing so intensely on the high-priority problem list is that participants learn how to see the whole picture and, therefore, become less susceptible to spending too much attention on tangents of lesser value. This skill is one that project heads require in order to manage effectively. It is also a skill seen most often in the more productive and effective project leaders.

8

Product Requirements: Understanding the Customer's Problem to Solve

A software product is built for a customer in mind. The "customer" can be internal to your company or outside your company, one customer or many customers. Each customer has specific *problems* and *needs* that your product must address. A *problem* might be that the customer needs to improve productivity or decrease expenses or increase customer satisfaction or expand to new market opportunities. Problems tend to be associated with the big picture.

 Lesson: Before investing in building a new product, take the time to understand the prospective customer's problems and needs that you must satisfy.

Needs are specific tasks or functions that a customer *needs* to be able to perform as part of solving the *problem.* For example, if a customer's *problem* is low productivity because the word processors used in the company do not satisfy the *needs* of employees, then the customer might seek out a new word processor. The *needs* that the word processor must satisfy might be to support special letter templates that can be shared among all employees through a local area network, automatically address labels for mass mailings, and perform automatic backups of data at user-selected frequencies so that users cannot lose large chunks of work when a power interruption or a serious user mistake occurs. Before you begin to build a new product or enhance an existing one, it is important to understand what customer *problems* you are expected to solve and what customer *needs* you are expected to satisfy.

The place in the software development process to define your customer's problems and needs that your product is to address is in a document called the requirements, also referred to as the *product requirements*. As Figure 8.1 shows, the requirements document represents the first significant activity to be worked in the software development process.

Many software products are developed with a weak or nonexistent product requirements document. This situation can have a devastating effect on a project's costs, schedules, quality, customer satisfaction, and profits as a project's members can only hope that the product, or *solution*, they are building does indeed solve real customer problems and satisfy real customer needs.

The most common requirements-related problems are:

- The customer's problems and corresponding needs are not understood.

- The customer's problems and needs are not fully documented.

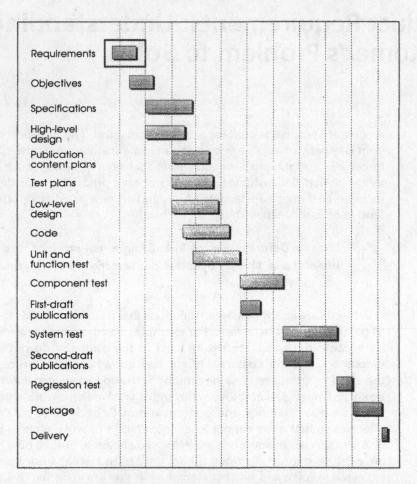

Figure 8.1   Product requirements in the software development process.

- Agreement has not been reached on the validity of the contents of the requirements document.

- Changes to an agreed-to requirements document are not controlled.

This chapter addresses these and other requirements-related problems. This chapter also identifies the topics that a well thought out requirements document should address.

A Project Tale

The following tale helps to highlight why you must understand your customer's problems and needs before embarking on the costly journey of building a new product.

It is time to plan and build a new product. Revenue from the current product line, although strong, is expected to decrease in about a year—the same amount of time estimated to build a new product. The marketing group has some ideas for a new product and is eager to have the developers begin building the product right away. The developers also are enthusiastic to begin work on the new product. New products are always more fun than performing "repair" work on current products or adding enhancements.

The marketing group calls a meeting with the developers to kick off the new product. In the meeting, marketing presents their ideas. Most developers quickly accept marketing's view that the product has acceptable potential to bring in the desired revenue; however, a developer, Larry Whittington, asks, "What exactly is the problem that the new product is expected to solve?" A dialog ensues.

"That should be pretty obvious. The new product will increase a customer's productivity and result in decreasing overall expenses."

"Can you be more specific? Can you give me an example of how that is expected to happen? Have you worked with any customers and received assurance that the proposed product would have the impact that you anticipate?"

"Well, we don't have any specifics, but based on our knowledge of the industry the new product will serve, we feel confident that it will be well received. We don't think that we have to play this out with any potential customers; however, at some point during the development of the product, we plan to begin promoting it to potential customers."

"What if we wait until the product is nearly built before we get customer feedback and we discover that the product does not solve the problems and meet the needs that our potential customers expect? This has happened to us with earlier products, and it has always been costly to redesign a product so late in the development cycle."

"Don't be such a pessimist. With your attitude, we would be afraid to build any product. We have to take some risks in this business. Besides, we know what our customers need—even if they don't."

Whittington backs off, seeing that he was getting no support from others at the meeting. He was beginning to think that maybe he is wrong about wanting to better understand customers' problems and needs before developing a product. After all, the marketing group should know best.

A few weeks pass and the product objectives are available for review and approval. The proposed product has an abundance of "bells and whistles" that would seem to appeal to many customers. The developers are proud of its function. The objectives are approved with only minor changes. Whittington suggests that marketing pass the product objectives by several potential customers as reassurance that the product will meet their needs. Marketing declines, saying that they are understaffed for performing "optional" work. "Trust us," trumpets a marketing representative. "We know our customers and they will love this product."

Six weeks pass and the product specifications are completed and available for review. Several significant changes are suggested by marketing and other groups. Whittington suggests the recommended changes not be made until they can be verified by potential customers. He is concerned that a lot of time and expense will be invested to make these changes without anyone checking with potential customers. Again he is unable to obtain the needed support to have his concerns considered seriously, although some project members are beginning to give a bit more credence to his ideas. The project's leaders responsible for the product specifications and the design of the product agree to making almost all the changes and begin to update the product specifications.

A few weeks later, the product specifications are fully updated and distributed for approval. Because most of the recommended changes from the review draft were made, the document's approvers mostly request only minor changes and the product specifications are approved. However, at the meeting of the approvers, Whittington tries again and suggests that marketing take the approved product specifications and solicit feedback from potential customers while the developers proceed full steam in building the product. Whittington argues, "As it is today, the project's schedules are so aggressive that there will be many months of overtime ahead for almost all members of the project; however, if late customer feedback indicates that we need to make additional major changes to the product, we will all work heavy overtime and have to forfeit vacations and most holidays, not to mention a loss of revenue and profit for our company." With the potential loss of months of the project's members' personal time, Whittington is beginning to gather an interested following and marketing agrees to go out and get "some" feedback.

Several months pass. The developers are tracking reasonably on schedule, although more overtime has been required than originally expected. In the weekly tracking meeting, Whittington asks marketing about their progress on obtaining potential customer feedback regarding this being the "right" product. Marketing says they haven't yet found the time but will begin to work on it within the next few weeks. Whittington, seeing what is happening, logs this as an action item to be tracked weekly and given a target close date. Everyone agrees and the "problem" is now openly tracked.

More time passes and the new product has been fully designed, coded, and tested by a team of developers. It is now being tested by a group independent of the original developers. If all goes well, the product is expected to be ready for delivery to the first customer in three months. The project's leadership agree to announce the product now and to begin to talk with potential customers.

What about the "action item" for marketing? Marketing never seriously worked it. They were "too busy" with preparing the new product for public announcement. Whittington had escalated marketing over their repeated missed commitments to gather feedback from potential customers, but the result was that "we are so close to announcing the product now that, even if we did hear that potential customers need significant changes made to the product, we have no time to incorporate the changes." This position by the project's higher leadership did not make good business sense to Whittington, but the position was final.

Testing is now complete and the product is ready for delivery to customers. The project's members are proud of the hard work they put into creating the product. The overtime on the project averaged about 30 percent over the past six months. Most members consider this overtime "normal." Many people begin taking their delayed vacations before the next project starts.

During the first three months that the product is available, a major realization occurs. With sales at only 30 percent of expectations, it is becoming apparent that the customers are viewing the new product to be deficient in solving their basic problems and meeting their needs. Although many customers judge the product to have potential, most cannot use it until some major changes are made. This puts the developers into the mode of "repair" work on the new product. Instead of performing "repair" work, the developers and marketing had hoped to be enhancing the new product to broaden its appeal even more.

How does this tale end? Not well. Six months after the product was available for delivery, sales are hovering at about 25 percent of expectations. The "repair" work is still under way and is not expected to complete for another three to four months. Because the company was banking on this product being a success, cutbacks in expenses have had to occur partially to accommodate the significant loss in revenues. Part of the expense savings is the reduction in the workforce by 20 percent. Unfortunately, the project's leader who so adamantly resisted performing the necessary "homework" with potential customers—the leader who "knew what was best for the customer"—is not part of the reduced workforce. Whittington? His job remains; however, he left the company. He was frustrated over the same problems occurring from project to project, problems that are not difficult to overcome but that require discipline and vision. He now works for a former competitor intent on being the best in the business by working closely with customers and providing them what they need to be successful.

Had the right up-front work on developing the requirements document been done, would this have guaranteed success for the product? No. Nothing guarantees success; however, it would have significantly increased the likelihood of building the right product the first time and getting to market as soon as possible with a "good bet" product.

The Value of Product Requirements

 Lesson: The product requirements document focuses on the problems and needs—not the solutions—of the customer.

Many projects define requirements as an initial description of the product to be built; that is, the *solution* to a customer's problem. The primary focus is on the solution. This book takes a contrary view and represents requirements as focusing on understanding the *problems* to be solved, not on the actual solutions. (The product objectives and the product specifications, discussed in the next two chapters, address the solution.)

 Lesson: Never assume you understand your customer's problems and needs if you have not worked closely with the customer for this purpose.

Why focus the requirements document on the problems and not the solutions? Simple. The members of a project can never feel certain that they are building the right product if, indeed, they do not fully understand the problems that their product is expected to solve. It is arrogant for members of a development shop to assume they understand their customer's problems so well that they dismiss working with the customer and immediately jump into defining the solution. A software development process is far more productive if the initial focus is on understanding the targeted audience's problems that must be solved.

 Lesson: More will be learned about your customer's problems and needs when you put them in print and verify their accuracy and completeness with your customer.

Furthermore, the project's members learn a lot by understanding and writing down the perceived problems of the customer. Then the customer, or a sample subset of customers if there is more than one, is given the opportunity to review the documented problems. The customer is very likely to add new insight to the problems, insight that will prove invaluable when a high-level description of the solution is prepared in the forthcoming product objectives. (See Chapter 9.)

 Lesson: A requirements document forces important issues to surface at the start of a project that might otherwise be overlooked, incorrectly assumed, or discovered late in a project.

Focusing on the customer's problems allows important issues to be raised that might otherwise be overlooked, incorrectly assumed, or discovered late in a project. The more the members of a project understand their customer's needs, the greater the likelihood that those needs will be satisfied—and satisfied as soon as possible.

 Lesson: A requirements document provides a tangible means against which to validate the solution.

Another benefit of documenting the needs to be solved is that the product objectives can now be categorically validated for addressing each need defined in the requirements. This technique of *mapping to requirements* helps to ensure that the customer's needs are being satisfied.

You might be wondering, "But what about combining the customer's problems and needs with the proposed solutions into a single document?" The problem with this approach is that the document's reviewers will focus most of their attention on the solutions. After all, the solutions represent the future work of the project's members. There seems to be a tendency quickly to accept the problems and needs and just get on with the developing the solutions. Instead, it is important that the customer's perceived problems and needs be studied carefully and understood. After the requirements are documented, they should be verified by one or more prospective customers before a great deal of time and cost is invested in developing the solution.

The product requirements document literally represents the foundation from which the product's solution will evolve. The time and energy invested in ensuring a sound review by prospective customers may be the best investment that can be made throughout the software development process.

Gathering Requirements

 Lesson: The most successful product developers will be those who consistently and tirelessly work at understanding their customer's problems and needs that must be satisfied.

The primary reason for gathering requirements is to better understand the problems and needs of current and prospective customers. The more you understand your customer's problems, the better you are able to offer the best solutions to them. This is a classical example of the truth in the saying *Information is power*. In today's increasingly competitive and technologically changing world, the most successful product developers will be those who best understand their customer's needs and can provide the best solutions to satisfy those needs.

It is helpful to collect requirements in a manner that allows easy access and categorization of the information. You can use a standard word processor to arrange this information or enlist one of many specially designed databaselike tools for this purpose. As requirements information is collected, it can be filed in a number of ways. One such method is to review the section headings found in the "What Should Product Requirements Address?" section later in this chapter. You can use these headings as categories under which to file requirements information.

Another useful technique is to file the information with some designation of its importance, or *priority,* when compared to the many other requirements. For example, the designation of *H, M,* and *L,* for high, medium, and low priority, can be recorded with each requirement. These designations can be associated with the perceived customer importance of satisfying the particular requirement or need.

Another helpful technique is to designate whether the requirement needs to be satisfied in the long, intermediate, or short term: *L, I,* or *S.* You will discover that it is possible for a requirement to be a high priority yet does not need to be satisfied short term. The opposite also can be true: A requirement can be designated as a low priority, even though it is tagged to be satisfied in the short term.

Creative techniques are available to help weigh the importance of each requirement against the others. One such example is *quality function deployment* (QFD). This technique not only includes the customer in identifying his or her own needs but prioritizes these needs according to the customer's own priority rating. QFD doesn't stop here. It provides a technique to continue to include the customer's voice throughout the development process. (See the bibliography for more information about QFD.)

Requirements can be collected in many ways. Some common methods are listed in Figure 8.2. Requirements gathering works best when it is accomplished over a sustained period of time—as a person's mind becomes increasingly attuned to the presence of pertinent information. Moreover, collecting information over a long period helps the gatherers spot trends that show the changing moods and needs of prospective customers. Also, the longer people work with current and prospective customers, the more can be learned about how their businesses operate and the greater the understanding for their problems and needs.

Writing the Product Requirements Document

The primary audience of the product requirements document is the development organization that has the mission of building, testing, and maintaining a product that will satisfy the needs identified in the document. The secondary audience is prospective customers. Prospective customers are included in the audience so that they can review the document and validate its completeness and accuracy.

Typically a marketing-oriented organization writes the requirements document because that group is viewed as being the closest to understanding the customers and the marketplace those customers make up. It also is helpful that the organization writing the requirements document be different from the group that must respond with a proposed solution to satisfy the requirements. This approach better focuses

- Feedback from customers of similar products
- Customer surveys
- Users' groups
- Conferences and workshops
- Competitive products and literature
- Public literature

Figure 8.2 Common methods for collecting product requirements.

each group to concentrate on its specific mission: either to identify the needs or to propose a solution. Having the same organization perform both roles can weaken the attention needed to fully understand the customer's problems and needs. Also, there can be a tendency to focus overmuch on a solution and attempt to force-fit the solution to solving the customer's problems.

 Lesson: A requirements document should be clear on the priority of each need to be satisfied.

Perhaps the greatest challenge in writing the requirements document is sifting through the numerous requirements that have been gathered and selecting those that are the highest priority to satisfy. After these requirements have been identified, some probably will be considered mandatory, some desirable, and some optional. These designations of priority must be communicated clearly to the audience of the requirements document to increase the likelihood that the *right* product is built. A common method to relate these designations of priorities is to use the verbs *must* (or *shall*), *should*, and *may* when describing the needs that the eventual product is expected to satisfy. These verbs represent the priority categories of *mandatory, desirable,* and *optional*, respectively, and are often required when working with government agencies.

Another method that can be used to relate the three categories of priorities is to designate separate sections in the requirements document for each category. In other words, when describing the problems and needs to be solved, group them according to whether they are mandatory, desirable, or optional.

The requirements document needs to describe the customer's problems and needs as completely and accurately as possible. Sufficient information must be provided to allow the developers to feel comfortable that they really understand the customer's needs. This information also must be complete enough to convince the customer that the *correct* problems are being focused on.

Sometimes the problems to be solved are so complex that it is helpful to understand them in an iterative fashion. For example, imagine a customer who has a large, complex manufacturing operation and is intent on having software developed that not only controls the entire operation, but that is integrated to the point where data from each of the many active applications can be shared across applications as well as collected for reporting and tracking purposes. In this case, a project might choose to use the iterative software process model introduced in Chapter 1. This model allows the requirements to be developed iteratively so that the portion of the requirements that is known can be documented and the corresponding portion of the solution developed. As that piece of the solution is being developed, then the next iteration of requirements are described, and so on.

Obtaining Agreement

After requirements are documented, they must be reviewed and approved by all interested parties. Typical groups to approve the requirements document are planning (those who write the product objectives), "development" (those who write the product specifications and design and code the product), publications (those who write the product's user documentation), test (those who test the product), and service (those who must troubleshoot and maintain the product after it has been purchased by a customer). In this chapter the term *development* usually is generic and refers to all the groups just mentioned; in this section, however, it is used in a narrower sense.

Each group reviews the requirements document from a different perspective. First and foremost, each group must be comfortable that the document provides sufficient information so that they better understand the needs that the to-be-proposed product must satisfy. Even though the requirements document focuses on the problems and needs—and not the solutions—these review groups can perform their jobs with greater confidence if they understand the problems and needs they must address.

 Lesson: Writing the requirements is not enough; they must be agreed to by all interested parties, including a subset of prospective customers.

A subset of prospective customers also should review the requirements document. If the document contains proprietary information that prospective customers should not see, then the requirements document should be written with the sensitive information in sections that can be removed easily. The importance of prospective customers reviewing the requirements document cannot be overstated. After all, the new product is intended to satisfy the needs of customers. What better way to ensure that those needs are stated accurately and completely and understood adequately than to have prospective customers validate the contents of the requirements document? You are certain to discover new views and information from these prospective customers that will greatly help you in choosing the right solution—the first time.

Controlling Changes

After the requirements document is approved, it is placed under change control. This means that any subsequent changes to the product requirements first must be examined carefully and agreed to as per the change control process, which is defined in Chapter 10.

Typically only a small number of project documents is ever placed under change control. These are documents that are particularly critical to the project and must be controlled carefully to maintain order and control the flow of communications and work in the software development process. Documents that are usually placed under change control include the product requirements document, the product objectives document, and the product specifications document.

 Lesson: The creation of a requirements document is the first significant action that a project undertakes to help start out in control; placing the agreed-to requirements document under strict change control helps a project stay in control.

Requirements are a "moving target", that is, the problems and needs of customers are in a constant state of change largely brought about by fierce competition and rapidly changing technology. The longer the duration of a software development project, the greater the likelihood that it will experience changing requirements. Because changes in requirements can have a profound effect on the function, costs, schedule, and quality of a product, it is imperative that all changes be controlled carefully. Let's look at how this might work.

> A project is midway through the development cycle and has committed schedules, costs, and quality for the new product. Several new requirements surface from a customer. What do you do? Accept them? Reject them? Or something else?

Many development shops accept the changing requirements because they come directly from a customer. However, this is *not* the automatic proper behavior in spite of the common rhetoric that says the customer is always right. Automatically rejecting changing requirements also can be the wrong thing to do. Instead, the new requirements should be examined carefully and *sized*, and the cost, in terms of schedule delays and increased project costs, should be presented to the customer. If the customer is willing to pay the "price," then you should accept the new requirements. If the customer is not willing to pay the price, then you should not accept the new requirements.

As you know, things are usually not so simple as black or white. For example, if the new requirements will result in minor work that can be absorbed easily in the existing schedules and costs, then perhaps they should be satisfied as goodwill to the customer. If the customer is but one of many for which the product is being developed, and the other customers do not desire the new requirements at the risk of delaying completion of the product at its committed schedule and cost, then you should reject the new requirements. You can consider the possibility of modifying the new product later to satisfy the one customer who asked to change the requirements.

There are other options as well; however, the point here is that you always must behave in a manner that allows you to stay in control. This is your business and you are responsible for making the decisions that will support your continued success. A sound change control process that is fully supported by the project's leadership will help you achieve the desired control.

What Should Product Requirements Address?

This section identifies many of the typical subjects to be addressed in the product requirements document. All of these subjects might not need to be addressed—or perhaps additional subjects need to be added—depending on the problems and needs that a customer has to be solved.

As each subject is introduced, a brief, supportive example is used to further illustrate the type of information to be addressed. For illustrative purposes, the examples assume that the requirements are for a single customer only.

Overview of Problem to Be Solved

Describe the fundamental problem to be solved.

The customer is a company that was formed three years ago with 20 employees. Today the company has 100 employees and expects to grow by an additional 100 employees over the next three years. Most employees, as a significant part of their job, frequently write and distribute a large number of letters and brochures, and occasionally produce reports and manuals both for customers and in-house use. There is no standardization across the company for the computers and software applications that are used to perform these tasks. It has been estimated that, based on current spending rates and employee productivity, $1 million can be saved annually if a consistent and compatible set of the appropriate hardware and software was adopted for use across the company. The customer is looking for a solution that will result in an overall savings of about $1 million.

Tasks/Functions

List specific needs that the solution must satisfy related to function and tasks.
The solution must make the following functions and tasks available to the user:

- Standard word processor functions
- Standard database functions
- Creation and use of letter templates
- Automatically addressing of envelopes
- Mixing graphics, text, and spreadsheet data into documents (includes letters)
- Be accessible to multiple users at a time
- Allow computer-based data to be faxed directly to another computer or a fax machine
- Scanning of data for inclusion into documents and for fax transmissions
- High-quality printing
- WYSIWYG (What-you-see-is-what-you-get; that is, exactly what the user sees on the computer display is exactly what the printed representation will look like)
- ...

User's Current Mode of Operation

Describe how the user currently operates.

Most company employees either use a Macintosh or an IBM-compatible personal computer, while a few continue to use typewriters. Although most of the letters written could be derived from standard letter formats and shared across the organization, very little sharing is performed. A mixed collection of software applications of word processors and databases (for mailing lists) are being used. In fact, some applications are several years old and are no longer supported by their manufacturers. Although there is a need to include some graphics or spreadsheet information in the letters and brochures, little of this is done because the software applications being used either do not support these features or the users do not understand how to exploit these features.

Most employees have a printer connected to their personal computer. These printers come in all varieties, from dot matrix to laser. The employees with computers but no printers print their material by transferring, via diskette, their data to another employee's computer that has a printer.

While most of the personal computers, with their hardware and software components, represent costs between $1,500 and $3,000, others have costs in excess of $5,000. Only a handful of computers are linked to one another, and virtually no correspondence between employees is done on the computer. Instead, the telephone or hard-copy mail system is used. Letters that must be mailed to large numbers of people are typically hand-addressed.

Environment

Describe the environment that must be taken into account with the solution.

The employees have a common need to communicate with one another. The employees are scattered across three buildings that are located about 10 miles from each other. The buildings are not wired with cables other than standard telephone lines.

Ease of Use

Describe the needs related to ease of use to be addressed.

The solution must be easy to learn and use for all employees. Emphasis should be on a solution that requires minimal help from support personnel. The education level of the employees resides mostly in the range of high school graduate to master's degrees. Seventy percent of employees are college graduates.

Hardware/Software

Identify any hardware and software needs that must be satisfied.

The solution must satisfy the need to fax computer-based data directly to its destination—without requiring the use of a standard fax machine. At some point in the future, the solution must allow all fax data to be sent or received via an employee's computer. This need requires that data can be scanned into a computer if needed.

The solution must consist only of off-the-shelf hardware. The hardware chosen must be expandable to meet future anticipated needs. To the extent predictable, the hardware also must be adaptable to improved technologies so that the company's hardware investments are protected.

To the extent reasonable, off-the-shelf software applications should be utilized. All software should run on an industry recognized and well-supported operating system.

Quality

Describe the quality-related needs.

The solution must be reliable to the extent that data are never lost and that backup procedures exist to restore back-level files and continually and automatically save work being performed.

Performance

Describe the performance-related needs.

The solution must operate with an efficiency that leaves the employee with the perception that almost no time is spent waiting for the computer program in use to respond.

Security

Describe the security-related needs.

The solution must allow all employees access to data that has common use across the organization (such as letter templates, databases, and application software) but must protect each employee's private data from access by others.

Compatibility/Migration

Describe any compatibility and migration needs.

The solution should be compatible with most of the software currently being used in the company. Where compatibility is not possible or reasonable, then careful consideration should be made for migrating existing databases and other computer data to the solution.

International

Describe any international needs.

The solution must be able to support foreign language fonts at some later time when the company expands to international markets.

Service and Support

Describe the support-related needs.

The solution should allow an in-house-trained person to resolve most questions and problems. In those few cases when outside company help is required, an 800-type number should be accessible during normal working hours.

Pricing/Licensing

Describe the pricing and licensing needs to be addressed.

Quantity discounts must be available for hardware and software purchases. Terms and conditions of licensing must allow multiple employees to use the same software applications.

As stated earlier, more subjects could be added to this sample list. The objective is to present the underlying *problem* and the supporting *needs* that later must be satisfied by the *solution* that will be proposed in a product objectives document. Examples of more subjects that can be addressed in the requirements document include:

- Publications: Describe any publications-related needs.
- Standards: Describe any needs related to corporate, industry, or government standards.
- Employee laws: Describe any needs related to complying with employee rights, labor laws, and the like.
- Product integration: Describe any needs related to integrating the solution to existing or planned products.
- Packaging: Describe any packaging-related needs that the solution must satisfy.
- Competitive offerings: Describe any existing or in-development competitive offerings that satisfy a portion or all of the problems and needs.

When the requirements document has been written and is distributed to the various groups for approval, be prepared for questions to be raised so that the requirements can be better understood. Examples of questions that might be asked about the supportive examples used in this section are:

- What is an acceptable price range for the solution? What data are available to measure the current productivity against the new productivity when the solution is fully operational? (Overview of Problem to Be Solved)

- What is the maximum number of users expected to be actively using the new system at any point in time? (Tasks/Functions)

- What are the software applications currently being used? How many users for each? (User's Current Mode of Operation)

- Is there a need to deal with power fluctuations and the potential impact to losing data? (Quality)

- Are there any specific timing objectives when using the solution, such as switching between screens in one second or less, or printing letter-quality pages within 10 seconds each? (Performance)

- Does future capability to support foreign fonts include languages that are not left to right? (International)

- Does an "800-like number" mean having access to "free" support? (Service and Support)

Notice that the needs presented in the examples were designated by the terms *must* and *should*. (*May* was not used.) These terms signify to the reviewers of the document the priority of the needs identified.

Solving the Right Problem

 Lesson: If your product fails to satisfy your customer's expectations, competitors will be happy to help.

The requirements activity commonly is one of the weakest performed activities of the software development process. Yet, if not performed well, it can have a devastating impact throughout the development process and on the success of the product with customers. Now more than ever, software development shops can no longer afford to spend hundreds of thousands of dollars—even millions of dollars—developing a solution that does not satisfy the problems and needs of its intended audience. If a development shop fails to meet the customer's expectations, other competitors will appear quickly who are more than happy to work with and satisfy the customer.

The requirements activity requires very little time to perform relative to the overall software development process. But it can return such a high value on the small investment. Would any serious businessperson competing in the market for the long haul, intent on being the most successful world-class software development shop in a particular market, consider anything less than personally understanding customers' problems and needs *before* commiting huge resources? Not for long.

9

Product Objectives: Providing Direction for the Solution

"If you don't know where you are going, then how will you know when you get there?" These familiar lines could have been written about software projects in general and product objectives in particular. Every project, when it is conceived, needs a set of higher-level objectives to provide *direction* in the creation of a new product. The focus of the objectives is on defining a product, *at a high level*, that will satisfy a marketing opportunity and the perceived needs of the targeted customers. The vehicle for doing this is a document called the product objectives.

As a product is being developed, virtually thousands of decisions must be made that will, collectively, define the final product. Ultimately, each decision will have some impact on the schedules and costs of the product and on the level of satisfaction with it after it is available to customers. The goal, of course, is to make the *right* choices whenever decisions are made throughout the software development process.

A common problem with many software development projects is that the project members often are busy working on defining the wee detail of the new product long before the basic functions and features have been defined and agreed to by the participating organizations. Without agreement on the big picture of what the product will look like, spending so much time on defining and making decisions on the details is wasteful. The result can be that, when agreement on the basic functions and features finally is reached, a great amount of redirection and rework must occur, leaving an aftermath of throwaway work, frustrated participants, poor communications across the project, slipped schedules, and increased costs—or, worse, the cancellation of the project.

This chapter presents the need for product objectives in the software development process. It also identifies the topics that a well thought out product objectives document should address.

A Project Tale

The following scenario shows how inattention to product objectives can have an unwelcome toll on a software development project.

The project is off to a good start. The product requirements document has been written and agreed to by all the appropriate groups. This means that the customers' problems and needs appear to be reasonably understood. Now a solution must be defined that satisfies these problems and needs.

Many of the people on the project have their own ideas on what the "right" solution should be. After all, the solution to many of the problems and needs defined in the product requirements are "common sense." Because software development cycles always seem to take too long, the project leaders decide to take the "calculated" risk of dispensing with formal product objectives. Instead, they decide that a small set of charts, created by the development group, would do just as well, as long as certain project leaders in the direct chain of command can reach a consensus on the contents of these charts. Anyone outside of this direct chain of command who disagrees with the charts can log an objection, or issue. There will be "plenty of time" to work on these issues later.

Two charts are created in place of the product objectives document. The charts, comprised of abbreviated bulleted information, are approved quickly by the selected project leaders. The charts also are made available to other groups; however, without exception, these groups quickly discover problems with the information provided in the charts and raise issues with the development group. The development group resists immediately working the issues but agrees to log the "problems" for later resolution. Example issues are: the bulleted items are too vague ("product must be easy to use"), almost no mention is made of how the new product must compare against competitive offerings, and potential customers are not consulted as to the acceptability of the proposed solution. The issues raised normally would be resolved during the review and approval phases of the product objectives document—had there been one.

Several product designers are recruited quickly to form a product development team to begin work on the product specifications and design. The team's size is intentionally kept small to limit the number of people that must interface with one another across the team. The team also is told to work primarily in a vacuum—that is, as a self-contained team with little to no communications with any groups outside the team. This is viewed as a "productive" way to streamline the decision-making process for the new product.

Day by day, the team is faced with making product definition and design decisions. As there is no completed and approved product objectives document to refer to when making these decisions, the team attempts to reach a consensus for the more important decisions. Frequently, a consensus cannot be reached, due to conflicting perceptions of the direction the product should take. When this happens, the team leader or project leader makes the decision. In spite of the confusion over the big picture of what the product should look like, it appears that something must be going right because the product specifications are on schedule to be available for review within a few weeks. The groups outside of the small product development team are eager to review the product specifications.

The product specifications are now available for review and are distributed across all groups. After studying them, many reviewers believe that the product, as defined, doesn't size up competitively. The product would have been fine for a product of five years ago, but today's users are looking for increased ease of use. Information systems (IS) managers are looking for connectivity to computers already purchased and in use by their companies. Company managers are looking for compatibility with their existing hardware and software. Retailers are looking for something that sets a new product apart from competitors. The customer service department is looking for improved serviceability aids. Furthermore, upon closer examination of the product specifications, there appears to be broad inconsistencies in the product functions. Some product areas are strong in function, while others are weak. Again, these are issues that normally are resolved during the review and approval of the product objectives—had there been one.

But the developers like the product. After all, they defined it. It always can be enhanced in the next release offering of the product. Isn't that what new releases are for?

All issues raised against the product specifications are logged. A third of the issues are accepted as work items to resolve. A third are negotiated to a future release of the product. And the remaining third are rejected.

Many weeks pass as the product specifications are reworked and finally distributed for approval. The revised specifications are an improvement. But still more issues surface, most of which should have been resolved with the product objectives. For example, marketing learns that it must sell "x" number of packages of this product in order to meet the forecast, which is based on a minimum return-on-investment figure. Consequently, several of the issues that had been negotiated to a future release now seem too important to be ignored until then. To make matters worse, the next release will follow this one by at least a year, and a lot can happen in the software industry in one year. However, because development already has completed so much work, more compromises are made and the specifications, with moderate changes, are deemed to be at an acceptable level of completeness. With the detailed definition of the product "complete" in the product specifications, the detailed design of the product begins.

By now the project is fully staffed. The developers are halfway through the coding phase. The testers are defining, designing, and writing test cases from the product specifications. The product publications writers are working on the initial drafts. The marketing and support people are preparing their brochures, tutorials, and support plans. Some members of the project feel that progress is proceeding acceptably, while others are uneasy and don't like the uncertainty that seems to be looming.

News comes in that a competitor, who currently dominates the industry among this product's target audience, has just announced the ability to connect its product to other programs in other machines. The company's marketers had predicted this. Now major product changes must be made to add this enhancement into the first release of the product. Unfortunately, this addition will impact product schedules and will increase the selling price. Also, some work that had been completed now must be thrown away. This change in direction for the product has caused the project leadership to take a closer look at the plans for the next release. It is discovered that the enhancements slated for the next release that now must be moved into the first release will cause up to 25 percent of the code in the first release to be discarded. Unfortunately, most of this code has been written already.

Several months pass. The product is now being system tested. The original schedules have been extended by several months. Once again marketing has decided that the product is no longer desirable at the current level of function. Either the project must be scrapped or more of the enhancements that were to be provided in the next release must be moved into the first release. A scramble takes place to rework the product specifications document again and to redirect the momentum that has taken months to build.

How does this scenario end? The damage is high. Schedules, costs, and resources have all been impacted negatively. Could this scenario have been avoided? Nobody can say for sure. But it definitely could have fared better had the product objectives homework been done up front, when mistakes and delays are much less costly and project groups are more receptive to negotiating changes in product function and design.

The Good Sense ($ Dollars and Cents $) for Product Objectives

 Lesson: The product objectives is the first project document to focus on the solution to the customer's problems and needs.

As shown in Figure 9.1, the creation and approval of the product objectives document is the second significant activity to be worked in the software development process—just after product requirements—and is the first activity to define the solution to the customer's problems and needs. This is the document that provides the initial direction to all the groups that must build, test, market, and service the product. This fact should suggest how important and influential the product objectives document can be in helping a project start out on the right foot. But let's look from another perspective at the impact of this document on a project.

 Lesson: The product objectives is a relatively small document that defines the new product at a high level.

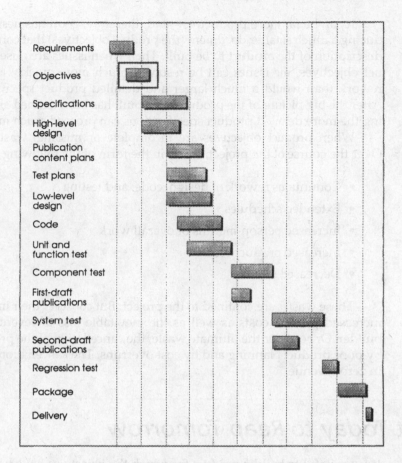

Figure 9.1   Product objectives in the software development process.

The product objectives document typically is one-tenth the size of the product specifications document, can be written by a fraction of the people required to write the product specifications document (sometimes by only one or two people), and can be written in one-fourth or less calendar time. When a project fails to create a product objectives document and instead begins investing its time and resources into creating a product specifications document, a lot of guesswork can be involved. After all, a product specifications document defines the solution in far more detail than a product objectives document. When the product specifications are finally available for review, it is very possible that major issues will be raised that require many areas of the product specifications to be reworked. Reworking parts of a product can be the major waste of a project's time and budget.

 Lesson: A product objectives document is good business—well written and agreed to, it can have a significant, positive impact on reducing rework on a project.

It can be far more productive—and, therefore, good business—to begin by producing a much smaller document (the product objectives) that contains a higher-level description of the product to be built. Then when issues are raised against the product objectives, the issues can be resolved much more quickly and require far less rework than would a much larger and detailed product specifications document. After the big picture of the product to be built has been defined and agreed to, building the more detailed product specifications can proceed much more smoothly.

When product objectives are incomplete or missing, waste typically results. Over the course of the project, waste in the form of the following items occurs:

- Continuous rework of design, code, and testing
- Extended schedules
- Increased person-months of overall work
- Increased product costs
- Decreased morale

These wastes are confined to the project. But consider their impact to the user by increased product costs as well as the inevitable loss of revenue to the product's builder. Or consider the ultimate waste, the cancellation of the project brought about by poor product planning and by cost overruns. The cancellation of a project results in zero revenue.

Invest Today to Reap Tomorrow

It is wasteful to build a product for which the objectives have not been defined and approved. Know the objectives for the product you are building and carefully control any changes that are proposed later. Follow the simple process shown in Figure 9.2.

Interesting and often unexpected things happen when product objectives are put to paper (Step 1). For example, product planners suddenly might realize that many of the product's basic functions and features are unclear to other groups. Although the overall scope of objectives for the product might seem "obvious" to some, it now might become apparent that an additional level of refinement is needed before the product objectives are ready to be turned over to the product builders. Another example is that the marketing group might decide that more analysis of competitive product offerings is needed to better ensure that the functions and features chosen for this product will lead to the success of the product.

For maximum productivity and minimal disruption throughout the product development cycle, the product objectives must cover many aspects of the product. The next section, "What Should Product Objectives Address?" will identify specific areas that need to be addressed when writing product objectives.

 Lesson: A product objectives document forces important issues to surface early when they can be addressed most efficiently.

> **1** Document the product objectives.
>
> **2** Obtain agreement from the "approvers."
>
> **3** Control proposed changes.

Figure 9.2 Define and control the product objectives.

Putting product objectives on paper for all to see is often an enlightening experience for yet another reason: When the objectives are at a high level, perhaps written simply as "bullets" on several charts, interpretations of each bulleted item can vary widely. However, it is difficult to understand just how widely these interpretations vary until more detail behind the bullets is documented and studied. With the documentation in hand, a sudden unexpected flurry of issues may appear. When everyone has had the chance to study the product objectives thoroughly and realizes that they all will share responsibility for the success of the product defined, a very thoughtful and interested group of participants emerges. The marketers suddenly recognize that the product is insufficiently function-rich to be competitive. The service group sees it as deficient in serviceability aids and believes those deficiencies will restrict their profit margins. The human interface "gurus" believe the product is not intuitive enough for the typical user. The financial and forecast departments say it won't generate enough revenue. Representative users feel the product won't satisfy their primary problems and needs. And the development shop views the product as too much to deliver too soon.

So who's right? Not the point. The point is that, before this project gets on the road, a consensus of the right people (Step 2) or groups must be reached in order to avoid serious roadblocks later or, worse, the project being scrapped. And the most important element in this equation should not be overlooked: the user. If the intended users of a product (or at least a representative subset) have not participated in some significant fashion in defining and approving the product's objectives, how can there be any certainty that it will meet their requirements? This reasoning applies to a product built for a single customer, a product intended for use only within the company that built the product, or a product targeted for multiple user groups and customers. No matter what type of customer or the number, some valid representative sample of the targeted users must be included in the product objectives process. If this user involvement is weak or missing, you can expect rough going throughout the product development process—and beyond.

 Lesson: A contentious environment is almost always healthy for the product.

It is healthy for all the key groups that are required to build, launch, and support a new product to be heard and to be free to debate and negotiate their views and needs. A contentious environment can challenge a team to run lean and make decisions early—when they are the least expensive and the least emotional. Getting the *right people* to agree and feel ownership is like buying stocks low in an emerging bull market. It feels good and significantly increases the project's chance for success.

If "new" news appears later in the project and it is felt that a change must be made to the product objectives, then this alteration must go through a change control process (Step 3). This is a defined process that can be followed when a change is proposed in a critical, and therefore *controlled*, document—in this case, the product objectives document. The change control process ensures that the proper documentation and approvals are obtained; otherwise, the proposed change is rejected.

 Lesson: Changes solicited against an approved product objectives document must follow an enforced change control process.

Remember, the objectives literally define the basic direction of the entire project as the solution is being defined, built, and tested. The product objectives must be sufficiently complete and agreed upon to risk betting the company's allocated financial investment against—because that is exactly what is being done. Every time a product departs from the objectives, it costs. The farther into the development process, the greater the cost. Therefore, any changes made to the product objectives document should be controlled carefully once the product objectives have been approved. The recommended change control process is presented in Chapter 10, along with a discussion of product specifications. The change control process discussion is deferred to that chapter because it takes on a greater importance after the product specifications are approved, the project is nearly staffed to its maximum level, and the efficiency of communications among the project members requires greater attention.

It literally pays to do the required homework up front, before the full deployment of dollars, people, material, and time has occurred. While no activity in the software development process should be rushed, building complete product objectives is among the activities leading the list of those *not* to rush.

What Should Product Objectives Address?

Product objectives should address several different aspects of the product they define. These topics and the extent to which they are discussed can vary, depending on the type of product to be built. Compare the product objectives for a real-time, multitasking network program to handle the routing of telephone calls throughout the southeastern United States with the product objectives for a stand-alone, sort utility program that runs on a personal computer. Obviously there are many more factors to consider in defining the product objectives for the network program than those for the stand-alone, sort utility program.

Also keep in mind that product objectives are just that—objectives. They do not describe the product in detail. Certain areas might be, such as the intended audience for the product or the exact hardware it will support, but the way in which the product will be built and the syntax and semantics of its function should not be part of the product objectives. As you can see, this leaves wide room for the builders of the product to exercise their creative energy in developing the best possible product description (product specifications) and design.

The following categories, while not exhaustive, represent the more common areas to address in a product objectives document. Some are more important than others in that they are defined and agreed to very early in the product development cycle. Examples of these important categories include the overview of the solution, deviations from product requirements, definitions of the product audience, basic function, ease-of-use considerations, and overall architecture. These items need to be understood before the product design and detailed function can be described. Categories in which objectives can be delayed a bit might include product license agreements and packaging. If the objectives for these items will not be fully defined in the product objectives document, then a *place-holder* for these items should, at minimum, appear in the product objectives. This place-holder then acts to reference a forthcoming document of objectives for these items.

With each category that follows, a supportive example—in the form of questions—is used to illustrate further information that should be addressed in product objectives. A word processor program has been chosen as the product example because of its familiarity among readers and simplicity of concept.

Overview of Solution

Describe the overall solution to the problem defined in the product requirements document. If there is no product requirements document, then define the problem to be solved and the primary needs that must be satisfied by the new product. Explain how the solution solves the underlying problem and satisfies the primary needs of the intended users.

> Will the solution solve the problem that it is intended to address? Are the users' primary needs satisfied? Will potential customers reading this section be convinced that the new product will meet their needs? Enough so that they will want to invest in it?

Deviations from Requirements

Describe any aspect of the problem to be solved and the needs to be satisfied that are not being addressed fully. This is a place where a matrix can be built that maps the information in the product objectives document against the needs defined in the product requirements document. A matrix can help ensure that the full set of requirements are being addressed adequately.

> What are the requirements, if any, that the new product will not fully satisfy?

Audience

Define both the customer and the customer's environment for the product.

Is the word processor user expected to be computer literate? And if so, how much computer and word processing experience is assumed? For what reading grade level should the publications be targeted? Will the product user be expected to install the product, or will a data processing staff or even the authorized product dealer perform the installation? What level of problem determination is the user expected to handle? The dealer? The manufacturer?

Functions

Present the fundamental capabilities that the product should provide for its intended audience.

What are the basic required functions and features of the word processor? Examples are:

- Automatic installation
- Correct mistakes with multiple-level undo
- Cut and paste
- Borders and shading
- Create forms to fill in on-screen
- Create templates
- Provide and allow creation of on-line help screens
- Select fonts and type sizes
- Delete, insert, copy, move of characters, words, lines, blocks
- Set margins and page numbers
- Highlight text
- Check spelling
- Create address labels
- Select pages to print; spooled printing
- Fast mode for the experienced user

(Of course, these items must be described sufficiently in the product objectives document.)

Ease of Use

List all ease-of-use needs. These needs should be stated in terms of typical **usability tasks** that the user is expected to perform with the product. These tasks should be defined in terms of examples of typical customer hardware/software configurations and ease-of-use criteria that are measurable in a test environment. (See Chapter 11 for more on this topic.)

What are the typical tasks that a user is expected to perform? How much time, and with what assistance, if any, should it take for the customer to install the word processor? To begin to be productive? To recover from specific error situations? To learn how to use a specific function? To retrieve information from the product publications?

Architecture

Identify the architecture of the new product. The architecture defines the product in reference to its total environment; that is, the hardware and software configurations and communication protocols. It also can define the product's design at a very high level, particularly when a specific design is crucial in order to support the product requirements.

What hardware and software products and components make up the overall configuration? What communication protocols are used? What special design characteristics are expected to be followed? What areas of the new product will exploit the reuse of existing products, components, and modules in order to save time, resource, and expense and possibly improve quality?

Hardware Supported

List all hardware devices to be supported as well as the specific features of each device to be supported. Also, state the minimum machine configuration to be supported, including memory and disk storage requirements.

What printer models will the word processor support? What video display modes will be supported? What is the minimum memory size required? Will extra memory be exploited?

Software Supported

List all software products to be supported as well as any limitations of their use.

What software will the word processor operate with? What are the version and release levels? What limitations, if any, are there when operating with the software?

Performance

Define the critical performance needs that the product builders must satisfy. These needs should be stated in specific, measurable terms. It is here that any memory or DASD storage size requirements or program execution path performance requirements are listed.

How much time, expressed in user terms, will it take the word processor product to perform such actions as initializing and becoming ready for use, switching from one screen to another, retrieving or saving a file, or searching and replacing character strings?

Publications

Define the number, size, and types of publications; define what each publication will address and its specific audience. Also, list any special considerations, such as color or black-and-white publications and physical page size. This section also must satisfy those needs that apply from other sections defined in the product objectives. For example, the publications must be written to the proper reading grade level and experience level of the intended audience.

What consideration is being given to the layout of each publication in order to support ease of use for readers? What is the goal in providing examples? Will there be none, some, or many? For just some sections or all sections? What areas of the publications, if any, will be provided on-line? What special accommodations are provided for the new user? For the experienced user?

Standards

List the standards that must be followed. These standards may be the manufacturer's or specific industry standards, or both.

What data format types will the word processor product support? If documents will be distributed over a network, then what voice, graphics, imagery, and other data standards must be supported?

Reliability

Define the level of reliability of the final product.

What is the acceptable failure rate for the word processor in the user's establishment? How many problems are expected to be reported to the manufacturer for correction? What percentage and types of problems are expected to be corrected by the user? In the event of a failure or power outage, to what extent will the data and work files be preserved?

Serviceability

State how and where the product will be serviced and by whom.

Will the word processor customer and/or dealer have tools to aid in identifying problems? In resolving problems? Will failing modules be field-replaceable? Will a hotline number be available to handle problems by telephone? If so, for how many hours per day? Days per week?

Compatibility/Migration

State the level of compatibility that this product will have with other software and hardware products currently in use. If follow-on releases are planned, state the degree of upward compatibility expected.

Will the word processor user be able to use existing data and document files in their current format, or will a migration path be defined? Will this migration path require new software or hardware tools? To what degree will the user's existing hardware investment be protected? Will any new hardware be required? Software? With what release levels of existing and new software, including operating systems, will the word processor product run?

International

State the international-related functions and features of the product.

What foreign languages will be supported? What design features will be incorporated to ease translating the product for foreign markets?

Pricing/License Agreements

State the acceptable pricing range. Also, state the primary terms and conditions that apply to the purchaser, the seller, and the manufacturer.

How will a buyer of the word processor product be charged to allow one copy of the product to be used by multiple users within a network? Can the publications be purchased separately?

Competitiveness

State the degree of competitiveness this product has with similar products that are already available and with those that are anticipated to be available.

Will the word processor be a competitive price/performance product? What is its anticipated life span? Is this a one-time product or will it be replaced by follow-on products?

Packaging

Define all the options to be made available in packaging the product. State all media on which it will be distributed.

Will the word processor be made available on a personal computer with 3.5-inch diskette drives, 5.25-inch floppy drives, or both? On CD-ROM? Other? Will the product be packaged as one unit, or will it consist of multiple, individually packaged units? Will the product have the capability to be distributed electronically?

Security

Define security-related needs.

Will the word processor generate and use documents that have been encrypted? Can files be password-protected?

Futures

List future enhancements expected.

Will the word processor be enhanced to support the new generation of graphics displays anticipated to be available the following year?

The "Futures" category is useful in helping guide developers in selection of the design that will best support future enhancements. A list of future enhancements also provides a way to satisfy those approvers of the objectives who do not get everything they want in the first release, but at least feel that their desires are being planned for as the product evolves.

You might have noticed that several of these categories have no direct relevance to the programmers who design, code, and test the product or to the writers who write the product's publications. Many different organizations and skills are required to launch and support a new product successfully. The product objectives must give direction to *all* participating organizations so that each one is "singing from the same hymnal." This direction serves to ensure a unified, consistent, and complementary approach to building the product.

Invest the time very early in the software development process to create completed and approved product objectives. You will find the returns to be handsome indeed.

10

Product Specifications: Defining the Final Product

The continual addition of function enhancements to a product, throughout the software development process, is called *creeping function*. These enhancements creep into the product, line of code by line of code, until the weight of the code exceeds the committed schedule capacity of the project. It does not matter why these changes were accepted into the product. The result is that these constant changes literally can destroy a project, a product, and the morale of the people building that product.

It is essential that the answer to the following question is understood early in the software development process: What is the product to be built?

When the answer to this question is spread across the entire software development process, it usually will come as bad news. Why bad news? Because it is impossible to schedule a project's activities, to commit deliverables, to anticipate problems with the expectation of avoiding them, or just plain to act responsibly when certain planning-related activities have been neglected. These important activities are:

- Describe the full product, in detail, early in the software development process.

- Get agreement from the right people or organizations on the functional detail of the product to be built.

- Define, implement, and enforce an orderly process to follow when a functional change must be made to the product.

This chapter addresses these important activities. It also identifies the topics that a well thought out product specifications document should address.

A Project Tale

The following comprehensive scenario is an example of how creeping function can undermine a project. Do parts of this story sound familiar?

A new project has started. Both the product requirements and the product objectives have been written. Furthermore, all the right people and organizations have agreed to the contents of these two important project documents. The product's definition is off to a good start.

The detailed description of the product must now be defined. (This typically is accomplished through a document called the product specifications.) A small group of programmers has been working off to the side, prototyping the basic function and design of the new product. With the help of a generous amount of **scaffolding** or **stubbing** (temporary code that will later be discarded), a portion of the group's prototype is running. As with most projects, a great need exists to develop this product as soon as possible. Not only is there an attractive market for the product today, but the competition allegedly is planning to unveil a similar product. The company's management is supportive of the project and, at the request of the project's leadership, has already approved the required staffing of people for the project.

The project leaders have had experience in developing several other products, so there is a high level of confidence in their wisdom to plan and direct this project. Because the project is on a fast track, the leaders decide that time restrictions do not allow the "luxury" of writing full product specifications and getting the early agreement of participating organizations. Instead, an *overview document* will be produced. This document will record the portion of the product that is supported by the prototype work and appears to have general agreement by groups who have seen it. The overview document will be distributed, for information purposes only, as "this is what we are building," and no agreement will be solicited.

The person writing the document is one of the more knowledgeable project members and, unfortunately, also is needed to help lead in the remaining design activities. Since his time is critical, the project's leadership decides that he must complete the overview document as soon as possible. The document is "completed" within two weeks. The new people on the project find the document to be valuable as an educational aid in getting them on board. Schedules are now firmly in place and committed throughout the project as well as up through the project's leadership chain.

The leadership has divided the development organization into groups that will each work on developing specific components of the product. At this early juncture in the project, communication across the different groups appears relatively easy to manage. The groups' leaders meet regularly to resolve problems and present status information. The overview document that was intended as a substitute for the product specifications continues to evolve into more detail to accommodate each of the group's components. The leadership has decided that these changing "product specifications" must be "frozen" in order to stabilize the design activities. Even though schedules indicate that all changes to the "product specifi-cations" were to be completed by now, more work is required. However, the groups believe that the remaining work is relatively minor.

Time passes and this "minor" work seems never to end. Increasingly, more of the design assumptions are proving to be incorrect, and additional design changes are necessary. This is recognized as a result of neglecting to finalize the product specifications. Some frustration is beginning to surface due to the changing design coupled with the fixed, committed schedules.

Several groups are now falling behind their schedules. No serious concern is shown since it is still relatively early in the overall project schedules and "there is plenty of time to recover." The project continues to recruit new people to take on activities not yet in full gear. The test organizations are being assembled. So too are the writers for the product's publications. Excitement continues to mount as peo-ple are assigned to the various areas of the project.

Until now, the problem of incomplete product specifications has been con-fined primarily to the programmers charged with designing the product. But as the project grows in size and momentum, other groups have an increasing need to understand the specifications. The test group must design and write test scripts that verify the product performs as required. Members of this group need to know precisely how the user will install and use the product. They need to know what each screen will look like and what the product's responses to the user will be. The writers of the product's publications need the same information. In fact, the testers will verify the accuracy of the publications against the specifications.

The need for completed product specifications is growing urgent. Even though testing is not to start for quite some time, this period of the software devel-opment process is expected to be used productively in writing the first set of test scripts and in preparing the initial drafts of publications. Several options are explored to address the serious problem of incomplete product specifications. These options range from one extreme—the writers will create the product speci-fications under close direction from the designers—to another extreme—a large weekly education meeting will be conducted to share the latest information on specifications. The alternative chosen is to isolate the designers for three weeks so they can concentrate on completing the product specifications. While this will leave many of the project's people idle during the three-week period, it is decided that, over the long haul, this is the least painful approach.

Three weeks pass. The designers emerge with a document that they say is "all but complete." It is their view that, although remaining design activities might continue to impact some areas of product specifications, the specifications are now current and are sufficiently complete for the dependent organizations to proceed with their activities. The designers return to designing. This three-week slip also has meant at least a three-week delay in starting the detail design and coding. Sev-eral groups request that the product specifications be reviewed by all the depen-dent groups and updated until all groups approve their completeness and level of detail. The project leaders decide against this. Their rationale is: There is no time remaining in the schedules to allow for an approval phase for the specifications and at least 80 percent of the specifications are not debatable anyway. Debating the remaining 20 percent will only tie up the key designers. And if the key designers are consumed in meetings and debates, many people and groups dependent on the completion of their design work will suffer.

As the testers and writers begin their activities from the new product specifications, they freely admit that additional productive work can be done now. However, the farther they proceed into their activities, the more questions they have about the specifications. When they are analyzed carefully, the product specifications appear to have numerous weak areas. (These weak areas would have been identified and corrected had the product specifications been through review and approval phases.) The testers and writers are told they can have only minimal access to the designers. Frustrations abound, but restraint is shown. The designers also are getting increasingly frustrated by their inability to satisfy all the demands made on them to provide additional information and clarification. The numerous requests they receive to include additional functions in the product adds to this frustration. It seems some people just don't seem to understand or appreciate the designers' predicament. The designers rationalize that these people probably never worked on a software development project. (Or could they instead be people who sense something very wrong and are hopeful the same mistakes made on past projects will not be repeated here?)

As the designers continue to make changes to their copies of the product specifications, bits and pieces of their changes find their way to the dependent groups. It is becoming more apparent across the project that these changes must be given to everyone at the same time. A procedure is established to document and distribute changes to the product specifications. Everyone (except the designers) is ecstatic. Now change information is flowing from the source to the people who need it. While the designers recognize the need to do this, it is costing them time for which they had not planned. For everyone else, things begin to look up.

It is time to reevaluate schedules. There is, of course, much need (and pressure) to prevent schedule slippage. After several days of negotiations across the project, new schedules are established. Some relief is felt, but not enough to feel "right." Everyone will have his or her own challenges to overcome. Spirits, however, are reasonably high.

The product is now being unit and function tested. The first test by an independent group, called component test, is right around the corner. The initial drafts of the publications are also just around the corner. Things should be looking up. Unfortunately, this is not the case for all. It seems that the product specifications are still changing. Although the changes are not all major, the collection of numerous, small changes is making it impossible for the writers and testers to maintain their schedule commitments. Something needs to be done to shut down, or at least significantly reduce, the number of these changes. The designers say the changes are necessary because "the schedule" never allowed them the time to complete the product specifications during the early stages of the software development process. Also, they say that, as they proceeded into the design activities, corresponding changes were required in the product specifications.

The project's leaders decide that drastic steps must be taken to reduce, if not eliminate, the number of changes being made to the product specifications. These leaders form a "review board" and decide that all new changes must be approved by them personally and individually. Not everyone welcomes this bureaucratic step. However, it does cause fewer changes to be proposed and accepted. Apparently, two conditions are causing the product specifications to change. The first is that specifications were never completed and locked tight by a strict change control process. The second condition is the eternal desire of programmers to make things better—to add things that are "nice to have" but are not required. A consensus cannot be reached to determine which condition is more at fault. A consensus is reached, however, that both are factors in the creeping function equation. Regardless, things are looking better again; while current schedules still are not met, progress is proceeding at a more productive and predictable pace.

The project is now several weeks into component test. The first drafts of the publications are now available for review. A new concern is surfacing. Areas of the product specifications were misinterpreted due to the sketchy information available for some sections of the document. Misinterpretations also resulted because writers had limited access to designers, who could and should have made necessary clarifications to the specifications. Also, many of the commands, display screens, and product responses to the user are not consistent across the product. Because the product specifications were not "baselined" early, the different design groups evolved their pieces independently. This incompleteness and inconsistency must be corrected, which means more specifications, design, coding, test script, and publications changes—and, ultimately, more schedule slippage.

All these changes are made, including the revision of schedules—again. (Unfortunately, it will be shown later, that the original project schedules bear no resemblance to the final ones.) Due to the need to maintain schedules throughout the project, compromises continually have been made in the functions defined in the product specifications. Testing and publications trade-offs are made also. The resulting product not only looks different from originally anticipated, but there is now some pressure for the quality to be less than originally expected. No one specifically states or votes for lower quality. It is not an overt desire. It is a result— a result of the chaos brought about by incomplete product specifications and by a weak or missing process to control changes to product specifications.

Does this example have a happy ending? It is too late for that. A lot of irreversible damage has been done. The best that can be hoped for is that the product survives the cost and schedule overruns, is still competitive, is of acceptable quality, and is finally delivered to customers. Could this mess have been avoided? A definite "yes." Read on for how.

Controlling Creep

Three steps must be followed if you are serious about controlling creeping function. These steps are stated at the beginning of this chapter and are shown in Figure 10.1.

> **1** Establish the baseline: fully describe the product.
>
> **2** Obtain agreement from the "approvers."
>
> **3** Maintain control: Enforce a change control process.

Figure 10.1 Steps to control creeping function.

 Lesson: The product specifications fully define, early in the software development process, the product to be built.

You first need to describe the product to be built fully. This description must be in sufficient detail to allow the many diverse project groups to proceed with their missions. These missions include designing and writing the code, developing test scripts, writing product publications, and preparing the market and support plans for selling, distributing, and maintaining the product. The product description must be available early in the software development process so that all groups can proceed in a parallel and productive manner.

Because each group within the project needs the product definition for different purposes, all groups need to review and approve the product description, hereafter called product specifications. Each group needs to ensure that the proper level of information is documented and complete. Also, they must ensure that product specifications adequately reflect and support the product objectives.

Some changes to the product specifications as the product proceeds through the software development process should be expected. A process must be defined and followed to ensure that all changes that must be made to the product specifications documents are made in a strictly controlled manner. In fact, as stated in two earlier chapters, the product requirements document and the product objectives document also must follow an enforced change control process.

The discussions in the sections that follow expand upon the three steps featured in Figure 10.1.

Step 1. Establish the Baseline: Fully Describe the Product

Chapter 9 presented the importance of driving to approved product objectives early in the software development process. Briefly stated, product objectives are a crisp statement of direction, or framework, from which the project's money, people, material, and time will be committed. This early declaration of direction uniformly focuses a project's resources.

 Lesson: The product specifications define the product to the level of detail that allows all project groups to perform their activities productively.

But you cannot build a product from product objectives alone. The objectives are at too high a level. Much more detail about the product is required, detail provided in the product specifications document. Figure 10.2 illustrates the relative position of

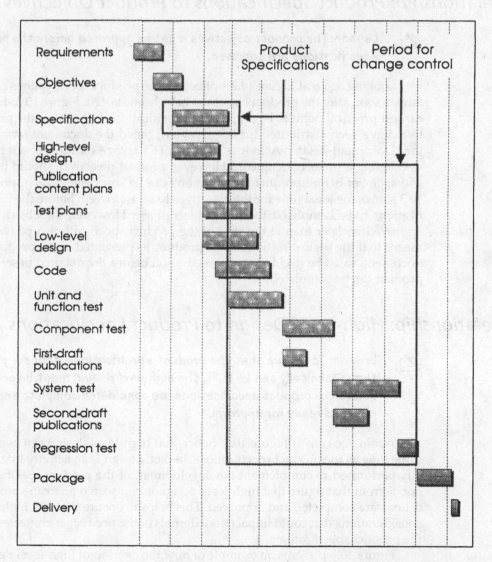

Figure 10.2   Product specifications and change control.

the product specifications in the software development process. The product detail found in the specifications is the same level of detail that potential users would require to understand and use the product. As stated earlier, it is also the level of detail required by the many organizations within the project to proceed productively with their activities. The product specifications *baselines*, early in the software development process, what the product that must be built looks like. With so many people and groups dependent on this detailed description, it should be easy to understand why it is important to document product specifications.

Relationship: Product Specifications to Product Objectives

 Lesson: The product objectives must be approved before the product specifications are approved.

Looking again at Figure 10.2, notice that the product specifications can begin relatively soon after the product objectives have been started. Figure 10.3 shows that the earliest practical point to begin product specifications is just after the product objectives have been distributed for initial review, called the document *review phase*. (See the "Document-Related Activities" section of Chapter 4 for more about the phases in developing a project document.) However, product objectives should be completed and *approved* before product specifications can be completed and approved. Figure 10.3 shows the ideal time for the objectives to be approved: before the product specifications have completed the preparation phase. However, the objectives must be approved no later than at the start of the product specifications update phase. This means that the basic direction for the product, as presented in the product objectives document, must be decided and agreed upon before the detailed description of the product can be completed.

Relationship: High-Level Design to Product Specifications

 Lesson: To ensure that the product specifications define a product that technically can be built, the high-level design must be complete before the product specifications are considered complete and accurate and ready for approval.

Again, looking at Figure 10.2, notice that high-level design can begin about the same time as the product specifications; in fact, design is an activity that is intentionally performed to complement the development of the product specifications. Also notice from that figure that high-level design is completed *before* the product specifications are completed and approved. This helps to ensure that any high-level design considerations that could impact the externals of the product are reflected properly in the product specifications.

Figure 10.3 presents an example of how the overlap of high-level design and the development of product specifications might be scheduled. The goal is to create an

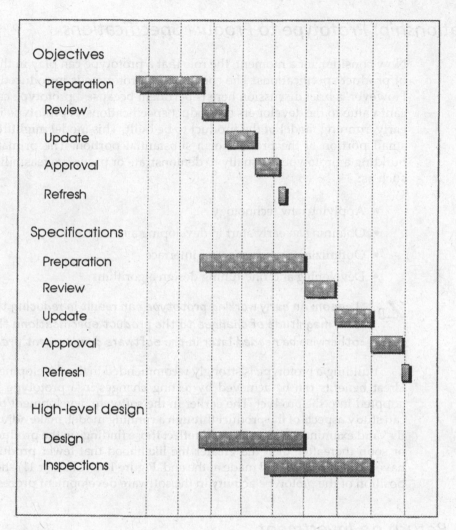

Figure 10.3   Overlap: Objectives, specifications, high-level design.

approval draft of product specifications that is fully supported by the high-level design. This means designing the product as it is defined and described in the product specifications. Inspecting the design can begin somewhere during the preparation of the product specifications, when sections of the specifications have been completed and also designed. Inspections must end by the time the update phase of the product specifications is complete. The approval phase of the product specifications consists of a document that fully reflects a complete and inspected design.

As you can see, the example provided in Figure 10.3 also shows how the product specifications and the high-level design overlap with the product objectives. For information on what is meant by inspections within the high-level design sequence of activities, see the "Defect Removal Activities" section of Chapter 6.

Relationship: Prototype to Product Specifications

Now consider, for a moment, the role that a prototype can play in the development of product specifications. The concept of a prototype is introduced in Chapter 11. However, a brief discussion here is pertinent because a prototype can have significant value to the developers of product specifications. A prototype is defined as an early, running model of the product to be built. This model might represent only a small portion of the product or a substantial portion. The primary purpose for building a prototype is usually to demonstrate or prove the feasibility of a concept, such as:

- Applying new technology
- Obtaining an early start in developing a new product
- Optimizing a product's user interface
- Developing and fine-tuning design algorithms

 Lesson: An early working prototype can result in reducing the volume and magnitude of changes to the product specifications that might otherwise be needed later in the software development process.

Building a prototype is strongly recommended in the development of a product. Great benefits can be achieved by testing changes in a prototype before they are adopted into the product. The earlier in the software development process that you can study aspects of the product through a running model, make adjustments "on the fly" and examine their impact, and reflect those findings in the product specifications or soon thereafter, then the greater the likelihood that fewer product changes will have to be requested and made at the end. Figure 11.2 (Chapter 11) shows the relative position of the prototype activity in the software development process.

The Return on Investment

To write the product specifications to the level of detail recommended here, you should expect to spend a bit more schedule time than is typical for some projects. However, this investment should be more than recovered later in the software development process. Why? Because the entire organization starts off on a more productive footing. Also, significantly less rework is expected since fewer functions should need to undergo change.

 Lesson: The product specifications document is the most important project document in the software development process.

Once again, it is in the best interest of the product and the project to establish a baseline for what the product will look like by defining *all* of the final product in the product specifications. People and organizations depend on complete and accurate information in order to do their work. The longer the development of *complete* product specifications is delayed, the longer completing the product will take. This translates to higher expenses and lower revenues. The investment in completing the product specifications as recommended here will likely draw interest for the remainder of the software development process, and beyond.

The recommended information to be included in the product specifications document is discussed later in "What Should Product Specifications Address?"

Step 2.   Obtain Agreement from the "Approvers"

The next step in controlling creeping function, as shown in Figure 10.1, is to get agreement from the product approvers. The phases to follow when developing project documents are discussed in the "Document-Related Activities" section of Chapter 4. That discussion is relevant here because drafts of the product specifications are distributed for review and approval.

After the product specifications are written and distributed for review, you can expect some differences of opinion to emerge from various groups across the project. These differences should be viewed as healthy for the product and should be *welcomed input*. It is better to make changes that are right for the product now rather than to wait until the design, coding, and much of the testing has been completed. The costs of making product changes can increase dramatically the further along the product is in the software development process.

 Lesson: All groups dependent on complete and accurate product specifications must approve the document to ensure it meets their needs.

Literally every group in a project has some stake in the completeness and accuracy of the product specifications. Many groups will examine product specifications to ensure that the specifics and/or the spirit of the product objectives have been followed. The productivity of some of these groups will go into a nosedive if the specifications do not have the data or detail that the groups require in order to fulfill their commitments. Therefore, it is especially vital that this important project document receive the approval of all groups participating in the software development process.

There is another value in getting agreement from the participating groups, though perhaps not as obvious: The more that people believe in the product, the more their ownership will be demonstrated. Ownership can be translated into commitment—and it is commitment that will greatly increase a product's chances for success. People are much more interested in working on a product that they feel a part of than on a product that they perceive was dictated to them. Obtaining their approval helps in winning their commitment.

Step 3.   Maintain Control: Enforce a Change Control Process

The final step in achieving victory over creeping function (see Figure 10.1) is to define, implement, and enforce a process to follow for making changes to the product specifications.

 Lesson: Even the best-written product specifications will require some changes as the product is being built and tested.

The project that has, early in the software development process, documented product requirements, product objectives, and product specifications *and* has reached agreement on these documents is off to a strong start indeed. Starting a project with the product definition under control is an enviable (to projects that have failed to do this), but achievable, accomplishment. But what happens if some change in the approved functions is necessary? Even the sharpest minds cannot anticipate all future changes. Once the lowest level of design or the coding begins, deficiencies or oversights might be discovered. Also, product testing, particularly usability testing (see Chapter 11), might uncover undesirable user interfaces.

Figure 10.2 shows the lengthy period of time that follows the approval of product specifications. Throughout this period, changes to the product specifications might be required. Any changes to a product's description must be made with the considerations listed in Figure 10.4 in mind.

A **change control process** should be followed to ensure that the following occur:

- Only necessary changes are made to the product.
- Changes are communicated to all.
- Changes are implemented in an orderly fashion.

- Is the change necessary? In this release?
- What groups are impacted by the change? How will dependencies and schedules be impacted?
- Is there a more effective and preferred change to the one proposed?
- What documentation must be produced to document the change properly?
- How and when can the change best be made with the least negative impact?

Figure 10.4   Questions to ask before making a change to the product specifications.

There are many methods to choose from in implementing a change control process. Figure 10.5 provides one example of how a change to the product specifications might be made. The method shown can be supported by an on-line change control tool; however, for purposes of illustration, no dependency on an on-line tool is made.

Representatives from across the project are chosen to form a group. This group is commonly called a committee or *board*. When a technical change is deemed necessary, the originator of the change brings the change proposal before the board and attempts to convince the board members of its need. If the board agrees to accept the change into the next step of the change control process, the programmer with the responsibility to design and implement the change then must study the proposal. This study includes doing the following:

- Documenting the precise change that must be made to the product specifications
- Completing the high-level design
- Understanding the impact to all components of the product
- Developing an implementation schedule

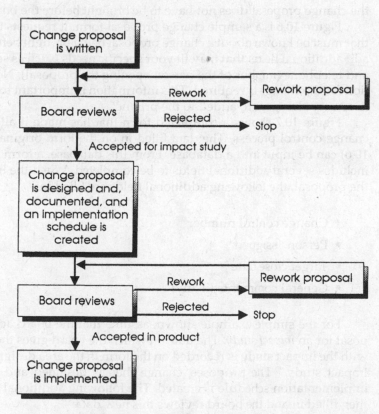

Figure 10.5   Change control process.

This "homework" is done to ensure that the true impact of the change proposal is understood before a final vote is taken by the board. Then the board reviews this new information and can make a much more educated decision as to whether to accept or reject the change. If the change is accepted, the proposal becomes part of the product plan and is tracked along with other product work items.

If the change proposal is not accepted, then it is slated to be reworked and then resubmitted to the board, or it is rejected. If the change proposal is rejected at any time in the change control process, one of three actions can occur:

1. The originator can escalate the proposed change to higher management in an attempt to win support for the change proposal.

2. The change proposal can go into the *product outplan* and be considered for inclusion in a future release.

3. The change proposal is rejected, with no intention of future consideration.

If the change proposal is trivial, or the previously mentioned homework is completed before the proposal is first taken to the board, the board may act immediately on the fate of the proposal. This can save time in the change control process because the change proposal does not have to be brought before the board twice.

Figure 10.6 is a sample change proposal form. It requests the initial information that must be known about a change proposal being brought before the board. You can add additional fields that may fit your specific needs (such as severity of the problem and telephone number of the person opening the proposal). Notice that the justification for the change is required. This information is important to help ensure that only necessary changes are added to the product.

Figure 10.7 shows a completed form that has made it all the way through the change control process. The data filled in on the form originally submitted (Figure 10.6) can be input into a database. From this database, a form can be generated that includes several additional fields to be completed. When the board initially reviews the proposal, the following additional fields are filled in:

- Change control number
- Person assigned
- Target close date
- General comments (if any)

For the simple example shown, assume that the board accepts the change proposal for an *impact study*. The date on which the board gives the go-ahead to proceed with the impact study is recorded on the form in the area designated by "accepted for impact study." The proposed change then is designed and documented, and an implementation schedule is created. The following additional fields on the form are then filled in and the board reviews this new data:

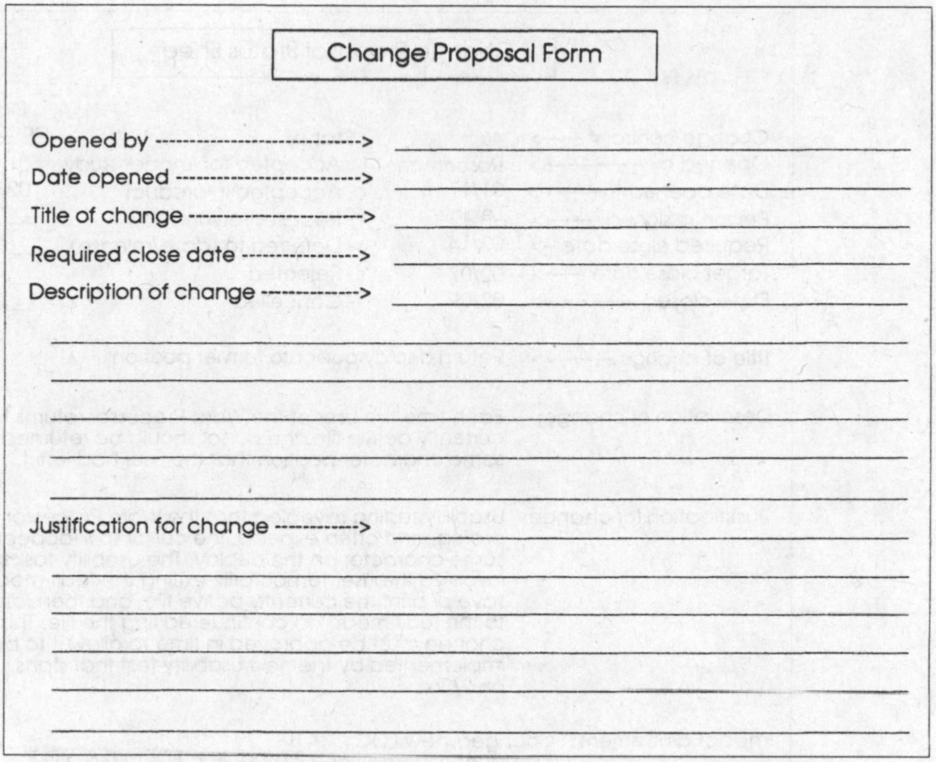

Change Proposal Form

Opened by ----------------------------> ______________________

Date opened ---------------------------> ______________________

Title of change -------------------------> ______________________

Required close date ------------------> ______________________

Description of change ----------------> ______________________

Justification for change -------------> ______________________

Figure 10.6 Change proposal form.

- Impact assessment
- Check mark to show that the product specifications section has been completed
- General comments (if any)

If the board accepts the change proposal, the date is recorded in the area on the form designated "accepted in product" and "date closed." In this simple example, the board might have approved the change proposal the first time it was reviewed. Why? Because the board may be able to recognize that the design, code, test, and documentation impacted was minimal and needed no more study. (The 10 LOC depicted in Figure 10.7 means 10 lines of code.) However, some projects might insist that all changes undergo a thorough evaluation to prevent unexpected problems later.

The example just discussed is included to give you some insight into how the "board" operates. For some projects, the data gathered here might be too much; for others, too little. For instance, you might want to consider other factors before a change proposal is accepted in your product. These factors may include:

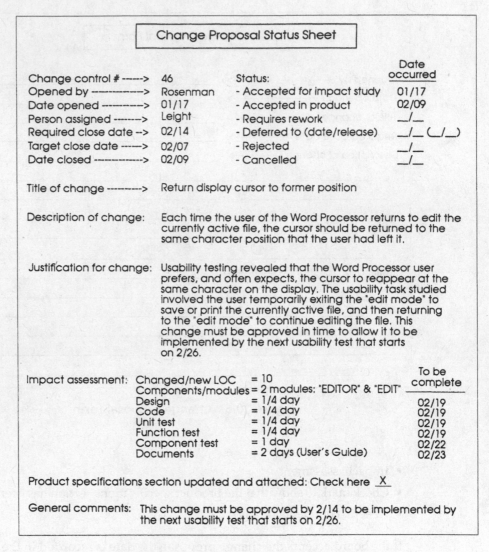

Figure 10.7   Change proposal status sheet.

- What alternative solutions were investigated?
- What is the impact to the product's performance?
- What is the impact to the product's compatibility needs?
- How will the implementation be tracked to its completion?

 Lesson: A strictly *enforced change control process is essential for a* **well-managed software development process.**

A similar change control process should be followed in making changes to the approved product requirements document and the approved product objectives document. Whatever change control process is chosen, and whether it is the same or different for these important project documents, it is imperative that all changes to the product offering be made in a controlled environment. This ensures that only needed changes are made, that each organization can understand the impact the change has to their work activities, and that the change is made at the proper, orchestrated moment in the software development process. The goal is to maintain control throughout the software development process by strictly enforcing a defined change control process.

What Should Product Specifications Address?

The goal here is to define and document a reasonably complete and accurate description of the product. Emphasis is on *reasonably complete and accurate.* Describing all of a product perfectly the first time will be next to impossible. As stated earlier, some refinement to the product specifications is expected as design, coding, and testing unfolds. However, there is a major difference between refining some areas of the product and making major functional changes. If the necessary time and creativeness are expended early in the software development process, then changes to the product specifications during the software development process will likely be far less serious and far more manageable.

A precise description of *what the product is* should span the full product—from installation of the product to usage of the product to providing help in recovering from errors. The following topics are guidelines for use in determining what should appear in the product specifications document. Refer to Chapter 9 for more information on references made to the product objectives. If there is no product objectives document for sections of the product specifications to refer to, then the "objectives-level" information should be included in the product specifications.

Overview of Solution

If more detail is needed than that already described in the product objectives, expand on it here.

Deviations from Objectives

If the product to be described is different in any way from the direction provided in the product objectives, list those deviations here. This will prevent the need to update, redistribute, and reapprove the product objectives document, because the approvers of the product specifications document include the approvers of the latter. It also will ensure that the product objectives and the product specifications properly support one another.

Functions

Describe all the functions to be provided by the product. The functions described here also are called the product's **externals**—that is, what the user of the product will see and use. Externals include commands, programming interface instructions and linking conventions, and their complete syntax and semantics. Also, include what many think of as ease-of-use considerations. These include presenting all screens and their contents, the steps that the user must take in selecting each screen, displaying all the responses from the product that the user may see, and including all messages and return codes. If the product comes with an on-line tutorial, then that too should be documented here. This section, which describes the product functions, will be the largest in the product specifications document.

Remember, the goal is to document a reasonably complete and accurate description of all the product's function. Some changes to the description of the product are expected. The change control process will help to manage those changes in the controlled manner necessary.

Hardware Supported

There is no need to duplicate what is written in the product objectives. If, however, more detail about specific hardware devices must be clarified before the product can be built, tested, and documented completely, then do it here.

Software Supported

There is no need to duplicate what is written in the product objectives. However, if more detail about specific software must be clarified before the product can be built, tested, and documented completely, then do it here.

Resources

The system resources that the product requires should be listed. These include memory and DASD storage requirements, and buffers. Also, any related product information should be included. For example, if the product requires a specified minimum amount of memory, describe what happens if more memory is available. Will the product take advantage of the additional memory? If the product supports multiple users simultaneously, what is the impact to system resources of the addition or deletion of each user?

Installation

The precise procedure and tools for installing a product should be defined in full. This section also should include packaging information if it affects the installation.

For example, if the product is being shipped on diskettes, you should describe the number of diskettes that make up the product, the sequence in which they are used in the installation process, and the general layout of each diskette.

Performance

If there are performance requirements in addition to those already stated in the product objectives, state them here. Performance requirements typically state minimum expectations. However, given that additional system resources might be available, describe what performance benefit the user will see.

Publications

It is advisable to avoid discussing publications in any detail in product specifications. Instead, publication content plans (see Figure 10.2) should be created after the product specifications have been issued. The content plans describe, in detail, the layout of each manual to be produced, chapter by chapter. This layout cannot be defined until the product specifications have been completed and distributed for review. The layout cannot be defined and approved fully until after the product specifications have been defined and approved fully.

Standards

List all the standards to be followed in the development of the product. These include in-house standards to be used during the design, coding, testing, and maintenance phases of the project. Referencing a separate document that will define the standards and methodology to be followed for the project can be helpful. This will allow the approval of the product specifications to be distinct and separate from the internal development methodology that programmers will follow. Thus, the approval of one document does not hinder the approval of the other.

Standards that relate to industry acceptance also should be listed. An example might be the protocol to be used for transmitting a product's data from one computer system to another. Some of these standards already might have been listed in the product objectives. Again, if the product objectives list is complete, there is no need to duplicate it here.

Compatibility/Migration

If more detail is needed than that already stated in the product objectives, document it here. Remember, test groups will rely on the detail both in the product objectives and here to plan their testing, so be precise.

Security

State what the security-related product offerings are. Whether it is password protection, an encryption provision, a function that checks the infection and spread of computer viruses, or a physical key lock, the details of its use must be stated in the product specifications.

Other

Other features, some of which are introduced in the product objectives, may or may not need to be in the product specifications. You must decide whether additional information should be provided. The decision you reach will depend on the product you are building and whether there is an immediate need for more information by the users of the product specifications. For example, if the product will be marketed in foreign countries, a section on "international" might need to be added since this could affect the functional content.

Planning for Control

Throughout the software development process, there are many challenges to face and problems to be solved. Many of these obstacles are predictable and avoidable. As in the start-up of a small business, the failure rate of new software development projects is quite high if you define "failure" as not only the cancellation of the project but also a project that has overrun its original cost and schedule projections.

People usually think more clearly and are thought to be wiser with hindsight than when they are deeply entrenched in the middle of a demanding project. Your own most objective moments might seem to occur just when you are completing a project or when you are contemplating beginning a new one. Moreover, the farther removed you personally find yourself from a given project, the more objective your views seem to be about solutions to problems facing that project. At these times, you might quickly recognize what could have been done differently to improve the overall productivity, quality, and cost on a project. This is also the point when there would be little argument in insisting on well-defined and approved product specifications and a clearly defined and strictly enforced change control process. Do not ignore history and your instincts—two powerful sources of input in making decisions. Define what you will build *before* you build it.

Consider a final example to illustrate the importance of defining what you plan to build before you build it. When members of a company decide that they want some *other* company or group to build a product for them, what happens? The company looking for bidders does the obvious—it defines a *statement of work*. That is, the bidders interested in building the product need to understand what they are to build. The company that wins the bid must be certain that it fully understands what it is committed to build. Only then will the winning bidder be able to plan satisfactorily the costs, resources, and schedules to be committed.

 Lesson: It is good business to define what you are going to build before you build it.

Do not treat your own project any differently. If a full description of the product to be built is important both for the company asking for bids as well as for the bidding companies, it follows that this product description is indeed a critical exercise. It also follows that it is important to control changes that might be attempted throughout the software development process closely, because each change introduced into the product likely will result in an added cost. If these things are required of others, then also understand the value of imposing the same requirements upon your own project. Commit yourself to defining the product and the change control process early. Commit to this before you enter your next **thrashing zone,** where your biases, emotions, commitments, and good intentions will make it infinitely more difficult to implement a sound plan for controlling creep.

11

Product Ease of Use

Great strides have been made in recent years in understanding the importance of the term *user friendly*. The widespread popularity of personal computers has made computing available to a much wider audience and a much less computer-literate audience. The success of a growing number of program products has been attributed in large part to the ease with which users can both learn and become productive with these products. Today more thought goes into the design of the person-machine interface, called the **user interface,** than ever before.

Unfortunately, many products still come to market with obvious usability deficiencies. Many of these products are developed with little early consideration for the user interface. Often the most significant attention to product usability comes during the latter part of the software development process, sometimes more as an afterthought than as a significant planned activity. Not only does it cost more to make coding and documentation changes later in the cycle, there also is considerably less time to validate the acceptance of the user interface. Frequently, there is too little time.

This chapter reveals the major activities in the software development process where attention to usability can have the greatest positive impact on the product under development. It also introduces techniques that can be used to define, plan, test, and measure the new product's usability characteristics.

A Project Tale

The following scenario suggests how the level of attention invested in the **ease of use** of a product is, all too often, an afterthought.

A new software development project has started recently. The proposed product is recognized as being very important to the company's business. Its sponsor has convinced the company's higher management that the product can be built on a very aggressive schedule. The product requirements document has been written and approved. The product objectives document restates, from the product requirements, the important need for the new product to be user friendly. However, the product objectives mention no specifics that can be measured or tested.

Product specifications are in the process of being written. The technical leaders of the project are "heavy techies" and are focusing on the internal design structure of the product. They object to spending any appreciable time on "simple and less significant stuff" such as product ease-of-use features. They are staunch believers in their own ease-of-use philosophy, which proclaims: "There isn't any one right answer anyway, so our way is as good as another way." They feel that the product's usability will evolve as the product begins to be tested. "After all," they assert, "if the product can't run, what use is a friendly interface?"

The leadership in charge of the overall project, however, recognizes the need to focus early on the usability of the product. And to prove the commitment to ease of use, a junior programmer new-hire with usability experience, Angus Gladstone, is given the task of defining the user characteristics of the product. It is learned that Gladstone's usability experience consists of three human factors college courses and an expressed interest in usability.

It is expected that the user interface will be defined in the product specifications. However, some significant but "temporary" compromises are adopted to avoid delaying the completion of the product specifications. More specifically, these compromises are judged to be necessary because, first, the schedule to complete the specifications is very tight; second, any user interface features chosen require additional internal design to support them; and third, Gladstone is having a difficult time getting a consensus on his user interface preferences. Most of the compromises are contrary to his desires. The experienced programmers tell him that "We can always change the user interface later if and when we find a better interface."

Several weeks pass. The product specifications are available on schedule. Gladstone is happy in his belief that he has bought time to study the user interface alternatives further. Since he has minimal product development experience and minimal firsthand user interface design experience, he proceeds slowly, but enthusiastically. In the meantime, much of the product is being designed and coded. The temporary user interface described in the product specifications is now being implemented, with some minor improvements.

Several more weeks pass. Gladstone is now ready to introduce his proposed usability changes into the product. To his dismay, he finds that he missed the "window" for making changes of the magnitude he is proposing. He is hopeful, however, that he can lobby the programmers to make the changes "off to the side" and add them into the product during the component test activity of the software development process.

Gladstone soon learns that he is going to have an uphill battle. The aggressive product schedules are proving to be too aggressive. Independent of any usability changes, the schedules have slipped. Not only is a two-week development buffer lost, two weeks of component test also have been consumed. The few programmers who were on schedule with their modules now must wait for those late modules that they are dependent on for function testing. When component test finally starts, it has slipped another week and is now a full three weeks late. Gladstone is told that it is now too risky to jeopardize the stability of the code going into component test with the major user interface changes he is proposing. Most of these changes, incidentally, still have not been implemented. Many of the programmers who would have to implement these usability changes in their design and code are too busy trying to recover, or at least maintain, the already slipped schedule.

Gladstone is told by some of the seasoned leadership that there is still time to ensure that the product's usability is acceptable. (Notice that "acceptable" is the term used now.) Since a plan exists to have the testers evaluate the product's usability while they are testing it, there is still some hope for making usability changes if the testers support the need for them. As it turns out, some usability problems are identified by the test group as well as by a few outside people who have been tinkering with the product. Unfortunately, on closer examination, it is decided that the big-ticket, usability-related corrections must be delayed until the next release of the product. However, some minor, easy-to-fix usability problems are corrected. The product's publications are beefed up to compensate for usability deficiencies in the code. It is hoped, for a brief moment, that this customer set will do what most other customers of these types of products *don't* do: actually read the publications to discover how to circumvent some not-so-intuitive user interface problems.

What started at the beginning of the software development process as good intentions has ended the same old way. Good intentions, but little results. What can you do differently?

Objectives

A product's user interface consists of *all* aspects of a system's operation that are perceived by the user. It is much more than the *look and feel* of menus, mouse selections, and help screens. It is an understanding, an intuitive feel, that the user realizes when he or she is introduced to a product and the environment in which that product operates. Ideally, the goal is to create a product that the user will feel bears a remarkably close similarity in performance to typical noncomputer tasks, because these are tasks with which the user is intimately knowledgeable and comfortable. Examples of these tasks are shown in Figure 11.1.

This ideal product is one that allows the user to, in a very short time, feel at home with the concepts, logic, and interactions it provides. If the product is introducing a new concept in performing some common work task (such as discarding old files in a cabinet), then it must take full responsibility in guiding the user through the necessary actions. The user should not be given the opportunity to stray unwittingly to a

- Writing a note
- Checking a note for correct spelling
- Sending a note to a friend
- Retrieving a past note for reference
- Filing a note in a cabinet
- Searching for a telephone number
- Creating a budget for next month
- Calculating interest on a loan

Figure 11.1   Typical user tasks.

point at which problems arise (such as accidentally deleting the wrong file and being unable to recover).

 Lesson: Ease of use is basic product function—not something that merely is nice to have.

Having stated these things, now is a good time to assert that ease of use is basic product function. That is, ease of use must be *planned from the beginning* if there is to be any expectation that it will happen at all. If ease of use comes about as an afterthought, the user surely will recognize the inconsistent, incomplete, and unintuitive implementation. Also, when ease of use is planned and implemented as an afterthought, schedule slippages and higher product costs result.

Before the solution is planned, it is important to have a product requirements document state the ease-of-use needs of the intended users of a new product. With these usability needs documented, the people charged with proposing and developing the new product can feel more certain that the proposed new product will indeed satisfy its intended audience.

Planning the solution involves defining usability objectives in the product objectives document. Figure 11.2 shows the point at which the usability objectives (and the usability requirements) are addressed in the software development process. This figure also shows where the other major usability activities occur. The figure will be cited several more times throughout this chapter.

 Lesson: Ease of use is a primary topic addressed in the product objectives document.

Many meaningful statements can be made in the product objectives document that will provide ease-of-use direction. This direction is needed not only to develop the product specifications, but also to decide usability trade-offs that might need to be made throughout the software development process. Some examples of usability-

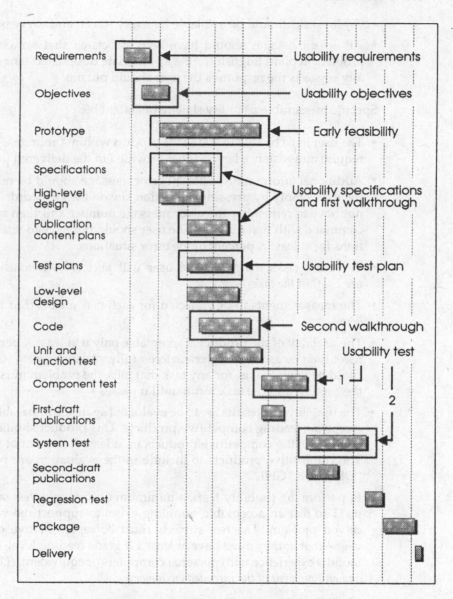

Figure 11.2 Major usability activities.

related statements that could appear in the product objectives (or the product requirements) are:

- The user should not be made to respond to, or input to the program product, anything that the program could have determined itself. Examples include having to remember data that the program already is capable of recalling or inputting information that the program could detect, such as how many disk drives are configured on the system.

- On-line help should be available for every screen and every prompt.
- All error messages should have help associated that not only explains the problem in plain English (or the appropriate designated languages) but actually suggests the responses the user should pursue.

Specific measurable usability statements might be:

- The user must be able to install the product within X minutes. The user should require no assistance beyond that provided in the delivered product.
- Additional information about an error message should be made available to the user simply by pressing a function key on the keyboard. The user should not have to remember the error message number and then type an operator command with that number. The user should not have to refer to the publications for at least X percent of the error situations.
- The basic tasks that a typical user will perform when using the product are . . . (*List the tasks here.*)
- The measurements to be collected for each task are . . . (*List the measurements here.*)
- The usability of the product is acceptable only if at least X percent of the tasks meet their measurable criteria successfully. (A simple pass/fail measure also could be used; that is, for any task that fails, the problem must be corrected in the product and the task rerun until it passes.)
- The usability test results are to be evaluated against comparable test data gathered from leading competitive products. This product should be equal to or better than the competitive products in at least X percent of the tasks tested. The competitive products to include in the evaluation are products "ABC," "DEF," and "GHI."
- In performing usability tests, a minimum of X people (test subjects) must be used so that an acceptable sampling exists to support the validity of a perceived problem. The test subjects must be representative of the product's user—that is, they must have at least a X grade reading level, have less than X months experience with personal computers or equivalent. (*Define the audience and environment of the intended customer.*)

For a product that is intended to have a superior user interface, ease of use must be defined as the entire product is being defined, because, to the user, the user interface *is* the product. Delaying attention to the crucial user interface increases the separation of the user interface considerations from the rest of the product function. This all-too-typical separation makes about as much sense as pairing a round peg with a square hole. If you are going to build a product, all aspects of that product must fit together naturally. The mutual design of different product aspects is paramount to ensure that they achieve a complementary and supportive fit with one another.

Usability Tasks

 Lesson: Identifying and understanding the tasks that a user is expected to perform with the new product is essential in validating that the usability objectives are met.

Figure 11.3 provides an example of some basic tasks that a user might perform with a new product. Notice that a task is typically a simple set of actions to be performed by the user of the product. The product chosen for this example is a word processor. The tasks listed will be used during the usability testing activities to ensure that the product's ease of use meets the usability objectives. The tasks should not be too complex or contain a large number of actions to perform. If a task is not defined simply, it could frustrate the test subject, not to mention the product's intended user, and it also might make determining how to correct the problem difficult.

Before going any further, this is a good point to define a frequently used term: **test subject.** A test subject is a person who helps to test a product as it is being developed. This person is expected to use the product in ways similar to those of the finished product's users. Consequently, the tasks that a test subject performs on the product are expected to be the same or similar to tasks that a user will perform. The

- Install.
- Create a new document (Document 1).
- Define margins and page length.
- Define heading and footing.
- Type several pages of text.
- Save Document 1.
- Print Document 1.
- Retrieve Document 2 (already created).
- Check for spelling errors.
- Set tabs.
- Change font of all section headings.
- Center all section headings.
- Move, copy, and delete groups of text.
- Search for and replace groups of text.
- Left and right justify all text.
- Save Document 2 under new name.
- Delete Document 2.

Figure 11.3   Sample tasks for a word processor product.

best test subjects are actual or potential customers. This *live user* involvement is, by far, the most beneficial form of testing to employ in order to certify that a product truly has met its ease-of-use objectives.

The second-best category of test subjects includes those who appear to meet a substantial number of the characteristics that define the product's users. For example, if a product is being developed for secretaries in the insurance industry, using secretaries who have no knowledge of insurance terms and operations yet have comparable secretarial skills can be beneficial. These secretaries first would be trained in insurance industry terms and operations before actually starting the tests. Choosing the right set of test subjects will aid greatly in ensuring that the right product is developed.

Measurements

> *People's minds are changed through observation and not through argument.*
> —*Will Rogers*

 Lesson: Observing and recording the impromptu actions of test subjects is an excellent technique to help measure a product's ease of use.

The type of measurements that can be collected from running each task include those shown in Figure 11.4. Of these examples, perhaps one of the best tools for measuring a product's ease of use is to record the spoken reactions and statements of test subjects as they proceed in performing the basic tasks of the product. These immediate verbal and facial expressions allow observers to gain insight into the journey that a user follows in exercising the product. This technique can be invaluable in discovering fundamental product design problems. By carefully studying the user's trail, the points in the product that caused him or her to go astray can be easily identified.

Consider the next example: identifying the number of unrecoverable errors. If an unrecoverable problem occurs, it could represent a serious defect in the product. It may mean that the product user will require assistance from the manufacturer, the dealer, or some other source. It also could mean that the user will perceive that the product's manufacturer delivered a product before it was ready.

An *assist* is help that a test subject requires in order to complete a task within a specified time limit. Identifying the number of assists is important because they indi-

> - Record impromptu statements made by test subjects.
> - Identify the number of unrecoverable errors.
> - Identify the number of assists.
> - Apply a user-satisfaction rating (1 through 5).
> - Determine whether tasks are completed successfully.

Figure 11.4   Sample measurements from performing each task.

cate how long a test subject takes to perform tasks. A product's user, given enough time, might be able to accomplish a given task without assistance. However, each task should have a reasonable time limit defined. A user will not want to spend his or her limited time trying to overcome ease-of-use deficiencies in the product.

A user-satisfaction rating is a useful tool for learning how the test subject really feels about the product's functions and ease of use. Figure 11.5 illustrates some sample questions that can be asked after each task has been completed. The best results are collected when the questionnaire is administered immediately after a task has been completed. This is when the test subject's views about that task will be the sharpest. These questions can do a lot to help pinpoint areas of annoyance to the user.

Notice that two types of questions can be asked of the test subject. One type involves questions that can be answered by choosing from a predefined set of responses. The questions listed in Figure 11.5 that fall into this category are numbers 1, 3, 6, 8, 10, and 13. A sample set of the response choices is shown in Figure 11.6.

The other type of questions are those that require the test subject to respond by writing his or her personal comments. Figure 11.5 lists these questions as numbers 2, 4, 5, 7, 9, 11, 12, and 14.

You also can develop a special set of questions for the test subject to respond to after all tasks have been run. Examples of these questions are:

- What did you like most about the product?
- What did you like least about the product?
- What improvements overall would you suggest?

1. How satisfied were you with performing this task?
2. What would have made this task easier?
3. How satisfied were you that the tutorial prepared you for performing this task?
4. What did you especially like about the tutorial?
5. What tutorial changes would you suggest?
6. How satisfied were you with the terms used?
7. List any terms that you did not understand.
8. How satisfied were you with the on-line help?
9. What on-line help improvements would you suggest?
10. How satisfied were you with the documentation?
11. What did you like about the documentation?
12. In what areas of the documentation would you suggest improvements?
13. How satisfied were you with the amount of assistance you required?
14. What changes would you suggest that would reduce the assistance you required?

Figure 11.5   Sample questions to ask after each task.

1	__	Very satisfied
2	__	Satisfied
3	__	Neither satisfied nor dissatisfied
4	__	Dissatisfied
5	__	Very dissatisfied

Figure 11.6   Sample response choices.

Five examples of measurements are listed earlier in this section. The first four have been discussed already. Now consider the fifth example: determining whether tasks are completed successfully. If you were to track only one measurement, this would be the one. However, the more measurements you collect, the higher your confidence will be that you can predict the user's acceptance of your product. For example, the test subject might have completed a task successfully within the allotted time but might have had to use trial-and-error techniques to get a function to work correctly. In this case, the user satisfaction rating would help reveal some of the test subject's specific frustrations.

Interpreting Measurements

Once you have collected measurements from each task, what then? Must all tasks have passed in order to declare the usability of the product satisfactory? This is one approach. Another approach is to define several, measurable criteria that can be used collectively in determining whether the overall usability test was successful. For example:

- Number of assists per task is less than or equal to .33.
- Satisfaction rating is "2" or better for 90 percent of the tasks.
- Ninety percent of the tasks are completed successfully.

   Lesson: The usability of a product can be measured.

Notice that some assists can be considered acceptable. In the case shown, if the average assists per task is less than or equal to one assist per every three tasks, then this is within acceptable bounds. Also, note that the satisfaction rating must be a "2" or better for at least 90 percent of the tasks, while at least 90 percent of all tasks must be completed successfully.

All of these criteria are somewhat arbitrary. They should be set at levels you believe are necessary to develop a winning product for your targeted audience of users. However, the criteria must at least meet or beat predecessor products and competitive products. The levels at which you set these criteria can depend on several factors. One factor is the skill level of the audience. If first graders will be using the product without assistance, then ease of use must be superb, and you should want 100 percent of the tasks to be completed successfully. If the product is intended for an office environment in which a programmer is expected to assist in installing the product, educate users, and be on call to assist when necessary, then development of a product with which users may require occasional assistance may be acceptable.

Other factors to consider in setting levels for measurable criteria include the type of product being developed, its number of users, its availability requirements, and the offerings from competitors. While many of the areas discussed in this chapter are quite subjective, it is essential that you set usability objectives very early in the development cycle so you can pace yourself against those goals.

Publications Objectives

As stated in an earlier chapter, the product objectives document also should provide direction for the publications that must be developed. An alternative is to provide a separate publications objectives document. In either case, the statement of direction for the product publications must be defined and documented at the beginning of the software development process. The type of usability-related areas to be addressed might include:

- The reading grade level for the targeted audience is to be set at the Xth grade.
- The publications will consist of four "books":
  —Installation pamphlet.
  —User's guide.
  —Reference manual.
  —Fold-out reference card.
- The introduction of every user command also must include at least one example showing how that command typically would be used.

 Lesson: If you want your product to have superior ease of use, then ease of use must be planned at the start of the software development process.

The examples offered in this section only scratch the surface of ease-of-use direction that can be provided in the product objectives. Remember, the crisper the direction, the more likely the final product will have satisfactory ease of use. Superior ease of use must be planned.

Specifications

 Lesson: The complete user interface is defined in the product specifications.

When the product specifications are defined in detail, all of the user interface also should be defined. This detail should be included in the product specifications. (See Figure 11.2.) The specifications should present the product just as the intended user will see and use it. (See Chapter 10 for general information on product specifications.)

User interface items that should be described in detail include those items listed in Figure 11.7. Other areas appear in the product specifications that also relate to usability but are better defined under a different topic. An example is the definition of the maximum time allowed for the product to respond to a user's request to switch screens. This has obvious usability impact but can be defined more appropriately under the topic of "product performance."

 Lesson: The user will judge the ease of use of a product by using both the publications and the programs that make up the product.

Ease of use also should be addressed when publication content plans are written. Content plans will describe the user interface to be designed into the publications. Keep in mind that the product's user will judge the *friendliness* of the product from both the publications (includes online text) and the programs. If either fails in ease of use, the product as a whole will be perceived as failing. Some ease-of-use items to be described in detail in the content plans include:

- Definition of specific, user-oriented tasks and how they will be used in the layout of each book
- Placement, scope, and variety of examples and illustrations
- Use of colors, bold printing, and italics
- Rules to be used in developing indexes

- All screens and prompts
- All messages
- How the user will get from one screen to the next
- How the user will select options from, or input to, each screen
- How the user will select the help functions provided
- Fast-path functions provided for the more experienced user
- On-line tutorials
- Use of screen highlighting and colors
- The precise product installation sequence

Figure 11.7   User interface information to be described in the product specifications.

Prototype

A **prototype** is defined as an early running model of the product to be built. This model may represent only a very small portion of the product, such as the interaction between several of the product's menu screens so that menu selection techniques can be studied. Or the model may represent a substantial portion of the product so that many of the product's functions can be demonstrated. The primary purpose for building a prototype is usually to experiment with, demonstrate, or prove the feasibility of a concept, examples of which are listed in Figure 11.8.

 Lesson: Building a prototype is an essential activity in a software development process.

The remainder of this section will focus on the benefit of a prototype in developing a product's user interface. You should view the building of a prototype as an essential part of product development. A lot can be learned about a product very early in the software development process by examining and "tweaking" its prototype. This valuable information can have a positive influence on the remaining development of the product.

Building a prototype to study the user interface characteristics of the new product can begin after the product objectives are understood reasonably well. (In some cases, often before a product has been approved for funding, a prototype actually might be built before the product objectives are started.) While it is possible that the development and study of a prototype will have some influence on the final product objectives, the major influence will be reflected in the product specifications and beyond.

Figure 11.2 shows the relative position of the prototype activity within the product development cycle. Notice that the prototype activity begins about the same time as the product specifications begin to be written. The benefit of prototype activity extends at least until the start of component test. Component test typically marks the first time that product code and publications are available for testing. With running product code and publications available, there is less dependency on the prototype. However, the prototype can be used throughout the software development process to

- Applying new technology
- Promoting a proposed product to higher managment or to customers
- Developing and fine-tuning design algorithms
- Obtaining an early start in developing a new product
- Optimizing a product's user interface

Figure 11.8   Benefits of building a prototype.

observe the effect of potential user interface changes before the changes are adopted into the product.

 Lesson: Expect a product being built to have ease-of-use deficiencies that were not as apparent when the product had only been defined on paper in the product specifications.

The prototype code typically represents a small fraction of the total amount of code that will need to be developed for a final product. Since significantly less effort is required to build a prototype than a complete product, prototype changes usually can be accomplished rather quickly. The ability frequently to alter various aspects of the user interface built into the prototype, and then to examine those changes for acceptance, offers a great opportunity to influence the user interface defined in product specifications. What looks good on paper often does not work in the "real world" with typical users. Consequently, each improvement made to the user interface early in the software development process can save a significant amount of rework later. Therefore, you want to maximize the benefit of the prototype as early in the software development process as possible.

As the product evolves through the development process, the prototype can continue to be used to anticipate ease-of-use problems before running product code is ready. Figure 11.2 shows the prototype activity ending at the start of component test, the usual point at which running product code is collected in a single driver. However, the prototype can continue to be enhanced as long as it offers a quicker and less expensive way to identify user interface problems early and to experiment in searching for the most acceptable solutions to identified problems.

It is a good idea to seek ways to port, as much as possible, the prototype code to the real product. Doing so can be especially beneficial if you anticipate that the prototype will grow to a significant size. If a sizable amount of code is developed that works identical to the way the product's code will work, then finding a lasting use for some of that code is a great additional benefit to draw from the prototype.

Test Plan

After usability objectives are in place, some method must be followed to verify that the usability defined in the product specifications and subsequently designed into the product meets requirements. Of course, the real goal here is to ensure that the ease of use built into the product is satisfactory to the intended audience. Any use of the term *product* now refers to the entire package that the user receives at the time of purchase. The product could consist of a tutorial, several programs, and several publications.

The *usability test plan* defines how the product's user interface will be *certified* as having met its objectives. This test plan should address answers to the following types of questions.

- What usability tests will be conducted?
- What are the entry and exit requirements for each test?
- What are the detailed schedules supporting these tests?
- Who are the persons responsible for the various aspects of each test?
- What are the detailed scenarios that support each usability task?
- What hardware, software, and tools are required to support each test?
- When and how will the use of a prototype be employed?
- How many test subjects are to be used for each test?
- What are the experience profiles of the required test subjects?
- What process is to be used in identifying, recording, and verifying the usability problems encountered?
- What training will test observers receive?
- How many test subjects per test observer?
- How will a task be recognized as passing? Failing?
- If a task has failed, how might it eventually pass?

The usability test plan is completed relatively early in the software development process, as shown in Figure 11.2. This ensures that each test becomes part of the official product process and is adequately planned. Tests that the usability test plan should define, at a minimum, are usability **walkthroughs** and **usability tests**. These are defined in the next sections.

Usability Walkthroughs

 Lesson: Usability testing can begin on a product before running code and publications are available.

These usability tests are called walkthroughs because running product code and publications drafts are not available yet. Usually the user interface is available only on paper, such as that found in product specifications, or a portion might be available in a prototype. However, the portion of the user interface to be inspected should be defined completely at this point. The user interface is examined by "walking through" the available user interface information. A walkthrough always should include the use of a prototype, if one is available, that addresses the portion of the user interface to be inspected.

A walkthrough usually consists of several people assembled to verify the correctness and acceptability of the user interface. These people include both test subjects as well as actual developers of the programming and publications user interface functions. The test subjects are asked how they would go about performing predefined tasks based on the known detailed user interfaces of the product defined in the product specifications. As the test subjects walk through the user interface, either on paper or using a prototype, or both, any problems found are logged. Care should be taken to ensure that the *product* is being tested and *not* the test subjects themselves. The goal is to identify as many product problems as possible now so they can be addressed and the product retested at the next usability test (as defined in the product's usability test plan). The earlier that these problems are identified, the easier and less costly it is to make the necessary product changes.

Performing two walkthroughs can offer a great benefit. Although three or more walkthroughs might seem to be even better, there is a point where more is not better. It takes time to prepare for the tests, conduct the tests, and correct the problems discovered during each test. Figure 11.2 shows the recommended points in the software development process for conducting each walkthrough. If your software development process is longer than 18 to 24 months, you might be able to accommodate additional walkthroughs.

 Lesson: After performing a usability test, always allow time to fix the problems identified before the next usability test is conducted.

The first walkthrough should occur after the user interface is defined and documented, but before the final level of product specifications is completed and distributed. This process allows time for any corrections to be made before the specifications are distributed. Once distributed, many groups use the specifications to plan their work activities (such as designing and coding programs, writing publications, and developing test scripts). The more complete and accurate the product specifications, the less rework that might be required later—rework that can impact several groups.

The second walkthrough should occur after low-level design has been completed and coding has started. This allows time for corrections to be completed for problems found during the first walkthrough. It also provides time for the developers better to understand any gray areas that surfaced either during the first walkthrough or from experience in being farther along in the development of the product.

The participants are the same for the second walkthrough with the exception of the test subjects, who are all new. This fresh set of views helps to ensure a more objective evaluation of the corrections made and increases the sampling size of test subjects. If the new test subjects find some of the same problems as before, and the problems were thought to have been corrected already, then careful analysis needs to be made before further product changes occur. If the test subjects find no new problems, the implementation of the user interface probably is on the right track. If only a small sampling of the test subjects from the first walkthrough discovered annoyances, then no corresponding corrections might have been made. However, if any test subjects from the second walkthrough encounter the same annoyances, then the likelihood increases that these annoyances are real problems and should be considered for fixing.

The great benefit of these walkthroughs is that problems are found early and corrected early. Notice that no running product code or publications drafts have been produced yet.

Tests

The next tests following walkthrough testing will evaluate the usability of the product with both real, running product code and complete drafts of the publications. These tests have been called by many names—customer tests, first-customer tests, user tests, user-oriented tests, and user product tests. They will be called simply usability tests here. These tests are similar to usability walkthroughs in that new test subjects are asked to perform a series of predefined tasks with the product. A significant difference is that the test subjects do not perform the tasks in a group setting or on a prototype. Instead, the test subjects are sitting at the computer (or at a computer display and keyboard) and are attempting to use the product just as a first-time user would.

The actions of each test subject typically are monitored for later analysis. A variety of monitoring techniques can be employed. Examples include those listed in Figure 11.9.

If a test subject needs help, it is given only after he or she has exhausted a search for ways to correct the problem within a reasonable time period. A time limit usually is set so the tests continue in a productive fashion. A time limit also helps to reduce the likelihood that a test subject will become seriously frustrated on any given task.

After each test subject attempts all tasks, the data are gathered for analysis. At this time, valuable data recorded from the monitoring process are compiled. The types of data collected and evaluated can be identified in the following questions.

- How many attempts did a test subject have to make before successfully completing a task?

- What was the precise sequence of steps taken as information was being retrieved from the publications?

- What book index entries were expected to be there but were not?

As part of the process in gathering this data, the test subjects are brought together in a room with the developers and publications writers. The test subjects then give their perceptions of the product: what was good, bad, confusing, easy, missing, and so on. The developers and publications writers are allowed to ask questions in an

- A test observer sits nearby and records every action made by the test subject.
- A video camera records the actions of the test subject.
- A software program records all keystrokes made by the test subject.
- Various combinations of the above.

Figure 11.9   Techniques used in monitoring test subjects.

attempt to understand the perceived problems better. After the data are collected and analyzed, a log of the problems is prepared. Then action plans are developed to address each problem. A prototype can be used to "correct" many of the problems and to verify resolutions before they actually are implemented in the product.

 Lesson: Run usability tests only on code that has passed a prede-fined set of tests to ensure its operational stability.

As with the usability walkthroughs, two usability tests seem to be optimum for most projects with a software development process of 18 to 24 months in duration. (See Figure 11.2.) The first usability test occurs halfway through component test. This allows time for the code being component tested to become more stable, with the first wave of bugs identified and corrected. If the usability test starts too soon, the code might have too many defects to allow a productive usability test to occur. It is a good idea to predefine a set of test cases that must be run successfully before the usability test can begin. Once these test cases have been run successfully, the usability tests can begin. Note also that the first draft of the publications is now available to become part of the usability test. Once usability problems are identified, the goal is to have them corrected in the product before the second usability test.

The second usability test starts shortly after system test begins. Again, there must be stable code in order for the usability test to be productive. The final draft of the publications is now available. Overall, the product is in its final stages and should be very close to what the user will see and use. Any problems found now must be corrected before system test ends, since system test provides the last opportunity to make product changes. If usability design and testing have proceeded as defined in this chapter, relatively few usability problems should be discovered at this point in the software development process.

 Lesson: Always be on guard to rationalizing away real usability prob-lems that have been fairly identified; ignoring these problems can have a long-term disastrous, perhaps even irreversible, effect on the acceptance of the product.

One more point: When product planners, designers, programmers, writers, testers, and so on are defining and building the product, the operational aspects of the product typically seem obvious to them. Yet to a user who has just been introduced to the product, there will likely appear a host of items that are *not* so clear. This chapter has introduced a sequence of steps that, when followed, can yield a superior ease-of-use product. However, beware of a danger that is common to many development projects: ignoring or attempting to rationalize away the ease-of-use problems that are identified by many test subjects participating in the planned usability tests. There are many reasons to argue about the validity of identified ease-of-use problems. Figure 11.10 identifies some of the common "excuses."

The face of the matter is that test data obtained from usability tests are invaluable if you are to provide a product that will be judged to have a superior user interface. Do not ignore these data or allow them to be argued away. You might find it benefi-

> - "Ease of use is too subjective a concept for me to seriously consider these changes."
> - "The test subjects represented too small a group of users for their comments to be considered statistically valid."
> - "The project schedules do not allow time to make these changes."
> - "It seems obvious to me."
> - "The user will have difficulty only the first time the function is attempted."
> - "The user will get used to it."

Figure 11.10   Common "excuses" for ignoring usability problems.

cial for this topic to be discussed among the project's personnel early in the software development process—before potential problems can surface. Also, the project leadership must fully support the ease-of-use journey that is chosen for your project.

Working at communicating the benefits presented in this chapter to others in a project will prove beneficial, both in the short and long term. Once tried, you also will be amazed at the speed with which these concepts are accepted on the *next* project. Most people will come around to understanding and supporting these benefits fairly quickly. After all, who wouldn't want to have the best user-friendly product available?

Ease of Use: The Competitive Edge

 Lesson: Products that have superior ease of use have a distinct competitive advantage.

The process defined here to yield a superior user-friendly product might seem like a lot of work. But it can result in a level of success for your product that would not be achievable otherwise, a success triggered from a perception that your product is truly easy to use. You get what you plan for. If you are not willing to invest in this process, one of your competitors will. Whatever product you are building, chances are that someone has or is building a similar product. Those who offer products that are easy to use have a distinct competitive advantage.

When your product is available to customers, will it stand out as a product that is easy to learn and use? The number of users of software products is growing rapidly. These users are increasingly less computer literate. They will purchase and stay with the products that allow them to get their work done with the least amount of effort. User-friendly products are becoming an essential customer requirement.

12

Development Testing: Strengthening the Weak Link

Product testing falls within two categories: **development testing** and **independent testing.** Figure 12.1 maps these two categories within the software development process. Development testing is that testing typically performed by the developer of the code. Development testing spans the unit test and function test periods. Independent testing, spanning the component test and system test periods, occurs after the development testing has been completed and is best performed by test personnel who have not developed the code to be tested. This chapter focuses on the *development test* period.

 Lesson: Development test is a common weak link—cause of problems—in the software development process.

The thoroughness with which code is tested during the development test period has a direct impact on the quality of code that will enter the independent test period. If code is poorly tested during development testing, independent testing will uncover many more problems than would be necessary otherwise. Furthermore, this increased volume of problems will result in longer independent test schedules. These lengthened schedules will tie up the programmers who developed the code as well as all support personnel, causing them to remain in force on the current release of the product longer than is planned or desirable.

There is yet another negative, often overlooked side effect of poor development testing: It has been shown that the volume of defects entering the independent test period is linked to the volume of defects that will still remain in the final code when

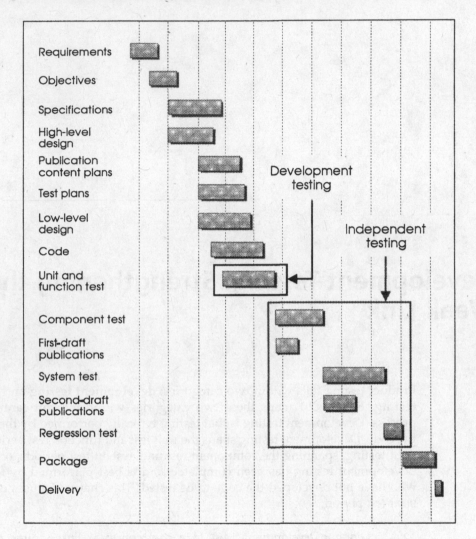

Figure 12.1   Testing in the software development process.

the product is delivered to the customer. This negative relationship not only causes additional expense in making repairs to the product after it has been shipped but also can undermine sales and, therefore, the overall success of the product.

If the independent test period is to be productive, two activities must occur.

1. Development testing activities must be planned and anticipated.

2. A trackable process for development testing must be defined and exercised to ensure conformance to the testing plans and to monitor schedule progress.

This chapter addresses these important development testing areas.

A Project Tale

The following scenario demonstrates how a poorly managed development test period can disrupt the remaining software development process significantly.

It is another new project. The general consensus is that the project is off to a good start. The product requirements, product objectives, and product specifications have been documented and approved. A control process is in place for any changes that might be made to these important project documents.

The schedule is in place and many of the developers feel it is reasonable. Why don't *all* the developers support the schedule? Some of the more experienced programmers feel that additional time is needed to do the right job on development testing. The project head declares, "Additional time for development testing would be nice, but I know you programmers. You would take all the time you could to drive your design, coding, and testing to perfection. And that time doesn't exist on any project." The project head also states that it is essential that the currently defined schedule be met if this product is to ship on time. Besides, the independent test is there to find bugs left over from the development test period. (Isn't it?)

The general view from within the trenches is that the people calling the shots on the project have developed other products, so they qualify as being experienced. And even though the schedules of many of these earlier products missed their original targets, the project leadership ultimately had accepted those schedule slips. (What *else* could they do?) Therefore, it is rationalized, this must be the accepted way to plan and manage a software development process.

Two months pass. The detailed design of the product is all but complete. Most of the coding is nearing completion. At this point, the product's work effort is defined in terms of program modules. Each module has an assigned owner, who is responsible for completing all the development testing on it.

To perform this development testing, two phases typically are required. The first, called unit test, is the isolated testing of each logic flowpath of code through the module. The second phase, called function test, checks to make sure each function executes properly through all modules that it spans. During unit testing, and sometimes function testing, artificial testing environments, also called scaffolding or stubbing, might be necessary. This is because most other areas of the product might not be sufficiently far enough along in their development to be included in the testing of a specific module or a specific function of the product.

There are several new programmers in the group. They ask if they must follow any specific process during the development test period and are told that they must have their unit and function testing completed on their modules by the start of independent testing. They also are told that, in effect, "If you want to do any functional testing that requires modules you don't own, you must negotiate dates to do so with the owners of those modules." However, the more seasoned programmers tell the newcomers that how they choose to do the development testing is up to them. To save time, some of the more experienced programmers say they often bypass unit testing. Furthermore, they frequently function test only the primary paths to "spot check" their overall code quality. After all, independent testing will test error paths and most, if not all, of each function. The newcomers are relieved to hear this. They estimate that if they had to test every piece of logic in the code, they would not be able to deliver it in time to meet the already committed schedule for the start of independent testing.

The development testing period has started. Some of the programmers have begun to develop test plans that identify the functions they want to test and the testing process they will follow. This approach was abandoned by most because there just was not time to do a complete job of planning. Besides, some owners of modules said they could not commit to any development testing dates. The buzz words were "It's available when it's available."

All are doing the best they can. When the project leadership collects status information, the answer always comes back, "We are on schedule." It was difficult not to be on schedule. Everyone knew the date when independent testing must begin. It was the same for everyone. The name of the game is to test "as much as you can" before that date.

The start date for independent testing arrives. All the product's modules are placed into a library controlled by the independent test group. This means that no developer can change any module's code without following a special process intended to control the type and frequency of module changes. The independent test personnel do not want the modules disturbed simply to make trivial changes, such as updating code commentary. Nor do they want random changes coming in at all times of the day or week. Changes must be made in stages to ensure that the more important problems are addressed and corrected first.

The modules are all linked together for what appears to be the first time. This linked set of modules, called a driver, is delivered to the independent test team. Independent testing begins, and immediately stops. The driver won't "come up." The developers are summoned to identify the bug. They do. The correction is patched into the driver, and the updated driver is delivered to the independent test team. Testing begins again. And stops again. This series of starts and stops consumes a full week. Translated, this means that the independent testing period has lost one valuable week.

The independent test team had developed charts that projected their progress each week. They had expected to be 10 percent through their test cases at the end of the first week. They are at 1 percent. No one seems to be too nervous. There were a couple of weeks of buffer in the test schedule. One experienced tester remarked rather confidently, "This is normal. It happens this way in every product I have ever worked on."

Some testing progress is made during the second week. However, not as much as projected. Five percent of testing has been implemented. Moreover, 40 percent more problems have been found than were projected. An experienced developer of the product code stated to a newcomer developer, "See, didn't I tell you that the bugs we didn't find would be found in the independent test?"

This rather slow progress continues for several weeks. The tests are now 35 percent complete. However, they were projected to be 85 percent complete by now.

The project leadership is beginning to feel worried. Not only is the schedule end date in jeopardy, the developers are tied up fixing bugs that the testers have found. Some of those developers were scheduled to move into other projects by now. Everyone is working overtime, some an excessive amount.

A work group is formed to determine what can be done to protect the schedule. Some creative ideas are found, but none that will support the existing schedule. The ideas considered include:

- Adding more developers to fix bugs.
- Performing inspections of the code for the error-prone modules.
- Canceling planned vacations.
- Doing more patching of code rather than fixing the source code and relinking modules.
- Adding developers to the independent test team who would possess the skill to determine the cause of a problem and immediately devise a corrective patch in the failing module(s).

All of these ideas are implemented to some extent. However, the schedule slips three more weeks. If these actions had not been taken, it is believed that the schedule would have slipped six weeks.

Better progress is now being made, but still not at the rate originally projected. One major obstacle is the numerous bugs being found in the interfaces between modules. These problems are surfacing in large number because modules from different owners were not sufficiently integrated during the development test so that their interfaces could be tested.

The scenario could continue, but you probably get the picture. In this scenario, before the product is ready for delivery to a customer, it encounters several more delays in the overall schedule. Especially painful was the need to pull the product out of packaging several times so that newly discovered bugs could be fixed and the code regression tested again. This is a sign that the product entered packaging before it was ready, probably because someone made a schedule-related decision rather than a quality-related decision. Had more time been provided to complete the unit and function tests properly, the overall schedule might have slipped only a little, or perhaps not at all, thus allowing independent testing to be more productive.

Unit Test

Recall the definition of unit test presented in the preceding scenario: It is the isolated testing of each flowpath of code within each module. All code should be executed. Also, all primary logic path combinations should be verified for correct design and coding. Figure 12.2 can be used to illustrate this point. Assume the flowchart shown represents the flowpaths within module ABC. Seven *distinct flowpaths* are identified and are labeled one through seven; however, as many as 12 *flowpath combinations* conceivably could be executed:

1 and 5, 1 and 6, 1 and 7

2 and 5, 2 and 6, 2 and 7

3 and 5, 3 and 6, 3 and 7

4 and 5, 4 and 6, 4 and 7

 Lesson: All code should be executed during unit test.

Unit testing of module ABC should result in, at a minimum, execution of *all* code. This requirement would be satisfied if the seven distinct flowpaths are executed. However, another factor must be satisfied: All *primary logic path combinations* also must be executed. A primary logic path combination is defined as a commonly used sequence of flowpaths that a module will be instructed to execute. Without knowing precisely what functions module ABC performs, one cannot know what the primary logic path combinations are for this particular example. The flowpaths that make up a primary logic path combination demonstrate a relationship to one another. This is not to say that the remaining logic path combinations, referred to as *secondary logic path combinations*, can be ignored. However, many flowpath combinations in a real module will never occur. Furthermore, the secondary combinations that are possible stand a good chance of being tested if both of these required conditions are satisfied:

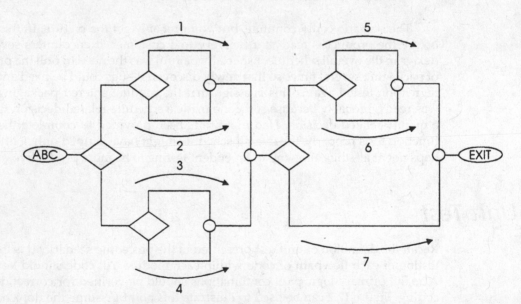

Figure 12.2   Flowpaths for module ABC.

- All code (therefore, all flowpaths) is executed.
- All primary logic path combinations are executed.

 Lesson: Not all flowpath combinations can be executed.

For almost any module, it is impossible to test every mathematical combination of flowpaths. This is because not all flowpaths bear a logical relationship to all other ones. By definition, if there is no logic relationship between two or more flowpaths, they will never be executed together. Let's look again at Figure 12.2 for a simple example to illustrate this point: If conditions that allowed flowpath 2 to execute, or conditions that resulted from the execution of flowpath 2 result in flowpath 6 never being executed next, then the flowpath combination of 2 and 6 will never occur.

Unit Test Plan

Having defined unit test, the next logical question to ask is: "What should a *unit test plan* talk about?" A unit test plan should provide the following:

1. For each module, identify the set of flowpaths that will be tested to satisfy the two required conditions presented in the preceding section:
   — All code (therefore, all flowpaths) is executed.
   —All primary logic path combinations are executed.
2. State the method to be used to create the test environment that will allow all these flowpaths to be executed.
3. List the entry and exit criteria for starting and ending the unit test period. Include dependencies on people and equipment.
4. State the schedule to be followed for starting and ending the unit test for each module.

Item 1 was discussed in the preceding section. Notice that if you follow these recommendations, you should find that all error conditions within a unit also will be tested.

Item 2, which states the method to be followed, primarily refers to the manner in which the unit testing on a given module will be conducted. Since other interface-related modules probably will *not* be available for the module's unit test, the environment on entry to the module (data areas, registers, and buffers) must be generated artificially to simulate the conditions necessary to test against. To prevent unpleasant surprises later, this temporary testing environment should be planned carefully and rigorously. Also, the expected output from the execution of each logic path should be identified so you can compare actual output against planned output. Care also should be taken to ensure that a comprehensive range of possible data values is tested. For example, if the valid range of values for an input field is 1 through 10, it is advisable to test at least the outside values of 0 and 11, as well as 1, 10, and some value in between. The point here is to include range-testing where appropriate.

Item 3 simply says to define what must be in place before the unit test can begin. One obvious example is to specify that each module's code has been written completely and compiled error-free. Another example is to have a completed unit test plan in place. Also list dependencies that must be satisfied in order to start unit testing, such as the necessary hardware or software that must be available. This hardware/software list should include any testing and debugging tools that are needed. Item 3 also requires that the exit criteria be defined. In other words, how does the programmer know when testing has been completed? Having specific exit criteria identified helps to keep one honest and better able to objectively view testing progress in the proper perspective. One example of unit test exit criteria: All unit test flowpaths and combinations of flowpaths must have been run and have produced expected results, with any problems corrected in the source code and verified.

For Item 4, if a module is very large and its unit testing will spread across many days, then more than just starting and ending test dates are required. Milestone dates that fall between the start and end dates should be identified for the module. These milestones could signify when certain percentages of code and/or flowpaths have been tested. This tracking approach helps the module owner to compare actual progress with his or her plan. It also provides the project leadership with a method to track the progress of unit testing routinely.

 Lesson: Always complete test plans before they are implemented; that's why they are called "plans."

The test plans should be written sufficiently in advance of the actual unit testing to ensure enough time to prepare for the unit test. The unit test plan for that module should be ready when code reviews are performed on that module's code, if such reviews are planned. It is strongly recommended that at least one peer or the team leader reviews the unit test plan. This offers a good check and balance to ensure the plan's completeness and accuracy.

Function Test

Function test is the testing of each product function through one or more modules, but more typically across two or more modules. This is the first time that modules are linked together and the interfaces across modules are verified. In fact, testing the interfaces across modules is a primary objective of function testing.

 Lesson: The less need there is to employ artificial test environments, the more reliable the testing.

Another objective is to do as little "jury-rigging" as possible. That is, you want to minimize the need to construct artificial testing environments. All modules of the product do not have to be available and linked together at the same time. However, it is strongly recommended that those modules related through functional dependence with one another be available at the time of testing for that function.

Figure 12.3 illustrates this point. The product shown is a text editor. The GET command can be used as an example of a function to be tested. Assume, for purposes of illustration, that every text editor command must first be parsed and syntax checked before it can be processed by its corresponding command module (in this case, the GET command). To test the GET command, the following modules must be available and linked to avoid creating an artificial test environment:

EDITOR, PARSE, SYNTAX, MESSAGES, GET, READ, ERRORS

Figure 12.4 is a matrix that shows the modules that are executed depending on the function being tested. This example lists seven functions: invalid command, three variations of the GET command, and three variations of the SAVE command.

Take a closer look at the GET command. Because other modules (such as SAVE and EDIT) are not necessary to test the GET <file> functions, they do not have to be linked with the needed modules. Notice that if only the error-free paths of the GET command are to be tested, then the modules MESSAGES and ERRORS would not be necessary. Figure 12.4 is grossly simplified to illustrate the basic concept of a "function versus module" test matrix. This matrix is a useful tool to ensure that all mod-

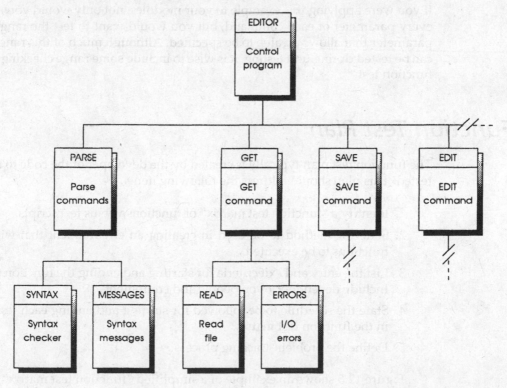

Figure 12.3   Module linkages for a text editor.

Function to test	Modules									
	EDITOR	PARSE	SYNTAX	MESSAGES	GET	READ	ERRORS	SAVE	EDIT	
Invalid cmd	X	X		X						
GET \<file\> No errors	X	X	X		X	X				
Syntax error	X	X	X	X						
Read error	X	X	X		X	X	X			
SAVE \<file\> No errors	X	X	X					X		
Syntax error	X	X	X	X						
Write error	X	X	X					X		

Figure 12.4 "Function versus module" test matrix.

ules required to test a function have been identified and planned for accordingly. This example has assumed only one parameter (\<file\>) on the GET and SAVE commands. If you were applying this example to your modules, not only would you need to test every parameter of each command, but you would want to test the ranges for each parameter that allows a value to be specified. Although much of this range checking can be tested during unit testing, it is wise to include some range checking during the function test.

Function Test Plan

The function test plan typically is created by the developer of the code to be function tested. This plan should address the following items.

1. Identify a "function test matrix" of functions versus test scripts.

2. State the method to be used in creating an environment that will allow all functions to be executed.

3. List the entry and exit criteria for starting and ending the function test period. Include dependencies on people and equipment.

4. State the schedule to be followed for starting and ending each test identified in the function test matrix.

5. Define the problem-tracking process.

Figure 12.5 shows an example of a simplified "function test matrix" that item 1 references. Item 1 requires that all the functions to be tested are listed, say, along the left margin of a matrix. The product specifications document should be used to identify *all* functions of the product. (See Chapter 10.) Listed along the top of the matrix are the *names* that identify the test scripts to be written. An X is marked for each function that a given test script will test. Ideally, you want to avoid testing a given function with more than one test script. However, this situation might be unavoidable for some products since the testing of different functions actually can invoke common functions and modules as part of the execution process. For example, Figure 12.5 shows that test scripts TEST02 and TEST03 both test the GET command. TEST02 thoroughly tests the GET command, while TEST03 merely tests the "no errors" portion. For purposes of illustration, one can conclude that the SAVE command cannot be fully tested without first retrieving a file (using GET) that can be saved.

Figure 12.5 implies a matrix of 25 test scripts. The actual number of scripts required is largely dependent on the amount of function that each test script has been designed to test. It is more productive, in the long run, to develop many simple test scripts than to develop only a few complex ones. Once this matrix is completed and approved, the corresponding test scripts can be written.

Item 2 addresses the method required to perform function test. Because a goal of function test is to minimize the creation of artificial testing environments, little may be necessary in this regard. However, if some scaffolding or stubbing (temporary code that eventually will be discarded) will be necessary, then it should be included as part of the plan.

As with unit test, Item 3 defines what must be in place before the function test can begin. Unit testing should have been completed on all modules to be included in

Function to test	Test scripts					
	Test01	Test02	Test03	Test04	//	Test25
Invalid cmd	X					
GET <file>						
No errors		X	X			
Syntax error		X				
Read error		X				
SAVE <file>						
No errors			X			
Syntax error			X			
Write error			X			

Figure 12.5   Function test matrix.

a function test. Also, an approved function test plan should be in place. Unlike unit test, the function test procedures, also called **test scripts,** probably are not trivial. In fact, they could even require several weeks to prepare. These test scripts also should be complete and as bug-free as possible before function test begins. Also, as with unit test, the dependencies that must be in place should be listed in full. These dependencies may span the range of hardware, software, special tools, and people required to help run the test scripts.

Do not overlook the exit criteria, which are especially important here since the next phase of testing—independent testing—likely will be performed by a separate test organization. Therefore, the function test exit criteria will be highly visible. One example of exit criteria: All function test scripts must have been run and all *major* problems corrected and verified in the source code. Another exit criterion might be that minor problems must be negotiated with the independent test group before the testers will accept the code into the independent test phase. The independent test group may require a *resolution plan,* which identifies all minor problems and committed dates by which each problem will be resolved.

The schedules (Item 4) should show when each test script will be run and, therefore, when each function will be tested. In developing these schedules, when various module groups will be available must be factored in. For example, in Figure 12.3, the MESSAGES and ERRORS modules can be among the last modules to be made available. Therefore, the function testing of the message and I/O error-handling facilities may be performed later in the function test period. Putting the schedules in place requires the developer to think through the way in which modules will be integrated. It also requires focusing on the dependencies for modules that are owned by others. These dependencies obviously need to be negotiated and committed in advance if they are expected to happen according to schedule.

The problem-tracking process (Item 5) should define the process by which a discovered problem is logged, corrected, and then verified. There are several reasons why a clearly defined problem-tracking process must be in place to support the function test. Because function testing requires multiple modules to be tested together, whenever an interface-related problem is found, there needs to be some orchestrated method for the module changes to be made simultaneously across all affected modules. The fact that the modules in question often are owned by more than one person magnifies the need to coordinate these changes.

Another need for a problem-tracking process is to provide a careful accounting of all problems found, both major and minor. The independent test group will have a great interest in assessing this list of discovered problems. Negotiations to enter the independent test phase will rely on the disposition of the problems comprising this list. The list also will be valuable for the function test personnel to help them decide the most important problems to correct first. The problem-tracking process, of course, provides yet another benefit—it allows the project leadership to follow the progress being made in the function test better.

 Lesson: The independent test group must approve the function test plan.

As with unit test plans, it is strongly recommended that the function test plan be reviewed by a peer or team leader. Also, the independent test group must review and approve the plan. Not only can the independent test group members add value from a functional test coverage point of view, they also have a vested interest in receiving quality-tested code when their own tests begin. The quality of the code they receive obviously will have an impact, one way or another, on their ability to meet their schedule commitments. Once again, it is easier and cheaper to find bugs earlier in the software development process than later.

Anticipating Quality's Weak Link

A decision to leave development testing to the whim of each developer to manage as he or she chooses usually will be regretted later. And the problems that result are usually not intentional or the result of recklessness. The development test period simply is often used as a scapegoat—is sacrificed—in the name of "maintaining schedules." Because tracking is usually very informal and has low visibility, the development test period often appears to be unproductive and of little use. The project leadership is anxious to get the code into independent testing where visibility, control, and tracking progress are high.

 Lesson: Development testing must be defined and tracked if the outcome is to be predictable.

Anytime you hear "But we don't have time to write the unit and function test plans," beware. It is a sure sign of impending disaster. Programmers are human too. (You heard it here!) When no formal plan exists for some activity, each programmer will implement a discipline that suits his or her skills, perceptions, or desires. Very experienced programmers may do a top-notch development test. Inexperienced programmers will do what they naively believe to be a thorough and conscientious effort. All others may do whatever the schedule or their other activities allow. Development testing should not be left to chance. If you gamble on the outcome, the odds favor failure.

Ensuring that unit test plans and function test plans are written, reviewed, and followed will significantly help to ensure that quality code enters independent testing. Whenever you have a plan, there then exists a vehicle to track against. The unit test plans and function test plans are a great tool for programmers to use in planning and pacing their activities. They are also great tools for the project leadership to use to track the progress being made during this development test period. This tracking is very important if the full benefit of these plans is to be derived. Quality's weakest link in the software development process is the period defined as development test. This chapter demonstrates how the "dark cloud" surrounding this activity can be removed. There is absolutely no reason why the development test period cannot be planned, anticipated, and tracked in an open and objective fashion.

With unit and function test plans in place, programmers also will feel better about their contributions during this phase of the software development process. They will understand what, specifically, is expected of them and will have visible plans to follow to demonstrate their compliance and progress. If you think it sounds like an investment that results in a win-win situation, you are right!

13

Vendor Relationships

Organizations performing software development activities are increasingly looking outside their companies for help in performing activities faster, cheaper, and with improved quality. Two popular approaches to enlisting outside assistance are the use of vendors and subcontractors. These terms, as used in this book, mean the following.

A **vendor** is a company that is hired to perform some type of software development work. As an example, the work might be to develop, test, and support one or more components of a product or perhaps even the whole product. The vendor typically resides at a location that is apart from the company that has purchased the vendor's services. Furthermore, the vendor typically is perceived as being in complete control of managing its own activities. Although grossly simplified, a vendor can be thought of in terms of a fast-food restaurant where the order is placed, a price is quoted, and the order is subsequently readied and delivered.

A **subcontractor** is a person who has been hired to perform one or more software development activities. The work to be performed might be to develop, test, and support several modules or components of a product. The subcontractor typically resides at the purchasing company's location and works alongside other subcontractors and company employees. The subcontractor might work under the direction of a representative of the subcontractor's company or might work directly under the direction of the purchasing company.

 Lesson: "You can exercise little control over your vendors and subcontractors" is a myth fueled by poor planning and follow-through.

Many problems can occur when working with vendors and subcontractors. These problems often are especially frustrating to a project's leadership because of the belief that a company can exercise little control over its vendors and subcontractors. This myth has been fueled by poor planning and follow-through. Attention to creating and executing a well thought out contract can make all the difference in dispelling this myth and asserting the control you need to be successful.

This chapter addresses the most common vendor- and subcontractor-related problems facing software development projects and discusses actions that you can take to get and remain in control. The subject of vendors is presented first, followed by a section that addresses subcontractors.

It is not the intent of this chapter to offer legal advice. You should contact your legal representative before proceeding with a contract or managing the performance of a contract with a vendor or subcontractor.

Project Tales

The following scenarios are played out somewhere everyday. They include situations to be avoided. Do any of these scenarios sound familiar? Too familiar?

Everyone knew there were not enough resources and the necessary skills in the organization to staff the new project fully. A vendor would have to be found to help out. The major concern, however, was that the regular employees would be denied the opportunity to learn new skills and new technology by hiring a vendor. The project's leadership said, with an air of confidence, "Not to worry! When the vendor's contract work is nearing completion, we will take the time to transfer the skills to our company employees." The project members were leery but accepted the project leadership's proclamation as a commitment.

Many months pass. The vendor's employees assigned to the project have been consistently behind schedule and producing code of a far lower quality than expected. There are no penalties in the contract for the vendor missing schedule and quality commitments. The vendor had overcommitted resources and skills to win the job and now can't wait to complete the contract work and move on to a newer project where it can begin afresh. Its aim is to walk as far away from this complex project as soon as possible.

Unfortunately, the vendor's poor-quality work and late schedules have caused the regular employees to work lots of overtime to help in testing the vendor's deliverables, diagnosing problems, and absorbing a small portion of the vendor's development work. As the project draws to an end and the product is almost ready for shipment—albeit six months late—the project's leadership suddenly becomes aware that no skills transfer has yet occurred. Even worse is the fact that the contract does not call for the vendor to remain to support any problems that may be discovered in the code at the customers' locations. Furthermore, the vendor refuses to extend the contract and stay to take on more work, even if the work is to formally train the company employees on the needed skills to support the vendor's code.

The product finally ships to customers. There is an expected, but dreaded, flurry of problems reported in the vendor-developed code. Many regular employees are called away from their new assignments to help support the vendor-developed code. There is a scramble to learn the skills and technologies needed to rework the code.

The vendor? It got paid, managed to "complete" the contract, and is "fat, dumb, and happy" working on new work for other companies. The vendor escaped being "accountable" for any of its actions.

The company is about to start two new projects: Meanswell and Doeswell. These projects are unrelated. Each project is led by a different set of project leaders. The leaders in each project decides that they must vend out the development of 50,000 lines of code. In both cases, the code is an important piece of the project. A "Request for Proposal," describing the work to be performed, is prepared for each project. The requests are sent to several vendors.

Unbeknownst to them, both projects select the same vendor to perform their work. The vendor tells the leader of each project that the code can be developed and delivered in 12 months. The project leader on the Meanswell Project is elated and closes the contract quickly.

The leader on the Doeswell Project is not so quick to close unless certain terms and conditions are accepted. For example, the vendor will be awarded extra money if it completes the contract early, but penalized if it completes late. Furthermore, if the code is better quality than called for in the contract, another award will be given. If, however, the quality is less than expected, a penalty will be levied. The vendor also must prepare a detailed project schedule plan and provide sufficient progress reports against that plan each week. The vendor is hesitant to sign, but does so with the goal of winning the extra financial awards.

Ten months pass. The leaders on the Meanswell Project are told consistently by the vendor that it is "pretty much on schedule—well maybe a week or two behind—but things are pretty much business as usual." There was never a detailed project schedule plan to track against, but "every worker remains very busy and dedicated." These progress reports are provided about once a month. Reality? The vendor currently is at least two months behind schedule and will probably be about four months late in delivering the code. After the code is delivered, it will be discovered that it is of poor quality.

The same 10 months pass for the Doeswell Project. Not only does the project's leadership know the progress made each week by the vendor, but the code is being delivered *today*, two months ahead of schedule (earning a big bonus award). Furthermore, the software development process used by the vendor and monitored by the project's leadership indicates that the code quality is significantly higher than expected. If it is confirmed during independent testing that the code is, indeed, of exceptional quality, the vendor will receive another fat bonus award.

"Here we go again. It looks like another overly aggressive project where there aren't enough people or the right skills to make the schedules. Don't we ever learn?"

These are the words that could have been muttered by just about anyone in the organization. But what's this? The project's leadership is going to hire skilled subcontractors to work alongside the regulars so that the schedules can be achieved? Wow! Could it be that we might be learning something from our past mistakes? Great!

The new project is planned to be 14 months in duration. There will be 30 regulars and 10 subcontractors. Even with 40 skilled people, the technical, schedule, quality, and costs aspects of the project will be challenging. The subcontractors are hired quickly; perhaps too quickly. Most must sit around for one to three months doing almost nothing until meaningful work can be defined and assigned.

The subcontractors are assigned to different project teams. Unfortunately, they receive little to no orientation to the project, the organization, what they can expect, or what is expected of them. They are not even sure of the software development process that they are expected to use. They feel they are treated more like objects than valuable people resources—objects that have been placed on a shelf and rudely ignored until they are needed. They don't feel at all like welcomed members of the project. "Oh, well," one sighs. "It's a job. I will do what I have to and move on to the next 'body shop' when this one has played out."

When the meaningful work arrives, the subcontractors—the only members of the project who have not worked any overtime—are happy to have something to break the boredom . . . and, boy, does the boredom break! Everyone tries to become productive as quickly as possible. Unfortunately, the team leaders seem to spend too little time with the subcontractors. It is as if the team leaders assume the subcontractors know the project processes to follow, have all the skills to do the job, and need almost no assistance.

Six months into the project, two subcontractors have acquired excellent reputations for their high skills and competence. Four subcontractors are viewed as "coders" who are contributing marginally to the project. The other four subcontractors are evaluated as not performing satisfactorily and are terminated. Six new subcontractors are hired to replace them. Why six? Because most of work performed by the four subcontractors must be reworked and a lot of valuable project time has been lost. It is hoped that the two extra subcontractors can help make up for the lost time.

It is learned that three of the four subcontractors who were terminated also had been terminated for poor performance from their previous jobs: working in a different organization *in the same company!* Project members were appalled. Everywhere, company employees could be heard saying "How could the project leadership not know? And why did it take so long for them to discover the four subcontractors who were terminated were not performing satisfactorily?"

The project continues to have a troublesome journey, but the project and the product finally complete—seven months late. In hindsight, many of the problems were traced to the weak leadership provided to the subcontractors and the poor or marginal performers who were hired. (Of course, the project had nonsubcontractor problems as well, but the problems related to the handling and performance of the subcontractors had a pronounced, negative impact to the overall project.)

After understanding the material in this chapter, you might want to revisit the scenarios and list the problem areas. Then decide, from the chapter material or from experiences of your own, how the problems could have been avoided or more effectively handled once discovered.

Benefits and Drawbacks of Using Vendors

There are numerous reasons for using vendors to perform many of your software development activities, but, as with most actions, there are both benefits and drawbacks. It is helpful to understand these pros and cons so that you can help your organization make the best decisions and be prepared for potential drawbacks.

The *benefits* of using vendors include:

- You can obtain skills or technology that are not readily available in your organization.
- Regular employees can be offered increased job security during financially tougher times by letting go of vendors before downsizing an organization.
- You can start activities sooner than your resources would otherwise allow.
- The project's overall schedules can potentially be shortened.
- You can associate your project with a well-known and well-respected vendor.
- You can perform activities for a *potentially* lower cost.

The first and last items (about acquiring skills and lowering costs) are often the most admitted reasons for using vendors. Companies will continue to utilize vendors for the foreseeable future, if for no other reason than the need to keep up with the wide-ranging and rapid changes in technology. Interestingly, it is not always the bigger and well-entrenched companies that have a corner on pushing technology's state of the art. Many smaller companies find themselves in an enviable position of having the skills and technology that are in great demand but short supply. This situation requires even the larger, high-tech companies to call upon smaller companies for assistance with applying the latest technologies.

 Lesson: Don't assume that the benefits of using a vendor outweigh the drawbacks—each case must be decided on its own merits.

Notice that the last bulleted item includes the warning: "potentially." Be careful not to fall into the easy trap of assuming that vendors always will be less costly than using your own resources. Often, after all the drawbacks (a list of which follows) of using a vendor are considered, the "lower" costs may not be the bargain you initially thought.

Here are the more prevalent *drawbacks* of using vendors:

- Some key skills can disappear from the project and from follow-on projects when the vendor contract completes.
- The employees whom the vendor chooses to apply to your project may not perform as expected and needed.
- In midproject, the vendor may decide to swap employees working your contract with employees working other contracts, leaving your project at a higher risk.

- Vendors often have a higher attrition rate than many companies; therefore, a negative impact might be felt if key employees of the vendor leave the company.

- You may have less direct control of the actions of the vendor's employees than you feel is comfortable or acceptable.

- The vendor can gain knowledge of sensitive "inside" information about your project and company that you would prefer is exposed to your employees only.

Recognizing the drawbacks to your project before a contract is completed is important so that you can address some in the contract and prepare for others. For example, you can add a clause to the contract that requires certain vendor employees to participate full time on the project. Moreover, the contract can forbid the vendor changing assigned employees without your consent after the contract has been signed.

Another drawback you can prepare for is the loss of skills when the contract completes. By planning ahead, you might have an employee work alongside a critical-skilled vendor employee during the later phases of the project so that a *skills transfer* can take place. Or perhaps you can hire the vendor's critical skills when needed by negotiating a retainer fee with the vendor.

 Lesson: When formulating a contract with a vendor, you get what you negotiate—nothing more, but often less.

The major point to be made here is for you to understand that this is *your* project. You must be proactive in driving a contract with a vendor that satisfies your business needs. If you don't drive assertively for the right contract and demonstrate the discipline and leadership to ensure the contract is executed properly, no one will.

The Vendor Contract Process

Figure 13.1 shows, at a high level, the vendor contract process. The **Request for Proposal** (RFP)—this may be called by a different name in your company—is a document that addresses two primary topics: the Statement of Work and the instructions to bidders (vendors). The **Statement of Work** (SOW)—this too may be called a different name in your company—includes information such as the work to be performed by the vendor, when that work is due, how the work will be measured for acceptance, and the working relationship between the vendor and your organization. The SOW becomes a major part of the eventual contract between the vendor and your organization.

The instructions to bidders, the other primary topic of an RFP, provides vendors with the information they need to follow in creating and submitting a bid proposal. It also contains information on the categories that each proposal will be evaluated against and the process they can expect your company to follow in selecting the best candidate vendor. Step 1 is the creation and distribution of the RFP (includes the SOW) to qualified vendors.

> **1** An RFP is created and distributed.
>
> **2** Vendors create and distribute proposals.
>
> **3** A vendor is selected.
>
> **4** A contract is negotiated, signed, and executed.

Figure 13.1   Vendor contract process.

Step 2 involves each vendor creating a proposal based on the information provided in the RFP. The proposals are then submitted to the company issuing the RFP. Step 3 includes the vendor proposals being carefully evaluated and the owner of the winning proposal being notified. The unsuccessful bidders also are notified and informed of the strengths and weaknesses of their proposals.

Step 4 involves writing, negotiating, and obtaining agreement on the contract. After agreement, the contract is executed according to its terms and conditions.

The vendor information presented in this chapter primarily focuses upon Steps 1, 3, and 4. It is not the intent of this chapter to discuss the contents of an RFP, SOW, or vendor contract exhaustively—many books can provide that detail. (See the bibliography.) Instead, this chapter alerts you to the most common vendor-related (and subcontractor-related) problems that continue to haunt software development projects. Of course, actions that you can take to avoid these problems on your next vendor contract are identified.

Defining the Vendor's Work

 Lesson: There is a direct relationship between the completeness of your RFP and the completeness of the bid proposals received.

The Statement of Work, as part of the Request for Proposal, must describe fully the work to be performed by the vendor. The better the work is defined, the better the vendor can submit a well thought out estimate. For example, if the product specifications are complete for the work to be performed by the vendor, then they would provide an excellent level of detail from which the vendor can bid. If you provide an incomplete description of the work to be performed, you can expect problems with the vendor's bid for months to come as you attempt to refine the work over and over. This moving target will continue to be elusive until you finally commit to define adequately, once and for all, an acceptable description of the work. The description of the work to be performed by the vendor also must include the specific deliverables that the vendor must develop and deliver.

 Lesson: When it comes to quality work from a vendor, you usually get what you ask for. Ask in the RFP!

The vendor is asked for a schedule that will yield a product of a specified quality level (for example, 2 defects per 1,000 lines of code). It is typical to provide a start date for the contract work and ask the bidder to provide the best delivery date possible. Don't forget to make it clear what the definition is for the "end of project" and the "end of effort," if different. Again, you want the vendor clearly to see the whole picture of what is being committed to so you receive a more realistic bid.

You also should ask vendors to identify any trade-offs that they feel they must make between quality, schedule, and cost. Some creative ideas may be offered to save some schedule time and cost. Beware, however; sacrificing quality for schedules and costs almost never pays.

 Lesson: Don't blindside your own organization—get your organization's agreement before releasing the RFP to vendors.

Before the RFP is delivered to vendors, it should be reviewed and *approved* by key project groups; that is, by any areas that can be impacted by the SOW and the terms and conditions of the RFP. At a minimum, these areas might be development, publications, test, finance, and assurance. A rule of thumb for the RFP and the subsequent contract: If it is important, then document it. If it is not written down, then it probably will not be performed or binding.

Performance Incentives

Performance incentives are an excellent tool to use in reducing the risk inherent in a contract with a vendor. Profit is a strong motivator. If a vendor has the opportunity to collect bonus money for delivering contract work ahead of schedule or with a higher quality level, you can bet it is going to do its best to make that happen. However, the flip side is also important; that is, there should be financial penalties if the vendor delivers its contract work later than required or of lower quality than required. How might this work? For illustrative purposes, let's look at a simple example:

As depicted in Figure 13.2, a vendor contract calls for work to be completed in 12 months, delivered into system test with less than two valid defects to be discovered per 1,000 lines of code (KLOC) and less than .2 valid defects discovered during the first 12 months the product is operational with customers.

There is a 5 percent bonus if the contract work is delivered one month earlier. There is a 10 percent bonus if the valid defects discovered in system test are between 1 and 1.5 defects per 1,000 lines of code, a 20 percent bonus if the valid

Contract:	Vendor-tested code available: 12 months Defects discovered in system test: < 2.0/KLOC Defects discovered after delivery to customers: < .2/KLOC
Bonus:	5% - Vendor-tested code available one month early 10% - Defects discovered in system test: 1.0-1.5/KLOC 20% - Defects discovered in system test: .5-1.0/KLOC 10% - Defects discovered after delivery to customers: < .1/KLOC

Penalty:	5% - For each month vendor-tested code is late
	5% - For each additional .5 defects/KLOC discovered
	     in system test over 2.0 defects/KLOC
	5% - For each additional .2 defects/KLOC discovered
	     after delivery to customers over .2 defects/KLOC

Figure 13.2 Sample performance incentives.

defects discovered are between .5 and 1.0 defects per 1,000 lines of code. Another 10 percent bonus can be earned if less than .1 valid defects are discovered per 1,000 lines of code during the first 12 months the product is used by customers. This means that a vendor has an opportunity to earn up to 35 percent in bonus money.

The vendor contract also has penalty clauses. For every month the contract work misses the 12-month delivery date, there is a 5 percent financial penalty. For every .5 valid defects over two valid defects per 1,000 lines of code that are discovered during system test, there is a 5 percent financial penalty. And for every .2 valid defects over .2 valid defects per 1,000 lines of code discovered during the first 12 months that the product is used by customers, there is a 5 percent financial penalty.

You might wonder why up to 30 percent in bonus money can be earned for higher-quality code. This might seem like too much money to provide in bonuses. However, when you calculate how much it costs—in schedule time, staffing, machine resources, lost revenue from delivering the product to customers later than the original schedule—to fix defects discovered in system test, you may find that bonuses are an inexpensive tool overall. But there is more . . . it costs a lot more money to fix defects that the customer discovers—not to mention the downside of dealing with dissatisfied customers. After you give a lot of thought to the costs of poor quality, paying bonuses for very good quality can look like a mighty good business decision.

 Lesson: All **contracts should have monetary incentives that include penalties.**

Every contract should have monetary bonuses for exceeding schedule and quality requirements and monetary penalties for missing schedule and quality requirements. These bonuses and penalties can be a percentage of the base contract or specific dollar amounts. Don't be stingy with the use of bonuses to improve schedules and quality, or with penalties for missed schedules and poor quality. You are running a business. Incentives are a time-tested, proven tool.

A Trackable Plan

 Lesson: Don't assume the vendor plans to work on an activity—spell it out in the contract.

The vendor must provide a project schedule plan that clearly states the items listed in Figure 13.3. The first six items are explained in Chapter 4. The next-to-last item—other duties of special note—is an important list that often is overlooked. These are items that are not always major activities individually, but collectively add up fast and can have a significant impact on the project's resources and schedules. Some examples of these "other duties" are:

- Reviewing project documents such as product specifications, publication content plans, quality plans, test plans, and test scripts

- Performing and participating in design inspections

- Reviewing drafts of the product's publications

- Reviewing changes being proposed to controlled documents such as the product specifications

- Responding to problems discovered by others during testing

The last item—contract funding plan—identifies financial payments to the vendor based on the work progress or completion of selected milestones. This item is important in planning and tracking the expenditure of funds, particularly for some types of contracts, such as a time-and-materials contract.

A sound project schedule plan is essential for appraising progress and identifying problems. Moreover, the project schedule plan ensures that each vendor participant knows what the overall vendor commitments are and knows his or her role in fulfilling those commitments.

- Activities to be performed
- Person responsible for each activity
- Predecessor activities (dependencies) of each activity
- Planned start and end dates of each activity
- Contract deliverables and the dates of those deliveries
- Assumptions behind the project schedule plan
- Other duties of special note
- Contract funding plan

Figure 13.3   Items to be addressed in the vendor's project schedule plan.

Measure Performance Routinely

 Lesson: Vendors should be tracked just as routinely and intensely as other groups within a project.

Many projects tend to track the groups that are farther removed, either physically or managerially, *much less rigorously* than they track their own project members who are nearby. This means that vendors frequently receive less attention and visibility than regular project members. All groups on a project should be tracked with the same regularity and intensity. After all, any link in the "chain" can become weak and threaten the success of the overall project.

Chapter 5 offers numerous suggestions on how to track a project, of which many of the suggestions also apply to working with vendors. However, some specific suggestions in tracking vendors are:

- Track the progress and problems of the vendor weekly.

- If the vendor resides at your site, include a vendor representative in your weekly project tracking team meetings (unless sensitive information about your company will be discussed).

- If the vendor does not reside anywhere near your site, then conduct teleconference (or equivalent) tracking meetings and face-to-face meetings, having a face-to-face meeting at least once a month.

- Make tracking meetings with your vendor formal; that is, distribute progress and problem status at each meeting so there is a written record of actual-to-planned progress.

- Alter the site where tracking meetings occur; that is, have them sometimes at the vendor's site and sometimes at your site.

- If the vendor always is included in the project tracking team meetings, then occasionally have a private meeting with only the vendor to help promote a close working relationship.

- Discuss contract funding with the vendor if the contract requires tracking of the expenditure of funds. This discussion may be for a limited audience.

 Lesson: Insist on obtaining information from a vendor that you feel you need to manage the project successfully.

Track the progress of a vendor just as you would track your groups of regular employees. Insist on the information you need to manage the project.

Who's in Charge

 Lesson: Take the helm of your project—you must be in charge!

As the purchaser of the vendor's services, *you need to be in charge!* Many project leaders have a hard time practicing this concept. The result is a vendor who runs all over you and is continually compromising your project plans. Don't accept this behavior—even once! The vendor may have legitimate problems, but you both agreed up front to the terms and conditions of the contract. Hold the vendor to the contract. The key here is making sure that you have the right verbiage in your contracts.

As you are writing contracts, picture scenarios where a vendor has (or might in the future) demonstrated behavior that had a damaging affect on your schedules, costs, or quality. Now think about the verbiage that you could have included in the contract that would have reduced the grief that you felt you had to endure. Make sure that this verbiage appears in your future contracts.

Let's look at an example.

The vendor is behind schedule on an important deliverable. You are aware that the vendor has been moving people from your contract to other contracts as the vendor's overall workload increases. Unfortunately for you, the vendor's behavior will cause it to miss a key delivery date to you.

How could you have prevented this from happening? Here are two actions that have been introduced in an earlier section. One method is to state in the contract that there will be no movement of assigned people off your contract work unless you agree to the change of personnel. An additional action would be to include performance incentives and penalties that would encourage the vendor to comply with the full conditions of your contract.

Let's look at another example.

The vendor's deliverable has entered your system test recently. Many more defects are being discovered than expected. The defects are not getting fixed fast enough to be able to complete system test on schedule. The vendor's personnel are working only 40 hours per week and have no intention of working additional hours per week.

What could you have done to exercise the control you need? One method is to state in the contract that you have control over deciding the shifts to be worked and any overtime up to a specified amount (say, 20 hours per week). Furthermore, state that you need the flexibility to decide the days of the week that must be worked overtime, including Saturday and half-day Sunday. (You could state that holidays are off limits and are totally in control of the vendor's employees.) Now you would be able to schedule all the key groups—system test, vendor's employees, driver build group, and needed others—to work the same days and the same hours overtime so that all the dependencies among the groups can be satisfied.

As you can see, the contract must define your authority to give direction. We have been focusing on giving direction administratively, but don't overlook the technical side of the equation. That is, make it clear who has the last say when technical decisions and trade-offs are made. If you have ever experienced poorly written vendor contracts where the vendor was able to take broad technical liberties, you quickly will see the value of staying in control on technical issues as well as administrative ones.

 Lesson: Expect and plan for the likelihood that escalations will occur.

When there is a disagreement between you and the vendor, the contract also should describe the process and chain of command on both sides that must be followed to resolve the problem. This is especially important when critical problems arise that the initial parties are at an impasse to resolve. In this case, an escalation should be initiated within two working days. (See Chapter 5 "The Role of Escalations" section for more on defining an escalation process.)

A contract is a legal document. It also is a document that allows each party to know what is expected of him or her. In order to exercise the control you believe you need to be successful, the contract is the place to clarify those items that you feel must be understood and agreed to.

Quality System

 Lesson: The vendor must have an acceptable quality system so that the quality result of the effort is largely predictable.

Before a vendor is selected, be certain you understand the quality system under which it will be operating. In this context, a *quality system* is a defined, documented process and supporting procedures that will describe clearly how the vendor will operate while performing the contract work. If the quality system is unclear or simply not defined, a bright red STOP flag should appear. This vendor should be avoided. The last thing you need is to increase significantly the risk to the project by allowing a vendor informally to "free-form it"; that is, perform contract work in such a loose manner that the quality result of the effort is unpredictable.

A reputable vendor recognizes the importance of a quality system in creating a defined, controlled, and predictable work environment. Such a vendor already will have a quality system in place, not because it expects you will look for it, but because it has learned the value that such a quality system brings to its own workplace.

Items to look for as you review a vendor's quality system include:

- Documentation that fully describes the quality system, including the processes and supporting procedures
- A quality plan that shows the adaptation of the quality system to this specific contract work
- The identification and availability of resources (staffing, equipment, fixtures) and skills required to achieve the desired quality

- Description of specific quality control, inspection, and testing techniques to be used

- Measurement techniques to be used to ensure that the quality system is being followed and the desired quality is being achieved along each phase of the software development process. This should include the identification and preparation of "quality records" that prove the quality system is being followed appropriately.

If the vendor has been registered or certified for following a recognized standard, such as ISO 9001 (a model for quality assurance in design/development, production, installation, and servicing), then you should find that the items just listed will be readily available.

Proximity to Main Location

When writing a contract, give careful thought to the proximity of the vendor to your organization. A vendor nearby in the same city can be optimal for communications between you and the vendor. But if the vendor is hundreds or thousands of miles away, beware! Why? Because one of the most common problems for software development shops is the communications among the project members. Adding a long-distance vendor to the project can challenge the communications all the more.

Does this mean that you should avoid vendors who are geographically undesirable? No, but you should take steps to ensure that communications does not become a problem. Some of these actions can be written into the SOW so that all parties know what to expect and how to interface with one another. The actions to consider include:

- Define the path of both verbal and written communications between you and the vendor. For example, should all queries go through a designated person, or can anyone call anyone at anytime?

- Define when, where, and how vendor progress status meetings will be conducted. For example, status meetings can be weekly, whereby the first three meetings can be by teleconference with written status faxed just before the meeting and every fourth meeting can be face to face. For the on-site meetings, decide which party will travel.

- Define the path for escalations when the resolution of an issue is at an impasse.

 Lesson: Don't overlook the added time and costs of working with a long-distance vendor.

Working with vendors that are not local costs more. This fact is often overlooked when the costs of hiring a vendor are determined. The additional costs can come in the form of:

- Telephone, fax, and electronic distributions
- Mailings, particularly documents or equipment being sent overnight
- Duplicating hardware, software, and tools that would have been shared locally
- Travel expenses for face-to-face meetings

There are also time delays while one party waits on a response from the other, say for mailings or travel. Furthermore, time zone differences can reduce the available hours in each day when communications can occur.

Another cost is the expense of one or more additional interface people who must travel to and from the vendor's location. Time can be more valuable than money, and often key project people must travel to participate not only in progress status meetings but also in design and document reviews, resolving architectural or design defects, and more.

The message here? Don't necessarily avoid working with nonlocal vendors; however, factor in the time and expenses necessary to deal with the long-distance relationship. And by all means, document communications processes and expectations in the SOW.

Acceptance of Deliverables

The SOW should state clearly the conditions under which the vendor's work will be accepted. For example, if the vendor is delivering a component into your system test, then the component should be in a reasonable operating condition before it is accepted officially. This could mean that a predefined set of test scripts first must be run against the component. If any major problems are discovered, then they first must be corrected before the component will be accepted into system test.

There are many opportunities to ensure that the vendor's contract work is proceeding in a satisfactory manner; that is, you do not have to wait for running code to be delivered. You can designate many points along the software development process for items to be delivered so that they can be judged acceptable. For example, after the vendor has designed contract work, a design document can become a deliverable and undergo an inspection. The inspection can serve as the vehicle to ensure that the development of the vendored work is proceeding acceptably.

 Lesson: All contracts should define acceptance conditions that must be satisfied before a deliverable is deemed acceptable.

As obvious as it may seem to have acceptance conditions clearly defined and satisfied before accepting work from a vendor, this is a common problem area. Often there is either no or vague acceptance conditions defined, or if defined, they are not strictly adhered to. The result is usually confusion as to what is or is not acceptable. If you define the acceptance conditions in the SOW, then the vendor will work to meet those criteria before attempting to deliver the designated work to you. This can save both you and the vendor a lot of time, aggravation, and frustration.

Support of Deliverables in Shipped Product

After the completed product is available to customers, there is this question: Who supports (services) the portion of the product that the vendor developed? The answer must be addressed in the SOW.

Often it is in your best interests to negotiate having the vendor support the portion of the product it developed. It has the technical skill. It has the knowledge of the developed piece of the product. It can make the resource available when requested. Furthermore, if the SOW has performance incentives and penalties based on the quality of the vendored-developed items in the customers' hands, then it makes sense to keep the vendor involved in the support of these items. The SOW might even state that the vendor must support, without charge, all defects discovered past an allowable level that has already been agreed to. As stated earlier, a recommended approach is to have the vendor pay for poor quality and be rewarded for quality that is shown to be better than expected.

If the vendor is to provide the support, then all the conditions behind that support must be made clear in the SOW. For example, the following questions must be satisfied.

- How long will the vendor support last? One year? Until the product is withdrawn?

- Who has the responsibility to screen customer problems initially before they are forwarded to the vendor to help ensure the problems are indeed in the vendor-developed piece of the product?

- Who is the primary interface to the customer for vendor-related problems? For example, must the vendor always go through your company's interface to work with a customer?

- What responsibility does the vendor have in absorbing the cost to fix defects in its developed piece of the product?

- What responsibility does your company have in paying the vendor for time, materials, and travel that is necessary in correcting defects in the vendor-developed piece of the product?

- What incentives or penalties come into play for the vendor supporting the piece of the product it developed?

- What hardware, software, and tools will the vendor use to support its developed piece of the product? Who is responsible for purchasing and maintaining this equipment?

 Lesson: A contract should look beyond the development of the specified work and also address how the completed work will be supported.

One area that receives the least attention when creating a SOW is what happens *after* the product has been developed and is in use by customers; however, the questions just listed show how important it is to think through these areas carefully. If you believe it is premature to lock in commitments today between you and the vendor for a period of time that is quite a distance away, that might be okay (providing they are addressed satisfactorily well in advance of their needed implementation). But don't forget that the performance incentives and penalties in the contract can have more clout when they also address the quality of the vendored developed piece *after* the product is delivered to customers.

Nonpreferential Treatment

Curiously, vendors often seem to get away with more than other members and groups working on a project. They may be tracked less, given less grief for missing commitments, and given more leeway in the software development process that they choose to follow. Be careful here. Poor work performed by a vendor can cause as much harm to your project as poor work by any other group on the project.

 Lesson: Treat vendors with the same expectations and discipline as you would any other group.

Just because the vendor resides far away and works under a different chain of command does not change the need for it to meet its commitments. Vendors will, to a large extent, behave in a manner that they learn from you. If your contract with them is poorly thought out or weakly executed by you, they will learn that you are not all that serious about running a tight, professional shop—whether this is the image you really want to project or not.

Selecting a Vendor

 Lesson: Spend the time and energy to select the best vendor—it is an investment decision you must live with for the duration of the project . . . and beyond.

Selecting a vendor can be a painstaking chore; however, the time invested in selecting the best candidate can become one of the best investments you will make on your project. Furthermore, the time and expense to select the best vendor candidate can be insignificant when compared to the overall time and expense that will be attributed to the selected vendor's participation on the project and the impact of its work after the product has completed and is being used by customers. Do not rush through the vendor selection process for your project.

Listed below are some actions to keep in mind as you search for a vendor.

- Always seek bids from at least three vendors.

Just as your competition keeps you on your toes to provide the highest-quality, lowest-cost products and services, so too are vendors challenged by other competing vendors. To take advantage of this competitive environment, seek bids from at least three vendors (whenever possible) for every one vendor you are looking to select.

• Make certain that vendor candidates are qualified.

The vendors you choose from must be "qualified"; that is, they must be capable of meeting all your essential requirements. For example, vendors under consideration should have the capabilities needed to comply with technical requirements, security requirements, confidential disclosure agreements, general business terms and conditions, quality, and schedule requirements.

• Prepare a complete and well thought out proposal.

This point was introduced in an earlier section but is so important that it bears repeating here. Vendors are responding to the proposal that you provide them. If your proposal is not complete, is not clear, or otherwise is inadequate, expect the vendor responses to be the same. Provide vendors with the information they need to provide you with a thorough bid. At the very beginning of the relationship with vendors set a professional example in letting them know what you expect from them. You will find that this investment will pay itself back many times over while working with the selected vendor.

• Evaluate vendors' responses as objectively as possible.

Before the proposals are completed and given to the candidate vendors, define the process you will follow to evaluate the responses. Also identify the categories to be examined when evaluating the responses and make sure that the competing vendors understand these categories. This planning will help you develop a well thought out RFP that identifies all the major areas you want the vendors to address.

 Lesson: Don't assume anything when evaluating a proposal—ask the vendor.

Let's look at a process you can use in evaluating the bid proposals from vendors. A chairperson is identified and a group of people is selected to form the committee to review the bid proposals. Each committee member reviews each proposal and performs a scoring for the main evaluation topics and subtopics. (If desired, committee members can be asked to evaluate only the general area of each proposal with which they are especially skilled; for example: technical, project management, quality, and business.) It is expected that questions will arise from the review of each vendor's proposal and that the vendor occasionally will need to be contacted for clarifications. Don't assume what the vendor meant or might do—ask.

Figure 13.4 shows an example of the scoring categories for project management. Notice that three vendors (ABC, DEF, and GHI) were evaluated. The scoring approach, shown in Figure 13.5, uses the values 3, 2, 1, and 0, where 3 is the best score. The numbers assigned to the subtopics (the bulleted items) are used to determine main topic scores. The main topic scores are, likewise, used to determine the general area score (project management). Finally, the general area scores are used to determine the overall score for each vendor. These overall scores are compared to select the best vendor from all the candidates. You can use many methods to score and select the best vendor. This example is provided only for illustrative purposes.

 Lesson: The lowest dollar bidder is not necessarily the best vendor to select.

It is recommended that committee members do not see the cost proposals during their evaluation process. This can help to avoid bias, allowing the best candidate to be identified regardless of cost. Then the cost can be factored in to help make the final decision. This means that the lowest dollar bidder is not always the best candidate to ensure that the best performance of schedule, quality, and support is obtained.

Project management evaluation categories	Vendor ABC	Vendor DEF	Vendor GHI
Project scheduling, tracking, and reporting methodology	1.75	2.25	2.00
• Clearly defined process, roles, responsibilities, tools	2	3	2
• Frequent and regular tracking meetings	2	2	2
• Dependency management	1	2	2
• Planned communication with company buying services	2	2	2
Project organization structure	2.00	2.50	2.00
• Supports software development process; built-in checks and balances	2	2	2
• Clear definition of roles and authority	2	3	2
Problem management approach	2.00	2.00	2.00
• Defined and responsive process	2	2	2
Staffing and skills	1.00	2.00	2.00
• Availability of headcount, skills, leaders, across required disciplines	1	2	2
Related experience	1.00	2.50	2.00
• Seasoned development; experience on similar products	1	3	2
• Indicators of learning from past experience	- - -	2	2
Software development process	1.67	2.67	2.00
• Clearly defined activities, roles, and responsibilities	2	3	2
• Comprehensive	2	3	2
• Effective checks and balances, entry/exit conditions	1	2	2
Facilities/equipment/tools	2.00	2.00	1.50
• Productive environment	2	2	2
• Security	2	2	1
Overall score for project management	1.63	2.27	1.93

Figure 13.4   Scoring categories for project management.

Score	Meaning	Definition
3	Exceptional	Exceeds performance or capability; high probability of success; no significant weakness
2	Acceptable	Satisfies evaluation criteria; good probability of success; any weaknesses can be easily corrected
1	Marginal	Currently fails to satisfy the evaluation criteria; low probability of success; significant deficiencies, but correctable
0	Unacceptable	Significant deficiencies; needs a major revision to bid proposal to correct

Figure 13.5   Scoring criteria.

After all the vendors have been notified whether they have been selected, you will work with the selected vendor to resolve any open problems and finalize the contract.

Replacing a Vendor

Most vendors do an acceptable job of performing to the contract agreement; however, occasionally a vendor will underperform. The reasons for violating the terms and conditions of the contract are varied and are not a point of discussion here. What is important is that you are aware that there can be times when it is in the best interests of your project to disengage from a vendor and seek elsewhere to complete the vendor's work.

Replacing a vendor can be a slow and tedious job. Usually a project waits too long to make the decision to terminate the vendor and find a replacement. Instead, there is the constant hope that the vendor's missed commitments or low quality will get better. In the meantime, valuable time is being lost—time that cannot be regained—and the success of the project can be hanging in the balance.

To be as prepared as possible for the situation when a vendor must be replaced, two actions must be performed.

 Lesson: Know the warning signs that a vendor is underperforming.

1. Identify those conditions that would alert the project's leadership that a vendor's performance is moving from low to medium or high risk. These are conditions that would have a disturbing impact on planned schedules, function, costs, or quality. (See the "Project Outlook" section of Chapter 5 for a discussion of risk values and actions that can be performed.) After these conditions are identified, monitor the vendor on a routine basis and be on the lookout for further deterioration of these conditions.

 Lesson: Have a contingency plan ready to help or replace a vendor.

2. Identify a contingency plan. It could be simply a brainstormed list of options from which to select. Or it could be something more deliberate, such as immediately bringing on board another vendor to work alongside the underperforming vendor until the original vendor is working satisfactorily ... to immediately distributing the vendor's work to several new vendors. A contingency plan will help you remain in control and deal professionally and thoughtfully with the situation.

As a project leader, it is your job to know if and when a vendor must be replaced. It is also your job to make it happen as expeditiously as possible so the least harm comes to the project.

Legal Considerations

 Lesson: Always consult with your legal representative before engaging in a contract with a vendor.

It bears repeating that it is not the intent of this chapter to offer legal advice. You should contact your legal representative before proceeding with a contract or managing the performance of a contract with a vendor or subcontractor. Listed here are some thoughts for you to discuss with your legal representative so you both feel prepared to proceed with a contract with a vendor. These subjects are commonly raised concerns when dealing with contracts with vendors.

- What conditions would allow you to terminate the contract? What are the implications of terminating the contract?

- What conditions would allow the vendor to terminate the contract? What are the implications of a vendor terminating the contract?

- What process must be followed to modify the contract?

- What conditions can lead to an escalation up either party's management chain? What is the escalation process to be followed?

- What authorization do you need to "lead" the vendor's activities? If you are considered the leader for its activities, what are the legal implications if the vendor's contract commitments are missed?

- What is the preferred approach to working with the vendor so that the vendor is fully accountable for its own actions (or inactions)?

- Are there changes that you feel must be made to the vendor's quality system?

- What are the legal implications of being a substantial part of the vendor's overall business?

- Is the vendor's work location sufficiently secured to protect confidential material and ensure uninterrupted work progress?

- Does the vendor have access to more information than it needs to know? Should some of the sensitive material be restricted to a small segment of the vendor's contract workforce?

- Who supplies the necessary equipment (hardware, software, tools, stationery supplies)? Who maintains the equipment and when must the equipment be returned?

- Who is responsible for the education and training of the vendor's personnel?

- What access, if any, will the vendor have to your development and test labs? After normal work hours?

- What rights, if any, does the vendor have to its contract-produced work items?

- Are sufficient financial incentives and penalties in the contract?

As you can see, if some of these subjects are not addressed sufficiently in the contract, they could cause problems later.

Subcontractors

Most of this chapter has focused on vendors because the use of vendors often represents a considerable expense and impact to a project. Repeating some of the more common mistakes when dealing with vendors can cost a project dearly—sometimes sinking the project before it can deliver to the first customer.

But what about subcontractors—those individual souls who are hired to perform pieces of work and who often are merged into a project to work alongside the regular company employees? As with vendors, companies increasingly are turning to subcontractors to satisfy their short-term (and sometimes longer-term) staffing and skill needs. Are there lessons to be learned when working with subcontractors? You bet! This section highlights the more common problems by recommending behavior and actions that can help you gain the most benefit from subcontractors, while reducing the overall risk to your project.

The following subjects address the most common problems.

- Rules of operation

 Lesson: Immediately take the time to inform subcontractors of the rules of working in the organization.

Subcontractors are like new hires to your company in that they do not know what the guidelines or rules are for working in your company and on your project. Whether a 30-minute introductory class or tagging them to a "buddy" who knows the ropes and can teach them what they need to know, the sooner they feel comfortable with your method of operation, the sooner they will be productive. However, subcontractors are *not* new hires in the sense of being company employees with full company benefits. There may be some areas of the organization, even some topics related to your project (financial information, customer lists, future plans, databases, and the like) that are outside their need to know. For example, can a subcontractor work overtime at your company location without a regular employee's "supervision"? (In most cases, it is strongly recommended that a subcontractor never have free access to the premises without supervision.) It is in everyone's best interest to reveal these rules as clearly and as soon as possible.

- Full members of the team

 Lesson: Welcome subcontractors as "full" members of the project team.

To draw the most from your subcontractors, they must be absorbed into your organization and treated as full members of the project team. Although a few rules are different for subcontractors (see above), in most cases the rules are the same as for regular project members they work alongside. They must be made to feel like wanted and needed valuable contributors of the project team. If you treat them as first-class members of the project team, they will perform as first-class members are expected to perform. The more they feel like welcome members of the team, the more they will want to contribute their fair share. For example, a subcontractor's progress should be tracked with the same frequency, intensity, and method that the progress of regular employees are tracked.

- Who's in charge?

 Lesson: Subcontractors clearly must know from whom they take direction.

It is recommended that subcontractors work under the direction of someone who is a regular employee of the company. However, there can be times when subcontractors might work under their own direction or lead a team of other subcontractors, or even lead a team that is comprised of regular company employees. Sometimes the company that supplies subcontractors also supplies a subcontractor to "supervise" all other subcontractors. This arrangement can work well; however, experience suggests that the most effective approach seems to be having subcontractors supervised by regular company employees. This way, your company can maintain the needed level of control for operating a successful project more easily. This is another area where it can be helpful to consult with your legal representative.

- Education

 Lesson: Unless otherwise stated, you have the responsibility to ensure the continual education of your subcontractors to keep them satisfactorily productive.

Subcontractors are hired for the knowledge and skills that they bring to your company. However, there will almost always be new information or technologies or processes that they will need to learn. After subcontractors are hired, you should expect to provide various types of training and education when needed. But be careful to provide only the education and training needed—and no more. Why? Two primary reasons. The first reason is that "overeducating" will cut into their productivity. The second reason is that subcontractors are usually considered a temporary resource; therefore, invest only to the point you must to get the job done.

- Awards

 Lesson: Awards can help you draw out the best from your subcontractors.

Unlike vendors who can receive monetary incentives for performing above expectations, subcontractors often have no opportunity to be recognized monetarily for outstanding performance. The solution? Allow subcontractors to earn awards similar to your regular employees. You might want to designate a specific award that only a subcontractor can earn. You are missing a great opportunity for motivating excellence among your subcontractors if you have no way to reward them individually for exceptional performance.

- Weeding out nonperformers

 Lesson: It is far more efficient to weed out nonperformers before they are hired.

Although most subcontractors whom you select will perform well, expect that occasionally you will discover a poor performer. Sometimes it can take months to do so. Moreover, to replace that person and get a replacement up to speed can take additional weeks or months. All the while, valuable time and money is being lost. Plan ahead to weed out the poor performers as early as possible. For example, when interviewing a potential candidate, also have two or three of your appropriately skilled employees interview the person. The extra interviews can help spot candidates that are not as qualified as they need to be. Another technique is to give newly hired subcontractors a specific piece of work that they can demonstrate their skills on immediately—something that can be completed within one to four weeks. Brainstorm other methods to spot potential nonperformers as early as possible.

- Don't rehire bad apples.

 Lesson: No successful enterprise can afford to ignore their past experiences.

Occasionally you will hire subcontractors who do not measure up to the requirements of the job and whose employment you must terminate. If the reason for termination is something that you feel needs to be "remembered" so a person is not inadvertently rehired into another organization in the company, then you must maintain a confidential accounting of these names. Too many times a company will, unknowingly, rehire these people (sometimes the very next day!) into a different area of the company, only to dismiss them again for poor performance or whatever. No company can afford to lose valuable time and expense in rehiring undesirable workers if it expects to remain competitive. Consult your legal representative to see what actions you can take to ensure the bad apples are not rehired.

A Changing World

 Lesson: Add to the ideas in this chapter to build a database of valuable information; then reference the information before engaging with vendors and subcontractors.

Rapidly changing technologies, global competition, shortage of critical skills, economic considerations . . . these are but a few of the reasons why the use of vendors and subcontractors is becoming increasingly popular. But to make the most of these resource aids, this chapter has revealed common vendor- and subcontractor-related problems that can plague projects . . . and what you can do to avoid or recover from these problems and remain in control. When a project is already in serious trouble or has completed, the best time to circumvent cost, quality, and schedule problems is lost. Take action immediately when problems arise, but better still, plan ahead—be proactive—by considering the hard-gained information presented in this chapter at the *start* of your next project.

Postproject Review: Understanding the Past to Improve the Future

Optimism is eternal. We are forever hopeful that the next software project will proceed infinitely smoother than the last. We know that we wouldn't be so dumb as to make the same mistakes again. But history has shown that we will make many of the same mistakes that were made last time and the time before that and before that. We will do this knowing full well that mistakes cost money, time, and resources. These mistakes could cause the cancellation of a project or even our jobs. Yet most projects continually replay many of the same problems.

History repeats itself in war, economics, love, and software development projects. This recurrence of history is not for lack of recorded information or good intentions. It is due to a lack of balance in *understanding* what went wrong on past projects, in applying the *experience* of past campaigns, and in exhibiting the *discipline* to apply this knowledge and experience.

This chapter shows you how to learn from your past mistakes through the use of a **postproject review** and demonstrates how to apply this knowledge to a current or new project. Two other beneficial reviews also are described: **project review** and **product certification review.** A project review is performed at selected points along the software development process and is a technique that allows you to make mid-project corrections while the project is still active. A product review is performed just before a product is announced or delivered to the first customer and allows you to "certify" that the product is indeed ready for announce or ship.

Project Tales

As the lessons of past mistakes are ignored and the project continues daily to sink deeper into a quagmire, warning signals can be heard. These signals come from both the lack of clear progress within the project and from the project participants themselves. The following collection of short scenarios reveals sample problems that are common across software development projects. Although costly to the overall well-being of a project, these representative problems are among a multitude that have a penchant for recurring.

The project is young, but already the frustrations of a new battlefront are surfacing. A team leader responsible for a small programming team feels a sense of helplessness and abandonment. When he committed his team to develop a 10,000 lines-of-code program, he also had stated requirements that his team be comprised of seven programmers with specific skills. Also he expressed the requirement that the team be fully staffed within two months of his commitment. Four months later, four semiskilled members comprise his team, and their product is six weeks behind schedule. He had feared this would happen, but gave way to his own optimism and his project leader's good intentions. The really distressing part is that his project leader still holds him and his team accountable for the original commitment. Because the team was short-handed, his project leader had personally dedicated most of the past four months in assisting the team with its design and coding. Somehow, the project leader has not gotten the message that his time would best serve the department if he was actively supporting the needs of the team and department rather than doing the work of a team member.

The project is in the midst of its numerous design inspection meetings. These meetings are intended to discover defects early rather than during the coding and testing phases. Unfortunately, all the inspection meetings are not being conducted in the same manner. Some of the moderators have had prior training or coaching, while others appear to be totally new to the inspection process. Some moderators are failing an inspection that has revealed *one* major problem, while other moderators are passing inspections that uncover *several* major problems. Some moderators document their meeting's results and then track the open problems to ensure their timely closure, while other moderators are not documenting any results from their meetings. Some inspections have all the required inspectors and organizations represented, while other inspections have poor attendance and often overlook inviting key inspectors. Two participants who have attended several different inspection meetings look at one another and agree, "We've seen this 'movie' before. I thought 'John' was supposed to fix this after the chaos from the last project. Oh, well, at least we're getting paid for all this nonsense and rework." (Paid, yes. But for how long?)

It is a new project. The design phase has been completed and the coding phase is just starting. In another three months, lab hardware will be required to implement various test phases. There never seems to be enough hardware for everyone to use, even when multiple shifts of six to seven days a week are employed. This situation existed on the past three projects. However, due to the griping and apparent awareness on the last project, the view is that this probably won't be as great a concern this time around. After all, everyone seems to have had an opinion on how to correct the problem, and it seemed as if it would have been an easy problem to fix if only a little advance planning would have been done.

Three months pass. Several groups converge on the available hardware almost simultaneously. It's déjà vu. Not only has the problem not been corrected sufficiently, apparently there still is no one to understand everyone's requirements and to put a mutually agreeable solution in place. "I can't believe this was allowed to happen again! This place is unreal! Won't we ever learn!" is heard—again.

Formal testing is finally ready to begin. The code has been delivered to the module build group and, after much pain, has been linked together successfully. But alas! The program won't run! Several developers swarm over the listings and the machines in an attempt to locate the problem. It is suspected to be in the piece of code that was delivered by a vendor. After two days of concentrated effort, it is discovered that the problem was not in vendored code, but within the in-house code. The problem is corrected and another attempt at running the program is made. It is unsuccessful. This time, after a full day of debugging, the problem is isolated to modules provided by a vendor. Complaints abound: "Why aren't people from the vendor here to debug their own code? Why aren't people here representing all the major departments?"

It seems no one has put together a comprehensive plan to support the independent testing. Although the development groups have agreed to fix their problems, no one has agreed to spend the needed time isolating a suspected problem to the failing module. What if a programmer spends all day isolating the problem down to someone else's code? No one has time for that. Said more accurately, no one has *planned* time for that. No one has planned to allocate any time or staff in performing this essential role. Someone quips, "Will we ever learn? This same thing happened last time! You would think a different project leader would be wiser than the last one."

The project is two-thirds complete. The performance test group members are swinging into full gear. They immediately discover performance problems that, after careful analysis by the development team, will cause up to one month in schedule slippage to correct. The performance team is proud that it was able to discover these problems so quickly. However, the development group is furious that the performance people had not identified these problems earlier. "Why didn't those performance guys participate in our design and code inspection meetings months ago? They could have gotten all the insight they needed to conclude that these performance problems would have resulted. It would have been a whole lot easier and less costly to have discovered these problems back then," says a frustrated developer to another developer.

This opinion trickles into the performance department, whose response is "We could have discovered these performance problems earlier if development would have invited us to all their inspection meetings. Also, why are we always the last to know when the function or design is changed? It seems the developers never learn!" In a developer's office down the hallway can be heard, "It seems those performance guys never learn!"

The publications work is already considerably behind the latest adjusted schedule. The first draft was nearly six weeks late. Even then, the magnitude and type of comments caused several chapters to go through major revisions. The next draft was a full two months late. The primary problem was that the product's functions continued to change drastically between drafts. Compounding the problem was the limited availability of programmers to review early chapters and to provide needed source material to the writers. Acknowledges a publications writer, "The programmers do this to us every time! I sometimes wonder how committed they are to putting out a quality product. Particularly an on-time, quality product."

The product is nearing completion. The publications are almost finished. Suddenly the assurance group realizes that the product manuals have too few examples. Unless more examples are added, the product will not be user friendly enough for the targeted audience. Someone comes up with the idea that the examples can be taken from some of the system test scenarios and test scripts. Someone else chimes in, "That's a good idea! I wish we would have thought of that before. It would have saved us a lot of time if we could have planned ahead." The idea originator responds, "It's not a new idea. On the last two projects I worked on, lack of examples in the product manuals was also a shortcoming in planning for the manuals. At the last moment, we also had decided to adopt many of the system test scenarios and test scripts. It seems we never learn."

A request for a plan is made to the product packaging and distribution (P and D) department. A plan is needed that defines precisely how and when the new product will be readied for customer delivery. The product is currently in the early stages of its development. Legal and other concerns from within P and D delayed the last product's announcement and delivery. The product leader hopes to avoid these delays on this product. The P and D leader insists that this won't happen again. She only needs six months of lead time, and there are 10 months from today. However, she also states that her department is tied up on other matters but will shortly begin to work on the request. The product leader, feeling his job of formalizing the request is complete, continues about his own business.

Four months before the product is scheduled for delivery, someone realizes that P and D has not been included in weekly status meetings. Once again, P and D's activities are holding up the announcement and delivery. Someone comments wearily, "This is exactly what happened last time."

As you read through these scenarios, some might have struck very close to home. Perhaps you were reminded of similar or even additional examples from your own pool of experiences. The upcoming sections will present an effective method that you can follow to avoid repeating these types of mistakes. You can use this method to better learn from your own wealth of experiences and from the knowledge and experiences around you.

Postproject Review

Those who cannot remember the past are condemned to repeat it.
—George Santayana, Spanish-born American philosopher, poet, humorist

 Lesson: Successive recurrences of the same negative situation are hardly a mistake—they are neglect.

The primary objective of this chapter is to explain how to learn from past mistakes. Mistakes are things that happen accidentally. They are blunders that result from misunderstandings. They are things that are done through ignorance, inattention, failure to think. If you accept any of these definitions, then you might conclude that using "mistake" as a reason for repeating the same errors from project to project is a misuse of the word. Don't people *consciously* repeat the same problems? The first time a problem situation occurs, then the word *mistake* might apply. But successive recurrences of that same situation is hardly a mistake. It is called *neglect*.

Neglect is the act of ignoring, disregarding, or failing to care for or give proper attention to something of notable importance. Said another way, neglect is the failure, either through oversight or desire, to utilize knowledge and experiences fully.

No one is infallible—we all make mistakes. So this chapter addresses neglect, that is, making the same mistakes more than once. This involves conditions that are not only often preventable but that can be downright nasty if not attended to early. These are conditions that, if left unchecked, can destroy a project and the spirit of its people.

The primary technique to counter neglect is the postproject review, which provides an opportunity to learn from past experiences. It is a sequence of activities that, when followed, will result in a conscious and planned attempt to prevent the next project from having to repeat the same neglects of its predecessors.

Postproject reviews have been called by many different names. Some of these names are *post mortem, autopsy review, project analysis review,* and *quality improvement review. Postproject review* is the name used in this book because it appears to be more universally accepted.

A postproject review is scheduled to occur at the end of a project. It can begin as early as the point when system test has completed and the code and product publications are "frozen" and are being replicated for delivery to customers. Or it can begin just after the first customer has received the new product. Depending on the product, the time between these two options can be on the order of days or weeks. It is recommended that the postproject review begin at the earliest possible moment so that more project members might be able to participate and the project's experiences are a bit fresher in the minds of the project members.

Figure 14.1 shows the sequence of steps to follow to yield a successful postproject review. Each of these steps is explained in the sections that follow. However, a simple overview of a postproject review is presented here.

A postproject review begins with the selection of people who represent all the major organizations within the project. These people then independently identify the elements of the project that went right and those that went wrong. Then each representative attends a group meeting to share his or her findings. The group then creates two lists: a *good list* of those things that went right and a *problem list* of those things that went wrong. The items in both lists are sorted independently in order of importance. A recommended solution is developed for each of the more important problems stated in the problem list. Then presentations are made to both the project's leadership and the project members. At this time the project leaders declare their level of support to ensure that both the good list and the list of identified solutions are implemented in upcoming projects.

 Lesson: Postproject reviews should be mandatory for all projects.

Learning from the mistakes and neglect of past projects is absolutely essential for a software development shop to become and remain competitive. The elements of schedules, cost, and quality all can be improved by examining our past behaviors and applying these lessons to our present and future actions. Postproject reviews are such a great investment into an organization's survival that they should be mandatory for

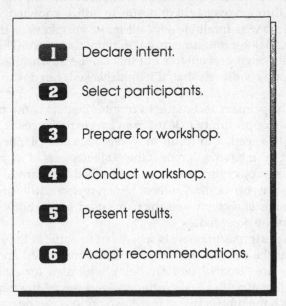

Figure 14.1 Steps for a successful postproject review.

all projects. What about projects that have been terminated? You don't want to waste your time performing a postproject review on them? Terminated projects are *especially important* to learn from. After all, if a project has terminated, then those expenses will never be recovered. Your only hope is to learn from those costly experiences so you do not find yourself reliving them again.

Step 1. Declare Intent

 Lesson: The project's leadership must be receptive to having their decisions reviewed in retrospect.

Early in a project, the project head should state his or her intention to have a postproject review at the completion of the project. This intention is best communicated verbally at an organizational meeting, then followed up with a letter to all project participants. The letter should state the goals of the postproject review. Everyone must understand that not only do the project leaders want to do things the best way, but they also are receptive to having their decisions reviewed in retrospect. The clear goal is to learn from both the errors of the past and from those things that went right, and to apply these lessons to future projects.

For maximum effect, the letter should include an attachment that describes the postproject review process. The attachment also should identify the questions or topics to which each organization will be responding. (More on this in the section entitled "Step 3. Prepare for Workshop.") Describing the postproject review process and the questions and topics to which each organization will be responding will result in some organizations paying closer attention to these areas of their processes throughout the software development process.

 Lesson: To ensure that the postproject review activity receives the necessary attention, it should be included in the project schedule plan.

If this is the first time this approach will be followed in your organization, then it probably will be met with mixed emotions. Most will view it with some skepticism, but everyone will hope it will come true—for it is easy to comprehend the merits of a postproject review. Take a "risk" and declare early your commitment to a postproject review. Make certain, however, that you follow up at the end of the project and make this postproject review happen. As a planning technique, add this event to the checklist of project activities that you track. There is much to gain from declaring these expectations early in the software development process.

Step 2. Select Participants

Once the project has completed, it is time to start the postproject review. The first act is to select the participants. At least one person should be selected from each major organization. Examples of major organizations are planning, development, test, publications, performance, usability, module build group, assurance, and any others that you feel are appropriate.

The people selected should have a strong knowledge of the processes that were used in the project. They also should be people who interfaced with groups outside of their own immediate areas. The best candidates are team leaders. The experiences that they originally brought to the project as well as their lead roles within the project make them the favored choices. The goal is to select people who will offer the breadth and depth of perception required for a comprehensive postproject review.

 Lesson: Managers should not participate on the postproject review team.

Managers, those project leaders in a position of evaluating the performance of people, should *not* participate on the review team. This is a time for the nonmanagers to use their hindsight to evaluate the process that they spent many months or even years developing and using. Nonmanagers are in the best position to offer both praise for the things that went well and criticism for those things that need improvement. Managers on the team can inhibit the candidness of the group and the free flow of ideas. The project's leadership need not feel left out, though. The recommendations by the review team must have support and commitment from the project's leadership before being implemented.

The chairperson should be chosen by the project's leadership and can be anyone in the review team. However, the person leading the team should be someone who is well respected by the team members. The team leader should be someone who can lead as well as be a good listener and facilitate discussion among the members. If the development representative is qualified to lead the team, then this person is recommended as the first choice. Because development often is the largest organizational group and often is the group with the greatest impact throughout the project, a special benefit is to be gained if development takes the team leader role. It may influence development to feel a stronger ownership for the team's final recommendations.

The participation of each representative in the review team must be mandatory. All organizations must be heard and must feel that the final results have their commitment. If the project's leadership is truly supportive, participation on this review team will be viewed as a positive form of recognition. People want to be heard, and they also want to be members of a progressive organization.

Step 3. Prepare for Workshop

 Lesson: A postproject review focuses on what went right, what went wrong, and what can be improved.

After workshop participants have been selected, the next step is to define the homework to be completed prior to the workshop meeting. Each participant is asked to respond to a set of topics. The responses should relate primarily to each respondent's mission in the project and should focus on what went right, what went wrong, and what can be improved. These topics can be generalized as shown in Figure 14.2. This way, each participant responds to the same general areas of interest. The list shown in the figure can be further expanded or shortened to accommodate the particulars of your project. These subjects are somewhat broad and can be stated, if desired, more pointedly. For example, the topic "productivity" could be addressed more finely with these additional questions:

- What level of productivity was achieved for your tasks? How did it compare with what you expected?

- What could have changed to improve your productivity? How much would each change improve your productivity?

Another approach is to customize a subset of topics that would be unique for each organization. Figure 14.3 provides an example of customized topics that would be addressed by the component test group. This approach can ensure that very specific topics will be addressed. These topics also can be refined to another layer of detail. As an example, the topic "problems discovered in product code" could be supported by the following questions:

- How many problems were reported found per every 1,000 lines of code? Of these problems reported, how many were found to be valid defects? Testers' errors? Not reproducible?

- Staffing
- Mission objectives
- Product definition and change control
- Customer involvement
- Schedules and tracking
- Education and training
- Productivity
- Tools
- Quality
- Vendors and subcontractors
- People communications
- Support from outside groups
- Software development process improvements
- Other processes that worked well; did not work well
- Financial budget
- Other problems and/or suggestions

Figure 14.2   General topics for a postproject review.

- Availability of needed product information
- Test plan
- Functional coverage of test scripts
- Developing the test scripts
- Test script inspections
- Running the test scripts
- Automation of test scripts
- Problems discovered in product code
- Self-documentation of test scripts
- Tools required and/or used
- Hardware availability

Figure 14.3 Postproject review topics for the component test organization.

- How did the actual number of problems reported compare to what you expected?
- What was the severity of the problems found? What was the average response time (in days) required to fix each category of severity assigned? Was the response time within the expected range? Was this acceptable?

Either of these approaches, generalized or customized, can be effective. Whichever method is used, do not overlook asking each organization to identify those things that went particularly well. A single focus on bad news can be depressing. In fact, in every organization, there are always activities that "went right." Make sure these positive areas are carried forward consciously to future projects.

Step 4. Conduct Workshop

The workshop meeting can be expected to last anywhere from one-half day to two days, depending on the size of the project and the number of workshop participants. One day might be a reasonable time for most projects. Every attempt should be made to prevent the meeting or anyone in the meeting from being disrupted by outside business. The meeting participants should be free to concentrate their attention on this valuable exercise.

The workshop is a working meeting. The first portion of the workshop should be allocated to listening to each representative present his or her responses to the topics that were distributed earlier. It is helpful if the order of presenters matches the general sequence of phases in the software development process. For example, the planning representative would present before the development representative, who would present before the test group representative, and so on. It is also beneficial to set a time limit for each representative—somewhere in the range of 10 to 30 minutes is sufficient for most workshops, but you may choose a more specific range that best suits your project. For example, allow 10 minutes for representatives of small organizations and 30 minutes for representatives of larger organizations.

 Lesson: The meeting atmosphere in the workshop must encourage full participation from all attendees.

Questions should be encouraged from the workshop participants. It is vitally important that the participants share their views among one another. You should expect that differing views will surface on many topics. This is healthy for the meeting atmosphere and provides a great opportunity for each group to understand the views of other groups. This insight and growing camaraderie is a wonderful side benefit of the meeting. Criticism of the process should be encouraged. However, criticism of people should be prohibited, regardless of whether it is directed at people in the meeting or people elsewhere in the organization.

After all responses have been presented and shared within the workshop team, the next step is to create two lists. The first list is of the things that "went right." These are things that you want to carry forward to future projects. It is helpful to order the list, with the most beneficial items placed at the top. These top items later will be shown both to the project's leadership and to all members of the project.

 Lesson: Don't "boil the ocean"—identify the most important problems to work, then propose solutions to these problems.

The second list is of the things that "went wrong" with the project (not defects in the product). This problem list must be sorted in priority order, with the most important problems listed first. What you really are interested in is focusing on the top five to 10 problems. Problems that do not make the significant list need not be ignored. Members of each organization that has these problems can resolve them independently to their own satisfaction.

After the more important problems have been identified, the next task is to develop proposals—to be submitted to the project's leadership—that address these problems. You can break into smaller teams or work collectively on these problem solutions. With either approach, the entire team should reach a consensus on each recommendation before it is presented to the project's leadership. These recommendations should address or answer the following questions.

- Who has the ownership to ensure closure of each problem?
- What constitutes closure of each problem?
- How will the solution be tracked until it is complete?
- What should be the frequency of tracking?

 Lesson: It is better to put a plan in place to solve a time-consuming problem later than to delay completing the postproject review excessively.

Note that it is unlikely that all these problems can be resolved in a single meeting. Some problems might require considerable research with data and skills not readily available at the workshop. In these cases, it is acceptable not to have a final solution. Instead, a plan can be drawn up recommending that a group be assembled to study a given problem further, with the goal of proposing one or more solutions. However, remember to ensure that an owner is assigned to work on each unresolved problem. This will better ensure that each problem is addressed successfully by focusing the responsibility on a single, accountable individual. Also, ensure that target dates are set so that progress can be tracked properly.

At this point, it is time to get the final charts together that will be reviewed by the project's leadership. These charts also will become part of the Postproject Review Report for follow-up and historical purposes. It is suggested that a good-news chart be presented first. This chart lists the things that "went right"—to the extent that these items are noteworthy.

The remaining charts list the problems that the review team felt were significant enough to receive special visibility. Each problem should be followed by a recommended solution or a plan that will yield a solution. Where appropriate, you may want to provide the project's leadership with more than one solution from which to choose. Not only does this give the project leaders flexibility, it also gives them a greater feeling of ownership of and commitment on the final solutions *they* choose.

Step 5.   *Present Results*

Two meetings are recommended at this point. The first meeting is used to present the workshop's results to the project's leadership. The second meeting is called to present the final results from the project leadership meeting to all the other project members.

At a minimum, the first and second levels of the project's leadership should be required to attend the project leaders' meeting. These levels are typically those defined as leaders of teams (first level) and of departments (second level). (On some projects, the leaders might all be defined as one "notch" higher: The first-level leader is defined as the department leader, and his or her leader is the second-level leader.)

The first level typically encompasses project leaders who are responsible for addressing the problems and their recommended solutions. The next level of project leaders is in attendance because they will need to know what resources are being committed and what the impact of these commitments will be. These leaders also will need to provide support to their subordinate project leaders as well as to measure the performance of the commitment of their project leaders in following through on plans.

You also will find it beneficial to include levels of project leadership higher than the second level. It is helpful for higher levels of the project's leadership to understand, firsthand, the problems experienced within projects. Often their support will be required to address some project problems. Also, their insistence on tracking the action taken by the first and second levels of project leadership can have a profound, positive effect on resolving the problems.

Lesson: Every attempt should be made to obtain the full support of the project's leadership in implementing the recommendations to the top problems as quickly as possible.

The goal of the project leadership meeting should be for the project review team to get the full support of the project's leadership to implement recommendations. This means an attempt should be made to get acceptance of the recommendations. Note, however, that some solutions might not lend themselves to quick decisions and might instead require further analysis by the project's leadership.

For the project members' meeting, the project leaders have an opportunity to express their commitment to the quality of the product, the processes, and the overall work environment. This event can show that the project's leadership is listening and responding with positive action.

The recommended presenter for the project leadership meeting is the workshop chairperson. The presenter at the project member meeting can be either a project leader or the workshop chairperson, depending on organizational structure and preferences.

Step 6.   Adopt Recommendations

> *The art of life lies in a constant readjustment to our surroundings.*
> —*Kakuzo Okakura, Japanese art critic*

The benefit of the postproject review does not end after the results have been presented to the project's leadership and to the project members. Quite the contrary. The real benefit of the postproject review is to learn from past errors and from those things that went according to plan, and to apply these lessons to other present and future projects.

The first order of business is to complete the Postproject Review Report. This report, at a minimum, should contain the charts that were presented to the project's leadership. The final recommendations that were adopted by the project's leadership also should be included. Optionally, the original charts that each representative presented at the workshop can be included.

 Lesson: When a new project is started, it should be mandatory that the results of past postproject reviews be examined for possible actions that should be taken on the new project.

After the report is completed, a copy should be sent to each project leader. In turn, each project leader should make the copy available to his or her employees. Another option is for the project head to distribute the report to all project personnel—both project leaders and project members. When new projects are started, a checklist or some list of activities should be in place to measure the project against. An activity should be added to this list that requires past Postproject Review Reports to be reviewed for possible action to be taken on the new project. This review must be tracked as a required activity before the new project's schedules and activities can be approved. Not only does this technique make it difficult to forget or overlook the results of a past postproject review, it is also insurance when major project players from past projects have left the organization. In this way, the valuable experiences of the past can continue to influence the future.

 Lesson: The "buck" stops with a project's leadership—if lessons are to be learned from past projects, the project's leadership must lead the charge.

The project's leadership is responsible for acting on these committed recommendations. If checks and balances in addition to those just described are required in any particular organization, this is the time to put those checks in place. All eyes will be on the project's leadership to see whether the promised support occurs. This is not a time for rhetoric, but a time for support and action.

Project Review

Up to now, the focus of this chapter has been performing a postproject review at the end of a project. Such reviews help future projects avoid many of the problems that plagued past projects and carry forth the actions that worked well. Every project, without exception, should undergo a postproject review. But for projects that have a duration of more than nine months, an additional projectlike review can be most beneficial. This additional review is simply called a project review.

The primary purpose of a project review is to examine the overall health of a project and recommend actions to address any significant problems that are identified. A project review is not the same as performing weekly project tracking team meetings. (See Chapter 5.) A project review is a special event to examine the current state of the project from an impartial source (more on this in a moment). A project review typically occurs near the end of a major project milestone, such as the completion of a product's design, coding, or development testing.

Figure 14.4 shows, at a high level, the steps to be followed in performing a project review. On the surface, this figure looks similar to Figure 14.1—the steps to follow for performing a postproject review. However, a project review not only serves a very different purpose, it also is conducted quite differently. Lets take a closer look at the steps shown in Figure 14.4.

Step 1. Schedule Project Review

The first step is to decide what strategic points along the software development process are most desirable for conducting project reviews—then schedule the project reviews. Typical points are near major project milestones such as those discussed earlier and in Chapter 5. This way, a condition for satisfying the milestone also can be the

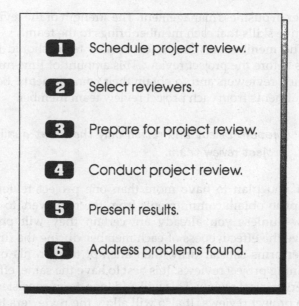

1. Schedule project review.

2. Select reviewers.

3. Prepare for project review.

4. Conduct project review.

5. Present results.

6. Address problems found.

Figure 14.4 Steps for a successful project review.

satisfactory closure of problems that have been identified from the project review. If your project has identified milestone points when additional funding is released for the next development period, these milestones are especially good candidates for project reviews to occur.

 Lesson: Project reviews should not occur more frequently than once every three to five months.

Depending on the length of the project, several project reviews may be performed; however, they should not be performed more frequently than once every three to five months. Why? Because the investment of time and people required to prepare for and conduct the project review, and then to address the problem identified, would be too disruptive for a project.

Step 2.   Select Reviewers

Project reviews often are coordinated by a person from assurance or by the project tracking team leader. (See Chapter 5 for a definition of the project tracking team leader.) The project review coordinator selects the members of the project review team. The review team is composed of several experts (typically three to five) from outside the project who possess experience and knowledge beneficial to the review. For example, one person might have technical expertise relative to the project, another might be an expert in project management, another in marketing, and yet another in business management. The strength of the review team is derived from the collective skills that each member brings to the team.

The members of the project review team should be selected at least several weeks before the project review. This amount of time might be needed to search for qualified reviewers and to obtain their commitments. Be certain that you have firm commitments from each project review team member.

 Lesson: Select and retain only the most qualified members for the project review team.

If you plan to have more than one project review for your project, do not attempt to obtain commitments from the reviewers to participate in every project review—unless you already are certain they will perform as needed. Instead, observe the effectiveness of each member during the first project review. If a member performs satisfactorily, then attempt to gain his or her commitments for the remaining project reviews. It is best to have the same, effective reviewers participate in every project review. This will add long-term consistency, stability, and credibility to the project reviews. It also will allow the reviewers to gain more familiarity and insight into the project's operations as the project evolves.

Hiring people from outside your company for a more impartial project review might be beneficial. The cost for consultants probably will be viewed as a bargain when compared against the potential insight they can offer you on your project—insight that can have a positive long-term benefit to the project.

Step 3.   Prepare for Project Review

 Lesson: If project organizations are given sufficient time to prepare for a project review, they likely will use that time to resolve some of the problems that would otherwise be revealed during the project review.

The project review coordinator prepares a set of topics for each project organization to address. The topics typically are reviewed and agreed to by the members of the project review team. These topics can be rather broad in scope or very specific. Figure 14.5 lists typical areas where the project review team members will ask questions of the project organizations. The project review coordinator distributes both these topics and an agenda to each project organization. Each organization will prepare a brief presentation addressing these topics. Project organizations usually should have a minimum of two weeks to prepare for the project review. You may find that the more time you allow project organizations to prepare, the more likely they will attempt to resolve problems before the project review begins. This is beneficial for everyone.

- Overview of product
- Staffing and skills
- Project organization, roles, and responsibilities
- Schedules and milestones
- Product definition and change control
- Processes
- Quality
- Productivity
- Project communications and morale
- Support from external groups
- Customer expectations
- Project financials
- Critical success factors
- Significant problems (including technical obstacles)
- Project outlook (including risk assessment)
- Other (including business and legal issues)

Figure 14.5   Topics of interest for a project review.

Step 4.   Conduct Project Review

 Lesson: The primary goal of the project review is to identify significant problems and to assess the overall capability of the project to meet its commitments.

The project review might take anywhere from one-half day to three days, depending on the size and complexity of the project. For most projects—those of 50 to 300 members—a full day should be sufficient. The goal is not to discover every possible problem but to discover the significant ones. The project organizations, following the planned agenda, present their information and answer questions from the project review team members. The team members are looking for problems that might have been overlooked or ignored. They also are attempting to understand all aspects of the operation of the project.

Immediately after the project review, the project review team members huddle together and prepare a set of charts to present to the project's leadership. The charts list their findings from the project review. The charts begin with good news, then list significant problems that need to be addressed, and conclude with an overall assessment of the likelihood of the project meeting its schedules, cost, and quality. Optionally, the project review team also will make recommendations to address some or all of the problems they have identified.

Step 5.   *Present Results*

 Lesson: Because the overall assessment from the project review is, in large part, a reflection of the effectiveness of the project's leadership, the assessment should be presented first to the project's leadership.

Now the project review team is ready to present its assessment to the project head (and possibly that person's superior) and his or her project leaders. Typically the assessment is presented first to the project's leadership. The discussion on problems and sensitive issues can become quite candid and is not conducive to a wide audience. Because the problems identified often are a reflection of the effectiveness of the leadership, it is important that the members of the project review team present their findings in a constructive, unemotional manner. The presentation usually is performed by the designated leader of the project review team; however, the team's members can present various pieces if desirable. The project review team might optionally prepare a formal report of their findings; however, in most cases, the charts presented should be sufficient.

After the project's leadership has seen the assessment, it is highly recommended that the assessment be presented to all members of the project. The project head might want to present the charts and reflect upon their messages. The project's members will be quite eager to see the assessment and to understand the actions that the project's leadership is proposing to address the problems identified.

Step 6.   *Address Problems Found*

 Lesson: The most important action of the project review process is for the project's leadership to satisfactorily resolve the significant problems identified.

Although the participation of the project review team members is now complete, the project review is not. The problems and recommendations identified from the project review team now must be addressed by the project's leadership. This means that an owner for each problem or recommendation must be assigned, target dates for plans to resolve the problems must be committed, and a tracking mechanism established. After these items have been logged sufficiently and are being worked and tracked, the project review can be considered complete. If another project review occurs, one of the actions for the next project review team is to examine the effectiveness of each project organization in resolving the identified problems from the last project review.

Project reviews are a powerful tool in managing projects. They act like a routine physical by a doctor; that is, the project undergoes a reasonably thorough examination and any problems identified are treated appropriately. The purpose is to ensure the project is and remains in the best of health. Project reviews allow midproject corrections to be made to reduce the risk in meeting schedule, cost, and quality commitments.

Some projects don't schedule project reviews in advance; instead, they are conducted either randomly or when perceived to be needed. This approach is not recommended. It is best to plan project reviews well in advance so that they become part of the base project schedule plan being tracked. This method alerts everyone in the project to work more deliberately in meeting commitments. After all, no one wants to be singled out as being the cause of a serious problem in the project. Just the opposite—it would be great to be acknowledged for being an example of meeting or beating commitments, or even performing activities in an innovative manner.

Product Certification Reviews

 Lesson: Product certification reviews serve your customers by ensuring that they receive the best product possible.

A product certification review is conducted immediately before a product is to be approved for announcement and again before the product is to be approved for delivery to the first customer. The steps to follow in a product certification review are similar to the steps discussed earlier for project reviews, with one major difference: The analysis of the product certification review is directed primarily toward the *product* rather than the *process*. More specifically, the focus of the review is on determining the readiness of the product. This analysis culminates with a "Go" or "No go" signal for announcing or delivering the product. The final decision is made by the project's leadership, but the recommendation is presented by the product certification review team.

Summary

Neglect always carries a high cost. By understanding past projects—that is, what went right and what went wrong—an organization can realize big savings. Applying this knowledge to future projects can mean taking greater profits to the bank.

I hope you will agree that the concept of reviews, whether they are postproject, project, or product certification, has great value to an organization and ultimately to the acceptance of the product by its customers. Organizations that demonstrate the foresight to plan for these reviews are also those organizations that are likely to report fewer problems during the actual reviews.

Glossary

NOTE: Highlighted terms within a definition are also defined within this glossary.

action item. A **project** problem that is logged, assigned an owner to resolve, and then tracked until it is closed.

activity. A defined portion of work within a **project** that typically has a designated owner, **entry conditions, implementation conditions, exit conditions,** duration, and schedules. Examples: creating the **product specifications** document, creating the **high-level design, coding,** and performing the **system test.**

activity responsibility matrix. A method of identifying the owner, approvers, and reviewers of each **activity.**

artificial test environment. *See* **scaffolding.**

bottom-up plan. A **project schedule plan** that has been developed with participation of virtually all members of a **project.** All the **activities** are identified, along with the activity owners, the activity durations, and the dependencies among activities. A bottom-up plan, if final, is *the* plan that should be committed to **management.**

brainstorming. A problem-solving technique whereby a group of people collectively pool their knowledge and experiences to focus on a problem or subject.

buffer. A designated period that is built into a schedule to serve as extra time, or a contingency, to help absorb delays that might occur unexpectedly.

bug. *See* **defect.**

burnout. A condition experienced by a person that typically results from working excessive hours across many days and taking an insufficient amount of time away from the workplace for rest and relaxation. Burnout results in a person making more mistakes, being less productive, and frequently being more irritable to coworkers.

CASE (Computer-Aided Software Engineering). The automation of well-defined methodologies that are used in the development and maintenance of software **products**. These methodologies apply to nearly every **process** or **activity** of a **software development process**, examples of which include **project** planning and tracking, **product designing, coding,** and testing.

change bars. A notation made in the margins of an updated document to highlight where changes have been made. These notations allow users of a document to locate the most recent changes to a document more quickly.

change control process. A defined **process** to be followed when a change to a **controlled document** or procedure is proposed. A typical use is to control changes proposed to **product requirements, product objectives,** or **product specifications** after these documents have been approved.

code. *See* **coding.**

coding. The act of writing instructions that are immediately computer recognizable, or can be assembled or compiled to form computer-recognizable instructions. Within a typical **software development process,** this **activity** typically follows the **low-level design** activity and precedes the **unit test** and **function test** activities.

component. A major design piece of a **product.** The collection of components comprises the **programming** portion of a product. A component is usually comprised of one or more **modules.**

component test. Typically the first independent test of a **product** where all or some of the components are tested together. Little or no **scaffolding** is required. The test includes the testing of all the product's **externals.**

content plan. *See* **publications content plan.**

contingency buffer. *See* **buffer.**

controlled document. A document that is especially critical to a **project**'s success. The completeness, accuracy, and control of this document is essential to the overall health of a project and, therefore, is typically updated through a **change control process.** Examples of controlled documents are **product requirements, product objectives, product specifications, project schedule plan,** and any agreements or contracts with groups, **vendors,** or customers.

critical path. The sequence of **activities** of a project that are neck to neck with one another and define the longest duration of a **project.** The path of these activities has no slack time in accomplishing the schedule.

customized project checklist. A **project checklist** that has been tailored to include only the activities of a specific **project** member or team.

defect. A deviation from the requirements of a **product** or **process.** Also called *bug*.

delivery. The distribution of the final, **packaged product** to a customer.

department. A group of people typically comprised of two or more **teams,** having a distinct mission and headed by a **manager.**

development test. The testing performed on a **product** that is often conducted in a loosely controlled environment and is performed by the programmers who developed the **code** to be tested. Both **unit test** and the **function test** are considered development test activities. Some amount of **scaffolding** typically is required during the development test period.

discipline. The act of encouraging a desired pattern of behavior.

document implementation phases. The **phases** that a **project** document typically passes through as it becomes approved and is used. The phases are *preparation, review, update, approval*, and *refresh*.

drift. A condition that applies to a **project** and its participants when the project's resources are not properly focused on solving the most important problems first. Drift can have a serious negative effect on a project by increasing rework, decreasing **productivity,** lengthening schedules, increasing project costs, weakening morale, and reducing **quality.**

driver. In a **software development process,** a collection of **modules** that are linked together to make a workable "**product**" that can be tested and evaluated.

ease of use. A basic **function** of a **product** that simplifies the operation of the product for users and aids in their understanding of other product functions. This **user-friendly** condition is typically attributed to the ease—the intuitive feel—with which users can both learn and become productive with a product.

entry conditions. Activities, resources, or actions that are required to have been started, completed, or be in place before a designated activity can begin.

escalation. The act of calling upon higher levels of **project leadership** to resolve an **issue.** When two parties cannot agree on the solution to an issue, and an earnest attempt to negotiate a resolution has occurred, then an escalation is pursued to resolve the issue.

exit conditions. Activities, resources, or actions that are required to have been started, completed, or be in place before a designated activity can be completed.

externals. The portions of a **product** that are directly visible and accessible to the product's user. Externals are documented in **product specifications.**

first-draft publications. The first draft of the **product**'s **publications** that is available for review by groups within the **project**.

function. An action that a **product** is capable of performing. For example, actions for a word processor might be: define margins, define page length, set tabs, change font for all section headings, search for words or phrases, and automatic document save.

function test. The testing of each **product** function across one or more **modules**. Some amount of **scaffolding** is typically required to perform this test.

high-level design. The level of design required to understand how the **components** of the product technically work (1) with one another, (2) with the surrounding hardware and software environment with which they must operate, and (3) internally. This design identifies the components that make up the product, defines the **functional** mission for each component, and defines, at a high level, the internal design of each component. (In some development shops, high-level design is called *architecture*.)

high-priority problem list. The list that is comprised of the project's **high-priority problems**.

high-priority problems. Problems that are considered the **project**'s most critical problems to solve—problems that have a major impact on the well-being of the project, the **product**, and the people involved. These problems are also called *high-risk areas*.

high-risk areas. *See* **high-priority problems.**

implementation conditions. **Process**-oriented requirements that define how a designated **activity** will be implemented.

independent test. The testing performed on a **product** that occurs in a controlled environment and is best performed by project personnel who did not develop the **code** to be tested. Independent test follows **development test** and spans the **component test** and **system test** periods. Limited to no **scaffolding** is required during the independent test period.

inspection. A group of people, typically peers, who meet with the goal of examining an **activity** (high-level design, code, unit test plan) to identify and remove **defects** and problems.

International Organization for Standardization (ISO). A worldwide federation of national standards bodies from various countries established to promote the development of standards to facilitate the international exchange of goods and services. ISO 9001 is an example of a specific international standard of a model for quality assurance in design/development, production, installation, and servicing that some software development organizations have embraced.

ISO. *See* **International Organization for Standardization.**

issue. A problem that, if not resolved, is believed to have a significant harmful effect on the outcome of a **project.** The effect can, for example, relate to such things as schedules, cost, resources, quality, or customer satisfaction.

low-level design. This term represents two levels of design. The first level is the design required to understand how the **modules** within each **component** will work technically with one another. This design identifies the modules that make up each component, the **functional** mission of each module, and the interface across these modules. (In some development shops, this level of design is called *high-level design*, not to be confused with the use of this term in this book.) The second level of design is required to define the design within each of the many modules that may comprise each component. This design level identifies each programming decision path within each module and may be documented by using a design language, graphic flows, and so on, or simply by writing English narratives. This is the lowest level of design prior to **coding.**

management. A collection of **managers,** from across one or more **projects,** who are viewed as responsible for the efficiency of the work environment and for the morale of the people involved.

manager. A person responsible and accountable for both employees and one or more work **activities.** This person is usually the head of a **department.** A manager is considered a **project leader.**

milestone. An important event, accomplishment, or turning point.

moderator. A person leading and controlling an **inspection.** This person is also responsible for ensuring that all problems discovered at an inspection are recorded and tracked properly to their satisfactory resolution.

module. Code that represents part of a single **function** or more than one function. A module is code that can be compiled independently. One or more modules usually make up a **component.**

negative discipline. Discipline that is not productive to achieving a **project**'s mission.

objectives. *See* **product objectives.**

observer. *See* **test observer.**

organization. A group of people, typically divided into two or more **departments,** who typically share a common mission (such as everyone working on the same **project**) or a common skill group (such as all **publications** writers or programmers or testers).

package. Collecting the pieces of a **product** together (for example, **code** and **publications**) for **delivery** to a customer.

phase. A defined portion of a **software development process** (such as **product requirements, product definition, product design, coding,** and so on). The portions defined as phases are arbitrary and are usually determined by the group that plans the project. Also, a subset of activities that make up a larger activity. For example, the implementation phases of a **project document** are comprised of five phases: *preparation, review, update, approval,* and *refresh.*

positive discipline. Discipline that encourages behavior that supports a **project**'s mission.

postproject review. The review of a completed **project** by a selected group of people who can represent all the major **organizations** that participated on the project. The group identifies those things that went right, those things that went wrong, and those areas where improvement can be made. The objective is to learn from past projects so that future projects can benefit.

process. A systematic approach that is performed to achieve a specific purpose. In the context of a **software development process,** a process is defined as an ordered set of **activities** that, after completed, results in a software **product** that is **delivered** to a customer. However, the term can be applied much more broadly: the manner in which a **project,** or any of its many integral parts, is planned, developed, or tracked. For example, the method of logging a problem, and tracking that problem to a satisfactory closure, is defined as a process.

process team. A group of people who are responsible for defining, documenting, simplifying, improving and managing the implementation of the **software development process.** The team represents all areas from across a **project.** Also called *software development process team.*

product. A **software package,** consisting of **code** and **publications,** that eventually is delivered to a customer. In a broader sense, the definition of *product* also includes the product support materials that are related to such **activities** as marketing and maintenance.

product certification review. The review of a **product** by a selected group of people charged with independently assessing the product's readiness to be announced or **delivered.**

product definition. A **phase** of the **software development process** that focuses on what the **product** will be. The completion of the **product objectives** and the **product specifications activities** are the major **milestones** for this phase.

product delivery. *See* **deliver product.**

product design. A **phase** of the **software development process** that focuses on how the **product** will be designed. The completion of the **high-level design** and the **low-level design activities** are the major **milestones** for this phase.

product function. *See* **function.**

productivity. A measure of accomplished work over a designated period of time, such as lines of **code** per person-month.

product manager. The **manager** typically responsible for the overall development of a **product.**

product objectives. A document that defines the solution to the problem (or set of problems) defined in the **product requirements** document. This document defines, at a high level, a **product** that will satisfy a marketing opportunity and focuses on the perceived needs of the targeted customer. This document also provides the underlying direction to be followed by the **project** members as **functional,** and design trade-offs are made throughout the **software development process.**

product requirements. A document that describes the customer and market problems that need to be solved. This document focuses exclusively on the problems that need to be solved, not the solutions to those problems. (The **product objectives** defines the proposed **product** solution.)

product specifications. A document that describes, in detail, precisely what the customer will receive and use when the completed **product** is made available. Every function, command, screen, prompt, and other user-interface-related items is documented so that all the participants involved in the software development process (including the customer) know the product they are to build, document, test, use, and support.

program. The **code** portion of a **product** or **test script,** or a collection of **components** linked together. *See* also **module.**

project. The combined resources (people, machines, materials), **processes,** and **activities** that are dedicated to building and delivering a **product.** A project has a defined starting point and defined objectives from which completion is identified. Also, a group of people, typically comprised of two or more **organizations,** working on the same product.

project checklist. A **project** exhibit that is derived from the **project schedule plan.** Its primary purpose is for use in routine **project tracking team** (PTT) **meetings** when gathering project status and anticipating problems. A project checklist typically shows the project's **activities,** the person responsible for each activity, predecessor activities, planned start and end dates of each activity, and space reserved for recording the actual start and end dates of each activity.

project document. A document that is generated within a **project** for use by that project (such as **product objectives, product specifications,** system test plan). Also, a document that is created outside the project but is adopted for project use (such as programming standards document).

project document implementation phases. *See* **document implementation phases.**

project head. The person responsible for an entire **project;** the top **project leader** within a project.

project leader. A person responsible for one or more work **activities** who provides direction to the employees assigned to these work activities. A project leader could also be a **manager** if the person also is responsible and accountable for employees.

project leadership. A collection of **project leaders** (includes **managers**) from across a **project,** all of whom are viewed as responsible for the efficiency of the work environment and the morale of the employees.

project review. An independent review that is performed at selected points along the **software development process** for a **project** in progress. A project review allows an active project to be examined to determine its overall health. Actions are then recommended to address immediately any significant problems that are identified.

project schedule coordinator. The person responsible for coordinating all the actions necessary in creating a **bottom-up project schedule plan** and resulting **project checklist.**

project schedule plan. The **project**'s plan that shows the **activities** that must be accomplished to achieve the project's goals. This plan includes information about the project such as the activities, the person responsible for each activity, the duration of each activity, the predecessor activities (dependencies) of each activity, the successor activities of each activity, the resource required to accomplish each activity, and the planned start and end dates for each activity. This plan defines the roadmap of activities that affects virtually every member of a project and is the keystone for communications across a project.

project tracking team. A group of **project** members who routinely meet (typically once per week) to present both their progress against the **project schedule plan** and any problems they have or foresee. Also called the *PTT.*

project tracking team leader. The person responsible for coordinating all the actions necessary in creating and using a successful tracking and problem-management **process** for use throughout the **project's software development process.** The **project schedule coordinator** might be the person chosen to perform the role of the project tracking team (PTT) leader.

project tracking team meeting. A meeting of the **project tracking team** (PTT) members, typically occurring once per week, that serves as a communications forum for tracking the progress of the **project.** The primary purpose of the meeting is to discover potential project problems before they occur.

prototype. An early-running model of a **product** whose primary purpose usually is to experiment with, demonstrate, or prove the feasibility of a concept.

PSC. *See* **project schedule coordinator.**

PTT. *See* **project tracking team.**

PTT leader. *See* **project tracking team leader.**

PTT meeting. *See* **project tracking team meeting.**

publications. The manuals or books, also called *user manuals* or *user publications*, that are included in the **delivery** of the **product** to the customer. Also, the manuals or books that are created to support the maintenance of the delivered product. The publications can be made available through electronic media as well as hardcopy.

publications content plan. A document that describes the content and layout of each of the **publications.**

publications drafts. Preliminary copies of the **publications** that are in the process of being reviewed and updated.

quality. Providing a **product** that satisfies the customer. The customer judges a product's quality by the product's ability to satisfy his or her problems and needs and by meeting his or her expectations. The expectations cover a broad area such as function, cost, minimal defects, reliable, good level of service, competitive, and so on.

quality assurance group. People assigned to perform an "outside check-and-balance" role of ensuring that a **product** is being developed according to an acceptable **process.**

quality improvement team. A group of people who meet to solve one or more problems.

quality plan. A document that can be used to define, track, and measure both **product** and **process** quality goals throughout the **software development process.**

regression test. The final test for a **product.** This test is comprised of a selected set of **component test** scripts and **system test** scripts that is run as a final verification that the product **code** is operating as intended. Also, a verification test that is run at various points throughout the development of the code and throughout testing. This test typically verifies that the **function** that used to work still does.

release. A fully functioning **product** to be **delivered** to a customer.

Request for Proposal (RFP). A document that addresses two primary topics: the **Statement of Work** (SOW) and the instructions to bidders (**vendors**).

requirements. *See* **product requirements.**

resource-constrained plan. A **project schedule plan** that is developed dependent upon staffing resources. The duration of each activity is estimated based on the staffing expected to be available.

RFP. *See* **Request for Proposal.**

scaffolding. Temporary **code** that has been developed to interface with one or more **modules.** This temporary code allows modules to be tested independently while waiting for the permanent interfacing modules to be developed and readied for use. This term often is used synonymously with the terms *stubbing* and **artificial test environment.**

schedule-constrained plan. A **project schedule plan** that is developed mostly independent of the staffing resources. The duration of each **activity** is estimated based on what seems "reasonable" or "hoped for." (After the project schedule plan is thought to be properly constructed, the impact of staffing on each activity can then be determined.)

second-draft publications. The second draft (usually the final draft) of the **product's publications** that is available for review by groups within the **project.**

software development process. An ordered set of **activities** that, after being completed, result in a software **product** that is **delivered** to a customer. A *software development process* can be defined to include activities that are performed *after* a product is delivered to a customer, such as fielding customer problems and fixing **defects** in the product.

software development process team. *See* **process team.**

software process model. A conceptual model that defines the sequence of **activities** to be followed for a **software development process.** Examples of software process models are code-and-fix, waterfall, incremental, and iterative.

SOW. *See* **Statement of Work.**

specifications. *See* **product specifications.**

Statement of Work (SOW). A document that is originally part of the **Request for Proposal** (RFP) document. The Statement of Work includes information such as the work to be performed by the **vendor,** when that work is due, how the work will be measured for acceptance, and the working relationship between the vendor and your organization. The SOW becomes a major part of the eventual contract between the vendor and your organization.

stubbing. *See* **scaffolding.**

subcontractor. A person who has been hired to perform one or more software development **activities.** The subcontractor typically resides at the purchasing company's location and works alongside other subcontractors and company employees. The subcontractor might work under the direction of a representative of the subcontractor's company or might work directly under the direction of the purchasing company.

system test. A test of a **product** in a total systems environment with other software and hardware product combinations. A portion of the test should be conducted in a real customer environment.

task. *See* **usability task.**

team. A group of typically two to 10 people that has a specific mission.

test observer. A person who watches, or observes, a **test subject** and records that subject's actions.

test plan. A document that describes the who, what, when, where, and how for a designated test. Test plans are completed before the corresponding test is conducted to allow for the satisfactory preparation of the test. Examples: **function test** plan, **usability test** plan, **component test** plan, and **system test** plan.

test scripts. Programs and procedures that are written to test specific aspects of a **product.** Examples: installation **process,** product **functions,** messages, and examples defined in the **product publications.**

test subject. A person who helps to test a **product** as it is being developed. This person is expected to use the product in ways that are similar to customers of the finished product.

thrashing zone. A period of time in a **software development process** when a person is so deeply entangled in daily **project** problems that his or her biases, emotions, commitments, and good intentions can interfere with making optimum decisions.

top-down plan. A **project schedule plan,** usually preliminary, that has been developed by one person or a small group of people. The top-down plan lists the more significant **activities** of a **project** and suggests a set of schedules that might be achieved for the project. The top-down plan does not involve the participation of all project members and, consequently, should not be conveyed to **management** as a committed schedule. Top-down plans are strictly estimating techniques to get a better feel for the size, cost, and complexity of a project.

unit test. The isolated testing of each flowpath of **code** within each **module.** Some amount of **scaffolding** typically is required to perform this test.

usability. *See* **ease of use.**

usability task. A simple set of actions that a user might perform with a **product.** These tasks are identified, and then their **ease of use** is tested as the product is being developed. For example, tasks for a word processor product might include: installing the product, creating a new document, and printing a document. Problems discovered are then corrected prior to the **delivery** of the product.

usability test. A test to evaluate the **ease of use** of a portion or all of a **product.**

user friendly. *See* **ease of use.**

user interface. The **functions** of a **product** that allow a user to interact with that product; also called *man-machine interface.* Examples: operator commands, user screens, and messages.

vacation factor. A useful planning tool that encourages **project** personnel to plan some, or all, of their vacation during the least busy periods of a project.

variable productivity potential. The flexibility a person has to vary his or her **productivity** to better match the needs of the task at hand.

vendor. A company that is hired to perform some type of software development work. The vendor typically resides at a location that is apart from the company that has purchased the vendor's services. A vendor is typically seen as being in control of managing its own activities.

walkthrough. A group of people who meet to verify the correctness and acceptability of a **product's user interface**. The people in the group include the product developers and **test subjects**. Because running **code** and product **publications** drafts are not yet available, the user interface is examined by "walking through" the available user interface documentation. This documentation typically includes the **product specifications**.

WBS. *See* **work breakdown structure.**

work activity. *See* **activity.**

work breakdown structure. The breaking down of **activities** into smaller and smaller pieces (*tasks*) to facilitate their planning, implementing, tracking, and budgeting. For detailed **project** planning, these smaller pieces typically might be one-week duration or smaller.

Bibliography

This bibliography provides additional reading material for many of the subjects presented in this book. Bracketed numbers at the end of each entry correspond with the chapter numbers of *Managing Software Development Projects: Formula for Success* in which material applies.

Aron, J. D., *The Program Development Process: The Programming Team, Part II*, Addison-Wesley Publishing Company, Inc., 1983 [4,5,6,7,10,12]

Basili, V. R., A. J. Turner, "Iterative Enhancement: A Practical Technique for Software Development," *IEEE Transactions on Software Engineering* SE-1, no. 4, pp. 390–396, December 1975 [1,4]

Beizer, Boris, *Software Testing Techniques*, 2d ed., Van Nostrand Reinhold, 1990 [11,12]

Blanchard, Ken, Spencer Johnson, *The One Minute Manager*, William Morrow and Company, Inc., 1982 [2,3]

Boehm, B. W., "A Spiral Model of Software Development and Enhancement," *Computer* 21, no. 5, May 1988, pp. 61–72 [1,4]

Branscomb, L. M., J. C. Thomas, "Ease of Use: A System Design Challenge," *IBM Systems Journal*, vol. 23, no. 3, 1985, pp. 224–235 [11]

Brooks Jr., Frederick P., *The Mythical Man-Month: Essays on Software Engineering*, Addison-Wesley Publishing Company, Inc., 1975 [4,5,6,9,10]

Burrill, Claude W., Leon W. Ellsworth, *Modern Project Management: Foundation for Quality and Productivity*, Burrill-Ellsworth Associates, Inc., 1980 [4,5,6]

Crosby, Philip B., *Quality Is Free: The Art of Making Quality Certain*, McGraw-Hill Book Company, 1979 [6]

Crosby, Philip B., *Quality Without Tears: The Art of Hassle-Free Management*, McGraw-Hill Book Company, 1984 [6]

DeMarco, Tom, *Controlling Software Projects: Management, Measurement, and Estimation*, Yourdon Press, 1982 [4,6,10]

DeMille, Richard A., W. Michael McCracken, R. J. Martin, John F. Passafiume, *Software Testing and Evaluation*, The Benjamin/Cummings Publishing Company, Inc., 1987 [12]

Deming, W. Edwards, *Quality, Productivity, and Competitive Position*, Massachusetts Institute of Technology, Center for Advanced Engineering Study, 1982 [2,6]

Dyer, Michael, *The Cleanroom Approach to Quality Software Development*, John Wiley & Sons, Inc., 1992 [1,6,10,12]

Dyer, Wayne W., *The Sky's the Limit*, Pocket Books, Division of Simon & Schuster, Inc., 1980 [2]

Dyer, Wayne W., *Your Erroneous Zones*, Funk and Wagnalls, 1976 [2]

Fagan, M. E., "Design and Code Inspections to Reduce Errors in Program Development," *IBM Systems Journal*, vol. 15, no. 3, 1976, pp. 182–211 [6]

Fallon, Howard, *How to Implement Information Systems and Live to Tell About It*, John Wiley & Sons, Inc., 1995 [2,3,4,5,6,12]

Fisher, Alan S., *CASE: Using Software Development Tools*, 2d ed., John Wiley & Sons, Inc., 1991 [1,6,8,10,11,12]

Gardiner, Margaret M. (ed.), Bruce Christie (ed.), *Applying Cognitive Psychology to User Interface Design*, John Wiley and Sons, Inc., 1987 [11]

Galitz, Wilbert O., *User-Interface Screen Design*, John Wiley & Sons, Inc., 1993 [11]

Gilbreath, Robert D., *Winning at Project Management: What Works, What Fails and Why*, John Wiley and Sons, Inc., 1986 [2,4,5]

Gitlow, Howard S., Shelley J. Gitlow, *The Deming Guide to Quality and Competitive Position*, Prentice-Hall, Inc., 1987 [2]

Gomaa, H., D. Scott, "Prototyping as a Tool in the Specification of User Requirements," *Proceedings 5th IEEE International Conference of Software Engineering*, March 1981, pp. 333–342 [11]

Guaspari, John, *I Know It When I See It: A Modern Fable About Quality*, AMACOM, 1985 [6]

Harrison, F. L., *Advanced Project Management*, 2d ed., Gower Publishing Company Limited, 1985 [4,5]

Hauser, J. R., D. Clausing, "The House of Quality," *Harvard Business Review* 66, no. 3, May–June 1988, pp. 63–73 [6,8]

Hausler, P. A., R. C. Linger, C. J. Trammell, "Adopting Cleanroom Software Engineering with a Phased Approach," *IBM Systems Journal* 33, no. 1, 1994, pp. 89–109 [1,6,10,11,12]

Humphrey, Watts S., *Managing for Innovation: Leading Technical People*, Prentice-Hall, Inc., 1987 [2,3]

Humphrey, Watts S., *Managing the Software Process*, Addison-Wesley Publishing Company, Inc., 1989 [2,4,5,6,12,14]

Ince, Darrel, *An Introduction to Software Quality Assurance and Its Implementation*, McGraw-Hill, 1994 [4,6,8,9,10,11,12,13]

Ince, Darrel, Helen Sharp, Mark Woodman, *Introduction to Software Project Management and Quality Assurance*, McGraw-Hill, 1993 [1,4,5,6,13]

Jones, C. J., "A Process-Integrated Approach to Defect Prevention," *IBM Systems Journal*, vol. 24, no. 2, 1985, pp. 150–167 [4,6,12]

Kan, S. H., V. R. Basili, L. N. Shapiro, "Software Quality: An Overview from the Perspective of Total Quality Management," *IBM Systems Journal*, vol. 33, no. 1, 1994, pp. 4–19 [6]

Kaner, Cem, Jack Falk, Hune Quoc Nguyen, *Testing Computer Software*, 2d ed., Van Nostrand Reinhold, 1993 [11,12]

Kaplan, Craig, Ralph Clark, Victor Tang, *Secrets of Software Quality: 40 Innovations from IBM*, McGraw-Hill, 1995 [1,2,6,12]

Levine, Harvey A., *Project Management Using Microcomputers*, Osborne McGraw-Hill, 1986 [4,5]

Linger, R. C., "Cleanroom Software Engineering for Zero-Defect Software," IBM Cleanroom Software Technology Center Technical Paper, IBM Corporation, Gaithersburg, Md., 1992 [1,6,10,12]

McNally, David, *Even Eagles Need a Push: Learning to Soar in a Changing World*, Dell Publishing, 1990 [2,3]

Miller, Dennis, *Visual Project Planning and Scheduling*, The 15th Street Press, Inc., 1994 [4]

Miller, William C., *The Creative Edge: Fostering Innovation Where You Work*, Addison-Wesley Publishing Company, Inc., 1987 [2,3]

Mills, H. D., M. Dyer, R. C. Linger, "Cleanroom Software Engineering," *IEEE Software* 4, no. 5, September 1987, pp. 19–25 [1,6,10,12]

Moder, Joseph J., Cecil R. Phillips, Edward W. Davis, *Project Management with CPM, PERT, and Precedence Diagramming*, Van Nostrand Reinhold, 1983 [4,5]

Myers, Glenford J., *The Art of Software Testing*, John Wiley and Sons, Inc., 1979 [12]

Myers, Glenford J., *Software Reliability: Principles and Practices*, John Wiley and Sons, Inc., 1976 [9,10,12]

Nielsen, Jakob, *Usability Engineering*, A. P. Professional, 1993 [11]

Nielsen, Jakob (ed.), Robert L. Mack (ed.), *Usability Inspection Methods*, John Wiley and Sons, Inc., 1994 [11]

Norman, Donald A., *The Psychology of Everyday Things*, Basic Books, Inc., 1988 [11]

Norman, Donald A. (ed.), Stephen W. Draper (ed.), *User Centered System Design: New Perspectives on Human–Computer Interaction*, Lawrence Erlbaum Associates, Inc., 1986 [11]

Norris, Mark, Peter Rigby, Malcolm Payne, *The Healthy Software Project: A Guide to Successful Development and Management*, John Wiley and Sons, Inc., 1993 [2,3,4,5,6,7]

Page-Jones, Meilir, *Practical Project Management*, Dorset House Publishing Company, Inc., 1985 [2,4,5]

Peters, Thomas J., Robert H. Waterman Jr., *In Search of Excellence: Lessons from America's Best-Run Companies*, Harper & Row, Publishers, Inc., 1982 [2,3]

Peters, Tom, Nancy Austin, *A Passion for Excellence: The Leadership Difference*, Random House, Inc., 1985 [2,3]

Peters, Tom, *Thriving on Chaos: Handbook for a Management Revolution*, Alfred A. Knopf, Inc., 1987 [2,3]

Project Management Institute, *Project Management Body of Knowledge (PMBOK)*, Project Management Institute, 1987 [1,2,3,4,5,6,8,9,10,13,14]

Rakos, John J., *Software Project Management for Small to Medium Sized Projects*, Prentice-Hall, Inc., 1990 [2,4,5,8,9,10,11,12,13,14]

Radice, R. A., N. K. Roth, A. C. O'Hara Jr., W. A. Ciarfella, "A Programming Process Architecture," *IBM Systems Journal*, vol. 24, no. 2, 1985, pp. 79–90 [1,4]

Radice, R. A., J. T. Harding, P. E. Munnis, R. W. Phillips, "A Programming Process Study," *IBM Systems Journal*, vol. 24, no. 2, 1985, pp. 91–101 [14]

Radice, Ronald A., Richard W. Phillips, *Software Engineering: An Industrial Approach, Volume 1*, Prentice-Hall, 1988 [4,6,11]

Roman, Daniel D., *Managing Projects: A Systems Approach*, Elsevier Science Publishing Co., Inc., 1986 [2,4,5]

Ross, Joel E., William C. Ross, *Japanese Quality Circles and Productivity*, Reston Publishing, 1982 [2,6]

Sanders, Joe, Eugene Curran, *Software Quality: A Framework for Success in Software Development and Support*, 1994 [1,6,8]

Shneiderman, Ben, *Designing the User Interface: Strategies for Effective Human–Computer Interaction*, 2d ed., Addison-Wesley Publishing Company, 1992 [11]

Simpson, W. Dwain, *New Techniques in Software Project Management*, John Wiley & Sons, Inc., 1987 [4,14]

Sommerville, Ian, *Software Engineering*, 4th ed., Addison-Wesley Publishing Company, 1992 [1,4,5,6,8,9,10,11,12]

Spencer, Richard H., *Computer Usability Testing and Evaluation*, Prentice-Hall, Inc., 1985 [11]

Spencer, Richard H., *Planning, Implementation, and Control in Product Test and Assurance*, Prentice-Hall, Inc., 1983 [4,9,10,11,12]

Thayer, Richard H. (ed.), *Tutorial: Software Engineering Project Management*, Computer Society Press of the IEEE, 1988 [2,4,5,6,9,10,12]

Thirty Years of Management Briefings, 1958 to 1988, published by IBM Corporate Communications, 1988, Mechanicsburg order number: ZZ04-1201 [2,3]

Thomé, Bernhard, *Systems Engineering: Principles and Practice of Computer-based Systems Engineering*, John Wiley and Sons, Inc., 1993 [1,2,6,10,11]

Vliet, J. C. van, *Software Engineering, Principles and Practice*, John Wiley & Sons, Inc., 1993 [1,4,5,6,8,9,10,11,12]

Walton, Mary, *The Deming Management Method*, Dodd, Mead, 1986 [2,6]

Watson Jr., Thomas J., *A Business and Its Beliefs, The Ideas That Helped Build IBM*, McGraw-Hill Book Company, Inc., 1963 [2,3]

Westney, Richard E., *Managing the Engineering and Construction of Small Projects*, Marcel Dekker, 1985 [4,5,6]

Whitaker, Ken, *Managing Software Maniacs*, John Wiley & Sons, Inc., 1994 [2,4,5,8]

Yourdon, Edward, *Decline & Fall of the American Programmer*, Yourdon Press, 1993 [1,2,4,6,7]

Index